CATO'S LETTERS

CATO'S LETTERS

OR

Essays on Liberty, Civil and Religious, and Other Important Subjects

FOUR VOLUMES IN TWO

BY JOHN TRENCHARD AND
THOMAS GORDON

*Edited and Annotated
by Ronald Hamowy*

VOLUME TWO

Liberty Fund   Indianapolis

Library of Congress Cataloging-in-Publication Data
Trenchard, John, 1662–1723.
  Cato's letters, or, Essays on liberty, civil and religious, and other important subjects / by John Trenchard and Thomas Gordon : edited and annotated by Ronald Hamowy.
    p.   cm.
  Originally appeared from Nov. 1720 to Dec. 1723 in the London journal.
  Includes bibliographical references and index.
    ISBN 0-86597-128-5 (set : hardcover : alk. paper). — ISBN 0-86597-129-3 (set : pbk. : alk. paper). — ISBN 0-86597-130-7 (vol. 1 : hardcover : acid-free paper). — ISBN 0-86597-131-5 (vol. 1 : paperback : acid-free paper). — ISBN 0-86597-132-3 (vol. 2 : hardcover : acid-free paper). — ISBN 0-86597-133-1 (vol. 2 : paperback : acid-free paper)
    1. Great Britain—Politics and government—1714–1727—Sources. 2. Church and state—Early works to 1800. 3. Liberty—Early works to 1800.   I. Gordon, Thomas, d. 1750. II. Hamowy, Ronald, 1937–   .   III. Title.
DA499.T7   1995
320.941′09033—dc20   95-17578

Liberty Fund, Inc.

8335 Allison Pointe Trail, Suite 300

Indianapolis, Indiana 46250-1684

12 11 10 09 08 07 06 05 04 03 C 7 6 5 4 3
11 10 09 08 07 06   P 6 5 4 3

Contents

CATO'S LETTERS

CATO's
LETTERS:
OR,

ESSAYS *on* LIBERTY,

CIVIL and RELIGIOUS,

And other important SUBJECTS.

In FOUR VOLUMES.

VOL. III.

The SIXTH EDITION, *corrected.*

LONDON:

Printed for *J. Walthoe*, T. and *T. Longman*, *C. Hitch*
and *L. Hawes*, *J. Hodges*, *A. Millar*, *J.* and *J.*
Rivington, *J. Ward* and *M. Cooper*.

M DCC LV.

❧ *Address to the Freeholders, &c. about the Choice of their Representatives.*[1]

SIR,

I beg leave to interrupt my discourse upon general liberty for one post or more, as occasion shall present; and desire you will publish the enclosed letter in your journal, in the place which used to be filled with one to yourself.

TO THE FREEHOLDERS, CITIZENS, AND BURGHERS OF THE COUNTIES, CITIES, AND TOWNS OF GREAT-BRITAIN.

GENTLEMEN,

There is no natural or political body but is subject to the variations and injuries of time. Both are composed of springs, wheels, and ligaments, all in perpetual motion, and all liable to wear out and decay: And as the parts are mortal, the whole must be mortal too. But as natural bodies may continue their existence, and preserve their duration, by action, by the addition of new particles, or by removing from time to time all occasional obstructions which clog their motion, and check their vigour, as long as their stamina, first principles, or original constitution, are capable of subsisting; so a political machine may do the same: And some writ-

1. New elections were called in March 1722, and the first session of the new Parliament opened in early Oct. of that year.

ers in politicks have asserted, that the same might be immortal;[2] which is not my opinion.

But whether this be true or not, certain it is, that in many respects a political body has the advantage of a natural one. We can often look into its inmost frame and contexture; and when any of its constituent parts are decayed or worn out, can supply it with new ones (which cannot be done in the other without a total dissolution of the fabrick): And we can frequently annex additional props and buttresses to support for some time a tottering building, and hinder it from falling upon our heads. This is often all that can be done in decayed governments, when a state is in a cachexy;[3] and this is what is every honest man's duty to do, when he can do no better. But, I thank God, the constitution of England is yet sound and vigorous: Many of its parts are active and strong; and if some members be corrupted or decayed, there are materials at hand to supply the defect. There is wealth and power in being: Our country abounds with men of courage and understanding; nor are there wanting those of integrity and publick spirit: There is an ardent desire and diffusive love of liberty throughout the kingdom; and many begin to be tired, sick, and ashamed of party-animosities, and of quarrelling with their neighbours, their relations, and often with their best friends, to gratify the pride, the ambition, and rapine of those, who only sell and betray them. It is yet in our power to save ourselves; most men have inclination to do it; and it is only owing to the art and address of our common enemies, if we do not agree on the means of doing it.

I dare therefore affirm, that there is such a general disposition towards liberty through the whole kingdom, that if there should be found in the next House of Commons as many honest, bold, and wise men, as would have saved Sodom and Gomorrah, England is yet safe, in spite of all the efforts of delusion and bribery: And I dare as freely affirm, that if some vigorous and bold resolutions are not there taken, to assist our most excellent King towards discharging the publick debts, and in redressing all sorts of publick corruptions, the liberty of Great-Britain—my heart can speak no more.

2. For example, Thomas Hobbes.
3. In a cachexy: malnourished and degenerating.

It lies upon you, Gentlemen, to give motion to the machine: You are the first springs that give life to all virtuous resolutions: Such as you shew yourselves, such will be your representatives: such as is the tree, such will be the fruit. Choose honest men, free and independent men, and they will act honestly for the public interest, which is your interest. It is not to be expected, that criminals will destroy their own handiwork; that they will either reform or punish themselves; or, that men, who have brought our misfortunes upon us, will go about in good earnest to redress them, or even own that there are any such. Besides, deep wounds must be probed and searched to the core, before they can be cured; and those who gave them can seldom bear to see the operation, much less will they pay for the cure, if they can be at ease by the death of the patient.

Let us not therefore, my countrymen, desert or deceive ourselves, or think we can be safe, if ever such men can get into power. Let us not again be deluded with false promises and deceitful assurances; but let us judge what men will do by what they have done. What warm and plausible remonstrances have you formerly heard and received? What impetuous storms and hurricanes of false and counterfeit zeal against oppressions and miscarriages in the late reigns; against exorbitant pensions, outrageous taxes, wild and expensive expeditions; against increasing the publick debts; against standing troops quartered up and down your countries; against oppressive companies, to the destruction of your trade and industry; against private men's raising immense estates upon your ruin; and against their bribing and corrupting the guardians of the publick liberty? And are you at last perfectly easy in every one of those complaints?

Now, therefore, my best friends, is the time to help yourselves: Now act honestly and boldly for liberty, or forget the glorious and charming sound. Let not a publick traitor come within the walls of your cities and towns, without treating him, as an enemy to your king and country deserves. Throw your eyes about your several countries, and choose your patrons, your protectors, your neighbours, and your known friends; choose for your representatives men whose interests are blended with your own; men who have no hands dipped in the public spoils, but have suffered by them as much as you yourselves have suffered; men who have not jobbed for stock, nor for wages, nor for you.

Make not so foolish a bargain, as for a little loose money to give up desperately all you have; your liberties, your estates, your families. Is it for your sakes, think you, that these jobbers of stocks, and of honesty, and of their country, come to caress you, flatter you, and bow to you? Do you, or can you believe that they come to impair their own fortunes, to increase yours? Or think you not that they will have their pennyworths out of you? Depend upon it, they will; and, for every bucket of water thrown into your wells, they will pump out tuns.[4]

Reason not therefore, as too many of you have done, and I fear yet do, that since those whom you trust make personal advantages of your confidence and credulity, you ought to share in those advantages. But throw your choice upon such who will neither buy you, nor sell you. Whoever purchases an office at more than it is honestly worth, must be supported by him who sells it, in all dishonest gains; or else he will call for his money again, if he know how to get it. No man will bribe you into your own interests, or give you money that he may have leave to serve you by his own labour, and at his farther expence; but will think himself at liberty to make reprisals: He will find no difficulty in himself to sell those, who have before sold themselves and their country: Nor can you have any right or pretence to reprove one that does so.

Mistake not, my countrymen, in believing that men in your condition and circumstances are too low for the scythe, and that you can shrink out of publick misfortunes. For you, gentlemen, are the first principles of wealth and power. From your labour and industry arises all that can be called riches, and by your hands it must be defended: Kings, nobility, gentry, clergy, lawyers, and military officers, do all support their grandeur by your sweat and hazard, and in tyrannical governments upon the people's spoils: They there riot upon the subsistence of the poor people, whose poverty is their riches. In corrupt administrations, your superiors of all kinds make bargains, and pursue ends at the publick expence, and grow rich by making the people poor.

4. Tuns: large casks.

You feel the first effects of tyrannical government; and great men are generally made the instruments of it, and reap the advantages. Exorbitant taxes, want of trade, decay of manufactures, discouragement of industry, insolence and oppression of soldiers, exactions of civil officers, ignorance, superstition, and bigotry, are all the constant concomitants of tyranny, always produce it, and are produced by it. And all these terrible evils must fall most signally upon the middle and inferior ranks of mankind: There must be a great number of slaves to furbish up one grand monarch, and the poor people must be those slaves. He must engage many in his interest, before he can establish a power which destroys the rest; all these many must be supported, and have their condition bettered by the change; and all this charge and expence the wretched people must work for and pay.

Forget therefore, Gentlemen, the foolish and knavish distinction of High Church and Low Church, Whig and Tory; sounds which continue in your mouths when the meaning of them is gone; and are now only used to set you together by the ears, that rogues may pick your pockets, I own myself to be one of those, whom one side in respect, and the other in contumely, call Whigs; and yet I never discoursed with a candid and sensible Tory, who did not concur with me in opinion, when we explained our intentions. We both agreed in our notions of old English liberty, in a passion for freedom to ourselves, and to procure it for every one else: We were both for preserving the English monarchy, and the legal constitution of the national church against its enthusiastick friends and enemies; and were for giving liberty of conscience to those, who through a prejudiced education, or as we believed, a less capacity of judging, were so unhappy as to think differently from ourselves, in an affair which concerned us not, and which we had nothing to do with.

We both honoured and resolved to preserve upon the throne our most excellent sovereign King George, and to endeavour to continue him a glorious king over honest men, and freemen; and not to attempt to make him, what he scorns to be made, a patron of parasites, and a lord of slaves: And we thought we could not shew our duty to him more effectually, than in bringing to exemplary punishment all who had betrayed him and us:

We wished the old names of distinction and faction buried deep as the centre; and nothing heard in their room but court and country, Protestant and papist, freemen and slaves. It will lie at your door, Gentlemen, to put an end to the above silly and wicked gibberish. Choose those who have no interest to continue it, and it will not be continued.

Consider, my dear friends and countrymen, what I have said, and think what you are doing, while you are raising hue and cry after men who will betray you; while you are sending afar for courtiers, for directors of bubbles, for company-men, and publick pickpockets, to represent you; while you are giving up, perhaps for ever, to the mercy of bloodsuckers, your honest industry, and the just profits of your trade, for a poor momentary share of their infamous plunder; and thereby bringing a canker upon your subsistence, and the just resentment of heaven upon your endeavours. Shew yourselves once, and once for all, Britons and freemen, and not foreign and saleable slaves; shew that you know how to honour your king, and yet to keep your liberties; that you obey him out of choice, and not out of servile fear; that you know how to distinguish your loyalty to your prince, from a blind submission to his and your own servants; and that you can make your duty to him consistent with a vigorous resolution to punish all who betray him and you.

If you did but know, Gentlemen, how you are used above, by those who think it worth their time to flatter you below, and to your faces, you would not want my advice and admonitions. You are called the mob, the canaille,[5] the stupid herd, the dregs and beasts of the people; and your interest is never thought of by those men, who thus miscall you; men who have no more wit, and much less honesty, than yourselves; and men whose insolence and sauciness are owing to wealth, which they have plundered from you. It depends now upon yourselves, whether you will deserve these base and reproachful names, or not; shew that you are men, and you will be used like men; but if you sell yourselves like the beasts in the field, the purchasers will have a right to sell you again, and make honest gains out of a villainous bargain.

5. The canaille: the rabble.

For my own particular, I cannot give myself leave to despair of you, because I must at the same time despair of old English liberty: You are our Alpha and Omega, our first and last resource; and when your virtue is gone, all is gone. It is true, you have a wise and virtuous prince at present, who will not take advantage of your follies; and you may depend upon the same security from his son: but neither he nor his son, nor his family are immortal; and therefore I hope you will act wisely, and trust to yourselves alone. But whatever part, gentlemen, you shall think fit to take, you shall not do it blindfold, and in the dark. You shall have the fair and dark side of your conduct laid before you, and then you may choose whether you will be freemen or vassals; whether you will spend your own money and estates, or let others worse than you spend them for you: Methinks the choice should be easy. You shall hear more from me upon this subject; and you may believe me.

T

Gentlemen,

your very sincere,

and most affectionate,

humble servant.

NO. 70. SATURDAY, MARCH 17, 1721.

Second Address to the Freeholders, &c. upon the same Subject.

GENTLEMEN,

You are born to liberty, and it is your interest and duty to preserve it. The constitution which you live under is a mixed monarchy, where your governors have every right to protect and defend you, none to injure and oppress you. You have a large share in the legislature; you have the sole power over your own purses; you have an undoubted right to call to account and punish the instruments of your oppression: But it depends upon yourselves alone to make these rights of yours, these noble privileges, of use to you. The best laws give no security if they are not executed, but indeed become worse than no laws; and they never will be executed, unless those who are entrusted with the execution of them have an interest in their execution.

All men desire naturally riches and power; almost all men will take every method, just or unjust, to attain them. Hence the difficulty of governing men, and of instituting a government equally proper to restrain them and protect them; and hence the insufficiency of simple forms of government, to provide for the happiness and security of societies. An arbitrary prince will quickly grow into a tyrant; the uncontrolled dominions of the nobles will as certainly produce oligarchy, or the tyranny of a few; that is, pride, combination, and rapine in the sovereigns, and misery and dejection in the many; and the unrestrained licentiousness of the multitude will beget confusion and anarchy. To provide against these certain and eternal evils, mixed forms of government were invented; where dominion and liberty are so equally tempered, and so mutually checked one by another, that neither of them can have interest and force enough to oppress the other.

These institutions have provided against many evils, but not against all; for, whilst men continue in this state of degeneracy, that is, whilst men are men, ambition, avarice, and vanity, and other passions, will govern their actions; in spite of all equity and reason, they will be ever usurping, or attempting to usurp, upon the liberty and fortunes of one another, and all men will be striving to enlarge their own. Dominion will always desire increase, and property always to preserve itself; and these opposite views and interests will be causing a perpetual struggle: But by this struggle liberty is preserved, as water is kept sweet by motion.

The nature and reason of this sort of government, is to make the several parts of it control and counterpoise one another; and so keep all within their proper bounds. The interest of the magistracy, which is the lot and portion of the great, is to prevent confusion, which levels all things: The interest of the body of the people, is to keep people from oppression, and their magistrates from changing into plunderers and murderers; the interest of the standing senate, which is, or ought to be, composed of men distinguishable for their fortunes and abilities, is to avoid ruin and dissolution from either of these extremes: So that, to preserve liberty, all these coordinate powers must be kept up in their whole strength and independency.

Names will not defend you, Gentlemen, when the thing signified by them is gone. The emperors of Rome were as absolute with the shew of a Senate, and the appearance of the people's choosing their praetors, tribunes, and other officers of the commonwealth, as the eastern monarchs are now without these seeming checks, and this shew of liberty: And in some respects they were more secure; as the infamy of their tyranny was shared by these assemblies, the advantages were all their own, and the condition of the people was rather the worse for these mock magistrates and pretended representatives, who, under the colour and title of the protectors of the people, were, at the people's expence, the real helpers and partakers of the iniquity of the tyrant. The kings of France have parliaments, but parliaments which dare not dispute their royal pleasure; and the poor people would not fare one jot the better, if these parliaments were bribed not to dispute it.

This wretched case, Gentlemen, will be yours and the wretched case of your posterity, if ever an ambitious prince and designing minister shall hereafter be able to corrupt or awe your representatives. And whatever wicked bargains are then made, will be made at your expence, and you must pay the terrible reckoning at last. You have a king at present, from whom you have none of these things to fear. But, alas! Gentlemen, how few Tituses and Trajans were there found amongst the Roman emperors! and how few can England shew since the Conquest! It requires therefore your best thoughts and most vigorous resolutions, to preserve your constitution entire in all its parts, without suffering any one part to prevail so far over the other, as to reduce it in effect, though not in name, to a simple form of government, which is always tyranny. It will be all one to you, whether this is brought about by confederacy or by force. Whatever be the villainous means, violence, oppression, and every rank of evil, will be the end.

In order to this honest or publick design, you ought to choose representatives, whose interests are at present the same with your own, and likely to continue the same; representatives, who are not already pre-engaged, nor, from their circumstances, education, profession, or manner of life, likely to be engaged, in a contrary interest. He will prove but a sorry advocate, who takes fees from your adversary; and as indifferent a plenipotentiary, who receives a pension from the prince whom he is commissioned to treat with: Nor can there be any security in the fidelity of one, who can find it more his interest to betray you, than to serve you faithfully.

Virtue and vice will be but ill balanced, when power and riches are thrown into the wrong scale. A great Protestant peer of France having changed his religion, in compliance with his master, Henry IV of France, who had changed too, was soon after asked by that monarch publickly, which of the two religions he thought the best? "The Protestant, sir, undoubtedly is the best," said the peer, "by your own royal confession; since, in exchange for it, your Majesty has given me popery, and a marshal's staff to boot."[1] Where boot is given, there is always a tacit confession that the exchange is unequal without it. Choose not therefore such who are likely to truck away your liberties for an equivalent to themselves, and to sell you to those against whom it is their duty to defend you. When their duty is in one scale, and a thousand pounds a year, or more, or even less, is thrown into the contrary scale, you may easily guess, as the world goes, how the balance is like to turn.

It is the right and duty of the freeholders and burghers of Great Britain, to examine into the conduct, and to know the opinions and intentions, of such as offer themselves to their choice. How can any of them be truly represented, when they know not who represents them? And as it was always their right, they had once the frequent means and opportunity to resent effectually the corruptions of those who had basely betrayed their sacred trust; of rejecting with scorn and detestation, such traitorous parricides; and of sending up honester and wiser men in their room. This, my dear countrymen, we had once the frequent means of doing: Make use now, O worthy and free Britons! make good use of this present dawn, this precious day of liberty, to recover once more that invaluable privilege. Do not wildly choose any one who has given up, or attempted to give up, your birthrights, and, above all, that right which secures all the rest. Admit no man to be so much as a candi-

1. The reference is probably to François de Bonne, Duc de Lediguières, a Protestant, who was given the rank of marshal by Henry IV in 1609. It was not, however, until 1622, twelve years after the King's death, that Lediguières formally abjured Protestantism.

date in your counties and boroughs, till he has declared, in the clearest manner, in the most express and solemn words declared, his most hearty and vigorous resolutions, to endeavour to repeal all laws which render you incapable to serve your king, or to punish traitors, or to preserve your original and essential rights. This, Gentlemen, is your time; which, if you suffer it to be lost, will probably be for ever lost.

There are a sort of men who prowl about the country to buy boroughs; creatures, who accost you for your votes with the spirit and design, and in manner of jockeys; and treating you like cattle, would purchase you for less or more, just as they think they can sell you again. Can you bear this insult, Gentlemen, upon your honesty, your reason and your liberties? Or if there be any amongst you, who countenance such vile and execrable bargains, which affect and involve you in all their consequences, ought they not to be treated like publick enemies, as indeed they are, and be hunted from amongst you? I have often wondered how a little contemptible corporation, consisting, as some of them do, of broom-makers, hedge-breakers,[2] and sheep-stealers, could stand the looks and rebukes of a rich and honest neighbourhood, after these dirty rogues had openly sold at the market-cross, perhaps for forty shillings a-piece, not only their own liberties, but, as far as in them lay, the liberties of that rich neighbourhood and all England. Such saleable vermin ought to be treated as persons excommunicate, as the pests and felons of society, which they would sell for porridge: And if proper abhorrence were every-where shewn towards them, and no commerce held with them, they would soon grow honest out of necessity; or if they did not, they might justly fear, like guilty Cain, that every man whom they met would kill them. If this method were taken, it would cure corruption of this kind: Let those who sell their country be everywhere renounced and shunned by their neighbourhood and their country, and such sale will soon be over.

The majority of you, Gentlemen, are yet uncorrupted: Indeed none but a few of the worst and poorest of you are yet corrupted. The body of the freeholders know not what it is to take money; and choose their representatives from amongst them-

2. Hedge breakers: breakers of the peace.

selves, and from a thorough acquaintance, either with the men, or with their characters. The little beggarly boroughs only are the pools of corruption; with them money is merit, and full of recommendation. They engage for men without knowing their names, and choose them sometimes without seeing their faces; yet their members, when they are chosen, are as good as yours; that is, their votes are good. It is in your power, Gentlemen, and in that of your honest neighbours to cure this mighty evil, which has hitherto been incurable, or not suffered to be cured. They are but a few, and an inconsiderable few, in comparison of you; and cannot live without you, though you can without them.

Try the expedient which I propose; neither buy nor sell with those reprobate mercenaries, who sell themselves and you. Consider how much it imports you; your all is concerned in it. This is not a dispute about dreams or speculations, which affect not your property; but it is a dispute whether you shall have any property, which these wretches throw away, by choosing for the guardians of property men whom they know not, or who are only known to them by a very bad token, that of having corrupted them.

Lay not out your money with those who for money sell your liberties, which is the only source of your money, and of all the happiness which you enjoy. Remember, when your all is at stake, as it always is in an election of those who are either to guard, or to give up your all; I say, remember how wantonly and blindly upon that occasion, these wretches surrender themselves, and you, and your all, and all England, to the best bidder, without knowing, often, who he is. What mercy do these cruel slaves deserve at your hands? The most horrible thing that they can do against you and your posterity, they do.

When Hannibal had gained his last and greatest battle against the Romans, and many of the nobility were deliberating about leaving Rome, the young Scipio entered the room with his sword drawn, and obliged every man present to bind himself with an oath, not to desert their country.[3] And will you, Gentlemen,

3. The *Scipio* to whom Gordon is referring is Scipio Africanus Major, who is reputed to have rallied the Roman nobility to continued resistance against Hannibal's forces after the Roman defeat at Cannae in 216 B.C.

suffer the little hireling inhabitants of boroughs, who receive from you and your neighbours their daily bread; will you, can you suffer them to betray you, to give up your fortunes, and to comprehend you as they do, in the sale which they make of themselves? Do you not know how much you are at the mercy of their honesty, how much it depends upon their breath whether you are to be freemen or slaves: Yet will you stand stupidly by, and see them truck you away for loose guineas? Would you allow the common laws of neighbourhood to such as steal or plunder your goods, rob you of your money, seize your houses, drive you from your possessions, enslave your persons, and starve your families? No, sure, you would not. Yet will you, can you continue to treat as neighbours and friends, those rash, wicked, and merciless profligates; who, as far as in them lies, would bring upon you and your posterity all those black and melancholy evils, by committing the mighty and sacred trust of all your lives and properties to men, who hire them to betray it; and having first made them rogues, may afterwards, for ought they know, make them slaves, and you with them?

Can you bear this, Gentlemen? It is the root of all your heavy sufferings, and may yet produce worse and more heavy. You are freemen, and men of reason and spirit; awaken your spirit, exert your reason, and assert your freedom. You have a right to petition the Parliament, you have a right to address the king, to propose your thoughts and grievances to both; and to be heard and relieved when you suffer any. And from the same reason and equity, you, Gentlemen freeholders, have a right and a near concern to advise your neighbouring boroughs in the choice of their members, and to warn them of the consequences, if they make a bad one.

For God's sake, Gentlemen, and for your own, and for all our sakes, shew your spirit, your understanding, and your activity, upon this occasion; and the hearty prayers and wishes of every honest man will attend you.

Alas! Gentlemen, with tears I tell you, that the cure of corruption is left to you. A cure from another quarter is cruelly denied to us. A worthy attempt was lately made to destroy it effectually; and we hoped that no man, or set of men, pretending to common honesty, would have had the face to discourage or frustrate that attempt; but it was frustrated, and we know where, and by whom, and for what ends.[4] Those who owe their whole figure, and fortune, and force to corruption, rather than part with it, seem determined to see the nation consumed and perish in it. Your help must be from God and yourselves; be honest, and make your neighbours honest; both are in your power, and I glory that they are. As you love your liberties exercise your virtue; they depend upon it. Remember the true but dismal picture that I have given you of slavery and arbitrary power; and if you would avoid them, be virtuous, scorn bribes, abhor the man that offers them and expose him. Consider him as an accursed tempter, and a barbarous ravisher, who would buy you out of your integrity, and spoil you of your liberties.

Give me leave now, Gentlemen, to mark out to you more particularly what sort of men you ought not to choose. Choose not those who live at a great distance from you, and whose abilities, probity and fortunes, are not well known to you. When you have chosen them, it will be too late to know them. Choose not the eldest sons of noblemen, who must be naturally in the interest of the nobility, as the nobility generally are in the interest of the court, whatever it be. Reject bigots of all kinds and sides: Those men, whose minds are shut up in band-boxes,[5] and who walk upon stilts, have not thoughts large enough for governing society. Even their honesty, when they have any, is useless to the publick; and is often, on the contrary, made an ill instrument in the hands of those who have none. Reject also all timorous, fearful, and dastardly spirits; men, who having good principles, either dare not own them, or dare not act according to them. Choose not men who are noted for non-attendance, and who have been members of Parliament, without waiting upon the business of Parliament; men, who will probably be engaged in a

4. This is apparently a reference to the House of Commons "trial"—an unprecedented inquest into the participation of members of Parliament and officers of the administration in the South Sea swindle—of Charles Stanhope, Secretary of the Treasury. Stanhope's was the first of these hearings, held on Feb. 28, 1722; despite overwhelming evidence of his guilt, Stanhope was acquitted by a vote of 180 to 177, a large number of MPs having abstained.

5. Band-boxes: small, lightweight boxes, originally used for storing apparel.

fox-chase, in a tavern, or in other debauched houses, though the kingdom were undoing. While your happiness or misery depends so much upon the breath of your representatives, it is of great importance to you, that their attendance be as constant, as their behaviour be honest. What excuse can they offer for themselves, when by their wanton absence a vote may pass, which may cost you millions? We know what bold advantages have been taken in former Parliaments, of a thin House, to raise great and unexpected sums from the nation, to enable its worst foes to carry on an unnatural conspiracy against it.

Reject with indignation those men, who, in the late execrable South-Sea conspiracy, took stock for votes; and for an infamous bribe in stock, voted your liberties and purses into the merciless claws of the South-Sea traitors, and are since many of them justly undone by the bargain. Think you, Gentlemen, that these men, who could sell their country, when they had a stake in it, will not sell it for less, when they have none? You ought to add to the same class, and treat in the same manner, all those who headed and abetted that destructive scheme, or endeavoured to protect those who did so.

You are to be particularly careful, that those whom you choose be duly qualified according to law, and that no deceit be practised in obtaining temporary qualifications. You ought to enquire into their estates, and how they came by them; and if they have none, as many who stand candidates, I am told, have not, you may guess who assists them, and what hopeful services are expected from them. Such men you may be sure will never speak your sense in Parliament, nor even their own, if they have any; nor be suffered to consult your interest. They must work for their masters against you, who ought to be so.

Neither can you expect to be well served by men, whose estates are embarked in companies: They themselves will be engaged with their fortunes in the particular interest of such companies, which are always against the interest of general trade; and they will be but too apt to fall into the juggling and artifices of courts, to raise their stock to imaginary values. A certain and known method to promote cheating, and to sink trade.

Shun likewise all those who are in the way of ambition; a passion which is rarely gratified by integrity, and an honest zeal for your good; shun all men of narrow fortunes, who are not for your purpose from obvious reasons; shun all lawyers, who have not established practice or good estates, and who are consequently more liable to corruption, and whom the court has more means of corrupting, than other men; shun all men involved in debt, all men of ill morals, and debauched, and dishonest lives; all gamesters, and all men who spend more than their income. Their extravagance makes them necessitous, and their necessities make them venal.

We do not ordinarily trust a man with a small sum without a note, or mortgage, or a bond; and such security is but reasonable: And is it not as reasonable, that, when we trust men with all that we have, as we do our representatives, we ought to seek and procure all the security which the nature of the thing will admit? Would it not be direct madness to trust our all, our whole accumulative portion in this life, to those whom no man would, in a private way, trust for five shillings? Call to mind, Gentlemen, whether some of you have never formerly made such a rash and dangerous choice; and for God's sake mend it now.

I suppose thus far you will all agree with me; as I dare say you will, when I tell you that the gentlemen of the sword are not proper representatives of a people, whose civil constitution abhors standing armies, and cannot subsist under them. The fortunes and expectations of these gentlemen depend upon observing the word of command; and it is but natural that they should support power in which they are sharers. You must not therefore expect that they will ever concur in a vote, or an address, to disband or reduce themselves; however desirable or necessary the same may be to you. Those of them who deserve well of you, as very many of the present officers do, are doubtless entitled to thanks and good usage from you; but to shew them respect by giving them seats in Parliament, is by no means a proper, prudent, or natural way of doing it. Besides, it will create a great and unjust partiality to particular boroughs, and some shall be burdened with soldiers, when others shall be free from them; just at the mercy and expectations of the commanding officer.

It is indeed a misfortune to the army itself, to have any of its officers members of the House of Commons, since the greatest merit in the field shall not recommend a man so much to just preferment, as the want of merit sometimes shall in that House. A complaint, however, which, I hope, there is no ground for at present.

Choose not, Gentlemen, any sort of men, whose interest may, at any time, and in any circumstance, consist in confusion. Neither are men in employments the properest men for your choice. If ever your interest comes in competition with their places, you may easily guess which must give way. I think there are but few instances, where they themselves suffer, and fall in that struggle. Under this head, I would desire you, Gentlemen, to observe the behaviour of the officers of the customs and excise upon the ensuing elections; and remember, that they forfeit one hundred pounds, if they persuade or deal with any person to vote, or to forbear voting, and are made for ever incapable of holding any employment under the crown. If you find them busy and intermeddling in this election, take the advantage which the law gives you, and see it honestly put in execution against them. Besides, such conduct of theirs, and prosecution of yours, may give occasion to a new law, with more terrible penalties upon that sort of men, whom our misfortunes have made numerous.

For a conclusion. Consider, Gentlemen, Oh! consider what you are about, and whether you will bring life or death upon us. Oh! take care of yourselves, and of us all. We are all in your hands, and so at present are your representatives; but very quickly the scene will be shifted, and both you and we will be in theirs. Do not judge of them by their present humble speeches, and condescending carriage; but think what they are like to be, when they are no longer under your eye, when they are no longer suing to you, nor want you. These humble creatures, who now bow down before you, will soon look down upon you. Oh! choose such as are likely to do it with most pity and tenderness, and are most likely to relieve you of those burdens, under which we all sadly groan, and under which we must certainly sink, never to rise again, if we be not relieved.

I am, Gentlemen, with exceeding sincerity, and all good wishes,

G   *Your most affectionate humble servant.*

NO. 71. SATURDAY, MARCH 31, 1722.

Polite Arts and Learning naturally produced in free States, and marred by such as are not free.

SIR,

In the first rise and beginning of states, a rough and unhewn virtue, a rude and savage fierceness, and an unpolished passion for liberty, are the qualities chiefly in repute. To these succeed military accomplishments, domestick arts and sciences, and such political knowledge and acquirements, as are necessary to make states great and formidable abroad, and to preserve equality, and domestick happiness, and security, at home. And lastly, when these are attained, follow politeness, speculative knowledge, moral and experimental philosophy, with other branches of learning and the whole train of the muses.

The Romans were long masters of the arts of war and policy, before they knew much of the embellishments of letters.

> *Serus enim Graecis admovit acumina chartis,*
> *Et, post Punica bella, quietus quaerere coepit,*
> *Quid Sophocles & Thespis, & Aeschylus utile ferrent.*[1]

These were the effects of ease, leisure, security, and plenty, and the productions of men retired from the hurry and anxieties of war, and sequestered from the tumults of the world; of men not ruffled by disappointment, nor scared with the noise of foreign

---

1. "It was not until late that Romans turned their minds to Greek writing, and, in the peaceful days following the Punic Wars, began to ask to what use Sophocles and Thespis and Aeschylus could be put." Horace, *Epistulae*, 2.1.161–63.

invasions, nor disturbed with civil tumults; and of men not distressed by want, or wholly employed with the cares of life, and solicitous for a support to themselves and families;

—*praeter laudem nullius avaris.*[2]

The Romans had secured their conquests, and settled their power, before they grew fond of the ornaments of life.

> How should my Mummius have time to read,
> When by his ancestors fam'd glory led
> To noble deeds, he must espouse the cause
> Of his dear country's liberties and laws?
> Amongst rough wars how can verse smoothly flow,
> Or 'midst such storms the learned laurel grow?

L. Mummius[3] was one of the principal men of Rome; yet so late as the taking of Corinth, he was so ignorant in the polite arts, that when he was shipping off the glorious spoils of that great city to Rome, he ridiculously threatened the masters of the vessels, that if they broke or lost any of the statues, paintings, or of the other curious Greek monuments, they should be obliged to get others made in their room at their proper expence.

But the Romans quickly improved in their taste, quickly grew fond of works of genius of every kind, having now leisure to admire them, and encouragement to imitate them. And the Greeks, from whom the Romans had them, were first great in power, and their civil oeconomy was excellently established, before they grew eminent in politeness and learning.

But neither will the single invitations of leisure and ease prove sufficient to engage men in the pursuits of knowledge as far as it may be pursued. Other motives must be thrown in; they must find certain protection and encouragements in such pursuits, and proper rewards at the end of them. The laurel is often the chief cause of the victory. The Greeks who encouraged learning and the sciences more, and preserved them longer than any people ever did, kept stated, publick and general assemblies, on purpose for

2. "They desired nothing but glory." Horace, *Ars poetica*, 323–24.

3. Lucius Achaicus *Mummius*, Roman consul who defeated the Achaean Confederacy in 147 B.C. and who plundered the Greek treasures found at Corinth.

the trial and encouragement of wit and arts, and for the distinguishing of those who professed them. Thither resorted all who had any pretensions that way, or had engaged in performances of that kind: All the most illustrious men in Greece, the nobility, the magistracy, the ambassadors of princes, sometimes princes themselves, were the auditors and judges: By these merit was distinguished, the contention for glory decided, the victory declared, and by these the rewards of it were bestowed. Thus glorious was the price of excelling; thus equitable, publick, and loud was the fame of it. It is therefore no wonder that it was courted by the Greeks with as much ardour and application, as the chief dignities in a state are courted by others. And, considering how strong were the stimulations of the Greeks to study, Horace might well say,

> *Graiis ingenium, graiis dedit ore rotundo*
> *Musa loqui.————*[4]

Before this august assembly, Herodotus repeated his history with great applause; which so animated Thucydides, then very young, that, in emulation of Herodotus, he wrote a better history than that of Herodotus. Here Cleomenes recommended himself, by only repeating some verses skilfully collected out of Empedocles;[5] and here Euripides and Xenocles[6] contended for preference in the drama.

Indeed, the honours attending a victory upon these occasions were excessive, and, according to Cicero, did almost equal those of a Roman triumph. The victors were reckoned to have arrived to the highest human felicity, to have entailed glory upon all that belonged to them, upon their families, friends, their native city, and the place of their education. Elogiums[7] were made upon

4. "The Muse gave to the Greeks the gift of genius and the ability to speak with perfect voice." Horace, *Ars poetica*, 323–24.

5. The *Cleomenes* to whom Gordon is referring is the rhapsodist who is reputed to have recited Empedocles' poetry at Olympia (Athenaeus, *Deipnosophistae*, 14.620d). *Empedocles* was a Pythagorean philosopher, poet, and historian from Agrigentum, in Sicily, who flourished during the late fifth century B.C.

6. The tragic writer *Xenocles* is reputed to have defeated Euripides for the poetry prize in 415 B.C., through bribery.

7. Elogiums: eulogies.

them, statues were erected to them, and, ever after, they met every-where the same preference, which they had met at the Olympick assemblies. A preference which so fired the emperor Nero, that, when he had ridiculously stood competitor at a singing-match, and taken a journey to Greece on purpose, he first declared himself victor, and then, to destroy all marks and memory of those who had been so before him, he commanded all their pictures and statues to be pulled down, and thrown into the privies.

The Romans, as soon as they had leisure from their long and many wars, fell quickly into the same studies, and into the same emulation to excel in them. They no sooner had any acquaintance with Greece, but they were possessed with a fondness for all her refinements.

> *Graecia capta ferum victorem cepit, & artes*
> *Intulit agresti Latio.*————[8]

The fierce Romans subdued Greece by their arms; and Greece made rustick Italy a captive to her arts. All the youth of Rome were charmed with the beauties of learning, and eager to possess them: Many of the Senators were caught by the same passions; even the elder Cato,[9] who was at first against these improvements, which, he feared, would soften too much the rough Roman genius, yet changed his opinion so far afterwards, as to learn Greek in his old age.

This prodigious progress of the Romans in learning had no other cause than the freedom and equality of their government. The spirit of the people, like that of their state, breathed nothing but liberty, which no power sought to control, or could control. The improvement of knowledge, by bringing no terror to the magistrates, brought no danger to the people. Nothing is too hard for liberty; that liberty which made the Greeks and Romans masters of the world, made them masters of all the learning in it: And, when their liberties perished, so did their learning. That eloquence, and

8. "Captive Greece in turn captured her savage conquerer and brought the arts to rustic Latium." Horace, *Epistulae*, 2.1.156.

9. Marcus Porcius *Cato* (214–149 B.C.), who made every effort to restore what he regarded as the elevated morality and simple life characteristic of the early days of the Roman Republic.

those other abilities and acquirements, which raised those who had them to the highest dignities in a free state, became under tyranny a certain train to ruin, unless they were prostituted to the service of the tyrant.

That knowledge, and those accomplishments, which create jealousy instead of applause, and danger instead of reward, will be but rarely and faintly pursued; and for the most part not at all. No man will take great pains, spend his youth, and lose his pleasures, to purchase infamy or punishment: And therefore when such obstacles are thrown in his way, he will take counsel of self-love, acquiesce in the fashionable stupidity, and prefer gilded and thriving folly to dangerous and forbidden wisdom.

Ignorance accompanies slavery, and is introduced by it. People who live in freedom will think with freedom; but when the mind is enslaved by fear, and the body by chains, inquiry and study will be at an end. Men will not pursue dangerous knowledge, nor venture their heads, to improve their understandings. Besides, their spirits, dejected with servitude and poverty, will want vigour as well as leisure to cultivate arts, and propagate truth; which is ever high-treason against tyranny. Neither the titles nor the deeds of tyrants will bear examination; and their power is concerned to stupify and destroy the very faculties of reason and thinking; Nor can reason travel far, when force and dread are in the way; and when men dare not see, their eyes will soon grow useless.

In Turkey, printing is forbid, lest by its means common sense might get the better of violence, and be too hard for the imperial butcher. It is even capital, and certain death there, only to reason freely upon their Alcoran. A sure sign of imposture? But by imposture, stupidity, and janizaries, his throne is supported; and his vast, but thin dominions, know no inhabitants but barbarous, ignorant, and miserable slaves.

Nor is printing in other arbitrary countries of much use but to rivet their chains: It is permitted only on one side, and made the further means of servitude. Even in Christian countries, under arbitrary princes, the people are for the most part as ignorant and implacable bigots as the Turks are. And as it is rare to find a slave who is not a bigot, no man can shew me a bigot who is not an ignorant slave; for bigotry is a slavery of the soul to certain religious opinions, fancies, or stories, of which the bigot knows little or nothing, and damns all that do.

The least cramp or restraint upon reasoning and inquiry of any kind, will prove soon a mighty bar in the way to learning. It is very true, that all sorts of knowledge, at least all sorts of sublime and important knowledge, are so complicated and interwoven together, that it is impossible to search into any part of it, and to trace the same with freedom to its first principles, without borrowing and taking in the help of most, if not all, of the other parts. Religion and government, particularly, are at the beginning and end of every thing, and are the sciences in the world the most necessary and important to be known; and as these are more or less known, other knowledge will be proportionably greater or smaller, or none: But, where these cannot be freely examined, and their excellencies searched into, and understood, all other wisdom will be maimed and ineffectual, indeed scarce worth having.

Now, in all arbitrary governments, and under all created and imposing religions, nothing must be found true in philosophy, which thwarts the received scheme, and the uppermost opinions: The most evident mathematical demonstrations must not disprove orthodox dogmas, and established ideas; the finest poetical flights must be restrained and discouraged, when they would fly over the narrow inclosures and prison-walls of bigots: Nor must the best, the strongest, and the most beautiful reasoning dare to break through popular prejudices, or attempt to contend with powerful and lucrative usurpation. A bishop was burned before the Reformation, for discovering the world to be round; and, even in the last century, the excellent Galileo was put into the dismal prison of the Inquisition, for maintaining the motion of the Earth round the Sun, as her centre. This proposition of his, which he had demonstrated, he was forced to recant, to save his life, and satisfy the Church.

Where religion and government are most deformed, as religion ever is where it is supported by craft and force, and government ever is when it is maintained by whips and chains, there all examination into either, and all reasoning about them, is most strictly forbid and discouraged: And as one sort of inquiry and knowledge begets another; and as, when the wits of men are suffered to exert themselves freely, no body knows where their pursuits may end; so no tyranny of any kind is safe, where general, impartial, and useful knowledge is pursued. Inhuman violence, and stupid ignorance, are the certain and necessary stay of tyrants; and every thing that is good or valuable in the world is against them.

In the East (if we except China) there is not a glimmering of knowledge; though the eastern people are, from their natural climate and genius, vastly capable of all knowledge. Bernier, mentioning the cruelty of the government, and the great misery of the people there, says,

> From the same cause, a gross and profound ignorance reigns in those states: Nor is it possible there should be academies and colleges well founded in them. Where are there such founders to be met with? And, if they were, where are the scholars to be had? Where are those who have means sufficient to maintain their children in colleges? And, if there were, who durst appear to be rich? And if they would, where are those benefices, preferments, and dignities, which require knowledge and abilities, and animate young men to study?[10]

I will not deny, but that, in arbitrary countries, there are sometimes found men of great parts and learning. But these are either ecclesiasticks, who, even in the greatest tyrannies, at least in Europe, are blessed with great liberty, and many independent privileges, and are freemen in the midst of slaves, and have suitable leisure and revenues to support them in their studies; or they are men invited and encouraged by the prince to flatter his pride, and administer to his pomp and pleasures, and to recommend his person and power. For these reasons alone they are caressed, protected, and rewarded. They are endowed with the advantages of freemen, merely to be the instruments of servitude. They are a sort of Swiss, hired to be the guards of their proud master's fame,

10. The passage appears in the "Letter to Colbert Concerning Indostan," in Bernier's *History of the Great Mogul*, pp. 77–78.

and to applaud and vindicate all his wickedness, wildness, usurpations, prodigalities, and follies. This therefore is the worst of all prostitutions, and most immoral of all sort of slavery; as it is supporting servitude with the breath of liberty, and assaulting and mangling liberty with her own weapons. A creature that lets out his genius to hire, may sometimes have a very good one; but he must have a vile and beggarly soul, and his performances are at best but the basest way of petitioning for alms.

France could boast many men of wit and letters in the late reign, though it was a very severe one, and brought infinite evils upon all France and Europe. But these great wits were many of them the instruments and parasites of power, who bent the whole force of their genius to sanctify domestick oppression and foreign usurpation: Such were the characters and employment of Pelisson, Boileau, Racine,[11] and several others. France saw at the same time several churchmen of great and exalted talents, such as the late Archbishop of Cambray, the Cardinal de Retz, Claude Joly,[*] the present Abbot Vertot,[12] and many more excellent men, all lovers of liberty, which, by being churchmen, they possessed.

But though it be true, that the late French king encouraged all sorts of learning, that contributed to the grandeur of his name and court, and did not contradict his power, and courted great writers all over Europe, either to write for him, or not against him; yet the nature of his government was so constant a damp upon general

11. Paul Pellisson (1624–1693), author and historiographer of Louis XIV. Nicolas Boileau Despréaux (1636–1711), French poet and critic and the author of the extremely influential *L'Art Poétique*. Jean Baptiste Racine (1639–1699), the greatest French dramatic poet of the age.

* Claude Joly [(1607–1700)], Canon of Notre Dame, Paris, has published a treatise entitled *Recueil de maximes véritables et importantes pour l'institution du roy. Contre la fausse [et pernicieuse] politique du cardinal Mazarin* [Paris, 1652], wherein he shows that the power of kings is limited by that of their estates and *parlements*, and gives authentic proofs that such is the original constitution of the government of France. He died [in] 1700.

12. "The late Archbishop of Cambray" is François de Salignac de la Mothe Fénelon (1651–1715), the noted author, who was consecrated archbishop in 1695. Jean François Paul de Gondi (1614–1679), Cardinal de Retz, the implacable opponent of Cardinal Mazarin, wrote his *Mémoires* after retiring to private life in 1662. René Aubert, Abbé de Vertot (1655–1735), authored, among other works, *L'Histoire des révolutions de Portugal* and *L'Histoire de la république romaine*.

learning, that it was at last brought to a very low pass in that kingdom, even in his time. Monsieur Des Maizeaux tells us, in his dedication of St. Evremond's works to the late Lord Halifax, that the great geniuses of France were, about the time I speak of, so constrained, as either to have forbore writing at all, or to have expressed what they thought by halves; that La Bruyere complains, that the French are cramped in satire; that Regis, the famous philosopher, solicited ten years for a licence to publish his course of philosophy, and at last obtained it only on this condition, to retrench whatever displeased the censors; That monsieur de Fontenelle hath been obliged to depart from the freedom which he used in the first works he published; that but few of the present French authors distinguish themselves either by their learning or wit; and that all this is to be attributed to the nature of the government;[13] which is unquestionably true.

What Mr. Des Maizeaux says upon this argument is so judicious and just, that I shall borrow another paragraph from the same dedication: "Liberty," says he,

> inspires a noble and elevated confidence, which naturally enlarges the mind, and gives it an emulation to trace out new roads towards attaining the sciences; whereas a servile dependence terrifies the soul, and fills the mind with a timorous circumspection, that renders it mean and groveling, and even debars the use of its most refined natural talents. Greece and Italy never had illustrious writers, but whilst they preserved their liberty. The loss of that was followed by the decay of wit, and the ruin of polite learning. Greece, formerly the seat of the Muses, is now involved in a frightful barbarity, under the slavery of the Ottoman Empire; and Italy, which, under the influence of a Senate, was so fruitful in great and learned men, now subject to the tribu-

13. Pierre Desmaizeaux, "Dedication," in *The Works of Monsieur de St. Evremond [Charles de Marguetel de Saint-Denis, Seigneur de Saint-Evremond] made English from the French original. With the author's life by Mr. Des Maizeaux* (2d ed.; 2 vols.; London: J. Churchill, 1714, I:8–9). Desmaizeaux is referring to Jean de la Bruyère (1645–1696), the French moralist and historian, Pierre-Sylvain Regis (1632–1707), the eminent Cartesian philosopher; and Bernard le Bovier de Fontenelle (1657–1757), the distinguished man of letters.

nal of the Inquisition, produces no considerable works of erudition or politeness.[14]

All the great geniuses, who lived in the days of Augustus, were born and educated in the days of liberty; and he borrowed from the commonwealth all the ornaments of his court and empire. In spite of all his boasted taste of letters, and the encouragement which he gave them, I do not remember one extraordinary genius bred under his influence: On the contrary, all that were so, died in his time, without leaving any successors. *Quicquid Romana facundia habet quod insolenti Graeciae aut opponat aut praeferat, circa Ciceronem effloruit. Omnia ingenia quae lucem studiis nostris attulerunt, tunc nata sunt. In deterius deinde quotidie data res est,* says Seneca.[15] "Every improvement in the Roman eloquence, which either equals or excels that of assuming Greece, flourished in the time of Cicero. All the great wits, that now animate and direct our studies, were then born. But, ever since then, wit daily decays, and grows lower and lower."

This decay began in the time of Augustus, who began his reign with butchering Cicero,[16] his patron, his father, and his friend, and the prodigy of Roman eloquence and learning; and that decay increased so fast, that from the first Roman emperor to the last, for the space of about five hundred years, the great city of Rome did not produce five great geniuses; and those that it did produce, were produced near the times of liberty, when they were yet warmed with its memory, before the tyrants had yet time utterly to abolish all that was good, though they made infinite haste. Tacitus was their last great historian, and Juvenal their last great poet, both passionate adorers of liberty. It is melancholy what the former says upon this subject, *Post bellatum apud Actium,*

14. Desmaizeaux, "Dedication," I:6–7.

15. "Whatever Roman oratory that may be placed alongside or even set above haughty Greece flourished at the time of Cicero. All the geniuses who have illuminated our studies were born then. Since, things have gotten daily worse." The Elder Seneca, *Controversiae* 1, praef. 6–7.

16. Because of his enmity toward Mark Antony, Cicero's name was included in a list of those to be killed following the establishment of the Second Triumvirate, comprising Antony, Lepidus, and Octavian. He was assassinated in Dec. 43 B.C.

atque omnem potestatem ad unum conferre pacis interfuit, magna illa ingenia cessere.[17] The Romans had no longer any great geniuses, than while they were free.

The Greeks preserved learning some time after the Romans had lost it; for, though they were conquered by the Romans, many of the Greek cities were suffered to enjoy their ancient liberties and laws: They paid only an easy homage, and no troops were quartered among them, as in the other provinces. However, as they were at the mercy of foreign masters, the vigour of their spirit was gone, and they produced but few good authors: Dio[18] and Plutarch are, I think, reckoned the chief. It is the observation of the learned, polite, and ingenious author of the *Reflexions critiques sur la poesie & sur le peinture*,[19] that Greece had more great men of all kinds in the age of Plato alone, when its liberties flourished, than in all the many ages between Perseus, the last king of Macedon, and the taking of Constantinople by the Turks, amounting to seventeen hundred years.

The several attempts made by Vespasian, Titus, and Trajan, to restore learning, proved almost vain. The Muses, who, frightened by tyranny, were now fled out of the world, could not be allured back to Rome, where baseness, terrors, and servitude had long reigned, and where their seats were filled by pedantick praters, by babbling and hypocritical philosophers: For, the itch and name of learning still subsisted; and therefore Seneca says, *ut omnium rerum, sic literarum quoque intemperantia laboramus.*[20]

The root of the evil remained; the empire of mere will had usurped the throne of the laws, and the place of learning. The genius, that bold and glorious genius inspired by liberty, was gone;

17. "After the battle of Actium, when the interests of peace required that all power should be conferred on one man, great geniuses ceased work." Tacitus, *Historiae*, 1.1.

18. *Dio* Cassius (*c.* A.D. 155–235), Roman statesman and author of a history of Rome.

19. Jean Baptiste Dubos (1670–1742). The citation appears in Dubos's Third Reflection: "That eminent painters have been always contemporaries with the great poets of their own country." *Reflexions* (2 vols.; Paris: J. Mariette, 1719); bk. II, p. 235.

20. "We suffer from excess in all things, so also in letters." The Younger Seneca, *Epistulae morales*, 106.12.

and the trial to restore learning, without restoring liberty, only served to shew that they who would do good to a community, which is ill constituted or corrupted, must either begin with the government, and alter or reform that, or despair of success. All that the best Roman emperors could at last do, was, not to butcher nor oppress their people; which yet they could not restrain their ministers from doing. Mucianus[21] blackened the reign of Vespasian by his pride, insolence, and cruelties; and the ministers of Nerva, under colour of punishing the informers, a crew of rogues licensed and encouraged by the former emperors, to ensnare and destroy their dreadful foes, the innocent and virtuous, made use of that good prince's authority, and his hatred of these vermin, to banish, plunder, kill, and ruin, many of the best men in Rome.[22]

The government, the arbitrary single government, had long discouraged and banished every thing that was good; and, with the rest, learning irretrievably.

G   *I am, &c.*

NO. 72. SATURDAY, APRIL 7, 1722.

In absolute Monarchies the Monarch seldom rules, but his Creatures instead of him. That Sort of Government a Gradation of Tyrants.

SIR,

The advocates for absolute monarchy argue as ignorantly as perversely, and build without a foundation; since, while they contend for unlimited submission to the monarch's will, they must either suppose, that all acts of power proceed from his will, or else that the will of his ministers is also unlimited, and their orders are

21. Gaius Licinius *Mucianus*, military commander who supported Vespasian's claims to the office of emperor and whose chief advisor he remained. He is reputed to have urged that all philosophers be banned from Rome.

22. Despite the humane policies adopted by Nerva upon becoming emperor in A.D. 96, he was unable to check the vengeful spirit of his councillors in prosecuting the army of informers active in the last years of Domitian's reign.

irresistible. So that either all his servants, instruments, and executioners, are absolute monarchs too; which none but a madman will say: Or that he himself does immediately direct every thing that is done; which no man of common sense will affirm. Indeed such princes have the least share of their own power, and seldom know what is done, or care.

Monsieur Thevenot tells us, that the Grand Seignior minds nothing but his pleasures, the pranks of mutes and buffoons, who are his constant attendants, and always studying new freaks and grimaces to divert him; and the dalliances of women, sent to him from all quarters by his bashaws. His power is absolutely despotick: His will, that is to say, his lust, his maggots, or his rage, is his only law, and the only bounds to the authority of this vicegerent of God. By virtue of his sacred power, he may rob any man, or all men, of their estates, and no man has a right to complain: He may put the best men to the most ignominious and barbarous death, and exalt the vilest criminals to the highest dignities; and no man must ask why. "This unlimited power of the Sultan," says Monsieur Thevenot, "is founded on the Mahometan religion, which enjoins a blind submission to all his commands, on pain of damnation."[1]

A blessed and beneficent religion this! and a single sovereignty with a witness! But this monstrous and formidable power, which is holden by him, is directed by his ministers without him. They employ both him and themselves; him, far from his duty, in unmanly pleasures; themselves, in the mismanagement of his affairs, and in prostituting his name and authority, to serve their own views. He wears the crown, and lives in a brothel; they sway the sceptre, suck the people's blood, and fill their own coffers. The Grand Vizier, or first minister, is, in effect, king over his master: He has the custody of the imperial power, and discharges the office of the Grand Seignior: And as to the bashaws, who are likewise so many kings in their provinces, Thevenot says, they abuse their authority, and are more arbitrary than the Sultan himself,

1. Jean de Thévenot, *The travels of Monsieur de Thevenot into the Levant* (3 vols. in 1; London: Printed by H. Clark for H. Faithorne, J. Adamson, C. Skegnes, and T. Newborough, 1687), I.xlv.61 and I.li.72. Thévenot's account originally appeared in French under the title *Relation d'un voyage fait en Levant* (3 vols.; Paris: L. Billaine, 1665–1684).

their design and business being to raise sudden fortunes by their spoils and oppression: And the Grand Seignior is forced to dissemble his knowledge of this rapine and exorbitancy, for want of power to punish or redress them; for that these men have the soldiers more at their devotion than he has.[2]

As to the Turkish civil officers and judges, he says they do what they will, and judge as they please; for all their written laws being contained in the Alcoran, which is but a short book, they are so ambiguously expressed, and so loosely delivered, that the cadi,[3] as well as the bashaw, wrests them as he pleases; and, judging without appeal, both these greedy and rapacious officers turn justice into oppression, and make it a stale[4] to their avarice.

Such is the spirit and effects of lawless power, lodged in one man; every officer and creature of his will have it; and, by setting up one tyrant, a thousand are set up. As this power is never to be got or preserved, but by violence and oppression; all men who have any share in executing and ministering, and defending the same, must be oppressors too. As no man is an oppressor for the mere pleasure and security of another, but only for his own sake and gratification; so all the servants of tyranny do, in their master's name, but rob and spoil for themselves; and every servant is a master. All over the Ottoman Empire, there is a great Turk in every town, and he at Constantinople is perhaps the idlest and most harmless of them all; and the exercise of the Turkish government is nothing else but a daily and general plunder, a contention between the governors who shall spoil best and get most. Nor, let them plunder and butcher as they will, is there any redress to the oppressed and expiring people; for though the imperial oppressor often forces his ministerial oppressors to disgorge, and spoils the spoiler of his booty and his life, where he dares; yet, there being no

2. Neither this nor the following paraphrase appear in Thévenot's *Travels*. While Thévenot does report on the abuses of power of the Sultan's chief civil officers, at no point does he directly attribute this to their relation to the military. Nor are Thévenot's discussions of the Koran, the source of all civil and canon law, and of the Ottoman judiciary quite as negative as are Gordon's descriptions.

3. Cadi: the chief judge of a town.

4. Stale: step.

restitution made, the condition of the oppressed is not mended: It is mock-justice, and worse than none; every act of power, every degree of office there, is robbery and violence, and every officer, the least and lowest, is an irresistible tyrant.

Single and absolute monarchy therefore, or the ruling all by the will of one is nonsense and a contradiction; it is rather a multiplication of monarchs, and in fact the worst sort of oligarchy. Now, suppose we were to obey blindly the will of the prince; are we also to obey blindly the will of his eunuchs, mistresses and janizaries, who oppress without his knowledge, or against his will? Sure the instruments and delegates of tyranny are not also the Lord's anointed. How therefore shall we know their mind from his, which perhaps contradicts theirs? Or how shall we know whether he wills any thing at all, and whether they do not will for him? This is almost always the case; and then here is a monarchy of ministers, and parasites, pathicks, buffoons, women, and butchers, rule for him, and over him.

Is this government too by divine right? If it be, let us rail no longer at anarchy; which, being the absence of all government, though it leaves every man to do what he lists, yet likewise leaves every man a right to defend himself: Besides this sort of anarchy, where every one is absolutely free, will quickly settle into order, and indeed cannot subsist long. But single monarchy, which is a long gradation of tyrants, where many on one side do what they will against the most on the other side; where cruelty and lust revel without control; where wanton and inhuman power has no limits, and heavy and sorrowful oppression no remedy nor end; where the innocent and harmless suffer most, and the worst and vilest thrive best, and where none are secure; where wickedness supports power, and property is the spoil of armies: I say, this absolute monarchy is worse than absolute anarchy, by not being so general. It is a partial anarchy, with worse effects, and no remedy.

All this still further proves, that men and societies have no possible human security but certain and express laws, setting express bounds to the power of their magistrates, ascertaining the measure of power as well as subjection, and restraining alike the exorbitances of both prince and people. It is eternally true, that such as is the nature of the government, such will be the nature of the people; and that as they are happy or miserable, so they will be good or bad, as their government and governors are good or bad; and that their whole integrity and virtue, or all their corruption and baseness, does arise from that single source.

"Princes," says Machiavel,

> do, but with little reason, and an ill grace, complain of the transgressions and faults of their subjects, since by the negligence and debauched example of their prince alone, the people are, and must be, debauched: And, if the people of our times are infamous for thefts, and robberies, and plunderings, and preying upon one another, and the like enormities, it is all owing to the exorbitances and rapaciousness of their governors. Romania was a place full of all dissoluteness and iniquity, every day, and every trivial occasion, producing notorious murders and rapines: Which evils were not derived so much from any depravity in the nature of the people (as some would falsely suggest) as from the vile corruption of their princes: For, being poor themselves, and yet ambitious to live in splendor, luxury, and magnificence [*the true causes of their poverty!*] they were forced upon execrable courses for money, and indeed refused none that could supply them.
>
> To pass by their many other sponging projects: One of their detestable schemes was to make laws against such and such things, and after these laws were published, they themselves would be the first to break them, and to encourage others to do the same: Nor was any man ever rebuked and punished for his unobservance, till they saw enough involved in the same penalty and praemunire;[5] and then, forsooth, the laws were to be executed with all strictness and severity, not out of any zeal for justice, but from a ravenous appetite to be fingering the fines. From whence it followed, that, by grievous mulcts and explications, the people being impoverished, were constrained to use the same violences upon those, who were less potent

5. In English law, an offense against the sovereign that is not subject to capital punishment.

than they themselves were. By which means the people were not corrected for doing evil, but instructed how to do it. And all these mischiefs proceeded solely from the baseness and iniquity of their princes.[6]

Thus it is that such courts, being continually in a conspiracy against the property and felicity of their people, and preying continually upon them by vile means and pretences, teach their people to conspire against honesty, and to prey upon one another; nay, by robbing them, they make it necessary for them to rob. Thus readily, necessarily, and naturally, is the spirit of the governors transfused into the governed, who are ever taught civil corruption by their superiors, before they practise it themselves.

Father le Compte, giving an account of the government of China, and shewing the wise provision made by the laws to check the great power of the Emperor, says,

> Nor is interest a less motive than reputation to the Emperor, to be guided by the ancient customs, and to adhere to the laws, which are framed so much for his advantage, that he cannot violate them, without obvious prejudice to his own authority, nor alter them, without bringing his kingdom into confusion; for such is the temper of the Chinese, that when the Emperor is governed by violence and passion, and grows negligent of his affairs, the same perverse spirit possesses his subjects: Every mandarin thinks himself sovereign of his province or city: The chief ministers sell offices and places to worthless wretches: The vice-roys become so many little tyrants: The governors observe no rule of justice; and the people thus oppressed, are easily stirred up to sedition: Rogues multiply, and commit villainies in companies, and court all occasions to do mischief, and to break the peace. Such beginnings have occasioned fatal consequences, and put China under the command of new masters; so that the Emperor's surest way to preserve his crown, is to observe the laws, and give an entire obedience to them.[7]

6. *Discourses*. II.29.1–2. The phrase in brackets is Gordon's.

7. Louis Daniel le Comte (1655–1728), *Memoirs and observations topographical, physical, mathematical, mechanical, natural, civil, and ecclesiastical. Made in a late*

An absolute prince and his deputy-tyrants are only the instruments of one another. By their hands he executes his lust, avarice, and rage; by his authority they execute their own. He is their dupe; they are his tools: However they may differ in particular views; they are always strongly united in cruelty and oppression. And therefore, whenever there is any contention amongst them, it is only who shall be the uppermost tyrants; for tyranny is the aim, the darling and the practice of all: And when the superior and subordinate tyrants butcher one another, as they often do; the people, though they see the revenge, yet feel no relief. Whoever bears the iron rod, they feel its sharpness and its weight: For almost every tyrant grows worse and worse; yet generally leaves a successor worse than himself. What unutterable and increasing woe must be the lot of their poor subjects under continual harrows of iron, made daily more poignant and heavy! Nor is the killing of a tyrant any cure, unless the tyranny be killed with him. The nature of this power breaths nothing but destruction, private ruin, and publick desolation; the common maxims of justice and mercy are not known to him, or known only for high treason; the very contrary are constantly practised; and his ministers, to be faithful servants, must be the worst of men, and all of them tyrants like himself.

These kings (of the East) says Monsieur Bernier, see no men about them, but men of nothing; slaves, ignorants, brutes, and such courtiers as are raised from the dust to dignities; who, for want of good education, do almost always retain somewhat of their original, and of the temper of beggars enriched. They are proud, insufferable, cowardly, insensible of honour, perfidious, void of affection, and of all regard for their king and country.

These kings, says he, must ruin all, to find means to defray those prodigious expences, which they cannot avoid, for the support of their great court, which has no other source of subsistence, but their coffers and treasures; and for maintaining constantly the vast number of forces necessary to keep the people in subjection, and to prevent their running away, and to force them to work, in

---

journey through the empire of China, and published in several letters (Third ed., corrected; London: B. Tooke, 1699), pp. 256–57. The passage appears in the section entitled "Of the Policy and Government of the Chinese."

order to draw from them the fruits of their work. For the people being kept continually under the dreadful yoke of oppression, and made to labour through fear, for the benefit of their governors only, and perfectly wild and desperate, and ready to do any act of despair.[8] Captain Perry says the same of the Muscovites; that, made desperate by oppression and want, they run eagerly into tumults, murders, and rebellions:[9] And Dr. Fletcher says, that they are so enraged with hunger and cold, that they beg in a wild and desperate tone, "Give me, and cut me; help me, and kill me," &c.[10]

I would observe here, how much more easy, as well as glorious, it is to govern freemen than slaves. It is true, that freemen go sometimes much farther in their opposition to unjust power, than slaves go or can go; because they have more spirit, sense, virtue, and force: But that they are with more difficulty governed, is absolutely false. It is indeed difficult to oppress them, and their rebellion is generally no more than their distinguishing of government from oppression; a distinction which their governors but too seldom make, and which slaves, born to oppression, know not how to make. In truth, government is a thing not so much as known in the greatest, by far the greatest part of the earth. Government supposes, on one side, a just execution of rational standing laws, made by the consent of society; and on the other side, a rational subjection to those laws. But what has arbitrary will, wanton and outrageous lust, cruelty and oppression, to do with government, but to destroy it?

But to shew yet further the anarchy of absolute monarchy, I shall insert here what Monsieur Bernier says of the education of such sort of princes. He says, that one of the principal sources of the misery, of the misgovernment, of the dispeopling, and the decay of the eastern empires, proceeds from hence, that the children of their kings are brought up only by women and eunuchs, who generally are no other than wretched slaves from Russia, Circassia, Gurgistan, Mengrelia[11] and Ethiopia; creatures of mean and insolent, servile and ignorant souls.

8. "Letter to Colbert Concerning Indostan" in his *History of the Great Mogul*, pp. 80–81.

9. John Perry (1670–1732), *The State of Russia Under the Present Czar*, p. 260.

10. Giles Fletcher, *Of the Russe Commonwealth*, pp. 116–117.

11. Circassia, Gurjistan (present-day Georgia), and Mingrelia are all located in the Caucasus.

These princes become kings, without instruction worthy of men, and without knowing what it is to be a king. They are amazed when they come out of the seraglio, as persons coming out of another world, or out of some subterraneous cave, where they had spent their whole lives. They wonder at every thing which they meet, like so many ignorants. They either fear all and believe all, like children; or nothing at all, like idiots. They are commonly high and proud, and seemingly grave: But this their loftiness and gravity is so flat, so distasteful, and so unbecoming them, that it is visibly nothing but brutality and barbarousness, and the effect of some ill-studied documents. Sometimes they run into some childish civilities, still more unsavoury; or into such cruelties as are blind and brutal; or into the vile and mean vice of drunkenness, or into a gross and excessive luxury; and either ruin their bodies and understandings with their concubines, or abandon themselves to the pleasure of hunting, like some carnivorous animals, and prefer a pack of dogs before so many poor people, whom they force to follow them in the pursuit of their game, and suffer to perish with hunger, heat, cold, and misery.

In a word, they always run into one extreme or another, and are entirely irrational or extravagant, according as they are carried away by their temper, or by the first impressions made upon them. And thus remaining, almost all, in utter ignorance of their duty, and of the state of their country, and of all publick concernments, they abandon the reins of the government to some vizier (in English, a first minister), who entertains them in their ignorance, and encourages them in their passions and follies; and their ignorance, passions and follies, are the strongest supports that these viziers can have to maintain their dominions over their masters.

These kings are also frequently given up entirely to these slaves, to their mothers, and to their own eunuchs, who often know nothing but to contrive plots of cruelty to strangle and banish one another; sometimes they murder the king himself: Nor is any one else safe in life or property.[12] Thus far Bernier.

12. The excerpt is taken from Bernier's chapter entitled "Parlicular Events, or the Most Remarkable Passages after the War," in his *History of the Great Mogul*, pp. 59–60.

Thus do these princes live shut up in brothels, strangers and enemies to their people; and when an appetite for war is added to their spirit of cruelty and oppression, all the advantage from it to their subjects is, that in the warlike havock a quicker end to put to their miseries, by ending their lives with a gun or a scimitar, instead of famine.

As to the redress of their grievances, and the doing justice upon the authors of them, it is absolutely impracticable in any country which has no states and representatives; and certain and irretrievable misery, as absolute as its government, is entailed upon it to all generations, till there be an utter end either of the government or of the people. The governor of Schiras[13] pays for his government, to the King of Persia, vast sums of ready money, with fine horses, and all the fine things and rarities to be found within his province: Besides these excessive presents to the king, he is obliged to make the like to all the great lords and favourites at court, who are never to be gained but by continual bribes; so that to defray this great and endless expence, the wretched people must suffer great and endless burdens and exactions, and the governor must be a tyrant to preserve his government. Nor can they have any possible relief, though they have sometimes attempted to find it: But when two or three villages at a time have come to complain to the king, they have, after long waiting, been forced away without any redress, with empty purses and hungry bellies, because they who should have given them admission, were bribed to debar them: So that they must stupidly submit to the barbarous extortions of a ravenous vizier. This, says Bernier, is the policy practised by all the governors and kans[14] in the Persian dominions: And he tells us, that one day, when Sha Sefi[15] was hunting (a prince whose justice and punishments were only acts of cruelty), a poor man deputed by a neighbouring village to make some complaint to the king, appeared behind a rock with a paper in his hand: But while

13. Shiraz, that is, the Persian province extending around the area of the city of Shiraz, along the northern shore of the Persian Gulf.

14. Khans, i.e., princes.

15. Shah Sufi, King of Persia from 1627 to 1641, who was infamous for his savage cruelty and malevolence.

the poor wretch was declaring his errand, and praying for justice, his most gracious Majesty, without making any answer, drew his bow, and shooting two arrows into his body, instantly slew him.[16]

Nor was this execrable royal act of his any more agreeable to the genius of that prince than to the genius of that sort of government, which is naturally barbarous and savage. An arbitrary prince is only the most exalted and successful beast of prey in his own dominions, and all the many officers under him are but so many subordinate beasts of prey, who hunt and rob and devour his people for him and themselves; and he and his officers do but constitute a long link of armed tigers terrible to behold, who leap furiously upon every man and every thing that tempts their eye or their appetite.

So that under a tyrant, there is no end of tyrants: From him that sways the scepter to him that carries a musket, all are tyrants, and every one for himself as far as he dare.

If any thing concerning these unintermitting pests of [the] human race, could possibly raise in a human soul any other passion but grief and horror, it would create mirth to hear mention made, as sometimes in books of history and travels there is mention made, of a tyrant's sitting in his seat of justice once in so many days, to hear equally all causes and persons. What mockery! It is really a farce, but a melancholy one, to hear the word *justice* come out of the mouth of a tyrant; who, by being so, is a settled enemy to the common laws of justice and mercy, and common sense, and to all that is good or lovely, or desirable amongst men. As well may he set apart one day in six to cure all the diseases of his subjects, or to make their clothes, and cook their victuals, if he leave them any to make and cook. As every subject in his dominions is oppressed, and he and his instruments are the oppressors, I know no way upon earth for him to do them any general justice, but to destroy himself and all his deputy tyrants.

G   *I am, &c.*

---

16. Gordon is in error in attributing these comments to Bernier. The description in fact appears in *The Six Voyages of John Baptista Tavernier*, V.iii.206.

NO. 73. SATURDAY, APRIL 21, 1722.

A Display of Tyranny, its destructive Nature, and Tendency to dispeople the Earth.

SIR,

I intend to finish in this paper, what I have so largely handled in so many others, the subject of liberty and tyranny;[1] a noble subject, superior to all others, and to the greatest genius, but fit for the consideration of every genius, and of every rank of men. It concerns the whole earth, and children ought to be instructed in it as soon as they are capable of instruction. Why should not the knowledge and love of God be joined to the knowledge and love of liberty, his best gift, which is the certain source of all the civil blessings of this life? And I have shewn that religion cannot subsist without it. And why should not the dread and hatred of Satan be accompanied with the dread and hatred of tyrants, who are his instruments, and the instruments of all the civil miseries in this life? I have often thought that the barbarians, who worship the Devil, must have borrowed their idea of him from the character and behaviour of their own princes. One might indeed defy any thing out of hell, or even in it, and all that are in it, to do half the mischief upon this earth that tyrants do.

They reduce mankind to the condition of brutes, and make that reason, which God gave them, useless to them: They deprive them even of the blessings of nature, starve them in the midst of plenty, and frustrate the natural bounty of the earth to men; so that nature smiles in vain where tyranny frowns: The very hands of men, given them by nature for their support, are turned by tyrants into the instruments of their misery, by being employed in vile drudgeries or destructive wars, to gratify the lust and vanity of their execrable lords, who suffer neither religion, nor virtue, nor knowledge, nor plenty, nor any kind of happiness, to dwell within the extent of their power.

1. See Letters 59 through 68 (Dec. 30 to March 3, 1721), and Letters 71 and 72 (March 31 and Apr. 7, 1722).

Nothing that is good or desirable can subsist under tyrants, nor within their reach; and they themselves subsist upon nothing but what is detestable and wicked. They are supported by general ruin; they live by the destruction of mankind: And as fraud and villainy, and every species of violence and cruelty, are the props of their throne; so they measure their own happiness, and security, and strength, by the misery and weakness of their people; and continued oppression and rapine are their studied and necessary arts of reigning, as is every art by which they can render their people poor, abject, and wretched; though by such methods they do in effect render themselves so, and consequently become easy preys to the next invader. That wealth, which dispersed amongst their subjects, and circulated in trade and commerce, would employ, increase, and enrich them, and return often again with interest into their coffers, is barbarously robbed from the people, and engrossed[2] by these their oppressors, and generally laid out by them to adorn their palaces, to cover their horses or elephants, or to embellish their own persons, and those of their concubines and attendants, or else locked up in dark caverns far from human sight and use.

Whilst it is yet in the mine, it is within the reach of pickaxes and shovels; and by the labour and industry of men, may be made useful and beneficial to men: But in the den of a tyrant, it is more securely, more irretrieveably buried and guarded from the use of men. Here are literally Pluto's brass walls, and adamantine gates; here are thousands of real Cerberuses, who never sleep; all to encompass and secure this dead treasure, and to restrain a general gift of God from the use of his creatures: From thence it is rarely fetched, even upon the greatest emergencies, or for any purposes but ill ones, 'till at last it becomes the prize and booty of a conquering enemy. Alexander found more riches in the Persian treasures, than in the hands of freemen would have conquered the world; and 'tis thought that there are more at this day in that of the Great Mogul, than would purchase the greatest and wealthiest kingdom in Europe; and it has been computed that there are thirty millions of wealth buried in the secret vaults of the Turkish seraglio, the

2. Engrossed: amassed.

plunder of the people, or of those who plundered them; yet they are still plundered and miserably oppressed, to increase this dead, useless, and pernicious store.

By these and the like inhuman means, the countries of tyrants are come to be in the condition which I have elsewhere described, desolate and uncultivated, and proper receptacles for such savage monsters, and ravening beasts of prey, who rather choose to live in barren fields, unhospitable deserts, and in dispeopled and empty towns, than amongst freemen in happy climates, filled with rich and numerous cities, abounding in inhabitants who are possessed of liberty, and will be bold to defend it.

Now where can all this dismal ruin, this growing depopulation end? If a continued decay in the natural body certainly ends in the extinction of life; in what can a continued and hasty decay of mankind end, but in the extinction of men? So that if the world last many centuries more in its present wasting and mournful situation, there must be a dissolution of [the] human race, before the world is dissolved.

Several new tyrannies have sprung up, like so many new plagues, within the memory of man, and like them have laid waste, but with a more regular and continued ruin, countries once strong in liberty and people: And as tyranny, like every other full-grown mischief, becomes more and more insupportable every day, the condition of mankind under it must necessarily, and does actually, grow every day worse and worse, and they themselves fewer. And even when their numbers and their substances are lessened, or rather exhausted, the demands of the tyrant upon them are not lessened, nor his rapine abated, nor his expences and exactions restrained.

When a tyrant has reduced a million of people to half that number by his cruelty and extortions, he madly expects from the remaining half the same revenue and assistance of men, which he had from the whole; and like the rest, they must perish to make good his expectations; and he often increases his troops as fast as his people decrease. So that his expence is enlarged as there becomes less to support it; but he will be supported, and his poor perishing people must do it, though they destroy themselves.

Such is the pestilent, savage, and unsatiable nature of this sort of monster, whose figure, throne and authority is established upon the ruins of reason, humanity, and nature: He takes all that his subjects have, and destroys them to get more.

A late great prince,[3] when he had lost and destroyed two millions of his people out of twelve, and reduced the whole to a degree of poverty and servitude scarce to be expressed, what impositions did he recall, what taxes abolish, what troops disband, for their relief? Not one. On the contrary, the swellings of his insolent heart continued, as did his merciless extortions upon his people, and his perfidious designs and encroachments upon his neighbours; and he lived and died the plague and curse of Christendom. Nor can it be shewn, that other princes who govern by the same authority, that is, according to their own whims and caprice, leave their subjects more plenty or happiness, or cheat or harass their neighbours less, according to the measure of their power. In truth, the whole tribe are perpetually taking advantages, and usurping upon one another, and are constant goads and thorns in one another's sides, and in the sides of their people: nor can the subjects of a prince of this cast have one tolerable reason under the sun to defend him against another, but that he lives amongst them, and spends with them part of their own plunder, and probably the other would not: As his whole reliance must be upon his soldiers, he must increase them in proportion to his distrust of his people; which is a confession of mutual enmity: Neither is it enough that his soldiers oppress and famish his people, for his sake and their own (for both he and they are supported by the spoils of the people), but he must keep them as constantly employed as he can; because if they be not employed in plundering, invading, and shedding of blood, they will grow unfit for such beneficent and necessary work, and may probably degenerate into humanity and mercy; than which a more terrible change could not befall their royal master; so that in mere duty they must be constantly practising mischief and rapine at home or abroad.

Thus do these general destroyers proceed to lay waste the world: The best and most countries in it are already, many of

3. Louis XIV.

them, almost desolate, and some of them altogether, as I have shewn in many instances; and the desolation gains ground daily: Nor, when some countries are dispeopled, are there sufficient recruits, or indeed any, to be had from others as formerly. The north, formerly the hive of nations, is now as much dispeopled as any of the southern countries, which some centuries ago, were peopled from it; and both north and south have been dispeopled by tyranny. Arabia, which once over-ran the world with multitudes, is now as desolate as the rest of the world which they over-ran. The country of the Chozari,[4] which was a vast empire, within these four hundred years, is now quite uninhabited, though great part of it is a fertile and beautiful country; and in its last struggle with Tamerlane, brought five hundred thousand men into the field: Such a force of people were there so lately in a country where now there are none! I think Rubriquis says, that he travelled two months through it, and in all the time saw neither man nor beast, but many great ruinous towns and cities, particularly one which had eight hundred churches in it less than four hundred years ago, but now has not one inhabitant.[5]

What can be more affecting than this instance! Not a single soul to be met with in a vast and noble country, which a few centuries ago was a potent empire, and contained millions! In all probability, countries and empires, which now make a great noise and bustle in the world, will be lying, two or three centuries hence, in the same woeful and silent solitude, if they last so long; for depopulation makes every-where, except in a few remaining free states, a prodigious and flying progress; even in Europe, as I have before proved in many instances. And in some of those free states, the seeds of servitude, the true cause of depopulation, and of every misery, seem to be sown deep. Alas! Power encroaches daily upon liberty, with a success too evident; and the balance between them is almost lost. Tyranny has engrossed almost the whole earth, and striking at mankind root and branch, makes the world a slaughter-

4. That is, the country of the Khazars, situated west of the Volga River and north of the Black Sea.

5. Willem van Ruysbroek, "The Journall of Frier William De Rubruquis, a French-man, of the Order of the Minorite Friers, unto the East parts of the World," in Samuel Purchas, ed., *Purchas his Pilgrimes*, III.i.49.

house; and will certainly go on to destroy, till it is either destroyed itself, or, which is most likely, has left nothing else to destroy.

The bulk of the earth being evidently almost a desert already, made so by tyrants; it is demonstration that the whole must be so, and must soon be entirely so, if the growth of tyranny be not restrained; else if the general and wide waste goes on, men will become too few for the management of societies, and for cultivation and commerce; all which are supported by numbers; and then degenerating into absolute savages, they will live straggling and naked in the woods and wildernesses, like wild beasts, and be devoured by them; or, like them, devour one another, or perish with hunger. And thus there will be an end of men; unless those states that are yet free, preserve, in the midst of this general waste, their own liberties and people, and, like the ancient Egyptians and Greeks, fill the world again, in process of time, with colonies of freemen.

That there is such a terrible waste of people in the world, cannot be denied; and it is as evident, that tyrants, are the constant, regular, and necessary cause of it. They are indeed so manifestly the authors of all that is ruinous and wicked, that if God Almighty had left it to Satan to invent an engine for the destroying of the world, and for defacing every thing beautiful, good, or desirable in it, that minister of vengeance, and enemy to God and man, would doubtless have invented tyrants, who by their wonderful success in such ministration, have ever shewn, and do still shew, their eminent fitness for it. They shew every-where such a constant and strong antipathy to the happiness of mankind, that if there be but one free city within their ken, they are restless in their designs and snares against it, and never defend it but against one another, and practice the vilest and the meanest rogueries to become masters of it. There are instances in this age of free cities falling into the claws of tyrants, and of the miserable difference between their former opulency, and their present poorness: They have never since put off their mourning, which grows daily more black and dismal.

The breath of a tyrant blasts and poisons every thing, changes blessings and plenty into curses and misery, great cities into gloomy solitudes, and their rich citizens into beggars and vagabonds: I could name cities, which, while they governed themselves, could maintain armies, and now enslaved can scarce maintain the poor proud rogues who govern them. It is certain, that whatever country or place is subdued by a prince who governs by his will, is ruined by his government.

It is confessed, that the arbitrary princes in Europe have not yet, like those in Asia, declared themselves masters of the soil; and their people have a sort of property. How long this will continue, I know not precisely. This is certain, that the condition of their subjects, which was always bad, grows hourly worse; and their nobility, which were once rich and powerful, are now reduced very low, and greatly impoverished. These, who were the supports of royalty, having created jealousy as if they had eclipsed it, have felt the terrible effects of arbitrary power as well as others, though not so much. Besides, when the common people, already wholly exhausted, and starving under oppression, can supply the exorbitant demands of their prince no longer, the estates of the nobility will be the next resource; and, like the mastiff dog at the bee-hive, when he has sucked up all the honey, he will swallow the comb: And then most of Europe will be in the condition of Turkey, as many parts of it are at present not much better; and, like the Great Turk, most of its princes will be sole proprietors of the land, as they now make themselves of its product, which very near answers the same end. When tenants, exhausted by taxes, are unable to pay rent, the land yielding no profit, is as bad as none; and in some instances worse than none, as we are particularly told by the noble author of the *Account of Denmark*, where some landlords have begged the king upon their knees to ease them of their land, by taking it from them for good and all; for that it was taxed more than it was worth.[6]

Most of the princes of Europe have been long introducing the Turkish government into Europe; and have succeeded so well, that I would rather live under the Turk than under many of them. They practice the cruelties and oppressions of the Turks, and want the tolerating spirit of the Turk; and if some unforeseen check be not thrown in their way, the whole polity of savage Turkey will be

6. Robert Molesworth, *An Account of Denmark As It was in the Year 1692*, p. 77.

established by them in all its parts and barbarity; as if the depopulation which is already so quick, and taking such dreadful strides, were still too slow. It is not enough for tyrants to have consumed mankind so fast, that out of twenty parts, they have within these two thousand years destroyed perhaps nineteen (for so much at least I take to be the disproportion), but fresh machines of cruelty are still sought after, besides never laying aside any of the old, till the destruction be fully completed. They seem to think, that they shall have enemies as long as any men remain; which indeed is a reasonable apprehension: But it is astonishing at first view, that mankind should have so long borne these unrelenting slaughterers of mankind. But, alas! who knows not the force of corruption, delusion, and standing armies!

Oh liberty! Oh servitude! how amiable, how detestable, are the different sounds! Liberty is salvation in politicks, as slavery is reprobation; neither is there any other distinction but that of saint and devil, between the champions of the one and of the other.

And here I conclude this noble subject of liberty; having made some weak attempts to shew its glorious advantages, and to set off the opposite mischiefs of raging, relentless, and consuming tyranny: A task to which no human mind is equal. For neither the sublimest wits of antiquity, nor the brightest geniuses of late or modern time, assisted with all the powers of rhetoric, and all the stimulations of poetick fire, with the warmest and boldest figures in language, ever did, or ever could, or ever can, describe and heighten sufficiently the beauty of the one, or the deformity of the other: Language fails in it, and words are too weak.

Those who do not groan under the yoke of heavy and pointed vassalage, cannot possibly have images equal to a calamity which they do not feel: And those who feel it are stupefied by it, and their minds depressed; nor can they have conceptions large, bright, and comprehensive enough, to be fully sensible of their own wretched condition; and much less can they paint it in proper colours to others. We, who enjoy the precious, lovely, and invaluable blessing of liberty, know that nothing can be paid too dear to purchase and preserve it. Without it the world is a wilderness, and life precarious and a burden: Death is a tribute which we all owe to nature, and must pay; and it is infinitely preferable, in any shape, to an ignominious life: Nor can we restore our beings back again into the hands of our great Creator, with more glory to him, more honour to ourselves, or more advantage to mankind, than in defence of all that is valuable, religious, and praise-worthy upon earth, or include whatever is so.

How execrable then and infamous are the wretches, who, for a few precarious, momentary, and perhaps imaginary advantages, would rob their country, their happy country, for ever, of every thing that can render human life desireable; and for a little tinsel pageantry, and false and servile homage, unworthy of honest men, and hated by wise men, would involve millions of their fellow-creatures in lasting misery, bondage, and woe, and charge themselves with their just hatred and bitter curses! Such unnatural parricides, unworthy of the human shape and name, would fill up the measure of their barbarity, by entailing poverty, chains, and sorrow, upon their own posterity. And often it has happened, that such men have, unpitied, suffered in their own persons, the sad effects of those cruel counsels and schemes, which they intended for the ruin of all but themselves; and have justly fallen into that pit, which they had traitorously digged for others.

> ————*Nec lex est justior ulla,*
> *Quam necis artifices arte perire sua.*[7]

G   *I am, &c.*

NO. 74. SATURDAY, APRIL 28, 1722.

The Vanity of Conquerors, and the Calamities attending Conquests.

SIR,

The condition of an absolute prince is thought the highest lot of human life, in point of splendor, plenty, and power; and is perhaps the lowest in point of happiness. The greatest appearances of pleasure are no certain proofs of pleasure; and he who

---

7. "No law is more just than one that provides that those who plot the death of others should perish by their own devices." Ovid, *Ars amatoria*, 1.655–56.

can enjoy all things, has often the least enjoyment: Having little or nothing to expect, he is at a stand in life; than which there cannot be a greater unhappiness. It is an agreeable fallacy which men keep themselves under, that while they find themselves daily disappointed in the enjoyments from which they expected most pleasure, they still press forward to more enjoyments, without expecting to be disappointed in these, though they certainly will. Their happiness consists in being deceived without knowing it; and when they find that they are, they do not grow wiser, but go on to promise themselves satisfaction from things, which, upon a thousand trials, they have found gave them none.

Our only lasting pleasure therefore is expectation. And what have absolute princes to expect; they who are in possession of all things? Yet they cannot live without expectation: They grow weary of pleasures within their power, and are therefore for stretching their power to procure more or better; which yet it will not procure. But thus their hopes beguile them.

Hence great and famous conquerors, never content with their present condition, come to be the incessant troublers of the world: And they who should have protected it, and preserved its peace, have often sought their pleasures in the tears, misery, and sorrows of millions; nay, often found their own grief, ruin, and ill fate in doing so. That this has been their character, is too universally true; and I believe it will be hard to shew one such prince in an hundred, who never laid snares either against his own people, or his neighbours; and though he never did, yet it was their duty and near concern to be upon their guard against him. They might have depended upon it, as a proposition that had infinite odds on its side, that he was not satisfied with its present condition, and that he would alter it, if he could, at their expence. Either his power was not absolute enough, or his dominions not wide enough; nor would they ever have been, whatever accessions of both accrued to him. There was still some darling point to gain, dearer than any before gained, though they were all so before they were gained.

It is the hard fate of conquerors, that their only, or chiefest remaining pleasure, is that of doing mischief: but the fate of their subjects and neighbours is harder. They are often undone to furnish out employment for their governors, who find their pleasure in destroying their people, or in doing that which destroys them. To increase power is, no doubt, the maxim of these princes; but their practice generally contradicts it, while they lessen their people and their wealth to enlarge their territory; every addition of this kind being an addition to their weakness: And therefore great empires, from the moment they are at their height, are in a continual decay; the decay and discouragement of the people being the unnatural means of their first growth; and indeed their increase contained in it, and carried along with it, certain seeds of decrease and desolation.

It may seem a contradiction, to say, that the whole can be built upon the destruction of the parts: Yet it is true of absolute monarchy, which does ever subsist by ruining and destroying those by whom it subsists; and the people, without whom it is nothing, must be undone to make it what it is. It is a power erected upon the ruin of its own strength, which is the people; and when they are gone, the power must go, growing first impotent in proportion to their misery and thinness: And that it does make them miserable and thin, and must at last extinguish them, I have at large shewn in former letters;[1] I think demonstrated. It may bounce and terrify for a while, and extend its bounds; but even at the time when it looks biggest and strongest, it is wearing out, and by its conquest does but dig its own grave the deeper, by consuming its old people to acquire new, whom it also consumes, and with whom it must also consume; like a debauchee in private life, the faster he lives, the less time he has to live.

The conquests of the Spaniards made a great noise in the world, and them very terrible for a time. But their gold and silver mountains of Mexico and Peru, though they be such glorious prizes as never before fell to the lot of any conqueror, have not made that nation amends for the loss and fewness of their people at home. Those that remain there cannot be said to be enriched by these vast acquisitions, whatever some particulars may be, who by their inequality and insolence oppress the whole. And for the Turkish empire, which frighted Europe and the world, and subdued great part of it, it is so wretchedly sunk in its discipline and

1. See especially Letters 72 and 73 (Apr. 7 and 21, 1722).

forces, and its provinces are so desolate and poor, that, in all human probability, this generation will see it broken into an hundred pieces. It has spun itself out, as the Saracen empire did before it, into a thread too long and too small to bear its own great burden without breaking.

People are like wire: The more they are extended, the weaker they become; and the closer they are together, the richer they grow, and more potent. This is the language of common sense and experience: But ambition speaks another and a different language, for extensive empire and uncontrolled dominion; and being too well heard, puts men upon sacrificing their real strength to that which is only imaginary. Hence they become really impotent in quest of false power, and destroy men in gross for the venal breath of a few flatterers, which they call glory. But horrid and detestable are the ways to such glory, which incites them to ravage and plague, to fetter and kill [the] human race, for the sake of a pleasant dream; to which too they sacrifice all their waking quiet, and make themselves and all others miserable for this delusive vision of their own separate happiness, which, like a phantom, mocks their sight, and flies from them the more they pursue it.

Besides, whosoever considers the many difficulties and dangers, the endless uncertainties and anxieties, and the general horror and hatred, inseparable from such pursuits, will see how poorly they reward him who makes them; having long stretched out his arms to embrace happiness, he is at last forced to draw them back empty, or full of sorrows. He who seeks felicity this way, hunts a shadow, which he will never overtake: And, in truth, what can such a troubler of the earth expect, but the bitter aversion of his own people, whom he oppresses and exhausts; and the curses of mankind, whom he persecutes and lays waste? Conquest gives him no new security; but, far from it, multiplies those who have a mind to destroy him, and arms more hands against him. They who possess most, have more to fear; especially when coming to their possessions by injustice, they must maintain them by violence. Hence the endless fears and insecurity of conquerors and oppressors, and the many conspiracies against them;

Sine caede & sanguine pauci ————[2]

Such therefore is the bitter fruit, and such often is the terrible and bloody end, of such wild and pernicious pursuits. No wise man would, for the empire of the earth, live in perpetual or strong apprehensions of any kind; much less under a tormenting opinion, that whole nations detested him, and sought his life for making them miserable, as conquerors always do, and must consequently be considered by them as their worst enemies.

But the strange madness of conquest appears from another consideration, namely, that there is not a prince in the world, let his territory be ever so small, but must find full employment to govern it, if he govern it as he should do; and therefore there never was a great empire so well governed as private cities; and no city so well as private families. Where the governed are but few, or live in little compass, the eye of the magistrate is over them, and the eye of the law over him, where he is not above it: Complaints can be easily examined, and violence and injustice be quickly overtaken, or readily prevented. But in wide and overgrown empires, especially where all depends upon the will and care of one, let his heart be ever so upright, a thousand evils and injuries will be done, which he can never hear of, nor they who suffer them have the means of representing to him; and which probably are done or connived at by his own deputies, whom he employs to prevent or punish them.

All princes have indeed more business than they can well do; and when they look out for new business, they must neglect the old, and throw off necessary cares, to assume wanton ones, inconsistent with the other. Harmless amusements they ought to have; and whatever amusements those are, is all one to their people, provided the general security be consulted, and property and peace be preserved: But to embark in wars, and make conquests at the expence of the people, and not for the people, is a preposterous way of protecting them, and of fulfilling the duties of reigning.

2. "Few [kings] without slaughter and blood . . ." The line appears in Juvenal, *Saturae*, 10.112. The full text reads: *ad generum Cereris sine caede et sanguine pauci/descendunt reges et sicca morte tyranni.* ("Few kings descend to Ceres' son-in-law [Pluto] without slaughter and blood and few tyrants die a bloodless death.")

Such a war was that of Troy; where all the princes of Greece, leaving their several countries in a state of anarchy, and drained of their bravest men, beat their heads against stone walls for ten years together, because these walls contained, as they were told, a Greek beauty who was a great strumpet. And having sacrificed their time, their navy, and the forces of their country, to this wise resentment, at last, by a stratagem, they got their chaste and important prize,* and for joy and anger, burnt the city, putting the king and all the inhabitants, who had done them no wrong, to the sword.

Most of the wars in the world have been Trojan wars; but most particularly those in the Holy Land, whither most of the princes in Christendom made lunatic and ruinous expeditions, to rescue from the Saracens a grave which could not be known from other graves. Great preparations were lately made for a Trojan war at Astracan; and in Italy a Trojan war is apprehended.[3] We too, since the reigns of the Plantagenets, have had our Trojan wars; and our English Ajaxes and Achilleses have fought many bloody battles, in which England had no other interest, but the inward satisfaction and glory of losing its men and money.

Conquest, or fighting for territory, is, for the most part, the most shameless thing in the world. Government is either designed for the people's good, or else I know not what business it has in the world: And therefore in all contests among conquerors about territory, if natural justice and common sense were to decide it, that prince ought to carry it, who can satisfy the people that he will use them best. And sometimes they all vouchsafe to promise this, though very few of them perform it. But this consideration, which ought to be the only one, and is perhaps used by them in their manifestoes, has not the least weight with most of them. On the contrary, their chief argument to move people is often the most ridiculous, stupid, and absurd of all others, and really con-

* Herodotus says, that Helena, during all that long war purposely made for her recovery, was not in Troy, but in Egypt. [The claim appears at 2.119.]

3. In 1705, a rebellion against the authority of Peter the Great broke out in Astrakan, a city on the Volga River some fifty miles from the Caspian Sea and, at that time, the second largest city in Russia. The "apprehended war" in Italy appears to refer to possible hostilities between Spain and the Emperor over the Italian claims of the Spanish royal house.

cerns the people the least of any other. As to the great point of using the people well, and promoting their prosperity, these are considerations so much below the thoughts of your conquerors, and so opposite to their practice, that if the people were to throw dice for one of them, they would do as wisely as if they chose him by deliberate voices, if they were at liberty to choose him, since there is rarely a better or a worse amongst them. And therefore the Persian nobles did not amiss, when they delegated the choice of such a sovereign to the horses which they rode. If Philip II of Spain had in the least aimed at governing the Seven Provinces[4] for their good, he would never have disturbed their revolt; since he might see that they prospered a thousand times faster without him than ever they could with him. But as this reasonable and beneficent thought had no authority with him, he exhausted in vain the forces of that great monarchy, to reduce those new states under his tyranny, and to make them as wretched and desolate as he made his other dominions.

G   *I am, &c.*

NO. 75. SATURDAY, MAY 5, 1722.

Of the Restraints which ought to be laid upon publick Rulers.

SIR,

After all that has been said of arbitrary power, and of its hideous nature and effects, it will fall properly in, to say something here of the restraints which all wise and fortunate nations ought to put, and have ever put, upon their magistrates. This is what I promised nine months ago to do;[1] and this is what I propose to do in this letter and the following.

No wise nation in the world ever trusted to the sole management, mere mercy, and absolute discretion of its own magis-

---

4. The Dutch provinces that successfully rebelled against Spanish rule.

1. See Letter No. 33 (June 17, 1721).

trates, when it could help doing it; and no series of magistrates ever had absolute power over any nation, but they turned the same to its ruin, and their own wild gratifications and ill-judged profit. As long as the passions of men govern them, they will always govern by their passions, and their passions will always increase with their power. And therefore, whenever a whole people, or any part of them, cross the passions of any man that governs them, he will turn his passions against a whole people, or any number of them that offend him, and will destroy a whole people, rather than stifle his passions. This is evident in ten thousand instances; and the publick will ever, and certainly, be sacrified to private lust, when private lust governs the publick. Nothing but fear and selfish considerations can keep men within any reasonable bounds; and nothing but the absence of fear can set men at defiance with society, and prompt them to oppress it. It was therefore well judged of the Spartan Ephori,[2] when they erected an altar to Fear, as the most proper divinity to restrain the wild ambition of men, and to keep their kings within the confines of their duty.

A nation has but two sorts of usurpation to fear; one from their neighbours, and another from their own magistrates: Nor is a foreign usurpation more formidable than a domestick, which is the most dangerous of the two, by being hardest to remove; and generally stealing upon the people by degrees, is fixed before it is scarce felt or apprehended: Like wild beasts in a wood, beset with toils as yet unseen by them, they think themselves free; but striving to escape, find themselves caught in the chains, which had long been preparing for them, and stealing upon them. Besides, for one people undone by foreign invaders, ten have been undone by their own native rogues, who were entrusted to defend them; but instead of it, either betrayed them to these invaders, or seized traitorously for themselves those rights which they were sworn to preserve for others; and then, by oppression and cruelty, and the other consequences of their treachery, reduced them to an utter disability of defending themselves against any invasion whatsoever.

2. The five magistrates of Sparta, elected annually by the citizens and possessed of immense power, including certain powers over the monarchy.

What has made Italy and Asia deserts, and their remaining inhabitants starving and contemptible cowards? Not the inundation of barbarous nations; though that inundation was owing to the weakness of the inhabitants, weakened and undone by their base and tyrannical governors: But they have been made deserts by the continued depredations of their execrable princes, who have acted as if they had been scythes in the hand of Satan to mow down the race of men. There is a certain old Italian tyrant, now living,[3] who, though he has by studied rapine converted into a wilderness a country which nature has made a paradise, yet is not weary nor ashamed of his rapine, but goes on to suck and squeeze the remaining blood of his ghostly subjects; and next to his visiting seven altars a day (a way which he has of compounding with God for being a pestilent tyrant to his creatures), I say, his only employment, besides this his devout and impudent mockery of God, is to sit contriving with his faithful ministry, which of his subjects may probably be worth a hundred pounds, and how to cheat him or rob him of that hundred pounds.

This same grand prince has now scarce any other business for his soldiers, but that of employing them directly against his own people; nor are they fit for any other employment; for one English regiment would beat seven of his. So that his paltry forces, many of them, are placed upon his frontiers, not to defend him from an invasion, a task which they are not equal to, but to keep his wretched subjects from running away from famine and his government. A relief which is however barbarously denied them by this old polite tyrant! They must stay and perish under him; nor will he suffer them to seek elsewhere that support of life, of which his diabolical government deprives them at home; as if when he had robbed them of their labour and their life, he also wanted their skins.

There is not upon earth a nation, which having had unaccountable magistrates, has not felt them to have been crying and consuming mischiefs. In truth, where they are most limited, it has

3. Gordon is here referring to Cosimo III de' Medici, Grand Duke of Tuscany from 1670 until 1723 and a dissolute and avaricious despot. It is indicative of Cosimo's rapaciousness that one of his last acts before expiring was to sign a decree increasing the income tax.

been often as much as a whole people could do to restrain them to
their trust, and to keep them from violence; and such frequently
has been their propensity to be lawless, that nothing but violence,
and sometimes nothing but a violent death, could cure them of
their violence. This evil has its root in human nature; men will
never think they have enough, whilst they can take more; nor be
content with a part, when they can seize the whole. We are, indeed
told of some absolute princes, who have been very good men and
no oppressors. But the nature of their power rendered their good
qualities almost useless, and gave to others an opportunity of
doing in their name, and by their authority, mischiefs which perhaps they themselves abhorred. Besides, in any series of arbitrary
princes upon earth, scarce out of ten can one be named who was
tolerable, and who either did not himself prove an inhuman
tyrant, or suffered his ministers to be so: And when an absolute
prince has had great parts, they generally went to his grave with
him, and scarce ever proved hereditary. In truth, the children of
great princes have almost always proved very unlike them.

I own, the first of the line has sometimes acted plausibly,
and gained, by doing so, dangerous credit and popularity. But if
he were an angel, he is never to be forgiven, because it is out of his
power what his successor shall prove. The crocodile's egg does no
mischief whilst it continues an egg; but out of it is hatched a crocodile, and by it the cursed race of destroyers is continued. D. Heinsius says very justly, *Nec unquam servitus, ne speciosa quidem, legit
quibus serviat, sed accipit.*[4] "The most plausible slavery is attended
with this eternal misfortune, that it has no choice of a master, but
must accept of a master, such as chance sends." Vespasian left to
the Romans for their prince the beneficent Titus; but he also left
them the raging and bloody Domitian.

If Julius Caesar and Augustus had been really gods, as
their flatterers made them; yet their leaving behind them such a
race of successors (who proved a race of daemons) entitles them to
the characters of detestable tyrants to all eternity. Tiberius, Calig-

4. Daniel Heinsius (1580–1655), one of the great scholars of the Dutch Ren-
aissance. The Latin reads: "Those in servitude, no matter how reasonable it
might appear, do not choose whom to serve; they only accept him." The quotation is from his *De politica sapientia* (1614).

ula, Claudius, and Nero, were the precious and bloody blessings which these beneficent princes left! Names universally abhorred, whilst those of Caesar and Augustus are generally adored: And yet to Caesar and Augustus were mankind indebted for these pests of mankind: Nor were they so great pests as were Caesar and Augustus, who did much more mischief, and destroyed the world more than either Nero or Caligula, besides leaving them to destroy it still further.

People rarely think of this, but it is literally true. What! will some say, the generous Caesar and the mild Augustus do more mischief than the wild Caligula and the savage Nero! Yes, fifty to one: Nero destroyed his twenties, Caesar and Augustus their twenty thousands; and for Nero, we may thank Julius and Augustus. Tiberius, Caligula, Claudius, and Nero, took Rome chiefly for the scene of their cruelty, and destroyed many great and good men, some out of wantonness, and more out of jealousy: But Caesar and Augustus made Rome and the world their slaughterhouse, and destroyed more great and good men by far than the other four, as butchering monsters as they were: And as to publick rapine and general depopulation, they exceeded them still further. Indeed, as to heroick and diffusive mischief and villainy, the difference between them was as great as between Jack Straw and a late Grand Monarque. The truth is, Caesar and Augustus had art and great qualities, which are far from excusing the evils which they did; and their successors, having all their ambition, but wanting their great qualities and discretion, took the direct road to hatred.

An unrestrained power in one man, or in a few, over all, is such an extravagant deviation from reason and nature, that neither Briareus[5] with his many hands, nor the Hydra with its numerous heads, nor the Centaurs, half man and half beast, were things more unshapen, monstrous, and frightful: Nor would these fictions appear more fabulous and improbable, than such power would be to a free people, who never had heard of it before. What could seem to common sense a wilder chimera, than that one man,

5. One of the giants, who possessed one hundred hands and fifty heads.

not created with features and endowments different from other men, should have a lasting right from his blood, or his pride, or his madness, to domineer over all men, and to rule, kill, starve, famish, banish, and imprison, as many as he pleased?

This power is indeed so monstrous, that it turns men that have it into monsters; and therefore the most amiable and unexceptionable man upon earth is not to be trusted with it. Men change with their stations, and power of any sort rarely alters them for the better; but, on the contrary, has often turned a very good man into a very bad. This shews that men forbear evil, chiefly to avoid the ill consequence of it to themselves, and for want of opportunity and protection; and finding both in power, they prove, by making use of them, that their virtue was only self-love, and fear of punishment. Thus men of the best and brightest characters have often done most mischief, and by well serving their country, have been enabled to destroy it: And they were good and evil from one and the same motive; a passion for themselves, and their own security or glory.

Thus the house of the Medicis, by being very good commonwealth-men, and by serving and obliging almost every family in Florence, gained credit enough by this their generous behaviour, to enslave that great and powerful city. *Idque apud imperitos humanitas vocabatur, quod pars servitutis erat.*[6] Pericles administered the government of Athens with great sufficiency; but he broke down the fences of its liberty, and ruled arbitrarily all his days. Agathocles fought successfully for the city of Syracuse, and as successfully against it;[7] and having defended the citizens against their enemies, he afterwards shewed himself their greatest, by killing in one great massacre all the chief and best of them, and by crowning himself tyrant over all the rest. Marius and Sulla, Pompey and Caesar, were great and excellent commanders, and conquered many great kings and nations: But they made all the fruits of their victo-

6. "In their ignorance, they called this aspect of their slavery good manners." Tacitus, *Agricola*, 21.

7. *Agathocles*, tyrant of Syracuse, gained his kingdom in 317 B.C., after having overthrown the oligarchy that had ruled the city.

ries their own; and from being very good soldiers, made themselves most pernicious and arbitrary magistrates.

Now all these great men derived, from the good which they did, a capacity to do much more evil: So that as a power to do great good, does naturally include in it an opportunity of doing much evil; so those who are in the possession of power, as all magistrates are, ought, above all other men, to be narrowly watched, and checked with restraints stronger than their temptations to break them; and every crime of theirs ought to be more penal, as it is evidently more pernicious, than the same crime in any other sort of men. For, besides that *quales in republica principes essent, tales reliquos solere esse cives*;[8] that is, that people are generally virtuous or corrupt as their magistrates are; there is something exceeding solemn and important in the nature of this great trust; and accordingly as it is observed or betrayed, a country is happy or miserable: And when any one breach of it passes once off with impunity, another will soon follow it; and in time it will be considered no longer as a trust, but an estate.

So dangerous a thing is an ill precedent, which is often an inlet to an endless train of mischiefs; and so depraved is the nature of man, that we justify ourselves in wickedness by examples that cannot be justified. An action at first reckoned dishonest, by being practised once or twice, becomes unblameable; and that which was at first accounted an extortion, grows by use to be thought but a perquisite. Thus evil is mitigated, nay, cancelled, by repetition, which is a real aggravation of evil; and there are certain rogueries in office, which being long practised, and by many, are at last reckoned as sacred as the trust against which they are committed: A sufficient reason for providing, by great and certain penalties, that none be committed.

G   *I am, &c.*

---

8. "As the rulers are in the republic, so are the other citizens likely to be." Cicero, *Epistulae ad familiares*, 1.9.12. Cicero is here quoting Plato, *Leges*, 4.711c.

NO. 76. SATURDAY, MAY 12, 1722.

The same Subject continued.

SIR,

How cautiously and partially men in power are to be trusted, and how much to be restrained, appears from hence, that almost every civil evil begins from courts, and the redress of every civil evil from an opposition to the pretensions and excesses of courts. This is so universally true, that no nation ever continued happy, whose chief magistrate was its absolute master; and no nation miserable, whose supreme power was properly checked and divided. Nations are then free, when their magistrates are their servants; and then slaves, when their magistrates are their masters: The commonwealth does not belong to them, but they belong to the commonwealth. Tacitus says with great truth, *Nec unquam satis fida potentia ubi nimis est:*[1] "Power without control is never to be trusted." Every nation has most to fear from its own magistrates; because almost all nations have suffered most from their own magistrates.

Cicero, mentioning the condition of Cilicia,[2] of which he was proconsul, in a letter to Appius Pulcher, says, that he was "moved by pity, as well as justice, to relieve from their miseries the undone provincial cities; undone chiefly by their own magistrates."[3] It seems Cicero was that sort of whimsical man, that he had really at heart to do good to the people whom he governed: An odd and impracticable character; which, had he lived since, would have rendered him utterly unfit for any manner of preferment. He did not so much as know that he was to make the most of his place and his power, let what would become of the people. A lesson which other governors have amply learned.

1. "When a man possesses excessive power, he can never have complete trust." Tacitus, *Historiae*, 2.92.
2. A district in the southwest of Asia Minor directly north of Cyprus.
3. Cicero, *Epistulae ad familiares*, 3.8.5.

Aristotle makes it the great argument and proof of liberty, that they who command do also obey; and indeed all legal and just power being but a trust, whoever executes the same, does an act of obedience as well as command:[4] And every trust is best executed, where those who have it are answerable for it, else it never will be executed; but, where it is great and publick, is much more likely to be abused, violated, and turned to the destruction of those, who, for their own preservation, gave it. Nor is a people to be told, that such as want to be trusted with extraordinary power of any kind, have always been enemies to arbitrary power; for so are all men when they have it not, and expect no advantage from it. Who was a greater patriot than Sir Thomas Wentworth? And who was a more arbitrary minister than Thomas Wentworth, Earl of Strafford? All men are for confining power when it is over them; and for extending it when they are in it. Oliver Cromwell was once heartily in the principles of liberty, and afterwards more heartily in those of tyranny: And I could name two great parties in England, who, when they were out of power, seemed to place the sum of publick spirit, in intrenching upon the royal authority; and when they were in power, to know no other law but the prerogative royal. So unlike is the same man to himself in different situations; and yet still very consistent with the genius of human nature!

Men sometimes do actually good, in order to do evil, *Sejanus, incipiente adhuc potestate, bonis consiliis notescere volebat.*[5] "Sejanus, in the beginning of his administration, would found the reputation of a good minister in laudable measures." But there never proved a worse minister than Sejanus. Solyman, the Turkish emperor,[6] used to say, that a prince, to be well served by any minister, must never use any minister above once: And this saying is thus far true generally, that men, the longer they grow in power, the worse they grow. I think it is Tacitus who says, *Superbire homines*

4. See especially the *Ethica Nicomachea*, 5.6.4–6.

5. "Sejanus, still in the infancy of his power, wished to be known for good advice." Tacitus, *Annales*, 4.7.

6. Suleiman I, the Magnificent (1496–1566), probably the greatest of the Ottoman Sultans.

etiam annua designatione; quid si honorem per quinquennium agitent?[7] "If an annual election to power make men insolent; what must be their pitch of insolence, if they hold it five or seven years?" Aristotle finds great fault with the senate of Sparta, for being perpetual; and I think he says, that an unchanged or an hereditary senate falls into dotage.[8]

Many of the ecclesiasticks have been for trusting their favourite princes (and no other) with unlimited power over others: But in every thing that regarded themselves and their interest, they have never failed to stipulate for the strictest limitations upon all princes, even upon those whom over the rest of the world they wished arbitrary, and endeavoured by every means to make so. Nor did ever any man give up the freedom of his country, but he meant to preserve his own; and hoped to continue a freeman; as a reward of his helping to make other people slaves; and no man ever set up a tyrant, but in hopes of going shares in his tyranny: And upon these terms and expectations alone it is, that any body of men, or indeed any army, is brought to aid and establish any usurper. Passive obedience was always intended for other people than those who preached it. Interest cannot lie; though he does, who says that he will submit to servitude, when he can avoid it.

Who would establish a bank in an arbitrary country, or trust his money constantly there? In Denmark, the ministers and minions of the prince, think their money safest out of his dominions, and generally transmit the same to Hamburgh, and other free cities, where the magistrates have no divine right to lay violent hands upon what is none of theirs.[9] Even what we gain by rapine in a land of oppression, we are willing to save by the just laws of liberty, in a country of liberty. In England itself, and in our own free constitution; if the Bank of England were put under the abso-

7. "Men grew arrogant even though in office for a one-year term; what if their term had been five years?" Tacitus, *Annales*, 2.36.

8. *Politica*, 2.9.25 (1270b).

9. Denmark was at this time suffering under the despotic regime of King Frederick IV.

lute direction and power of the court,[10] I doubt stock would soon grow very cheap, and sellers multiply very fast. Or if the government of the Bank, which is purely republican, were improved into monarchical; I fancy our highest monarchy-men would rail at the change, and hasten to sell out, notwithstanding their inviolable attachment to the divine right of monarchy: Unless perhaps they think that absolute monarchy does best protect their power, but a free state their money. I am indeed of opinion, that upon such a change, the Bank would be broke, and shut up in three days.

All this shews, that even men who are against liberty in general, contend for it in particulars, and in all particulars which affect themselves. Even Lauderdale, a Tyrconnel, or a Jefferies,[11] who were all for making the crown absolute, as long as they could be as they were, the absolute ministers of oppression under it, would none of them, I dare say, have encouraged the maxim of the prince's rewarding his ministers and faithful oppressors with the bow-string; as well as they themselves were entitled to that reward, and as much as the Turkish genius of government did in other instances suit their own!

When we hear any sort of men complain, as some sort of men do frequently complain, that the crown wants power; we should ask them, whether they mean over themselves? And if they answer, no; as certainly they will, if they speak truth; we may further ask them, Why should they judge for themselves any more than others; or claim to themselves a liberty and an exemption which they will not allow to others? The truth is, they who complain thus, only want to increase the power of the crown, because by it their own would be increased, and other advantages acquired.

The fox in the fable, wanting to rob a hen-roost, or do some such prank, humbly besought admittance and house-room only for his head; but when he got in his head, his whole body

10. That is, the general court of the Bank of England, together with its governors, the Bank's ultimate governing authority.

11. John Maitland, first Duke of Lauderdale (1616–1682), Secretary of State for Scottish Affairs under Charles II and an uncompromising adherent of the crown's absolute power. Richard Talbot, Duke of Tyrconnel (1630–1691), Irish Jacobite and James II's lord deputy in Ireland. George Jeffreys, first Baron Jeffreys of Wem (1644–1689), Lord Chief Justice from 1682 and Lord Chancellor under James II; Jeffreys was particularly noted for his bias and brutality.

presently followed: And courts, more crafty, as well as more craving, than that designing animal, have scarce ever gained an inch of power, but they have stretched it to an ell;[12] and when they have got in but a finger, their whole train has followed. Pisistratus, having procured from the city of Athens fifty fellows armed only with cudgels, for the security of his person from false and lying dangers, improved them into an army, and by it enslaved that free state. And I have read somewhere, of the States of a country, who having wildly granted to their prince a power of raising money by his own authority, in cases of great necessity; every case, ever afterwards, was a case of great necessity; and his necessities multiplied so fast, that the whole wealth of the country was swallowed up to supply them:[13] As it always will be in every country, where those who ask are suffered to judge what ought to be given. A practice contrary to common sense, and which renders liberty and property perfectly precarious; and where it is continued, will end in taking without asking.

I have heard of a court somewhere abroad, which having asked upon a particular occasion four hundred thousand pounds of the States, found ways and means of stretching that sum to two millions. It was observed of the same court, that it had the art of raising mole-hills into mountains, and of sinking mountains into mole-hills; of disbanding armies without breaking them; of increasing debts by the means of paying them; of being engaged in an expensive war during a profound peace; of gaining for the country at a vast charge, advantages which the country never reaped, nor saw; of employing money obviously against the interest of that nation, and yet getting the nation to pay it; of purchasing other countries at the expence of their own, and against its interest; of procuring from the country at one time a great sum, without telling why it was wanted, but promising to tell, and yet never telling; and, in fine, after many other the like feats, of

12 An ell: a unit of measure equal to approximately forty-five inches.

13. This, and the following reference to "a court somewhere abroad," appear to refer to the events in Saxony during the reign of Augustus. Augustus became King of Saxony in 1694 and was elected King of Poland in 1697. His wars and extravagances proved a disaster for Saxony, large districts of which were pawned or sold to defray his expenses.

obtaining, by an arret of security, remission for all their past faults, without owning any, and yet going on to commit more: For as Tully well observes, *Qui semel verecundiae fines transierit, eum bene & naviter oportet esse impudentem.*[14] Cicer. epist. ad Lucceium, Quinti fil.

But these things concern not us; and I only bring them for examples, like other old stories of Greece and Rome. I hope that we shall never fall into the like misfortunes and mismanagements ourselves.

G   *I am, &c.*

NO. 77. SATURDAY, MAY 19, 1722.

Of superstitious Fears, and their Causes natural and accidental.

SIR,

As my design in these letters is to endeavour to free and man-umit mankind from the many impositions, frauds and delusions, which interrupt their happiness; so I shall, in this, and some of the succeeding ones,[1] attempt to remove the popular impressions and fears of spirits, apparitions, and witches; which more or less afflict and terrify the greatest part of the world: and consequently it will conduce much to their ease and felicity, if I can lay these phantoms.

There is a strange propensity in human nature to prodigy, and whatever else causes surprize and astonishment, and to admire what we do not understand. We have immediate recourse to miracle, which solves all our doubts, and gratifies our pride, by accounting for our ignorance. We are not affected by things which we frequently see; or if we can trace but one link of the infinite chain of causes, our admiration ceases; though we are then as far from

14. "Once having transgressed the limits of modesty, one might as well be openly and totally shameless." Cicero, *Epistulae ad familiares*, 5.12.3.
1. See especially Letter No. 78 (May 26, 1722) and Letter No. 79 (June 2, 1722).

our journey's end, as when we set out: for all the works of providence are miraculous to us, who cannot do them ourselves, or know how he, who is the author of them, does them. And in this sense every thing is a miracle to us; though we ought to be no more surprized at seeing a blazing star, which makes its revolution but once in five hundred years, than in seeing the sun every day.

For many ages the phenomena of meteors, eclipses and comets seemed unaccountable; and the causes of thunder and lightning were unknown to the world; as they are to most people in it at this day. Great guns were esteemed, by the Americans, to be angry deities; ships, floating monsters; the sun to be the God of the world; watches to be living animals; paper and ink to be spirits, which conveyed men's thoughts from one to another: And a dancing mare was lately burnt for a witch in the inquisition of Portugal.

All nature is in perpetual rotation; and in the great variety of actions which it produces, some must appear very extraordinary and unaccountable to us, by all the powers of matter and motion which fall within our narrow observations; and yet may, and undoubtedly have as certain and regular causes and effects, as the most obvious mechanick operations. We see into the bottom and internal frame and constitution of no one thing in the world, and probably never can do so, whilst we continue in these frail bodies. We see not into the principles and contexture of animal or vegetable beings; and consequently cannot know what nature can spontaneously produce, or how she works. We see only the outside and film of things; and no more of them than what is necessary to the preservation or convenience of ourselves, and not the thousandth part of what is so. Almighty God hath hid all the rest from our eyes; to baffle our foolish curiosity, to raise our admiration of his power, and to excite our homage and adoration to him, the great author of all things.

Nature (as is said in print elsewhere) works by infinite ways; which are impenetrable to our vain and fruitless inquiries.

The loadstone draws iron to it; gold, quicksilver. The sensitive plant shrinks from the touch. Some sorts of vegetables attract one another, and twine together; others avoid one another, and grow farther apart. The treading upon the torpedo affects, and gives raging pains to, our whole bodies. The bite of a mad dog causes madness. Turkey-cocks and pheasants fly at red. A rattle-snake, by a sort of magical power in his eyes, will force a squirrel to run into his mouth. Musick will cure the bite of a tarantula. The frights and longings of women with child, will stamp impressions upon the babes within them. People, in their sleep, will walk securely over precipices and ridges of houses, where they durst not venture whilst awake. Lightning will melt a sword without hurting the scabbard.

And there are very many other surprizing instances of the powers of matter and motion, which we every day see and feel; and without doubt, there are infinite others which we know nothing of.

If some men could follow scents, like dogs, or see in the dark, like cats, or have the same presages and prognosticks of fair weather or tempests, which other animals seem to have; how many things would they know and do, unaccountable to the rest of man-kind? If Almighty God had thought fit to have bestowed upon any man one or more senses above the rest of the species, many of his actions must have appeared miraculous to them.

But if these minute and pretty works of nature cause so much our surprize and astonishment, how ought we to admire and adore the Author of all nature, in the greater works of his creation! The Earth itself is but as a mustard-seed to the visible world; and doubtless that is infinitely less in comparison of the invisible one. It is very likely, that its many fellow-planets, which move about the sun, as we do, are filled with inhabitants, and some of them proba-bly with more valuable ones than ourselves: And 'tis next to cer-tain, that the numerous fixed stars, nightly seen by us, and the more numerous ones frequently discovered by new and better glasses, are so many different suns, and possibly with each a differ-ent chorus or system of worlds moving about them, and receiving vital warmth and nourishment from their beams; for 'tis impossible to believe, that the all-wise disposer of all things should place so many orbs, many thousand times greater than this Earth, in the vast abyss of space, far out of our sight, and of no use to us, unless to serve suitable purposes of his providence.

We are not, nor can we be, sure that there are no other beings who are inhabitants of the air or aether, with bodies subtle enough to be adapted to, and nourished by, these thin elements; and perhaps with senses and faculties superior to us: for the works of Almighty God are as infinite as is his power to do them. And 'tis paying greater deference to him, and having higher conceptions of his omnipotence, to suppose that he saw all things which have been, are, or ever shall be, at one view, and formed the whole system of nature with such exquisite contrivance and infinite wisdom, as by its own energy and intrinsick power, to produce all the effects and operations which we daily see, feel, and admire; than to believe him to be often interposing to alter and amend his own work, which was undoubtedly perfect at first; though in the pursuit of his eternal decrees, and in the course, progress, and unbroken chain of his original system, he seems to us sometimes to act occasionally; when, in compliance to our weak comprehensions, and in condescension to our low capacities, he speaks and appears to act after the manner of men. We have not faculties to see or know things as they are in themselves, but only in such lights as our creator pleases to represent them in to us: He has given us talents suited to our wants, and to understand his will, and obey it; and here is our *ne plus ultra,* the farthest we can go. We may be very sure that we are not obliged to know what is beyond our power to know; but all such things are as non-entities to us.

Whensoever therefore we hear of, or see any surprizing appearances or events in nature, which we cannot trace and connect to their immediate causes; we are not to call in supernatural powers, and interest heaven or hell in the solution, to save our credit, and cover our own folly, when there are so very few things in the world which we know any thing of, and of those few we know but very little. We are not to measure the works of God by our scanty capacities; and to believe that he miraculously interposes in the course of human affairs, but only when he pleases to intimate to us that he does, or intends to do so; much less ought we to introduce daemons into his system of the universe, unless as objects or instruments and executioners of his vengeance; but not to intrude into his government of the world, to trepan and mislead his creatures, and to thwart and oppose himself, and every now and anon to cut the chain, stop the wheels, and interrupt the course of his providence.

We are very sure that God can do, and impower any other beings to do, every thing which he would have done; but we are not obliged, by any precept, moral or divine, to believe every thing which weak, crazed, or designing men tell us in his name; and the disbelieving their foolish and fantastical stories, is not questioning the power of God, but the veracity or judgment of the persons who tell them: For sure there can be no occasion of recurring to super-natural causes, to account for what may be very easily accounted for by our ignorance of natural ones, by the fraud or folly of others, or by the deception of ourselves. There can be no wonder at all in a man's telling a lie, or in his being deceived.

Which of our senses does not often deceive us? Strangling, or strong pressure of the eyes, causes all things to appear on fire; that of the ears, makes us hear noises; straight things in the water appear crooked; bodies by reflexion or refraction appear other-wise, and in other places, than they are in nature. All things appear yellow to men in the jaundice: To those in calentures,[2] the sea appears like a green meadow; and if not restrained, they will leap into it: Melancholy and enthusiastick persons fancy themselves to be glass bottles, knives, and tankards; madmen often believe them-selves gods or princes, and almost always see spirits; and a rever-end divine, some time since, thought himself big with child, and could not be persuaded to the contrary, till a man midwife pre-tended to deliver him of a false conception.

In fevers and malignant distempers, people see visions and apparitions of angels, devils, dead men, or whatever else their imaginations render most agreeable or terrible to them; and in dreams all men see, or fancy that they see, such false appearances. Their imaginations, in sleep, are often so lively and vigorous, that

2. Calentures: a fever accompanied by delirium said to affect sailors in the tropics. Those suffering from the disease were reputed to fancy the sea as a green field.

they can scarcely be persuaded of their mistake when they awake out of it, and would not be so, if they did not find themselves in bed; and therefore, if a credulous, fearful, or melancholy man, should carelessly nod himself to sleep in his closet or his garden, and receive a vigorous representation of an angel, daemon, or dead man, speaking to him, or delivering a message, and after wake on a sudden, without observing his own sleeping (as often happens) I cannot see how he should distinguish this appearing phantom from a real vision or revelation, and I should be glad to have a rule to do it by.

The frame and contexture of our bodies betrays us to these delusions. For, as all objects and images from without are let in upon the mind by the windows or conduits of the outward senses, and the mind afterwards ranges, methodizes, operates, and reasons upon them; so it can only work upon such materials as it receives: and consequently, when the organs of sensation are wrong framed in their original contexture, or depraved afterwards by sickness or accidents, the mind must be misled too, and often mistake appearances for real beings: When the spies, scouts, and out-guards, are seized, corrupted, or deceived, the intelligence will be fallacious, or none at all.

It is evident, in a thousand instances, that the mind and body mutually act and operate upon one another; both grow and increase by age and exercise, both are impaired and enervated by distempers and accidents, and all the noble faculties of the former are often destroyed and extinguished by accidental injuries done to the latter, and by other fortuitous events and occasional strokes of fortune. Common experience shews us, that if men are born without one or more of their senses, so many conduits of knowledge are stopt: If a child comes into the world without the faculties of seeing or hearing, he can have no understanding at all, unless he afterwards acquire them; and if he loses them again, all further progress is at an end: The vigour and capacity of our mind depend very much, if not altogether, upon the organization of our bodies; and are altered, improved, and increased, by proper diet, action, or education; and oppressed, lessened, and sometimes quite lost, by drunkenness, gluttony, laziness or misfortunes. I have often almost fancied that men may be dieted into opinions; as experience shews us, they may be educated into the most absurd ones by custom, conversation, and habit.

Every passion or affection of the mind produces visibly a suitable and correspondent disposition of the muscles and lineaments of the face, and consequently must affect and alter the whole mechanism of the body; and by like reason every thought or motion of the mind must do the same in a lesser degree (though not equally subject to common observation) by forcing or directing the blood, juices, or animal spirits, into peculiar tubes, conduits, or vessels: and when by frequent use those channels and passages become habitual to them, they will often flow thither of their own accord, or are easily driven thither; and so, by working backwards, will cause those passions and perceptions which at first caused them, and in consequence the same impressions and dispositions of the organs of sense.

If this observation be true, it will account for our delusions in dreams, when exterior objects are shut out, which must otherwise control and overpower the weaker and more faint operations of the internal machine; and this too will account for the many panick and unreasonable fears and prejudices which we are subject to from education, custom, and constitution, as well as for the difficulty, if not impossibility, of our shaking off and conquering any other habits of mind or body acquired by early and continued practice.

I shall in my next apply these general principles to the system of spirits; and shew that philosophy and religion both contradict the commonly received opinions of them.

T   *I am, &c.*

NO. 78. SATURDAY, MAY 26, 1722.

The common Notion of Spirits, their Power and Feats, exposed.

SIR,

As I have shewn at large, in my last letter, that, in very many instances, our senses are subject and liable to be deceived in objects evidently material; so in this I shall endeavour as fully to shew, that we can have no possible ideas of any other. When we call God a spirit, we do not pretend to define his nature, or the modus of his existence, but to express the high conception which we have of his omnipotence, by supposing him most unlike to our-selves, and infinitely superior to every thing which we see and know; and then we are lost and buried in the abyss of our own ignorance: but we can have no other possible conception of what we mean by the word *spirit,* when applied to him.

We cannot have even the most abstracted images of things, without the ideas of extension and solidity; which are the mediums of conceiving all things that we can conceive at all. As the organs of our senses are all material, so they are formed only to receive material objects; and but a small part of those which are so. The ear cannot hear, the hands feel, the palate taste, the nose smell, or the eye see, bodies, but of certain magnitudes, dimensions, and solidity; and these vary too in different men, and in the same men at different times, and at different ages. There are millions of insects that cannot be seen without glasses; and probably infinite others, which cannot be seen with them: the subtle effluvia, or other minute causes of pestilential distempers, are not within the reach and observation of any of our senses. We cannot see wind and common air, much less pure aether, which are all too thin and too subtle bodies for the fabrick of the eye; and how should we see spirits, which we are told have no bodies at all, and in the dark too, when the contexture of the eye will not afford us the use of that organ.

I cannot conceive why the dreams of the old heathen philosophers should be adopted into the Christian system: or from what principles of reason or religion we should be told that the soul is *totum in toto,* and *totum in qualibet parte*;[1] that is, that all of it is diffused through the whole body, and yet all of it is in every part of the body: That spirits take up no place; and that ten thousand of them may stand upon the point of a needle, and yet leave room for a million times as many more; that they may move from place to place, and not pass through the intermediate space; and that they are impenetrable themselves, and yet can penetrate every thing else. Is not this fine gibberish, and pretty divinity? And yet it is esteemed by some a sort of atheism to disbelieve it; but neither philosophy nor scripture tell us any such matter. It is true indeed, we are told, that spirits have neither flesh nor bones; no more than wind, air, or aether, and thousands of other things, which yet are bodies: but we are no where told, as I remember, that spirits have no extension or solidity: And if we were told so, we could understand no more by it, than that they were beings of which we neither had, nor could have, any other than negative ideas.

I think, therefore, that I may venture to assert, that either God hath created no beings independent of matter, or that such cannot be objects of our senses: But if there be any such, they are of a nature so different from us, and so incomprehensible by the faculties which he has given us, that we can form no propositions about them; and consequently are not obliged to believe or disbelieve any thing concerning them, till he pleases further to inform us.

But there are an humble sort of philosophers, who want the sagacity to conceive how any substance can exist without extension and solidity; and consequently are modest enough to confess, that they do not understand the distinction between material and immaterial substances; and that they cannot, with their most refined imaginations, have any notion of a middle state of things, between extended beings and no beings at all; between real essences and shadows, phantoms or images of disordered brains; or that any thing can exist in the universe, and at the same time in

1. "All of it in all parts"; "all of it in any part."

no part of it. And yet these gentlemen will not give up the general system of spirits, but suppose them to be beings of subtle aerial contexture, that in their own nature are not objects of our senses; but gave powers, by assuming more dense bodies, to make themselves so, and have capacities to do many things unaccountable to us, and beyond the limits and reach of our apprehensions. All which I think no man will affirm to be impossible; but I think any man may safely affirm, that such agents are not permitted to molest human affairs, and seduce or mislead men, by doing supernatural actions, or what must appear to us to be so.

A contrary supposition must destroy the very use of miracles: for if other beings, either by the energy of their own nature, or the will and permission of God, can do miracles, or actions which we cannot distinguish from miracles; then nothing can be proved by them, and we shall lose the best evidence of the truth of our holy religion. For if signs and wonders may be promiscuously shewn and performed by the best of all beings and by the worst, they may be done and used to promote error, imposture, and wickedness, as well as virtue and true religion; nor can I find out any criterion, or sufficient mark, whereby we can distinguish which are done by the preserver, and which by the professed enemy, of mankind. To say that the truth of the miracle shall be tried by the doctrine which it is brought to propagate, or the precepts which it commands, is to invert the very use and end of miracles, which is, to give credit and authority to the doer, who is always supposed to act by God's power, in order to declare his will; and consequently, if the wonders which he does are to be tried by the doctrine which he teaches, there would be no use of any wonders at all, to prove not only what proves itself, but what is to prove the truth of the miracle, which is to prove the truth of the doctrine.

We are very sure, that the great Creator of heaven and earth, and the sole author of all our happiness, does not leave us in these uncertainties, to be tossed and tumbled in the thick mist and dark chaos of ignorance and deceit. How can we know the truth of any revelation, withot knowing the revealer himself to be true? We must be first certain, that a good and beneficent being speaks to us, before we can believe any thing which he tells us. Whenever therefore Almighty God, by means becoming his infinite wisdom, and from causes impenetrable to us, communicates his intentions by appearances and representations to our senses, or by any other ways out of the ordinary course of his providence, he always gives us sure marks whereby we can distinguish his works from delusion and imposture, which often ape truth itself, and mislead ignorant and unwary men. We are told in Holy Writ, that "young men shall see visions, and old men dream dreams";[2] which frequently happens; and that "false prophets shall arise and do wonders, which shall deceive almost the elect";[3] but we are bid to disbelieve them; which, if they worked true miracles, we could not do, without rejecting all miracles. For how can we believe any thing to be miraculous, and at the same time disbelieve another thing to be so, without being able to shew any difference between them? And therefore we may acquiesce in an assurance that such pretenders must be cheats, and their actions impostures and deceits upon our senses.

Whenever God works wonders, or produces those events which shall appear as such to us, he always does them for wise reasons, either to warn and inform men, to make them examples of his justice, or to communicate his will, and teach us some doctrine; and he takes the most proper and effectual means to attain his ends, and coerce our belief, by making such applications to our outward senses, and such impressions upon our understandings, as we must submit to and acquiesce in, unless we resolve to give up all certainty; or else by predictions which are justified by the event, and which are undoubtedly miracles. He does them in the most open manner before crowds at once; but our modern miracle-mongers do them all in secret, in corners, and in the dark; and their spirits and apparitions are seen only by melancholy, enthusiastick, and dreaming old men and women, or by crazy young ones, whose heads are intoxicated and prepared for these stories long before; and they are generally seen but by one at once, who is

2. "Your old men shall dream dreams and your young men shall see visions." Joel 2:28, Acts 2:17.

3. "And many false prophets shall rise, and shall deceive many." Matthew 24:11.

always in a fright when he does see them; or else they are the tricks and juggles of heathen and popish priests, or pretended conjurers, to pick men's pockets, and promote some knavish and selfish design. They are never done before a House of Lords or Commons, or in a prince's court, or in the streets before multitudes of people, or in the sight of several men at the same time, of clear and unprejudiced understandings, or of unquestionable integrity.

When our Saviour appeared to all his disciples together, he appealed to their senses, and bid them not be afraid, but to put their hands into his side, and believe themselves: He made his ascension before five hundred people at once: His miracle of the loaves and fishes was before five thousand: His turning water into wine was at a publick wedding; and the rest were of the same kind: He went through Judea from place to place, publickly doing miracles, confirming and convincing all, who were not willfully blind, of the truth of his mission; and teaching a doctrine of infinite advantage to mankind: Whereas our present workers or seers of miracles never tell us any thing worth knowing; and we have no other evidence that they are seen or done, but the veracity of those who tell them, who may be deceived themselves, or invent lies to deceive others. The proof ought always to be equal to the importance of the thing to be believed: For, when it is more likely that a man should tell a lie, or be deceived, than that a strange phenomenon should be true, methinks there should be no difficulty to determine on which side of the question we should give our assent; though in fact most men are so prepared by education to believe these stories, that they will believe the relation of them in these cases, when they will believe the relaters in nothing else.

If one or two men affirm that they saw another leap twenty yards at one leap, no one will doubt but they are liars; but if they testify that they saw a goblin with saucer eyes and cloven feet in a church-yard, leap over the tower; all the town is in a fright, and few of them will venture to walk abroad in a dark night. Sometimes these phantoms appear to one who is in company with others, and no one can see them but himself, and yet all the rest are terrified at his relation, without reasoning that they have the same or better faculties of seeing than he has; and therefore that his organs must either be indisposed, or that he designs to impose upon them: but it passes for a miracle; and then all doubts are solved, and all enquiries at an end. All men believe most of those stories to be false; and yet almost all believe some of them to be true, upon no better evidence than they reject the rest. The next story of an old woman inhabiting a cat, or flying in the air upon a broomstick, sets them a staring, and puts their incredulity to a nonplus. We often hear of a spirit appearing to discover a silver spoon, a purse of hidden money, or perhaps a private murder; but are never told of a tyrant, who by private murders has slaughtered thousands, and by publick butcheries destroyed millions, ever dragged out of his court by good or evil spirits, as a terror to such monsters: Such an instance would convince all mankind; and if Almighty God thought fit to work by such engines, and intended that we should believe in them, or any of them, it is impossible to believe but that he would take the properest methods to gain our assent.

From what I have said, and much more which might be said, I think I may with great assurance conclude, that these capricious and fantastical beings are not suffered to interfere and mingle with human affairs, only to mislead men, and interrupt them in the pursuit of their duty; nor can I see any foundation, in nature, reason, or scripture, to believe that there are any such as they are usually represented to us; which neither agree and keep up to the characters, dignity, and excellence of good angels, or the sagacity, office, and use of bad ones. Where are we commanded to believe that the Devil plays hide and seek here on earth; that he is permitted to run up and down and divert himself, by seducing ignorant men and women; killing pigs, or making them miscarry; entering into cats, and making noises, and playing monkey-tricks in churchyards and empty houses, or any where else here on earth, but in empty heads?

We know that he was cast headlong from heaven, is chained fast in the regions of the damned, and kept by the power of the Almighty from doing mischief to his creatures; and to say the contrary seems to me the highest blasphemy against heaven itself: For when we every day see and feel the many delusions to which human condition is subject, how we are the properties of impostors, the slaves to tyrants, and perpetual dupes of one another, and indeed are subject to daily and endless frauds and impositions; how shall we be a match for the most subtle and most sagacious being out of heaven? And is it possible to believe, that the good, merciful, and all-wise God should desert, leave, and betray us to so unequal a combat, without giving to us suitable precautions, capacities, and powers to defend ourselves?

I shall conclude by observing, that the heathen poets first invented these stories, and the heathen priests stole them from them; as badgers dig holes for themselves, and afterwards are stunk out of them by foxes.

T *I am &c.*

NO. 79. SATURDAY, JUNE 2, 1722.

꿔 *A further Detection of the vulgar Absurdities about Ghosts and Witches.*

SIR,

I have endeavoured, in my last, to shew, that no such beings as spirits and daemons are permitted by the good God to mingle with, and perplex, human affairs; and if my reasoning be good, the whole system of conjurers and witches falls to the ground: For I think it is agreed by all, if they have any powers supernatural, they receive them from evil spirits; and if these have no such powers themselves, they can transmit them to none else.

But, methinks, the advocates for Satan's empire here on earth are not very consistent with themselves; and in the works which they attribute to him, do not give credit enough to his abilities and power.

> They make this prince a mighty emperor:
> But his demands do speak him proud and poor.

They give him a power to do miracles; make him prince of the air, lord of the hidden minerals; wise, rich, and powerful, as well as false, treacherous, and wicked; and are foolish and presumptuous enough to bring him upon the stage as a rival for empire with the Almighty; but at the same time put a fool's coat and cap upon him. His skill has hitherto gone no farther than to cram pins down children's throats, and throw them into fits; to turn wort,[1] kill pigs; to sell winds (dog cheap too), to put out candles, or to make half-blind people see two at once; to help hares to run away from the dogs; to make noises, or to discourage his faithful votaries at Newgate,[2] by interloping upon their trade of discovering stolen goods; and such like important feats of daemonship. And, what is yet worse, I cannot find in these last eighteen hundred years, that with all his cunning he has invented one new trick, but goes on in the same dull road; for there is scarce a story told of a spirit, or a witch, who has played pranks in the next parish, but we have the same story, or one very like it, in Cicero's tract *De Divinatione*.[3]

He always plays at small games, and lives mostly upon neck-beef.[4] His intrigues are all with old women, whose teats he sucks (which, by the way, shews but a scurvy taste); and when he has gained his ends of them, feeds them only with bread and water, and gives them a groat in their pockets to buy tobacco; which, in my mind, is very ungallant, not to say niggardly and ungenerous, in so great a potentate, who has all the riches of the hidden world within his dominions. I cannot find, in all my reading, that he has expended as much in five hundred years last past as would have carried one election.

Methinks he might have learned a little more wit from his faithful emissaries here on earth, who throw and scatter about money, as if there was never to be an end of it; and get him more votaries in a week, than he can purchase for himself in a century, and put him to not a penny of charge neither; for they buy people with their own money: But to keep such a coil and clutter about an

1. To turn wort: to root.
2. The prison for the City of London and for prisoners from the Court of King's Bench.
3. In the *De Divinatione* Cicero subjects to a close, and unsympathetic, examination Stoic beliefs respecting Fate and the possibility of prediction. The work is filled with anecdote.
4. Neck beef: the cheapest cut of meat.

old woman, and then leave her to be hanged, that he may get her into his clutches a month sooner, is very ungrateful; and, as I conceive, wholly unsuitable to a person of his rank and figure.

I should have imagined, that it would have been more agreeable to the wisdom and cunning always attributed to him, in imitation of his betters, to have opened his purse-strings, and have purchased people of more importance, and who could do him more real service. I fancy that I know some of them, who would be ready to take his money, if they knew where he was to be spoken with; and who are men of nice honour, and would not betray or break their word with him, whatever they may do with their countrymen.

Besides, I conceive it is very impolitick in one of his sagacity, and in one who has so many able ministers in his own dominions and elsewhere, to act so incautious a part. It is very well known, that a plot discovered, or a rebellion quelled, gives new credit and reputation to the conquerors, who always make use of them to settle their own empire, effectually to subdue their enemies, to lessen their powers, and to force them for the most part to change sides; and, in fact, one witch hanged or drowned, makes old Beelzebub a great many adversaries, and frightens thousands from having any more to do with him.

For these reasons, I doubt, he is shrewdly belied by those from whom he might expect better usage; and that all the stories commonly told about, and believed concerning him, are invented and credited by such only as have much less wit, or not much more honesty, than himself. To enter into a detail of them is endless, as well as unneccessary to my purpose; it having been unquestionably shewn already by the worthy Dr. Hutchinson,* from very many instances, that these stories are fictions, cheats, or delusions, and that the belief of them is neither consistent with reason nor religion. But I shall add some more observations of my own, to what he hath with great piety and judgment published upon this subject; and shall begin with tracing the genealogy of these phantoms.

* Bishop of Down and Connor in Ireland. [That is, Francis Hutchinson (1660–1739), the author of *An historical essay concerning witchcraft* (London: Printed for R. Knaplock, 1720).]

The first inventers of them, as far as we know any thing of the matter, were the Egyptians; who believed, that the spirits of the deceased always attended their bodies where-ever they were deposited; and therefore embalmed them with rich gums and spices, to preserve their figure entire, and entombed them in stately mausoleums, with costly apartments for their souls to solace in: Which opinion gave occasion to their building the expensive and useless pyramids, to receive souls of a higher degree. From Egypt these airy beings were transplanted into Greece, and thence to Rome; and the Greek and Roman poets embellished their fictions with them, and the priests made their advantages of them; and both priests and poets added many more inventions of their own: They filled their woods, groves, rivers, rocks, houses, and the air itself, with romantick deities: They had their demi-gods, satyrs, dryads, hemi-dryads, penates, lares, fauns, nymphs, &c. And when the general belief of the existence of such beings was well established, without doubt they were often seen and talked with.

> For fear does things so like a witch,
> 'Tis hard to find out which is which.

They animated almost every thing in nature; and attributed even the passions and qualities of the mind to peculiar deities, who presided over them, or directed and caused them: Mars inspired courage and magnanimity; Venus, love; Mercury, cunning; and Apollo and his Muses, wisdom, and poetick raptures, &c. A good and evil genius attended every man, and his virtues and vices were esteemed to be spirits: A wicked man had an evil spirit; a virtuous man, a good one; a wrangler had a spirit of contradiction; people who could not speak, had a dumb spirit; a malicious man, a spirit of envy; and one who wanted veracity, a spirit of lying; and so on. Distempers too which were uncommon, and could not easily be accounted for, as apoplexies, epilepsies, and other fits and trances, were imputed to spirits and daemons; and at last these delusions, which were only the sallies of poets, or the inventions of priests, became the real opinions and religion of the common people, who are always ready to lick up the froth of their betters.

When the heathens came into Christianity, they brought in these phantoms with them, and accounted for oracular predictions, and the other cheats and juggles of their former priests, by the powers of these daemons; and the popish priests have since improved upon their pagan predecessors, and made their fictions turn to a much better account than putting them in verse. The heathen dryads and nymphs were changed into fairies; good and evil genii into conjurers and black and white witches; and saints are made to supply the offices of demi-gods: and by this lucky turn they made a very good penny of their charms, exorcisms, beads, relicks, and holy water; and were paid for many masses, to invoke their saints; in whom, it seems, they had a very good interest.

There was scarce a church-yard, an old or empty house, which was not pestered with these airy inhabitants; nor a man who had murdered himself, or who was murdered by another, or had forgot something in his life-time, who did not appear to tell his own story; nor could be persuaded to quit his new abode, till the holy man had laid him in the Red Sea; who, without doubt, was very well paid for his skill and pains. We may be sure so gainful a trade was duly cherished and cultivated by constant juggles and impostures, and all advantages were taken of surprizing and unusual phenomena of nature. By the help of glasses, unusual voices and noises, phosphorus, magick lanthorns,[5] feats of legerdemain, and collusion and confederacy, these prejudices were artfully kept up, and weak and enthusiastick people were made to believe, sometimes to see, and afterwards to publish to others their visions, or whatever else their deceivers had occasion for; whose power at the same time was so great, that the few intelligent men who saw and detested these impieties, durst not contend with the prejudices of the people, abetted by the rage of the popish priests.

Many of our first reformers were but weak men, and I doubt some of them were not very honest ones; and therefore generally fell into these stories: However, they lost a great deal of ground in Queen Elizabeth's reign; but were returned upon us with a full swing by her successor, who brought from Scotland with him whole legions of these subterranean inhabitants; who,

5. Magic lanthorns: magic lanterns.

methinks, should more properly have come from a warmer climate. That bright, sagacious, and royal author wrote and published a very learned book of daemonology, which effectually confuted all disbelievers;[6] for sure no man, who hoped for any preferment, ecclesiastical or civil, would have the ill manners to dispute his Majesty's great judgment and royal authority. When Nero proclaimed himself the best poet in his dominions by sound of trumpet, no man durst contend for the laurel with one who had fifty legions at his command. So an act of Parliament was passed for hanging of witches;[7] and his Majesty himself was graciously pleased to inform his judges by what marks they might be known; and many of them were hanged accordingly: But, as ill luck would have it, they multiplied like the blood of the martyrs; and the more they hanged, the more were left behind, during his whole reign.

In King Charles I's time they began to decrease again, by letting them alone; till, at the end of the Civil War, a new set of saints got into the saddle; and then again a fresh persecution began against old women, who were hanged plentifully at every Assizes.

> Some only for not being drown'd,
> Others for sitting above ground
> Whole days and nights upon their breeches,
> And feeling pain, were hang'd for witches.

There were professed witch-finders, who knew them at first sight; so that there was scarce a poor, withered, old wretch, with a mole or a wart in any part of her body, but was in danger of her life.

When King Charles II returned, and the nobility, clergy, and gentry resumed their proper seats, old women began again to live and die in quiet; and, during that prince's long reign, there were but few instances of witches hanged; and, considering the

6. In 1597, James I (then James VI of Scotland) published a work entitled *Daemonologie*, in which he argued for the existence of witches.

7. In response to James I's fanatical views on the existence of witchcraft, legislation was passed in 1603–1604 that declared it a capital crime to invoke evil spirits or to employ witchcraft to harm any person or his property.

prepossessions of the people, occasioned by so many late murders, under the pretences of zeal, it is not to be wondered at if there were a few: But since the Revolution there has not, as I remember, been one witch hanged;[8] nor do I think that one lawyer in England would condemn one, or any special jury of gentlemen find her guilty; though we are often told, and, if we may judge by other effects, have reason to believe, that Satan is as busy now as he has been in the memory of man.

But in a neighbouring country witches are almost as plentiful as ever; for as soon as the successors of the aforesaid holy men came into play again, and ruled the earth, they turned as they usually do upon their old benefactor, and hanged immediately a dozen or two of his accomplices; and did the same soon after in New-England, of which some were poor Quakers (whom they could not be permitted to hang merely for want of orthodoxy) and it is thought there was not an old woman in Fairyland (who was unfit for use), but would have undergone the same fate, if the government had not interposed.

Notwithstanding this, I do not find that the Devil has in the least changed his measures, or is more afraid of the saints than he used to be; but is constantly working under their noses, and every now and anon kidnapping some of their flocks; but it is always of such as can pay no tithes: for it is agreed by all, that a little money in their pockets will keep him out: But what seems very remarkable is, that at the same time that he makes so bold with these holy men, who have power to cast him out, he keeps a respectful distance from men of carnal sense, and plain natural understandings; and most of all from those incredulous persons, who cannot be persuaded to believe that the merciful God will permit him to outwit and destroy ignorant and unwary Christians, whom the Saviour of the world died to redeem from his power.

This is so true, that those stories are believed through the world, in exact proportion to the ignorance of the people, and the

8. The last English trial for witchcraft was in 1712, in which the defendant was convicted but not executed. The last trial and execution in Scotland, however, took place in 1722, the year this letter was first published.

integrity of their clergy, and the influence which they have over their flocks. In popish countries there is a spirit or witch in every parish, in defiance of holy water, and of constant *pater nosters*; and there are more of them in ignorant popish countries than in knowing ones, in poor than in rich ones; and they appear oftener in arbitrary governments than in free states. The King of Spain's and Pope's dominions have more of them than France and the German principalities, where priest-craft does not ride so triumphant; and these have more than Venice, Genoa, and the popish Hans towns.[9]

The same is equally true of Protestant countries: Muscovy, Sweden, Denmark, and Lapland, have more of them than Scotland and Ireland; and Scotland and Ireland more than England, where no clergymen of any credit abet these frauds; and consequently the Devil's empire here is almost at an end, how considerable soever it has been formerly: and in Holland he has nothing at all to do; though that country lies so near his other territories, that I wonder he should not sometimes shorten his journey, or at least now and then take it in his way, though only to try what may be done among the Hogan Mogans.[10]

From all that has been said I think I may reasonably conclude, that he is kept at home by the will of the Almighty, suffering the punishment due to his rebellion; and has no power over others, till, for their disobedience to the commands of heaven, they are delivered into his custody to be tormented, and made just objects of divine vengeance: And I shall take the liberty further to add, that true religion is so well supported by reason and revelation, that there is no necessity of telling lies in its defence, and putting it upon the same bottom with the heathen superstitions, and the popish forgeries and impostures; which, when discovered will make twenty infidels for one true believer that is made by such methods.

T   *I am, &c.*

---

9. That is, the Catholic Hanseatic cities.
10. Hogan Mogans: an eighteenth-century slang term for Dutchmen.

NO. 80. SATURDAY, JUNE 9, 1722.

That the two great Parties in England do not differ so much as they think in Principles of Politicks.

SIR,

Machiavel tells us, that it is rare to find out a man perfectly good or perfectly bad: Men generally swim between the two extremes; and scarce any man is as good as he himself, his friends, or his party, make him; or as bad as he is represented by his personal or party enemies.[1] Ask a Whig the character of a neighbouring Tory, and he represents him as a Jacobite, an enemy to publick liberty, and a persecutor; and, on the other side, if you enquire the other's character from his Tory godfather out of baptism, he shall pass for a commonwealth's man, an enemy to all sorts of monarchy, and an encourager of all kinds of licentiousness and faction: whereas an indifferent man, conversing with each of them, shall find both aim at the same thing, and their opposition to proceed only from their not conversing together, from an intention to thwart one another, or from the intrigues of those who reap advantage by setting them together by the ears. 'Tis too great a compliment to pay to our adversaries, to suppose them to act upon a mistaken principle against their real interest; and it is certainly the interest of every man to be free from oppression; and he will join in measures to be so, if he be not terrified by the fear of greater oppression. It is undoubtedly true, that there are many Jacobites in England; but it is thinking better of them than they deserve, to believe that they will be so against their own interests: And therefore, excepting the very few who can hope to receive the advantages of such a revolution, the rest may be converted, by shewing them that they can find better protection and security from the present establishment, than by hazarding their lives and estates, and their country's happiness, in bringing their designs to pass. The only dangerous Jacobites that I ever feared, were those

1. *Discourses*, I.27.

who took the same methods to keep out the son as turned out the father.

Whilst men enjoy protection, plenty, and happiness, they will always desire to continue them, and never look after revolutions; but when they lose, or fancy that they lose those advantages, which they ever will think they have a right to enjoy, they will endeavour to change their condition, though in the attempt they often change it for the worse. Whoever therefore would endeavour to preserve a present establishment, must make the people easy and contented under it, and to find their own account in the continuance of it. The instruments of tyranny (of which I hope we shall never have any amongst us) are never to be depended upon in any exigency; they will always be able to shift for themselves, and know how to make an interest with a new government, by betraying the old: which was the case of the late King James, and will ever be the case of others in the like circumstances.

Every man therefore, who is sincerely and heartily attached to the interest of his present Majesty, will endeavour to cherish, cultivate, and make a proper use of his excellent dispositions to protect and make his people happy, and to preserve our constitution in church and state upon its true and solid basis. Old land-marks are never to be removed, without producing contests and law-suits, which for the most part ruin both parties. We have an excellent constitution at present; and if not the best which can be formed in an utopian commonwealth, yet I doubt the best that we are capable of receiving. The present distribution of property renders us incapable of changing it for the better; and probably any attempt to change it for the better, would conclude in an absolute monarchy. There are so many interests engaged to support it, that whoever gets power enough to destroy these interests, will have power enough to set up himself; as Oliver Cromwell did, and every one else will do, in the same circumstances; or at least, no wise man will trust to his moderation.

No man of sense and fortune will venture the happiness which he is in full possession of, for imaginary visions; and throw the dice for his own estate: Such desperate gamesters carry their whole about them; and their future expectations depend upon confusion, and the misery of others: but such as have much to fear, and little to hope for, will acquiesce in their present condition. This being the true circumstance of the nobility, clergy, gentry, rich merchants, and the body of the people, I hope they will concur in such measures as will most effectually preserve our present establishment, and support the just rights of the crown, and the liberties of the people, oppose all usurpations on either side, and endeavour, in the most exemplary manner, to punish all who shall dare to interpose between the king and the subject, and spoil that harmony which alone can make them both happy.

This is the interest of all parties, and of every man in them (except a very few, who make their market of the others' differences), and I could never yet see a just bone of contention between them. It can be of no consequence to either party, if they are governed well, whether a man of one denomination or another governs them: and if they are oppressed, it is no consolation, that it is done by one whom they formerly called a friend; whereas if they would agree together, no one durst oppress them. Those who are called Whigs, have no intention to injure the legal establishment of the church; and seven years' experience, when they have had the whole power in their hands, may convince any one that they did not intend it; and the Tories tell us, that they desire no more than that establishment, and have no thoughts of breaking in upon the Act of Toleration, which is the right of all mankind.[2] The Whigs can have no motive to do the one, nor the Tories the other, when party opposition is laid aside: for how is a Whig injured by another's receiving advantages which he has no right to, and receives no prejudice by, but may receive benefit from, by providing for his children, relations, or friends? And how is a Tory injured in a quiet neighbour's worshipping God in his own way, any more than if he did not worship him at all; which is the case of thousands who are unmolested? The distinctions about govern-

2. The Toleration Act of 1689 permitted English nonconformists their own places of worship and preachers. They were, however, excluded from high public office until repeal of the Test and Corporation Acts in 1828.

ment are at an end: Most of the Tories are ashamed of their old arbitrary principles, and many of the modern Whigs ought to be ashamed of taking them up; and indeed they have no right to reproach one another with either practices or principles: for both have shewn their wrong ends in their turns; and they have brought matters at last to that pass, that whilst they have been throwing the dice for victory, sharpers have been drawing the stakes.

Indeed, I cannot see what we differ about: we fight at blindman's-buff, and fall upon our friends, as well as enemies. All the grounds of distinction are now at an end, and the honest and wise men of all parties mean the same thing, and ought to lay aside and forget the old names, and become one party for liberty, before that name is forgotten too. It is yet in our power to save ourselves. We are sure we have a prince, who has every disposition to help us, if we lend our own assistance, and shew him the means of doing it; and we are answerable to God, our country, and ourselves, if we do not use our own endeavours. The means are easy, obvious, and legal; and the motives as strong as ever did, or ever can, happen in any circumstance of human affairs. It is no less than the safety and preservation of the best king, and the best constitution upon earth, and indeed of almost the only people amongst whom there are any remains of liberty, knowledge, or true religion; all which depend upon the steady, loyal, and uniform proceedings of the next Parliament.

For my own part, I have no quarrel to names or persons, and would join in any just measures, or with any party, to save the kingdom; and will oppose, to the utmost of my power, all who will not; and I believe that there are thousands of the same sentiments; and methinks great men should accept so favourable a disposition to forget the mischiefs which ambition, covetousness, or inadvertency have brought upon us. We will not look with eagle's eyes into past faults, provided a proper atonement is made by future services; nor envy particular men's growing rich, if they will let the publick thrive with them; and it is certainly safer, and more creditable, to do so by the consent of their countrymen, than by constant struggles, broils, and contention, to overcome popular opposition;

which must get the better at last, or their country, and probably they themselves, must be buried in it.

England is yet in a condition to make the fortunes of a few men, if they are not in too much haste to make them; and will consent, or connive at their doing so, if they deserve well in other respects. There are many useless, and yet profitable, employments in England, and few men are concerned how they are disposed of; whether to lord's valets, or whether they are the perquisites of foreign or domestick favourites, provided the offices which regard the administration of justice, of the state, church, or revenue, be properly bestowed. Those who have the fortune to get into the highest stations, will expect to raise suitable estates, especially when they have in a great measure the means in their hands of making them, and the power of carving for themselves; and all but rivals will compound for their doing it by such ways as are consistent with the publick benefit, or such as the publick does not suffer much by; and I doubt the legal advantages belonging to few offices in England will answer the expectations of men in the first station.

It is often urged, that princes must be served upon their own terms, and their servants must sometimes comply against their inclinations, to prevent greater mischief; which I believe is rarely the case. I confess, princes ought and must be always treated with tenderness and delicacy, and regard must be had to their opinions or prejudices; but it is so much their interest to be honoured and beloved by their people (who from a thousand motives will be always ready to make them personally easy, and to gratify even their wanton desires, when they are not absolutely destructive to themselves), that there is much less address and management necessary to shew them their real interest, and bring them into it, than to engage them in designs which will ever produce disaffection and danger; and it is certainly the interest of their ministers and servants, rather to set themselves at the head of publick benevolences, and receive the thanks and applause due to such benefits, than to have them extorted from them always with general curses and detestation, and often with personal hazard.

T   *I am, &c.*

NO. 81. SATURDAY, JUNE 16, 1722.

The Established Church of England in no Danger from Dissenters.

SIR,

I have in my last letter said, that no wise man will remove ancient land-marks; and for the imaginary prospect of enjoying something which he does not enjoy, and has a mind to enjoy, run the hazard of losing what he is already in possession of. Those who have nothing to lose, can lose nothing by their feats of knight-errantry; but those that have, are seldom gainers by them. I considered this subject in that paper as it regarded the state; and I shall do it here with relation to our Church differences. The constitution of our Church is excellently well adapted to our civil government. The bishops answer to the Lords, and the inferior clergy to the Commons in the state; and all are subject to the legislative power mediately,[1] and immediately to the crown. The king has the power of creating the chief ecclesiastical officers, as he has of creating the civil; and they both receive their beings and existence from him; and consequently they must ever be in the interest of monarchy; and the monarch must ever be in the interest of an establishment from which he derives so much power. The nobility and gentry too, whose birth, character, and fortunes always give them the means of easy access to the throne, must be equally in the same interest; for, as no man can suffer by another's enjoying possessions which he has no right or pretence to; so they will share largely in these possessions, by having more frequent and better opportunities than their fellow-subjects, of preferring their children, relations, friends, and dependents; not to mention what presentations they have in their own power. Indeed, every man, of any condition, has an interest in them, as he has a chance of sharing preferments himself, or getting them for his family: and therefore it is wild to fear that any interest in England can shake an establishment which so many interests must concur to support;

1. Mediately: indirectly.

unless those who are in possession of its advantages should, by endeavouring to take away from others their rights, force them to make reprisals, and to do what, I dare say, no man in England now intends, and but few desire.

I have wondered, therefore, to hear some men of good understanding and unquestionable integrity apprehend any danger to the legal constitution of the Church, and cannot guess from what quarter they can fear it. The Independents, Anabaptists, and Quakers,[2] are no candidates for ecclesiastical power, but are by principle against all church establishments amongst themselves. The Quakers have no clergy at all; and the two former allow their ministers no superiority above the rest of their congregations; and it is certain, that all of them have much more favourable opinions of the national clergy than of the Presbyterians (the only rivals for church-power), from whom they apprehend, and have always found, much worse usage than from the Church. They desire nothing but liberty of conscience, and do not envy other preferments which they cannot enjoy themselves. It is true, the Presbyterians are candidates for church-dominion; and without doubt their priests have hawks' eyes at the church preferments, and wish often for them, if wishes would get them; but what facility, or, indeed, possibility, have they of obtaining them? They are an inconsiderable body as to their number; and as to their figure less; and as they grow rich, and leave estates behind them, their sons (for the most part) desert their congregations and interest: Besides, they are divided now into two parties, *viz.* the Subscribers, and Nonsubscribers;[3] the latter of which, much the most consider-

2. Independents were nonconformists (among them, Congregationalists and Baptists) who rejected both Presbyterianism and episcopacy and supported the autonomy of local congregations. The Anabaptists comprised an extreme sect of reformers, originating in Zurich in 1524, that rejected infant baptism in favor of adult baptism and opposed the use of force. The Quakers were a nonconformist sect founded in 1647 by George Fox; they renounced paid ministers, formal services, creeds, oath-taking, the bearing of arms, and tithing.

3. In 1717, John Abernethy, an Irish Presbyterian divine, was assigned to take charge of a congregation in Dublin, which he refused. This refusal was regarded then as ecclesiastical high treason and from it followed an intense controversy between those who supported Abernethy, the "Nonsubscribers," and those who championed the Presbyterian synod, the "Subscribers." Abernethy repudiated the sacerdotal assumptions of all ecclesiastical courts and

able for fortune and understanding, are come, for the most part, into the principles of general liberty and independency, nor will ever trust their clergy with the power which they pretend to, and which they claim from scripture; and by degrees many of these, in all probability, will come into the Church.

No prince can ever be in the interest of Presbytery; and I believe that there never was one in the world who was a true Presbyterian: for, as that government is purely democratical, so it is calculated only for a popular state; and, in fact, subsists no-where else in the world, unless in Scotland, where there have been frequent struggles between the crown and them. King James I was so plagued with them, that he was visibly partial to the papists against them: Charles I, by violence, destroyed their establishment; and King Charles II, though called in by them, and supported by them against his Parliament, yet immediately turned upon them: For, though they would have been glad to have had a king modelled to serve their purposes, yet that king had more wit than to have them. For the same reasons, the nobility and gentry of few countries, who by their births, fortunes, and near access to the throne, claim and enjoy a distinction above the inferior rank of mankind, can never be heartily in the interest of that sort of government; and it is certain, that many of the nobility and gentry in Scotland have never been favourable to it. And this is the true, perhaps the chief, reason why so many of them now are Jacobites.

The Presbyterian clergy claim a right, from scripture, to be independent of the civil power in all things which relate to spirituals, of which they pretend to be judges; and, in fact, their synods in Scotland, whatever they do now, formerly did not allow the crown power to adjourn or dissolve them, though they were forced to submit to it; and I am told, at present, they always adjourn by their own authority, though they take especial care it shall be to the same time that the crown appoints; which still keeps up their claim against a proper occasion. I do not avouch the truth of this, and hope that it is not true. Now it is certain, that the nobility and gen-

---

opposed the Test Act, for which he and his followers were cut off from the Irish Presbyterian Church in 1726.

try of England, who have actually the power of governing their clergy, will never be governed by them, whatever visions weak men of any denomination may flatter themselves with; nor will ever submit to the Presbyterian discipline, and to let monks and cynics govern their families, turn the heads of their wives, children, and servants, and control their own actions. Nor will the other sectaries, as has been said, who are already possessed of a free liberty of conscience, endeavor to put power into the hands of those who will be sure to take it away; as they did in New-England, though they went there to get it for themselves. So that the danger of settling Presbytery in England is a mere chimera; and when, by the chance of a long Civil War, they were actually got in possession of a power, which during the continuance of it they disclaimed, they could not hold it even for a few years.

The only ball of contention which seems to be now amongst churchmen, is the Sacramental Test,[4] which excludes dissenters from offices; which they think they have a right to in common with their fellow-subjects, having done nothing to forfeit it: But this seems to me to be a dispute only about a non-entity: for it is certain, that no one dissenter in England would be in any office of value, if that law was repealed, more than there are now; for they always qualify themselves, if they can get good places, and take advantage of the law to keep themselves out of chargeable ones: so that the churchmen alone suffer by the statute. The king, by act of Parliament, as well as interest and education, will be of the established Church; and the nobility are all, or almost all, so too, and no doubt but they will give the preference in all preferments to those of their own opinions: nor can it ever happen but that men, who can have qualifications to fill any considerable employments, will have wit enough to find out that there is no religious difference between the Church and Presbyterian establishments, except in the interests of their clergy; which no wise man will think considerable enough to differ about, and to separate upon that score from the national discipline, very few excepted,

4. The Test Act (25 Car. II, c. 2 [1673]), by which all holders of office under the crown were required to receive the sacrament of the Eucharist according to the usage of the Church of England. In addition, they were to take the oaths of supremacy and allegiance to the King and to repudiate transubstantiation.

who will find their account in setting themselves at the head of a faction, and selling it. So that this question appears to me only to be a party puncto,[5] and scarce worth asking on the one side, or denying on the other. Those amongst the Whigs, who most desire it, would not have the appearance of persecution stand in a law, when in effect there is no real persecution; and it is certainly the interest of the clergy to gratify and oblige their dissenting brethren in what costs them nothing: for one act of kindness will make more converts in a year, than they can make by preaching at them in twenty; however, till they see the advantage in doing it themselves, I think that no prudent man will give them any cause of jealousy, by doing it against their consent.

This being, as I conceive, the true state of our church differences, I shall conclude this letter, by application to our national clergy. It is not to be wondered at, that so many of their predecessors regretted the diminution which they suffered of their former revenues and grandeur at the Reformation; and that they often looked back with wishing eyes, and could not easily lose sight of so agreeable a prospect, without weighing enough the impossibility of recovering their lost power from the crown, and their lands from the nobility and gentry, who had got possession of them: Indeed it would have been a wonder if they had done otherwise. But now almost two hundred years' experience may convince them of the impossibility of succeeding in such a design. They have once lost all, by endeavouring to recover a part; and lately had like to have lost their possessions and religion too, by attempting to give the crown a power, which they intended should be employed for their own benefit, but was actually used against them; and I hope they are now pretty generally of opinon, that it is their interest to stand to their present establishment, and be contented with the same security for their own possessions as the rest of their fellow-subjects have, and to join with them in the defence of liberty, and the laws of the land.

I see, with a great deal of pleasure, many of them falling into these opinions; and hope, that it will soon be the opinion of the greatest part of them; and then I dare boldly affirm, that all

5. Puncto: a minor detail.

religious distinctions will soon be at an end, which are now kept up more by party animosities, than any essential difference of opinion: for men will always fly from the sentiments of those whose persons they hate, and whose oppression they fear; and such as are little concerned about metaphysical, and, as they think, useless, notions in divinity, will support any party against those who would oppress all; and therefore the most laudable, and indeed only way of the clergy's being safe themselves, is to make other people safe; and then they will have the good wishes, the respect, and protection of every honest man in England; and multitudes of the dissenters, who will not be frightened or bullied out of their opinions, will insensibly quit them of their own accord, if it be only to save the charge of paying separate ministers, and to be in the fashion, when they can once give themselves leave to consider coolly, that they differ about nothing, or nothing that is essential to religion, or their own interests. The heat of the sun made the traveller immediately quit his cloak, when the blustering of the north wind had made him wrap it closer about him.

T   *I am, &c.*

NO. 82. SATURDAY, JUNE 23, 1722.

꿏 *The Folly and Characters of such as would over-throw the present Establishment.*

SIR,

It gives equal occasion of mirth and concern to wise men, to see so many of the other sort, persons of seeming reverence, and with grave faces, exerting themselves with warmth and zeal for opinions and parties, with each a separate train or chorus of lesser and subordinate planets attending their motions, and dancing after them. Whoever views these solemn spectres at a distance, will see nothing but conscience, contempt of worldly honours and preferments, and minds superior to all temptations; whereas all this grimace, to a nice observer, will appear only to be a project for picking pockets, and getting away other people's money; which, in reality, at present makes, and ever did make, most of the squabbles which at any time have disturbed the world. This I may possibly hereafter shew to be true, in most of the conspicuous instances of publick and private life; but at present I shall confine myself to those gentlemen who deal in revolutions.

There are a considerable number of politicians in all governments, who are always enemies to the present establishment; not because it is an ill one, or because those who administer it betray their trust (which is a just and reasonable ground of complaint), but because they themselves are not in it: If they are so, all is well; but if they cannot be accepted upon their own terms, or are afterwards turned out for misbehaviour, then upon a sudden there is no faith in man, fundamentals are struck at, no honest man can serve, and keep his integrity, and there is no remedy but a total change, and if that happen, and they can get into power, nothing is mended but their own faces and their fortunes. Without a doubt, every man has a right to liberty, and to come at it by all ways which do not bring a greater inconvenience with it than the benefit proposed promises advantage; and all just attempts of that kind are commendable: but I speak now of a sort of cattle, who think nothing but their fodder, who do not care who feeds them, or who is their master, provided they have a belly-full; nor whether it be lawful pasture, or trespass and encroachment upon the neighbouring soil.

I am so unfortunate as always to think, that a man who is a knave in his private dealings, will never be a saint in politicks; and whoever does not do reasonable and just things in respect to his neighbours, relations, and acquaintances, which he knows, will have little real concern for the titles of princes whom he knows not. Indeed it seems to me, that there cannot be a greater ridicule in nature, than for any man to pretend to be concerned for the personal interest of another, whom he is not acquainted with, has no means of being acquainted with, and probably would not be acquainted with upon equal terms, unless he can hope to find a farther account in it, in going snacks with him.

It is certain, that every man's interest is involved in the security and happiness of a good prince, from whom he receives protection and liberty; but for one who has no concern for publick or private justice, who does not care what becomes of his neighbour's rights and possessions, who would make no difficulty of cheating any prince whom he served, or oppressing those in his power; I say for such an one to set up for loyalty, and the right line, and to hazard his life and family, for conscience sake, is such a farce, that if men's thoughts were not so wholly taken up with their own cheating, that they minded not other people's, no one could be deceived by such false appearances.

I must beg leave, therefore, of these gentlemen to take it for granted, that all this zeal is for themselves, and only a struggle for money and employments, and to get that by a revolution, which they want merit or means to get without it; and I will endeavour to shew them, that they are taking abundance of pains, and running much hazard to attain what they never will catch. But I would not be understood here to apply myself to those men who are in desperate circumstances, and whose condition may be bettered, and cannot be made worse by confusion; nor to the poor visionaries and enthusiasts, who are the cat's-feet[1] to the former, and are by nature prepared to be dupes and tools of ambition and design; but to the very few amongst them who are tolerably easy in their own affairs, and do not want common understanding; and to these I may safely say, that their passions and prejudices hurry them away from their real interests, to pursue shadows and imaginations, and to make those whose greatness they envy, yet much greater.

A prince long kept out of what he calls his dominions, will, upon a restoration, always bring back with him a junto of upstart Mamamouches,[2] with a huge train of half-starved beggars dangling after them, who through necessity have followed his fortunes, flattered his vices, and will expect to have his ear, and the disposal of his favours. This ragged crew, who have been long the outcasts of fortune, know, for the most part, nothing of government, or the maxims necessary to preserve it, unless to talk about

1. Cat's feet: cat's paws.
2. Mamamouches: the mock title conferred by the Sultan on Monsieur Jourdain in Molière's *Le Bourgeois Gentilhomme*.

the divine right of their master, and the injury done to so good a prince; but with arbitrary principles picked up in their travels, minds soured with wants and disappointments, hungry bellies, and ravenous and polluted claws, finding themselves at once metamorphosed from mock ministers and magistrates to real ones, glutted with sudden plenty, and rioting in profusion, which they before enjoyed only in imagination, will become of course proud, insolent, and rapacious, and think of nothing but to redeem the time which they have lost, to raise hasty fortunes, and will endeavour to get them as they can; and consequently will sell their master to those who can or will give most for him, which will be ever those who have got most by keeping him out.

The court language will be immediately changed: It will be said, that the prince must submit to the necessity of his affairs; that his enemies must be brought into his interest, who may be otherwise able to perplex his new government; and besides, having by long experience been used to employments, and the management of the publick revenue, must be continued till others are equally qualified to supply their offices; that his Majesty has a grateful memory of the faithful services of his true friends; that he will provide for them all by degrees, as fast as the others can be turned out; but they must have a little patience, and not be too importunate: And so, after two or three years daily attendance, with old coats new furbished, some good words, now and then a good dinner, and the honour of whispering and joking with his lordship, they will find themselves just where they set out, only with less money in their pockets; will see their enemies in possession of all the employments; find out at last, that courts and courtiers are alike, become new malcontents, and form themselves into a faction against the government which they ventured their lives to bring about.

This was the case upon the restoration of King Charles II when the Round-heads had all the offices, having got money enough, whilst they were in power, to buy them; and the poor starved Cavaliers, who had nothing but a good conscience, and past services to plead, were laughed at, and could hardly get admittance into the ante-chamber. The descendants of these are the modern Whigs; and of the other, for the most part the present Tories. Nor can it happen otherwise in the nature of things: for those who have no merit to offer but their money, will always offer enough of it; and those who want it, will always take it. Besides, such as are conscious of their own demerit to their prince, will use double diligence to please him, and to wipe off past scores; whereas those who pretend that they have sacrificed all for him, will esteem his favours received only as payments of just debts; and their expectations are seldom to be satisfied, or they to be persuaded that their services are enough considered. And it must proceed from a consummate ignorance in human nature, not to know, that almost all men, and especially princes and great men, would rather engage new debtors to themselves, than pay off old debts to other people; would sooner create fresh dependents, by conferring favours which will be esteemed obligations, than satisfy the clamours and importunities of such pretended creditors and duns, who will never be satisfied.

Besides, princes, for the most part, think all that can be done for them is no more than duty; and will throw off old servants, who can do them no more good, as easily as old shoes; grow weary of their long-winded tales about past services, and will think themselves at liberty to pursue their present interests, and employ such who are most capable of serving them for the present, as those undoubtedly are who have established interests, most experience in affairs, and money always at hand to back their pretensions.

Besides, when matters in any country are prepared for a revolution, the poor starved followers, or discontented well-wishers to an abdicated prince, will never have the merit and honour of making it; and can never, or very rarely, have power enough to do so: for those who enjoy the advantages of the government in possession, who are deep in its councils, command its fleets and armies, and perhaps made it odious by their wicked councils and actions, are always the first to veer about, and make their interest with the new government, by being instrumental to bring it in: They have it often in their power to do it, and great sums of money always at command to buy their peace, and very frequently to keep their employments; and so to go on where they left off: for a poor wandering prince, eager to get a crown (which he will conceit to be his own), will fall into any measures, or join with any persons, to obtain it; and for the most part to be ready to drop his necessitous followers, as easily as they would drop him, if they found it equally their interest.

Of this sort we have pregnant instances in the triumviri of Rome; of General Monk,[3] and others formerly among ourselves; and of a very great lord in the latter end of King James's time:[4] But why should I name particular instances, when every revolution which almost ever happened in the world, furnishes us with numerous ones, and will ever do so to the end of the world? unless the power by which the revolution is made is so great, and so much in the prince's disposal, that he is under no necessity of keeping measures with any person or party, but is wholly at liberty to follow his inclinations, and gratify his revenge and passions; or is so entirely an instrument of the power which he makes use of, or rather which makes use of him, that he must do whatever they would have him do; as was the case in a good measure of Marius and Sulla, but I think cannot be the circumstance of any person now living; and I hope that few of those who wish for a revolution would accept it upon those terms.

The starved crew who deal in revolutions, are seldom conjurers in politicks: for no man of fortune, or a grain of understanding, would venture a single hair of his head for the interest of another, educated in pride and ingratitude, and very probably one too of whom he knows nothing, and who knows nothing of him, nor will have the least regard to his hazard and services. Besides, is not such an one a worthy hero, and his particular interest a worthy cause for a man of common sense, and tolerable fortune, to ven-

3. George Monck, first Duke of Albemarle (1608–1670). Originally a staunch supporter of the Commonwealth, in 1660 Monck entered into direct communication with Charles II; he caused the election of a new Parliament which restored the monarchy and personally welcomed Charles II at Dover in May 1660.

4. There are any number of persons to whom Trenchard could be referring. One of the more likely is John Churchill, first Duke of Marlborough, who was advanced to the English peerage by James II and who was put in command of one of the royal armies assembled against the forces of William of Orange. To James's chagrin, Marlborough chose instead to join William's cause on the eve of battle.

ture his life and estate for, by involving his country too in a civil war?

But there is another reason still behind, which I fear these doughty politicians never think of; namely, that they are doing the work which they pretend to oppose; which has sometimes inclined me to believe, that they have been employed and hired to act as they do. It is certain, that their ill-digested libels, without the least notions of the principles of government, or shewing the least disposition to mend it; their stupid cant of a right in princes independent of the happiness of the society; their ill-mannered reflections upon the person of the sovereign, whom most of them have sworn to; and their constant invectives and reproaches upon all men, who are honester and wiser than themselves, do more mischief to this country, than their united force, counsels, and understanding could do good, if they were inclinable to do it.

Weak men, who know or suspect their designs, will take no measures with them for a common good; and those who laugh at their follies, and are not afraid of being over-reached and outwitted by them, are ever reproached with their silly designs. In fine, they are the only support of those whom they pretend most to abhor; and I believe I may venture to say, are the only friends in the kingdom, which some persons of figure lately had, without intending to be so.

In my next letter I will endeavour to shew, that it is impossible to bring their wild projects to bear; not with any hopes of making many of them wiser, but to convince better people, that they ought not to be bullied by the sound of Jacobitism, and so diverted from concurring in the necessary measures to serve their king, their country, and themselves, by bugbears and phantoms: for I dare venture to assert, that there is no possibility of restoring the Pretender to England, but by taking such measures to keep him out, as will be more terrible to the people than letting him in, if such can possibly be; and I am sure that every honest man ought to do all in his power to prevent any attempts of that kind, which we are certain will receive no countenance from his Majesty, and, I hope, from none of his present ministry.

T   *I am, &c.*

NO. 83. SATURDAY, JUNE 30, 1722.

ꝕ   *The vain Hopes of the Pretender and his Party.*

SIR,

I have promised in my last to shew, that the Pretender's game is altogether desperate in England, unless those whose duty and interest in the highest manner oblige them to keep him out, pave the way for his return: And this I shall do, by shewing, that there is no interest within the kingdom, or out of it, capable of bringing about such a revolution, and willing to do it. Indeed, such a convulsion would shake the very foundations of the earth, and turn all nature topsy-turvy. God knows, one Revolution is enough for one age. I do not deny, but such an event might have been brought about, if favoured by the crown, by the ministers and officers in power under it, and abetted by a great neighbouring potentate. Which case many people (I hope falsely) think was ours in a late reign;[1] and even then the success would not have been certain; and if it had succeeded, I dare venture to be positive, that those who had been most forward to have brought him in, would have been amongst the first to have turned him out again.

I think no man is now to learn, that conscience and the opinion of right have little or nothing to do in revolutions, but the resentments of men, and the gratifying the views and expectations of private persons, or of aggregate bodies; and no formidable set of men could have found their account amongst us, in continuing him upon the throne, upon the terms he must have sat there. He is certainly a very weak man, a great bigot, and of a saturnine and morose temper; and the near prospect of the possession of three crowns could not make him temporize with his then interest, nor disguise his religion to those who were contented to be deceived, that they might deceive others. And therefore it is impossible to

1. Trenchard is alluding to the attempts by Queen Anne's ministers during the last years of her reign to seat James Edward, the Old Pretender, on the British throne upon the Queen's death. The neighboring potentate is, of course, Louis XIV.

believe, that a prince so qualified, provoked by his expulsion, acquainted personally with few or none amongst us, and educated in the religion and maxims of France and Rome, restored by their means, and supported by them, would act afterwards upon other maxims than what he had before imbibed, and what would be constantly inculcated into him by his foreign tutors abroad, and his priests at home.

Such conduct would quickly have made those who most espoused his interest at first, soon turn upon him, as they did before upon his father; and so many interests in Europe were concerned to separate England from a dependence upon France, that they would never have wanted a strenuous assistance, as his father found to his cost, when all the popish princes, except France, preferred the interests of their states before the interests of their religion, as France itself would have done upon the like motives. I hope I shall be forgiven by the gentlemen of this cast of loyalty, if I say, that they have sufficiently shewn to the world, that they will espouse the interest of no prince any longer than he serves theirs; and I conceive it impossible to suppose a circumstance which that prince could be in, to answer both their views, considering his prejudices and dependencies.

But whatever might have been practicable then, the case is far otherwise now. We have a King upon the throne, who will not be sung out of his dominions, as the late King James was: He will have some troops at home, who will certainly stand by him: He has great dominions of his own abroad, and is sure of the support of powerful neighbors: His strength, and that of his allies, at sea, is so great, that no invasion can be made upon him, but by stealth; and that must be always a very inconsiderable one, and cannot be supported but by accidents. Very many, and I hope by far the greatest part, of the nobility, gentry, and people, are devoted to his person and title, and would be glad to serve him upon the bottom of liberty and his true interest: The dignified clergy shew their loyalty in the manner which is most acceptable to him, and every month adds to their number by new creations; and we may reasonably hope, that the rest will not be long left behind.

All who were concerned in the publick funds, which contain a fourth or fifth part of the wealth of the kingdom,[2] must support an establishment which supports them, and which if lost, they are undone and lost with it; and every man, who has property, or the means of acquiring property, and has an uncommon understanding, and a love for himself and liberty, must know that so many interests, and so supported, cannot be shaken but by a long civil war, and by making England the stage and field for all the nations in Europe to fight out their quarrels in; and that such a war must end in making us the prize of the victor, and subject us either to a foreign power or a domestic tyrant, if we have not the happiness to be restored to our present establishment again; and then we shall have had a civil war for nothing.

If we did not see by daily experience, that there is not an opinion in philosophy, religion, or politicks, so absurd, but it finds our heads wrong enough turned to embrace it; I should not think it possible, that any person, who is not a professed or concealed papist, could wish for such a revolution, or any one else fear it, and much less that they should fear it from abroad.

It is certain, that the Emperor[3] has so many personal as well as political ties and motives to engage him in the king's interests, arising from obligations received, from more expected, and as it is said contracted for in regard to his Italian dominions, from their mutual dependencies upon one another in Germany, and above all, from the interests of their several dominions, that it is politically impossible but that he must do all in his power to support him in his throne: for when two nations are so situated, that they have nothing to fear from one another, and have a common interest to watch and oppose a third power formidable to both, they must be natural allies without the help of treaties; and whatever little occasional or personal differences may happen between the princes who govern them, yet whilst the interest of their

2. The total national debt in 1722 was close to £50,000,000, while the value of all the lands in England at the time of the South Sea crisis was estimated by an early nineteenth-century source as somewhat less than £300,000,000.

3. The Holy Roman Emperor, Charles VI.

dominions are friendly, they will never long continue enemies; and though they do so, yet will always help one another upon any emergency.

I think I may safely say, that the King has much to hope, and nothing to fear, from the lesser princes of Germany, in respect to his English dominions; for many of them can and will help him, and none of them can do him any harm.

The safety and preservation of Holland is so entirely dependent and wrapped up in our present establishment, that they must venture all to defend it. We are obliged, by interest as well as treaties, to support them against every power that is capable much to offend them; and their interest is, to keep us in a situation and condition to do so: And though, without doubt, they emulate and fear the great naval power of England, and our possession of Gibraltar; and would please themselves, and laugh in their sleeves, to see us increase our burdens, and enervate our state, by airy and romantick expeditions to do their business, whilst they lie still, ease their subjects, and pay off their debts; yet they will never suffer England to fall under the dependence of France, Spain or Rome; though they very well know how to make mercantile advantages of the weakness of those whom they have to do with.

The crowns of Sweden and Denmark can never have a joint interest to insult us; and at present neither of them have so: For it is said, that we are engaged by alliances to support them against one another, and every one else who has power enough much to annoy them; nor can they be sure that ever England again will find its glory and advantage in the heroick gallantry of engaging in the squabbles of the north, when France and Holland (vastly more concerned with the event) find theirs in lying still, and letting them agree as they fall out.

The Czar can have no motives, from the interest of his dominions, to quarrel with a people from whom his subjects enjoy an advantageous trade, and with a power too which he cannot hurt, and which can hurt him: We are no rivals for adjacent territories; and he cannot rival us in maritime power and trade; and both of us can find our account in friendship, and neither in enmity. His encroachments in the Baltic have hitherto done us no mischief; but on the contrary, have opened a new market for naval stores, and rendered our supplies from Sweden and Denmark less precarious: Indeed his conquering either of those crowns would be very mischievous, but much more so to other nations than to us, who may be easily supplied with naval stores from our own plantations; and therefore if his neighbouring or distant trading nations apprehend such an event, they will certainly join together to oppose it, and implore our assistance upon our own terms; though undoubtedly they will be much better pleased, if we do it for them without asking theirs.

If, therefore, any subjects of ours have given him just cause of offence, and made him a personal enemy to our country, we ought to deliver them up, or punish them at home; and if any nation in alliance with us, and in enmity with him, can find their interest in quarrelling with him, let them quarrel by themselves, and make up their squabbles as they can, or get the assistance of those who have political motives to oppose his progress, and put a stop to his growing power: I doubt we shall have enough to do to defend ourselves; and therefore I hope we shall not undo ourselves yet further to conquer for others, and in instances too which in times to come may prove fatal to ourselves.

The states of Italy are interested to preserve the naval power and greatness of England, if we pursue the measures which are most advantageous to ourselves; namely, to meddle no farther with their affairs, than to carry on an advantageous trade with them; and, by friendly offices, proper negotiations, and perhaps sometimes by the shew of force, to protect them against the greater powers which threaten them. It is certainly their interest, that we should keep possession of Gibraltar and Port Mahon,[4] if we make a right and honest use of them; for we have nothing to desire from them, but what it is their interest to give, nor they to fear from us, whilst we act as Englishmen: but if we should ever sacrifice our

4. On the eastern coast of Minorca in the Balearic Islands, Port Mahon was seized from the Spanish by a British fleet in 1708.

own interests to such as are not our own, we must thank ourselves if we make enemies of those who would be glad to be our friends.

It is certainly the interest of the kingdom of France, to have an impotent administration, and a distracted state of affairs in England, and a prince at the head of them, that either from weakness cannot, or from other motives and dependences will not, obstruct the union of the Spanish monarchy to their own,[5] which would soon give them the possession of it as effectually as if they had conquered it; but the interest of the Regent, who governs France, is far otherwise: The appearing prospect, and probable chance of that crown's descending to him, or his posterity, will engage him to support a power which can alone support him, and which has every motive to do so. In such a circumstance of affairs, no interest in France, except his immediate dependents, can abet his personal pretensions against the interest of all France; and therefore he must depend upon foreign alliances; and England alone can be safely relied upon, who have no claim to any part of his dominions, or interest and desire to seize them; which cannot be said of the Emperor, or any other potentate, who has power and motives enough to assist him.

I have wondered therefore at the weakness of many among ourselves, who can be so often elated or terrified with the designs of the Regent, who can never conspire against us, without conspiring against himself; and no provocation even on our part could make him undermine or betray, in so tender an instance, his own interest. I doubt not but he wishes Gibraltar out of our hands; and if negotiations or big words can prevail upon us to part with it, I presume they are easily to be obtained, but he will never join with Spain to force it: This danger therefore is a mere bugbear, made use of to delude the Jacobites, and intimidate honester men, and, by making the first plot, or prate and bounce, to govern the others.

5. Philip V, Spain's first Bourbon king, was Duc d'Anjou prior to his accession in 1700; he was the grandson of Louis XIV and the second son of the recently deceased Dauphin and, as such, the uncle of Louis XV of France. Should Louis XV, who had ascended the throne at the age of five, have died, Philip V would ordinarily have succeeded to the French throne; he had, however, renounced this right in favor of Louis XIV's nephew, the Duc d'Orléans, the French Regent.

So that, the Pope excepted, who can do us no harm by his own force, the King of Spain alone is the power in Europe that can be concerned to favour the Pretender's interest; nor could he find his account in it, unless to open his way to the crown of France, in case of the young King's death.

The divine right of monarchy in the right line is so well established in arbitrary countries, that I dare say that prince[6] will be sorry to depend upon a forced renunciation and the power of Spain, to defend himself against his nephew, if other powers were not at hand to assist him; and no power in Europe can do it effectually but England: and whilst there is a king at the head of it, who will pursue his own and his people's true interest in protecting him, and preserving the friendship which for more than an age has been propitious to both kingdoms, and has the means, by the possession of Gibraltar and Port Mahon, of resenting any injury done on his part; it is wild to think, that at great hazard and expence he would attempt to bring about a revolution which may engage us in a long civil war, and disenable us to give him the protection he can receive no where else.

If, therefore, he is favourable to the Pretender's interest, it must be owing to personal resentments, or his views towards the crown of France. I hope that we shall give him no more cause for the first; and as to the latter, he has the interests of the Regent, of all Germany, Italy, the states of Holland, and indeed of all Europe, against him, as well as the united interest of his own subjects, who will not be contented to be a province to France; and I may venture to assert, that whilst we keep the possession of Gibraltar, and make a proper use of it, he can neither effect the one nor the other; namely, he can never make himself King of France, nor the Pretender King of England.

T   *I am, &c.*

6. The King of Spain.

NO. 84. SATURDAY, JULY 7, 1722.

əʕ *Property the first Principle of Power. The Errors of our Princes who attended not to this.*

SIR,

The subjects which men understand least are generally what they talk of most, and none so much as of government; which almost every man thinks he has talents to direct, and, like Sancho Pancha, believes he can make a very good viceroy: He thinks nothing is necessary, but to get at the helm, where his business is, to command, and that of others, to obey; and then, as the aforesaid Sancho (viceroy-like) says, "Who but I?" But to govern a state well, is the most difficult science in the world; and few men, who have ever been in the possession of power, have known what to do with it, or ever understood the principles upon which all power is founded; and their mistakes have made endless havock amongst mankind.

Government is political, as a human body is natural, mechanism: both have proper springs, wheels, and a peculiar organization to qualify them for suitable motions, and can have no other than that organization enables them to perform; and when those springs or principles are destroyed by accident or violence, or are worn out by time, they must suffer a natural or political demise, and be buried, or else smell above ground; and though neither of them ought to be murdered, yet, when they are dead, they ought to be interred.

Now it is most certain, that the first principle of all power is property; and every man will have his share of it in proportion as he enjoys property, and makes use of that property, where violence does not interpose. Men will ever govern or influence those whom they employ, feed, and clothe, and who cannot get the same necessary means of subsistence upon as advantageous terms elsewhere. This is natural power, and will govern and constitute the political, and certainly draw the latter after it, if force be absent;

and force cannot subsist long without altering property; so that both must unite together, first or last, and property will either get the power, or power will seize the property in its own defence: for, it is foolish to think, that men of fortunes will be governed by those who have none, and be plundered to make such whom they despise, and have every day new reasons to hate, rich and insolent: And, on the other hand, men will contentedly submit to be governed by those who have large possessions, and from whom they receive protection and support, whilst they will yet always emulate their equals. Though the people of Rome extorted a law from the Senate, that commoners might be admitted into the chief offices of the state jointly with the nobles;[1] yet all the address and power of the tribunes could not for a long time make them choose one of their own body into those offices, till commoners had got estates equal to the nobility; and then the balance of property turning to the people, they carried all before them.

The only true despotick governments now in the world, are those where the whole property is in the prince; as in the eastern monarchies, that of Morocco, &c. where every man enjoying what he has by the bounty of his sovereign, has no motive or means to contend with him, but looks upon him as his benefactor; and such as have no property, do not think themselves to be injured: But when men are in possession of any thing which they call their own, and think they have a right to enjoy it, they will ever contend for it, when they have the means to do so, and will always take advantage of every exigence in their prince's affairs to attain that right. Other princes, who have a mind to be as arbitrary as the former, and who want either the capacity or the power to acquire his natural dominion, seize by violence and productions of their subjects' estates and industry; which is a constant state of force on one side, and oppression on the other: It perpetually provokes the people, and yet leaves them often the means of revenging the injustice done them, and must end in restoring the old government, or in setting up some new form by the extinction of the present usurpation; whereas in states truly despotick, though the

1. Actually a series of laws enacted between 367 B.C. and 300 B.C., by which the plebeian class gained access to the magistracies and to the Senate itself.

monarchs be often destroyed, yet the monarchy is preserved entire, there being no interest in the state capable of shaking it.

But both these sovereignties have one mischief in common, and inseparable from them; *viz.* as they ever subsist by standing armies, so they must ever be subject to the caprices and disgusts of the military men, who often depose and murder their sovereigns; but in the latter much oftener than in the former: for whilst the people have the name, and, as they think, a right to property, they will always have some power, and will expect to be considered by their princes, and the soldiers will expect to have leave to oppress them, which will make continual struggles; and the prince, finding himself obliged to take part with one of them, often falls in the struggle; which was the case of the Roman emperors, most of whom were slaughtered either by the people, or their own soldiers: whereas in a natural absolute government, there is no danger but from the latter alone; and if he can please them, all is well, and he is safe.

But neither of these ought to be called by the name of government: both indeed are only violence and rapine, and the subjection of many millions of miserable wretches to the wild and wanton will of often the worst man among them: They deface human nature, and render the bountiful gifts of indulgent providence useless to the world; and the best which can be said of them is, that they make the grand tyrant and his inferior oppressors as miserable and unsafe as the poor wretches whom they oppress; nor should I have mentioned them as governments, but to make what I have further to say the better understood.

All other dominions are either limited monarchies, simple aristocracies, democracies, or mixtures of them; and the actions and operations in those governments, or the continuance of those governments, depend upon the distribution and alteration of the balance of property; and the not observing the variation and the frequent changes of the *primum mobile,*[2] causes all the combustions that we see and feel in states. Men who fancy themselves in the same situation, as to outward appearances, stare about them and wonder what is become of the power which their predecessors

---

2. *Primum mobile:* prime mover.

enjoyed, without being able to judge how they lost it by the float-ing of property: They think they have a right to enjoy the same still; and so, in spite of nature, use fraud and violence to attain what they cannot hold, if it were attained: However, they will struggle for it; and this struggle produces contentions and civil wars, which most commonly end in the destruction of one of the parties, and sometimes of both.

Now it seems to me, that the great secret in politicks is, nicely to watch and observe this fluctuation and change of natural power, and to adjust the political to it by prudent precautions and timely remedies, and not put nature to the expence of throws and convulsions to do her own work: I do not mean by altering the form of government, which is rarely to be done without violence and danger; and therefore ought not to be attempted when any thing else can be done, but by gentle and insensible methods. Sup-pose, for example, a limited monarchy, which cannot subsist with-out a nobility: If the nobles have not power enough to balance the great weight of the people, and support the crown and themselves, it is necessary to take some of the richest of the commoners into that order; if they have more power than is consistent with the dependence upon their monarch, it is right to create no more, but to let those already created expire and waste by degrees, till they become a proper balance: If the people by trade and industry grow so fast, that neither the crown nor nobles, nor both together, can keep pace with them; then there is no way left, but either, by using violence, to hazard, by an unequal contest, what the two latter are already in possession of, or, by using moderation and a beneficent conduct, to let the former enjoy all they can hope to get by a strug-gle, and voluntarily to give up all odious powers of doing mischief, though miscalled prerogative; which must ever be understood to be a power of doing good, when ordinary provisions fail and are insufficient.

Harry VII dreading the strengths of the nobles, who had always plagued, and sometimes destroyed his predecessors, found means to make them alienate a great part of their estates,[3] which

3. Not only did Henry VII fear a strong-willed and defiant nobility, but he was also unusually rapacious. As a consequence, his chief ministers, Richard Emp-

threw a proportionable power into the Commons; and his son, by seizing the revenues of the ecclesiasticks (who usually caballed with them), and dispersing those estates amongst the people, made that balance much heavier: which Queen Elizabeth wisely observing (though she loved power as well as any that went before her), yet caressed them with so much dexterity, that she preserved not only the crown upon her head, but wore it in its full lustre; and by encouraging trade, and letting nature take its course, still increased the people's wealth and power: which her successor early saw, and often lamented; but wanting her moderation, abilities, and experience, did not know how to temporize with an evil which he could not help, but took a preposterous way to cure it; and endeavoured, by the assistance of the governing clergy (who hoped by his means to recover what they lost by the Reformation) to regain a power, by pulpit-haranguing and distinctions, which he durst not contend for with the sword; and so his reign was a perpetual struggle between himself and his Parliaments: When they were quiet he bounced; and when he had thoroughly provoked them, he drew back, and gave good words again: but by such conduct he sowed the seeds of that fatal and bloody Civil War which sprang up in the reign of his son, and ended in the dissolution of the monarchy, and soon after of all liberty; for the general of the conquering army set himself (as all others will ever do in the same circumstance): But the property remaining where it was, this new tyranny was violent, and against nature, and could not hold long, and all parties united against it; and so the nation was restored to its ancient form of government.

King Charles II came in with all the exterior advantages requisite to enslave a people: The nation was become weary of the sound of liberty, having suffered so much in their struggle for it, and lost all that they struggled for: The clergy were provoked by the loss of their dignities and revenues; the nobility and gentry were universally distasted and alienated by sequestrations, and by being so long deprived of the offices and distinctions which they

---

son and Edmund Dudley, administered the English feudal law in such a way as to maximize the fines collected and to penalize with forfeiture of all goods as many landowners as possible.

claimed by their birth; and the body of the people had been harassed and exhausted by a long Civil War, and were weary of being tossed and tumbled once in a month out of one government into another; and all were prepared to accept and fall into any measures which might satiate their revenge upon those who had oppressed them, and to root out the very principles of liberty, the abuse of which had brought such mischiefs upon them.

That prince got a Parliament to his mind (as all princes will do upon a revolution, when parties run high, and will do any thing to mortify their opponents) and kept it in constant pension;[4] but property remaining in the people, it insensibly gained ground, and prevailed at last: The people grew universally disaffected, and looked upon the Parliament as a cabal of perjured hirelings, and no longer their representatives; and the nation was worked up into such a ferment, that their betrayers would not or durst not serve the court, nor the court keep them any longer. That prince had wit enough to drive things no farther than they would go, and knew when it was time to give back; but his brother, with less understanding, and a much worse religion than his predecessor openly professed;[5] hoped to accomplish what he had attempted, or despaired of bringing about; and how he succeeded we all know. I gladly throw a veil over what has happened since; and hope I shall hereafter have no reason to repent it.

I shall only observe, before I conclude this letter, that there is no need of the caballing of different interests, the uniting in joint councils, and concerting regular measures, to bring about some of the greatest events in human affairs; and consequently in great publick exigencies, oppressors will find no security in the appearing opposition of parties, who, like a pair of shears, will cut only what is between them, when they seem most to threaten one another. When nature has prepared the way, all things will tend to their proper center; and though men for some time will dally and play with their lesser interests, yet at last they will mechanically fall

4. In constant pension: constantly bribed.

5. By the terms of the Treaty of Dover of 1669, Charles II agreed to announce his conversion to the Roman Church as the price for an alliance with France. In fact, he was received into the Church only on his deathbed in 1685. Neither fact, however, was commonly known.

into their great ones, and often without intending or knowing it: Men will always feel their strength, when they cannot reason upon it, or are afraid to do so. I could name a party that for above thirty years together have acted in the interests of liberty, and for the greatest part of the time could not bear the sound of liberty, till at last great numbers of them are caught by the principles which they most detested;[6] which I intend as a seasonable caution to all those who have the honour to sit at the helm of states, or to advise princes, who may at any time hereafter want such a memento.

I shall, in my next letter, endeavour to shew, upon the principles here laid down, that England at present is not capable of any other form of government than what it enjoys, and has a right to enjoy; and that another neighbouring state will, with very great difficulty, preserve the constitution which they now are in possession of.

T   *I am, &c.*

NO. 85. SATURDAY, JULY 14, 1722.

Britain incapable of any Government but a limited Monarchy; with the Defects of a neighbouring Republick.

SIR,

Tacitus observed of the Romans in his time *Nec totam libertatem nec totam servitutem pati posse;*[1] That they could neither bear full liberty, nor perfect slavery. This is certainly the case of England at present, if by liberty be understood what I presume he meant by it, a republican form of government. But I conceive that liberty may be better preserved by a well poised monarchy, than by any popular government that I know now in the world, whatever forms may exist in imagination. However, whether this be true or

---

6. Trenchard is referring to the Tory party.

1. "Men who can tolerate neither complete freedom nor complete slavery." Tacitus, *Historiae*, 1.16.

not, it is certainly true that no man in his wits will lose the benefit of a very good present establishment, and run infinite hazards, to try to get one a little better, if he could have any prospect of attaining it: And I shall endeavour to shew, that the effecting such a project is impossible; and that during the present distribution of property, we can preserve liberty by no other establishment than what we have; and in the attempt to alter it, must run great hazard of losing what we are in possession of, or perhaps of falling into an absolute monarchy; or at best must return to the same form again, as we have done once already by such feats of gallantry.

It proceeds from a consummate ignorance in politicks, to think that a number of men agreeing together can make and hold a commonwealth, before nature has prepared the way; for she alone must do it. An equality of estate will give an equality of power; and an equality of power is a commonwealth, or democracy: An agrarian law, or something equivalent to it, must make or find a suitable disposition of property; and when that comes to be the case, there is no hindering a popular form of government, unless sudden violence takes away all liberty, and, to preserve itself, alters the distribution of property again. I hope that no one amongst us has a head so wrong turned, as to imagine that any man, or number of men, in the present situation of affairs, can ever get power enough to turn all the possessions of England topsy-turvy, and throw them into average, especially any who can have a will and interest in doing it; and without all this it is impossible to settle a commonwealth here; and I dare say, that few desire it, but such as having no estates of their own, or means and merit to acquire them, would be glad to share in those of other people.

Now it is certain, that the distribution of property in England is adapted to our present establishment. The nobility and gentry have great possessions; and the former have great privileges and distinctions by the constitution, and the latter have them in fact, though positive laws give but few of them: For their birth and fortunes procure them easy admittance into the legislature; and their near approach to the throne gives them pretences to honourable and profitable employments, which create a dependence from the inferior part of mankind; and the nature of many of their estates, and particularly of their manors, adds to that dependence. Now all these must ever be in the interest of monarchy whilst they are in their own interest; since monarchy supports and keeps up this distinction, and subsists by it: For it is senseless to imagine, that men who have great possessions, will ever put themselves upon the level with those who have none, or with such as depend upon them for subsistence or protection, whom they will always think they have a right to govern or influence, and will be ever able to govern, whilst they keep their possessions, and a monarchical form of government, and therefore will always endeavour to keep it.

All the bishops, dignitaries, or governing clergy, all who have good preferments in the church, or hope to get them, are in the interest of monarchy, for the reasons which I gave in a former letter,[2] and for some others which I choose not to give now. They know very well too, that a popular government would take away all possessions which it should think fit to call superfluous, would level all the rest, and be apt to reason, that Christianity would fare never the worse, if its professors were less politicians, of which they see before their eyes a pregnant and very affecting instance in Holland. All great and exclusive companies are in the interest of monarchy (whatever weak people have alleged to the contrary); for they can much easier preserve their separate and unwarrantable privileges by applications to the vices and passions of a court, than by convincing a popular assembly; and for the same reason, all officers who have great salaries and exorbitant fees must ever be sure friends to monarchy. Rich merchants, and indeed all rich men, will be equally in the same interest, and be willing to enjoy themselves, and leave to their posterity all the advantages and distinctions which always attend large fortunes in monarchies.

After these (many of whom are men of virtue and probity, and desire only to enjoy the rights which they are born to, or have acquired) there follows a long train of debauchees, and riotous livers, lewd women, gamesters, and sharpers; with such who get by oppression and unequal laws, or the non-execution of good ones: All these are ever for monarchy and the right line, as expecting

2. See Letter No. 81 (June 16, 1722).

much fairer quarter from the corruption of courtiers, than they can ever hope to meet with in popular states, who always destroy and exterminate such vermin, of which sort (I thank God) we have none amongst us at present; but who knows how soon we may?

Now, without entering into the question, which is the best government in theory, a limited monarchy, or a democratical form of government? I think I may safely affirm, that it is impossible to contend against all these interests, and the crown too, which is almost a match for them all together; so that the phantom of a commonwealth must vanish, and never appear again but in disordered brains. If this be the true circumstance of England at present, as I conceive it indisputably is, we have nothing left to do, or indeed which we can do, but to make the best of our own constitution, which, if duly administered, provides excellently well for general liberty; and to secure the possession of property, and to use our best endeavours to make it answer the other purposes of private virtue, as far as the nature of it is capable of producing that end.

I have purposely declined the speaking of aristocracies, because there can be no imaginary danger of establishing such a government here: for the nobility have neither property nor credit enough to succeed in such an act of knight-errantry, or will to attempt it; and the gentry will ever oppose them, unless their interests be also taken into the project; and both together are not able to contend with the crown and the body of the people, the latter of which will ever be in the interests of equality.

And now having mentioned aristocracies, I shall make some observations upon a neighbouring state,[3] which is vulgarly mistaken for a commonwealth, and is so in nature, according to the balance of property there; but is politically an union of several little aristocracies, in many respects like some states of Italy in the first time of the Romans, but contrived with much worse policy. As it was jumbled together in confusion, so it seems to me to subsist by chance, or rather by the constant dread of the two great successive powers of Europe, *viz.* that of Spain formerly, and France since; for the natural power being in the people, and the political in the

3. The Dutch Republic.

magistrates, it has all the causes of dissolution in its contexture. Every town is governed and subject to a little aristocracy within itself, who have no foundation of suitable property to entitle them to their dominion; and each of those is independent of its provincial state, and indeed of the States-General, nor have any check upon their own actions, but the tumult and insurrections of the people, who have the real and natural power: and indeed, to do the magistrates right, they judge so well of their own weakness and the power of the people, that they seldom or never give them just cause of provocation; but by frugality, public economy, wise and timely compliances, impartial justice, and not raising great estates to themselves at the other's expence, they make their subjects easy, and find their own account in the submission of those whom they want power to govern by the force of authority; and probably will continue to make them so, whilst they keep to the same maxims and their present conduct. But this is no steady and durable dominion; nor, unless mankind are formed there with other appetites and passions than in all other parts of the world, can the same prudence be always observed; which seems to me to be owing only to their necessities, and that virtue, moderation, and frugality, which is conspicuous in the first rise of states, and is not yet quite spent there, but cannot last much longer: for when they cease to be kept together by the constant dread of overgrown neighbours, they will certainly think themselves at liberty to play their own games at home. Those who are in possession of power will know what it is good for; and those who have great riches will fall into luxury, then into extravagance, at last into necessity; and others will vie with them, and follow their example.

When their magistrates have impaired their estates, or fancy that they want greater, they will plunder the publick; and others of equal condition will emulate them, and begin to ask what right the others have to the sole enjoyment of privileges and employments, which they think themselves to all respects equally entitled to, and will not be content to be always subjects to those who are no better than they are; and the people will be impatient in continuing to pay large taxes to such who pocket them, and will endeavour to right themselves, and have power enough to do so.

These opposite interests must raise convulsions in the body politick, and produce all the mischiefs which have happened in other states upon the like occasions. Those who have power, will endeavour to keep it; those who suffer under it, will endeavour to take it away; and the event will be in the will of heaven alone, but in all likelihood will be some other form of government.

I take my account of the constitution of this state from others, who possibly may not be well informed of it, and I hope are not so: for I should be very sorry to see the most virtuous and flourishing state which ever yet appeared in the world, perish of an internal distemper; a state which, ever since its institution, has been the champion of publick liberty, and has defended itself, and in a great measure its neighbours, from the two greatest tyrannies which ever threatened Europe and the Christian religion.

T   *I am, &c.*

NO. 86. SATURDAY, JULY 21, 1722.

The terrible Consequences of a War to England, and Reasons against engaging in one.

SIR,

I propose in this letter to shew, and I hope to do it unanswerably, that nothing can be a greater disservice to his Majesty's interest, more fatal to his ministry, or more destructive to his people, than to engage them in a new war, if there be but a bare possibility of preventing it, let the pretences be what they will. A new fire seems to be now kindling in Italy, which in all likelihood will blaze out far and wide;[1] and, without doubt, many princes will warm their hands at it, whilst their subjects will be burnt to death: But I hope we shall have wit enough to keep out of its reach, and

1. Probably a reference to the complex of disagreements between Spain and the Emperor over the Spanish claims in Italy and particularly to Austria's vacillation in supporting the succession of Don Carlos, son of Philip V of Spain, to the duchies of Parma, Piacenza, and Tuscany, to which Austria had agreed in the Treaty of the Hague in 1720.

not be scorched with its flames; but, like some of our wiser neighbours, lie still, and know how to make our markets of the follies and misfortunes of others. We have been heroes long enough, and paid the price of our gallantry and credulity. We are got near sixty millions in debt,[2] and have nothing for it but Gibraltar and Port Mahon; and it is said, that some of our allies have had the presumption to expect these from us too; and I am sure, if they should be lost, or given away, we have nothing left wherewith to compensate any power which we shall vanquish hereafter.

I hope no man will be wild enough to make any proposition for a new war to us; nor can I guess at any one argument for it, but what I hope will be called treason to his sovereign and his country. Old threadbare reasons will hold no longer: People will not always deceive themselves, nor be deceived by others. We shall not bear being told again, that England need but send a message, or a bucket full of water, and the fire will be extinguished. That argument has already cost us the terror and expence of providing against two invasions, or intended invasions; has lost or spoiled several great fleets, destroyed numbers of our merchant ships, increased our national debts many millions, perhaps brought upon us that noble project to pay them off,[3] and created the general want of trade, and, I doubt, that great disaffection which is so often complained of; and all the reward which we have met with, has been a struggle to keep what we were in possession of before, what was yielded to us by treaties, and what there was no pretence for demanding, if we had thought it our interest to have lain still.

I hope we shall never engage in a new war, before we have considered all the consequences which will necessarily or probably happen from such an engagement, and have thought how we shall get out of it, as well as how to get into it. The first step draws in all the rest; and when we are in, we must go through. We may begin with thousands, but must go on with millions. A message will produce a quarrel, but fleets and armies must end it.

2. The government's total long-term debt as of late Sept. 1719 was approximately £50,000,000 and could not have been appreciably higher than this amount when this letter was published.

3. The "noble project" is, of course, the establishment of the South Sea Company, which undertook to consolidate the national debt.

We well know, and have long felt, the moderation of our allies. We can no sooner engage in their squabbles, but they become our own; and then we must pay them for doing their own business, and largely too, or else they threaten to leave the war upon us; and when it is ended through our means, always divide the spoil amongst themselves, and endeavour to make us likewise for the peace. I would be glad to know what any of them have ever done for us, or would suffer us to do for ourselves, in return for all that we have done for them; or what courtesy they have ever shewn to us Englishmen, as Englishmen: I hope therefore, that we too shall at last, in our turn, consider only our own interests, and what is best for ourselves; and not ruin ourselves yet further, and let others have the whole advantage. But if we had no occasion given us for these complaints, we have another and shorter answer to give to our good allies; namely, that by helping them so long, we are rendered incapable of helping them any longer; and that all treaties must cease and become void, when it is impossible to perform them without utter ruin to one of the parties, and without destroying all the ends for which these treaties were made.

Let us take a short prospect of the journey which we are to go, and consider what will be the result of such an undertaking. All naval armaments must be made at our charge, and employed at a great distance from home, to the ruin of our ships and our seamen, and the obstruction of our commerce: Armies must be sent abroad, or money, in the name of subsidies, found out to pay those which are there already: More armies must be kept at home to oppose invasions, and keep the people quiet: Great land-taxes must be raised, our publick funds be every year increased, the people frightened with perpetual alarms, which will sink the price of the old stocks, and consequently set an exorbitant price upon the raising of new ones: We shall lose a beneficial trade to Spain and the Mediterranean; and probably Portugal will take that opportunity to execute what they lately attempted.[4] The Czar too may

4. The loss of a "beneficial trade" appears to refer particularly to the possible shifting of the woollen trade. The reference to Portugal is less clear; Cato is most likely alluding to recent Portuguese attempts to obstruct the trade of the East India and African Companies in Portuguese Africa and to limit English trade with Brazil.

think it a favourable one to acknowledge some past obligations; and other nations may judge it a proper time to bite the stone that was thrown at them; and then we shall have little or no trade at all, all our commodities and manufactures will lie upon our hands, and the people be starved, or subsist by ways which no honest man can wish, and all men ought to dread.

If France engage on the different side, we must have her too for our enemy; if on the same side, there can be no need of our assistance. But if she think it her interest to lie still, she, who is the next neighbour to both the combatants, and is vastly more concerned in the event; what have we to do with them at this distance, we who are no wise concerned whether the emperor or Spain uses the Italians worst, or who has the Provinces contended for? When Spain had them, we suffered nothing by it; nor do I hear what we have got by the Emperor's being in possession of them.[5] I purposely avoid saying any thing of the States-General, because they will certainly have wit enough to hug themselves in the folly of others, and profit by it.

And what shall we get by such feats of knight-errantry, but the disinterested glory of serving others to our own disadvantage, and the character of pious Christians, in treating those kindly who despitefully use us? Oh, but some tell us, that we are bound by treaties to preserve the neutrality of Italy. Whether this be true, or the contrary be true, I know not: but if it be true, I doubt not but we shall be told how England came to be a party to such a treaty; what were the motives for making it; what equivalent we had for it; what interest of ours was served by it; or what other country, which we were concerned to preserve, was to reap the advantage of it. And we ought to enquire too, how treaties, made for our benefit, have been kept by our allies; because we are told (I hope falsely) that one of them had once in his custody the Pretender to the King's throne, with several other traitors to the government; and yet, instead of delivering them up, set them at liberty: and lately one of them refused, or declined, to deliver up a much greater

5. The reference is to the Netherlands. Under the terms of the Peace of Utrecht ending the War of the Spanish Succession, the Spanish Netherlands were transferred to Austria.

traitor, when earnestly requested by the Parliament, and, without doubt, importunately pressed by the King's ministers.[6]

I do not find that we have any thing to fear from the King of Spain, if we do not give him provocation; for the Secretary of State assured the Lord Mayor, in his letter since printed, that no foreign potentate abetted, or gave any countenance to, the last intended insurrection;[7] and if he would not assist a conspiracy, actually, and, as we are told, deeply laid, there can be no reason to believe that he will form a new one against a state that intends him no harm, and can do him a great deal of good; and surely it is not our interest at this time of day to provoke him to do it in his own defence. If he and the Emperor have a mind to make a feast in Italy, let them bid whom they please to the banquet, which without doubt will be a long one, and many neighbouring princes will be gorged at it; but for us, we have no business there, unless to be caterers, to supply the greatest part of the provision, and to pay the reckoning for the rest. I once knew a wager of forty to one staked down to be spent. But instead of engaging our country in such expensive and wild whims, I hope we shall catch at so favourable an opportunity, when those who can most molest us are

6. There is no evidence of the Pretender's ever having entered the territory of any of Britain's allies. Although Robert Knight, the South Sea Company cashier who fled to the Austrian Netherlands in early 1721, was arrested by the local authorities, the Austrian government in the Netherlands refused to extradite him despite the persistent appeals of Parliament. The ostensible reason for their denial was that extradition would violate the ancient constitution of the duchy of Brabant, the *joyeuse entrée*, the terms of which the Hapsburgs had agreed to respect. In fact, it appears that the Earl of Sunderland paid a substantial bribe to the acting governor of the Netherlands to prevent Knight's extradiction.

7. In April 1722, the government was successful in forestalling a Jacobite plot to seize power as soon as the King had embarked for Hanover. However, news of the plot caused some panic and a run on the Bank of England. Fears that Spain might have countenanced the attempted insurrection were occasioned by the fact that Spain had in fact supported a Jacobite invasion of Scotland under the Duke of Ormonde in 1719. At that time, Spain had equipped ten ships of war, together with six thousand troops, for the purpose of supporting a Jacobite uprising in Scotland. The fleet, however, was scattered by a storm and the small Jacobite force that had assembled under the Pretender's banner was defeated by royalist troops at Glenshiel. The letter to which Trenchard refers was published under the title *Letter from the Right Honourable the Lord Viscount* [Charles] *Townshend, one of His Majesty's principal secretaries of state, to the Right Honourable the Lord Mayor of London* (London: S. Buckley, 1722).

together by the ears, to do our own business, pay off our debts, settle our trade, and reform all the abuses of which we so justly complain.

But if such a war were ever so necessary, how shall it be supported? We find by woeful experience, that three shillings in the pound has not maintained the current expence of the government, but we have run still in debt. The money given for the Civil List has not defrayed that charge, but new and large sums have been given to pay off the arrears; which, it is said, are not yet paid off. New salaries and new pensions have been found necessary to satisfy the clamours of those who will never be satisfied; and the greater occasions which the courtiers have, and the greater necessities which they are in, the more will still be found necessary: for it is no news for artful men to engage their superiors in difficulties, and then to be paid largely for helping them out of them again. The customs and excise are anticipated and mortgaged almost beyond redemption: The salt, leather, windows, and almost every thing else that can be taxed, is already taxed, and some of them so high, as to lessen the produce, and they are appropriated to pay off debts due to private men.

What new sources will be found out to maintain a foreign war, and a much larger expence in our own country, which will be necessary to defend us against enemies abroad, whom we shall provoke, and against discontented people at home, who, it is to be feared, may say that they are oppressed and starved? One additional shilling in the pound upon land, if the Parliament can be persuaded to give, and the people be easy in paying it, will be but as a drop of water thrown into the ocean, whatever may be pretended at first; and then for all the remainder we must run in debt, if we can get any one to trust us; and, where shall we raise new funds? Here I doubt our publicans and inventors of new grievances will be at their wits' end: It is certain that the greater the difficulty is in raising them, the greater must be the price for raising them; and the present stocks will be less valuable in proportion as new demands make more necessary.

But suppose, that, to the infinite dissatisfaction of the people, and the utter ruin and destruction of all trade, the little which

is not already taxed could be taxed, and turned into funds, to create new markets for stock-jobbers, and enough could be raised to
maintain a war two or three years; what shall we do next? It is most
sure, that the difficulty of obtaining a peace will grow in exact proportion as we become less capable to carry on the war; and what
assistance, think ye, my countrymen, shall we have from our good
allies to obtain a peace? Without doubt we shall pay the piper at
last, and they will parcel out the contended dominions amongst
themselves, and attempt to make us give up Gibraltar and Port
Mahon to bind the bargain; nay, to pay besides a large sum of
money for the ships which we shall have destroyed, and the other
mischiefs which we shall have done, and which we need not do. I
hope it will never be our lot to assist some of our neighbours at a
vast expence, and then reward them at a further expence for
accepting our assistance; and to beat others of our neighbours, to
our own loss as well as theirs, and pay them afterwards for having
beat them: What would the world think of us in this case, but that
as France had got the plague, England had got the frenzy; and that
we were weakening ourselves as fast with our own hands, as the
divine hand had weakened them?

But if, after all, we cannot get a peace, or shall think fit not
to submit to the honourable conditions which our honest and
faithful confederates shall judge good enough for hereticks, what
shall we do then? They will have no motives to serve us when they
have done their own business, or rather when we have done it for
them: They have sufficiently shewn already what inclination they
have to serve us; and if ever they have done it, they have been well
paid for their pains. What condition shall we then be in to oppose
one or more powerful neighbours, and perhaps victorious ones
too, when we are enervated and exhausted, when our people are
discontented at home, and we have no regular means to maintain
fleets and armies, who must be forced to maintain themselves, if
we cannot maintain them? These mischiefs (and terrible ones they
are) may be easily foreseen, and ought to be prevented, if we
would prevent absolute and conclusive ruin. What, think you,
must, in such a circumstance of affairs, become of the funds? If we
lie still, they are lost of course; and if we apply them to our neces-

sary defence, thousands and thousands of innocent people must be undone and become desperate, and infinitely inflame the popular discontents, and still make more taxes, more oppressions, necessary: And yet who will be found so hard-hearted, as not to sacrifice the interests of thousands to the safety of millions, when no other resource is left?

Beware, my friends, of the first step, and know your whole journey before you move one foot; when you are up to the ears in mire, it will be too late to look back. At first we may be told by our confederates and their creatures, that we need only bounce a little, and make a shew of force, and every thing will go to our mind; but a burnt child will dread the fire: When we are engaged, we cannot retreat; one step will draw another; it will not depend upon ourselves, whether we shall go on or not; the game will be then in other hands, who will play it to their own advantage, without regarding ours; and what we begin in wantonness, will probably end in our confusion.

What then must we think of any men amongst us, who would draw all these mischiefs, these inevitable mischiefs, upon their country! They must certainly be egregiously foolish, or consummately wicked. I hope, and believe, there are no such; but if there be, without doubt they have taken their measures, and have thought how to save themselves, whatever becomes of their country; but in that too they may chance to be mistaken.

If it be necessary to the publick safety to keep eight or ten camps in readiness for action in times of full peace, when there is no outward appearance of publick disturbances, and no foreign power promotes or abets any such; how many camps will be necessary when we have enemies assaulting us from abroad, and combining and intriguing with our own native traitors at home; especially if the people should be made still more uneasy, by laying burdens upon them which they cannot bear nor stand under? For my own part, I can see no steady source or continuing cause for the disaffection so much complained of, but the great and heavy variety of taxes, of which our ancestors knew nothing, and which it is a sort of a science now to know; and I doubt that disaffection will not be cured by adding to the number.

We can never, therefore, behave ourselves with more true duty to his Majesty, give better advice and assistance to his ministry, or acquit ourselves with more fidelity to our country, than by opposing, in the most vigorous manner, such measures as threaten them all with ruin; and by shewing the utmost resentment against any ill-designing persons, who would wickedly and traitorously sacrifice a great, free, and opulent kingdom, to mad whimsies, or the pitiful mean interests of little states.

T   *I am, &c.*

NO. 87. SATURDAY, JULY 28, 1722.

Gold and Silver in a Country to be considered only as Commodities.

SIR,

Boccalini tells us, that Archimedes was beat by the bravoes in Parnassus, for finding out a mathematical demonstration, by which it was plainly proved, that all the design of great, as well as private men, was dexterously to get money out of other people's pockets, and put it in their own.[1] And it is certain, that this is the grand design and business of all mankind, the chief if not the only spring of all their actions, and animates and inspires their best as well as worst performances. And how commendable soever this may be in private men, who already enjoy all the conveniences of life, it is certainly the interest and duty of states, by all prudent and just methods to increase their wealth and power, and in consequence their security and protection. As government is only the union of many individuals for their common defence; so they cannot attain that desirable end, unless by accident of situation, superior policy, or by sufficient number, they can render themselves strong enough to repel the injuries, and oppose the insults, of

1. Gordon is apparently referring to Boccalini's *Advertisements from Parnassus*, advertisement 76 (first century), wherein Aristotle, not Archimedes, is beaten by the crowd for contending that princes "who intended their own profit" were tyrants. For *all* princes—and all subjects—the crowd asserts, "Gain is the end of all merchandizing and the whole world one great public shop" (pp. 144–45 of the 1656 edition).

ambitious and unruly neighbours; otherwise they must submit to be undone, or throw themselves under the protection of some greater potentate, and accept such conditions as he pleases to give, and for no longer duration than he pleases.

As this is the greatest mischief which human nature can suffer, so every honest and wise man will endeavour to free himself, his family, and his country, from such an abject, lamentable, and forlorn condition, and contribute all in his power to make the state which he lives under great, rich, and formidable. I have already at large shewn, that no state in a small tract of ground can be so, but by liberty, which always produces riches, and every quality, which can grace and adorn the mind, and render mankind preferable to the brute creation.

Now nothing can be called riches, but as it is applicable, or rather as it is applied, to the use of men. The vast tracts of North-America feed only a few scattered and half-starved inhabitants, whilst the barren rocks of Switzerland maintain in plenty great numbers of wealthy and happy people. All Greece, Macedon, and Epirus, together, have not so much power now as single cities in them had formerly. Countries without inhabitants will not defend themselves, nor are worth defending; nor will they maintain inhabitants without their own industry and application. Every nation is rich and powerful, in exact proportion to the numbers, the employment, or the idleness of the people; and the power of the state is the accumulative wealth of the whole; that is, what every man can spare for the common defence, over and above what is necessary for his own subsistence: so that to make a state great, the people must be made rich and happy: Their private happiness will make them willing to defend their country, and their wealth will enable them to do it.

The riches of private men are such things as are necessary or conducive to their personal support, convenience, or pleasure; but many other things are necessary for the defence and augmentation of states. There must be fortresses, artillery, armed ships, and magazines of war, and proper encouragements given to skillful persons to make use of them: There must be often great armies at land, and fleets at sea, maintained and paid at the publick expence, for the publick security; all which must be maintained out of the superfluities of those who stay at home; and if they have not all those materials necessary to their preservation, or conducive to their private happiness, in their own country (as few countries have), they must purchase them abroad with the produce of their own country, or by silver and gold, which purchases all commodities. Indeed, by the universal consent of mankind, silver and gold is become the medium of all commerce; and every state, as well as private man, is rich and powerful in proportion as he possesses or can command more or less of this universal commodity, which procures all the rest: All other things are riches only *hic & nunc;*[2] but these will command every thing, and almost every person in the world.

Gold and silver are the natives but of few countries, and the propriety but of few persons in those countries, and can be obtained by others only by their consent, or by force and rapine; and consequently, no state can grow more considerable than their native soil will make them, but by robbing their neighbours of what they themselves want or desire, or by persuading them to part with it willingly; that is, either by arms or trade; and which of these two will conduce most to the happiness, security, and augmentation of empires, shall be the subject of this letter.

If we consider this question under the head of justice and humanity, what can be more detestable than to murder and destroy mankind, in order to rob and pillage them? War is comprehensive of most, if not all the mischiefs which do or ever can afflict men: It depopulates nations, lays waste the finest countries, destroys arts, sciences, and learning, butchers innocents, ruins the best men, and advances the worst; effaces every trace of virtue, piety, and compassion, and introduces confusion, anarchy, and all kinds of corruption in publick affairs; and indeed is pregnant with so many evils, that it ought ever to be avoided, when it can be avoided; and it may be avoided when a state can be safe without it, and much more so when all the advantages proposed by it can be procured by prudent and just methods.

All the advantage procured by conquest is to secure what we possess ourselves, or to gain the possessions of others, that is,

2. "Here and now."

the produce of their country, and the acquisitions of their labour and industry; and if these can be obtained by fair means, and by their own consent, sure it must be more eligible than to extort them by force.

This is certainly more easily and effectually done by a well regulated commerce, than by arms: The balance of trade will return more clear money from neighbouring countries, than can be forced from them by fleets or armies, and more advantageously than under the odious name of tribute. It enervates rival states by their own consent, and obligates them, whilst it impoverishes and ruins them: It keeps our own people at home employed in arts, manufactures, and husbandry, instead of murdering them in wild, expensive, and hazardous expeditions, to the weakening their own country, and the pillaging and destroying their neighbours, and only for the fruitless and imaginary glory of conquest: It saves the trouble, expence, and hazard, of supporting numerous standing armies abroad to keep the conquered people in subjection; armies, who, for the most part too, if not always, enslave their own country, and ever swallow up all the advantages of the conquests. I have often wondered at the folly and weakness of those princes, who will sacrifice hundreds of thousands of their own faithful subjects, to gain a precarious and slavish submission from bordering provinces, who will seek all opportunities to revolt; which cannot be prevented but by keeping them poor, wretched, and miserable, and consequently unable to pay the charges of their own vassalage; when, if the same number of men and the sums of money were usefully employed at home, which are necessary to make and support the conquest, they would add vastly more to their power and empire.

It is not the extent of territory, and vast tracts of barren and uncultivated land, which make states great and powerful, but numbers of industrious people under a proper oeconomy, and advantageously and usefully employed; and the same number will be always more powerful in a small tract of ground than a great one: They are here always at hand to assist one another, to carry on manufactures, and to promote and execute any great designs: All the materials of trade and industry are in place, and by that means the charges of carriage prevented, which swallows the advantages of commerce, and renders it unprofitable. The impossibility of subsisting by idleness renders them industrious, emulation rouses their ambition, and the examples of others animate them to desire to live in splendor and plenty; and all these passions concur to set their hands and wits to work, and to promote arts, sciences, and manufactures, to strike out new trades, form new projects, and venture upon designs abroad, to enrich their own country at home.

Great numbers of people crowded together, are forced by their necessities to turn every stone, and try every method to support themselves and families, and by doing so will trace and discover by degrees all the sources of wealth. All ways will be found out to make trade commodious and profitable; numerous contrivances be thought on to come at the materials of manufactures easily and at cheap rates, and to work them again at the lowest prices. Rivers will be made navigable, engines invented, which with the assistance of few hands, shall supply the labour of multitudes; store-houses will be built to deposit goods in, whilst they wait for markets; fisheries will be erected, colonies planted to furnish new commodities and new materials of commerce, and will vent too and carry off those turbulent and unruly spirits, who are unfit to live in a peaceable state, and must rob, hang or starve there. By all these laudable methods, and many more, riches will be amassed, money become cheap, and the interest of it lessened; and the lowering the interest of money will open new trades, and still bring in more money, as well as improve the native territory, increase vastly the purchase of land, and encourage the building of cities and towns: for the less men expect for the interest or profit of their principal, the more they can afford to lay out in trade, building, or husbandry, to return but the same income; and consequently can grow rich by the commerce and the same improvements, which will undo nations where the interest of money is higher.

There are few countries in the world, but by a due culture would maintain many times the inhabitants which possess it, better than they are at present maintained. Our indulgent mother will readily yield up her hidden stores to such of her children as make a proper courtship and application to her. The treasures of the earth and seas are inexhaustible: One acre of ground well manured, cultivated, and sowed with corn, will produce ten times as much for the sustenance of man, as ten acres not cultivated, or ill cultivated; and one acre in gardens will produce ten times as much as in corn; and it is much easier, cheaper, and profitable, to improve our own country, and so increase its productions, than to fetch the like productions by force from others. It is more safe, as well as virtuous, to accept the willing and chaste embraces of conjugal affection, than by violence to extort forbidden and dangerous pleasures, and which for the most part, if not always, fail our expectations.

But supposing the soil belonging to any nation should not be sufficient to support all its inhabitants, which I believe is the case of Holland; yet it is certain they may purchase from their neighbours what they want, for very much less than they can earn at home in arts and manufactures. Labour in husbandry is the least profitable employment in the world; and ten men so employed will not earn the wages of one good artist, and the meanest mechanicks and artificers earn more than husbandmen; and consequently have a surplus from their own labour, after they have bought the production of the other's industry. This is the circumstance of cities and trading towns, who have no growth of their own, and yet grow rich by retailing and manufacturing the growth of the neighbouring countries, over and above what they consume for their own subsistence and use; and the same is true of trading states. As Tyre,[3] and other free states did formerly, so Holland at present grows vastly rich and formidable, by keeping its neighbours employed in the poor and menial trade of husbandry, whilst they employ their own people in arts and manufactures; a small part of which supplies them with the productions of the other's labour, and with the rest they purchase a great part of the riches of the world. By those means they have made themselves more considerable in that little spot of land, than great empires have done by conquest, which always corrupts, and often enslaves, the conquerors as well as the conquered.

T   *I am &c.*

3. Tyre, on the Phoenician coast, was one of the great industrial centers of the ancient world and one of its major commercial hubs.

NO. 88. SATURDAY, AUGUST 4, 1722.

❧ *The Reasonableness and Advantage of allowing the Exportation of Gold and Silver, with the Impossibility of preventing the same.*

SIR,

Having in my last letter considered silver and gold as the only certain durable, and universal riches; and since the attaining them is the chief view and design of all mankind; I shall in this consider a question which puzzles the greatest part of the world, and which, as I think, they for the most part determine wrongly; namely, when a nation is once possessed of them, whether it is their interest to let them be exported again? In this I have the opinion of most states against me, who prohibit the carrying them out under the severest penalties, sometimes before, and sometimes after they are converted into their current coin; and to me nothing seems more injurious, impertinent, and impotent, than to make such laws.

No soil or climate produces all commodities, and no nation works all sorts of manufactures, which are of common and necessary use; nor can any man by his own skill and labour, make or acquire any considerable part of such things as he wants or desires; and consequently he can have no means of attaining them, but by exchanging what he does not want for what he does. But since it does and will most commonly happen, that the person who is possessed of the commodity which one man desires, does not want what he has to give in lieu of it, or not enough of it to answer the value of what he parts with; therefore something else must be found out to make the account even.

From hence mankind have found themselves under a necessity to agree upon some universal commodity which shall measure the value of all the rest, and balance all accounts at last. Hitherto nothing has been discovered which will answer that purpose so effectually as silver and gold: Their contexture hinders them from being perishable, their divisibility qualifies them to answer all occasions, their scarcity enhances their price, so as to make a great value lie in a narrow compass, and easily portable; and the more regular and equal supplies of them than of other commodities, render them proper standards for the valuation of other things. These therefore being, by general and almost universal agreement, the mediums of commerce, the balance of all traffick, and the ultimate view and chief advantage proposed by it; we are to consider how far those ends and advantages can be answered by exporting them again.

Now it is certain, that many commodities of absolute and indispensable use are in the possession of nations who do not want those which we have to give in exchange for them; or, knowing our necessities will not part with them but for silver and gold; and therefore we must have them upon their terms, or not have them at all. Some of them are the materials of our manufactures, which will return to us again many times the money which we advance in procuring them; and very often they are necessary to carry on trade in general, and enabling the merchants to make assortments of goods proper for particular markets; or are the materials of navigation, or magazines for war and common defence.

No country wants always the same supplies, or has the same growth and quantity of manufactures to purchase them; nor can any merchant have a clear view of the whole commerce of the country which he deals with; nor do the commodities always bear the same price: so that the balance will often vary, and must be paid at last in those universal commodities. No nation or private man will deal with another, who will not pay his debts; and if he has not other commodities to pay them with, or if those which he has are not wanted, or will not be accepted in payment, he must pay them in such as will; and, whatever it costs him, must deliver them into the custody, or to the order and satisfaction, of his creditor.

It is foolish to imagine, that any precautions, or the greatest penalties, will keep money in any country, where it is the interest of numbers to carry it out: The experience of every nation may convince us of this truth; gold and silver lie in so little compass, are so easily concealed, and there are so many conveniences, and opportunities to carry them off, that small encouragements will always find adventurers, and those adventurers will almost always succeed. There is no way in nature to hinder money from being exported, but by hindering the occasions of it; that is, by hindering the use and consumption of those things which it is sent out to buy; for when they are bought they must be paid for, or all traffick is at an end.

These propositions being, as I conceive, self-evident, it is next to be discussed, whether it be the interest of a state to permit their money to go out freely; or, by annexing penalties to the exporting it, enhance the difficulty, and raise the price of carrying it out, by obliging the exporter to pay himself largely for his own hazard, as well as the hazard of the seas: And I think nothing is more demonstrable, than that the greater the obstacle that is laid in his way, and the greater hazard which he runs, the more he will be obliged to export; for whatever he has agreed to pay beyond sea, must be discharged, whatever it costs him to get it thither, and he is to be paid besides all the charges of getting it thither.

Bills of exchange only serve the purpose, and save the expence of paying the carrier; for if one man has money due to him abroad, and the other wants the same sum here, they will both save the charges of carriage, by one's paying it where he does not want it, and the other's receiving it where he does: But if there be more demands by the merchants of one country upon their correspondents in another, than the others can pay by the produce of their effects, or from debts due to them elsewhere, which will be accepted as payment; the surplus must be returned in silver and gold, and they must pay too the persons who carry it; and other merchants seeing their necessity, will take advantage of it, and receive premiums for as much as they can return in bills, in proportion to the charge which it will cost to send it in specie, and the haste which their creditors are in to receive it: But herein they will not have regard only to the commerce between those particular nations, but to the course and balance of general trade; for bills often travel from country to country, and take a large circuit, before they center, and the account is finally made up at home. And this I take to be the whole mystery of exchange, which is either paying, or saving the charge of paying, the carrier; and if you do not do it yourself, others who do it for you, will reap advantage from it.

Since then money or bullion must be exported, when debts are contracted abroad, I think it is eligible to send out the first rather than the latter, or at least to leave the people at liberty to export which they please. Indeed they are the same thing; for all money is bullion, and all bullion is easily converted into money;[1] and all that is not otherwise manufactured, would be converted into it, if there were no disadvantage in doing so. The advantages are obvious, and the charge to the proprietors nothing; for the stamp of authority ascertains the weight and the fineness; and the dividing it into small parcels, makes it more useful for commerce, which renders it more valuable abroad as well as at home; and consequently foreigners will be contented to pay part, if not the whole, of the charge of coining it. It could in no circumstance be of less value, if it were not denied a privilege and advantage which it had before it was coined; which is the liberty of exportation, and being used in foreign as well as domestick trade: for, whilst free liberty of exportation is allowed to one, and denied to the other, and yet there are frequent and necessary occasions of exporting one or the other, it must happen that either money will be melted into bullion, and so the manufacture be lost, or bullion must be bought by money at a price answerable to the necessity or the hazard of carrying it in specie abroad, or of melting it down at home, and the expence of conscience afterwards in swearing it to be foreign bullion; which sometimes has raised the price 8 or 10 per cent.

Now it must be obvious to any one, who the least considers this question, how much such prohibitions must affect our general trade, they being equivalent to the putting an equal duty upon the

---

1. "Money" here refers exclusively to coin. Banknotes denominated in units as small as £1 or £2 and meant for general circulation did not appear until the end of the century.

exportation of our own commodities, which all wise nations encourage by all ways that they can, and often by giving premiums to the exporter. They give other nations the means and opportunity to trade so much per cent cheaper than we can; which must certainly carry away from us many valuable trades: They enhance the value of all foreign materials which we use in our manufactures, that are bought with bullion or money, as many of them are; which must in consequence raise the price of these manufactures, and hinder their sail; and above all, make the materials of navigation dear to us, upon which all trade in a great measure depends, and the carriage-trade wholly.

But not only those trades, which are altogether, or partly carried on by bullion or money, will be affected by them, but all trade whatsoever: For, as I have before shewn, that bullion, being the medium of the value of all commodities between nation and nation, as money is between people of the same nation; if the latter be of equal weight and fineness with the former, and yet less valuable; then of necessary consequence home commodities must be sold cheaper in foreign countries, and theirs must sell dearer here; which must alter the balance proportionably to our disadvantage: for we sell at home for our own money and buy abroad with bullion; which are equally valuable in themselves, the coinage excepted, and will be equally bought in foreign markets for the same quantity of commodities.

Suppose for example, that corn bore the same price in respect of silver and gold here as in Holland, and yet we must give more for it when that silver and gold is converted into money than they do, who get the difference by importing their silver; then it is evident that they can afford to buy it of us, and sell it again to foreign markets cheaper than we can, and sometimes to ourselves; and consequently must carry away that trade from us. These events are inevitable, unless we let our money be exported, or turn all our coin into bullion, and make that the medium of domestick as well as foreign commerce; which must soon be our case, and every day grows more and more so: for who will give himself the trouble of carrying his bullion to the mint, to have it made less valuable than before? Whereas if money had the same liberty of exportation as bullion has, all the silver not otherwise manufactured would immediately be carried thither and coined, and less of it be carried out afterwards for the reasons before given.

But whilst it remains upon the present foot, whatever contracts are made for English goods in English money, will be paid for with less bullion than will coin into the same quantity of money; and whatever are bought abroad will cost us more money than the same is worth in bullion: So that foreigners will choose to carry off our money, rather than our bullion or goods, and will afterwards melt it down, and find their account in returning it upon us again for more money; and so on till they have got all that we have; which can be prevented alone by putting coined and uncoined silver upon the same foot, and giving them equal advantages, the coinage excepted.

Till this be done, we must suffer in our exchange with most, if not all the countries in the world: For whilst our coin in quantity is less valuable than bullion, and theirs equal or more valuable, every thing that we buy or sell must be affected by it; and we must pay our debts with more silver, and receive them in less than they do; which must make a vast difference in the return of our whole trade.

This is so much the interest of every party, and almost every man in every party, that I have often wondered how so many able patriots that have sat at the helm should never once think of doing their country this great service. I cannot doubt but men of their great abilities must understand this plain proposition; and methinks they should sometimes find it their interest and duty to save a little money for their countrymen, and not always to be taking from them, especially when they themselves lose nothing by doing so much good to others; and though some people, who do not understand the benefit of such a law, may be at first distasted by it, yet I could wish to see that those who have had no regard to their opinions when they were doing mischief to them, would not be so over-scrupulous of offending them in once doing them and their country this great and general benefit.

T   *I am, &c.*

NO. 89. SATURDAY, AUGUST 11, 1722.

❧ *Every Man's true Interest found in the general Inter-*
est. How little this is considered.

SIR,

Most men see the advantage of trade to a country, and to every man in it; but very few know how to improve those advantages, and much fewer endeavour to do so. As soon as any law is enacted, or proposed for publick benefit, particular men set their wits to work how to draw separate advantages, from those provisions, whatever becomes of the publick; and indeed it is not to be hoped, must less expected, that they should ever do otherwise. But what is most to be lamented is, that the publick very often suffers by their not consulting their real interest, and in pursuing little views, whilst they lose great and substantial advantages. A very small part of mankind have capacities large enough to judge of the whole of things; but catch at every appearance which promises present benefit, without considering how it will affect their general interest; and so bring misfortunes and lasting misery upon themselves to gratify a present appetite, passion, or desire.

This is certainly true in almost every circumstance of publick and private life: The latter falls within all men's observation; and the other happens as often, though not as often taken notice of. How many are there, who do not prefer a servile office or pension before the general interest of their country, in which their own is involved; and so sacrifice their liberty and the protection which they receive from equal laws, for momentary and precarious advantages; and by such means lose or hazard a large inheritance, or make it much less valuable, for trifling benefits, which will not pay half the difference?

Nothing is so much the interest of private men, as to see the publick flourish: for without mentioning the pleasure and internal satisfaction which a generous mind must receive, in seeing all people about him contented and happy, instead of meagre and starved looks, nakedness and rags, and dejected and melancholy faces; to see all objects gay and pleasing; to see fruitful and well manured fields; rich splendid, and populous cities, instead of barren rocks, uncultivated deserts, and dispeopled and empty towns: I say, besides avoiding all this horror, every man's private advantage is so much wrapt up in the publick felicity, that by every step which he takes to depreciate his country's happiness, he undermines and destroys his own: when the publick is secure, and trade and commerce flourish, every man who has property, or the means of acquiring property, will find and feel the blessed effects of such a circumstance of affairs; all the commodities which he has to dispose of will find a ready vent, and at a good price; his inheritance will increase every day in value; he is encouraged, and finds it his interest, to build, and improve his lands, cultivate new trades, and promote new manufactures; and by these means the people will be employed, and enabled to live in plenty, to marry, increase, and pay for the productions of the land, which otherwise will have little or no production: foreigners will be invited to partake of our happiness, and add to the publick stock; and even the poor and helpless will have their share in the general felicity, arising from the superfluities and charity of the rich. But the reverse of this glorious and happy scene shews itself in enslaved and corrupted nations.

But as this is abundantly the interest of private men, it is much more so of princes: The riches of a prince are the riches of his people, and his security and happiness are their affections: They do not consist in pompous guards, splendid courts, heaped up and extorted wealth, servile and flattering parasites, numerous, expensive, and glittering attendants, profusion, and extravagance; but in the steady and faithful duty and devotions of a grateful and contented people, who derive and own their happiness to flow from his care and beneficence. Flatterers and parasites often will find it their interest to betray him (and what else can be expected from those who betrayed their country first?), his guards often revolt from him, and sometimes murder him, and neither can be depended upon in any exigency of his affairs; his amassed wealth shall be often their plunder, and his destruction the price of their new engagements. But a whole people can never have an interest separate from the interests of a good prince: Their diffusive wealth will be always at his call, because it is to be expended for their own benefit: Their persons will ever be at his command, to defend themselves and him: This is a source of wealth and power, which can scarce ever be exhausted. When men fight for themselves and their all, they are not to be conquered till they are extinguished; and there are few instances where they have been ever conquered, at least till they were not worth conquering.

Besides, the superfluities and wanton gifts of a free and happy people will bring more money into his coffers, than racks and armies can extort from enslaved countries. The states of Brabant[1] alone gave more money formerly to the Dukes of Burgundy and to Charles V than in all probability the whole seventeen provinces would have yielded to Spain since, if they had been all subdued; and I dare say, if England ever loses its liberties, its princes, in a little time, would not be able with whips and chains, to force as much money out of it in seven years, as we have seen it pay in one: They might fetch blood and tears from their subjects, but little else. It is undeniably therefore true, that the publick interest is the interest of both prince and people, which almost every one owns in words; and yet how few do so in their actions?

Every man sees the advantage of being formidable abroad, and safe at home, and knows that we cannot attain either but by being at the charge of it; and that the more equally and impartially taxes are laid, the fewer will be necessary, and more money raised: Yet how few men will come into equal and impartial taxes? And what have any got by contrary methods? It is certain, that less taxes than are now paid to one another, if fairly levied at first, would have ended all our wars, and not left us one penny in debt; whereas every landed man in England now owes the fourth or fifth part of his estate to the publick engagements, by declining the payment of perhaps the tenth part of it when it was due, or ought to have been due; and besides, has rendered all the rest insecure, by disabling the publick to defend it.

1. That is, those territories which, from the end of the twelfth to the middle of the fifteenth centuries, formed the duchy of Brabant (at the time covering the northern portion of the Austrian Netherlands and the southern portion of the United Provinces). In 1427, the duchy passed into the possession of the dukes of Burgundy and, at the end of the century, into Hapsburg hands.

Who, that is interested in the national funds, does not see, that if some method be not soon taken to pay them off, they can never be paid at all; that no nation will deliver themselves up to a foreign enemy, or be contented to languish, expire and perish, at home, to make good juggling and extorting bargains, cooked up between courtiers and brokers; that publick necessities will happen in the course of human affairs, and those necessities will justify or colour uncommon measures; and that corrupt ministers, in times to come, may advise their masters to extraordinary courses, and desperate acts of power? And yet how many are there among these gentlemen (the greatest part of whose fortunes depends upon these events) who will fall into any effectual measures to make the payment of these debts due to themselves practicable, or that are not ready to catch at and to promote the raising of a new fund; though they must see that every step which they take towards it renders the payment of the old ones desperate?

How many courtiers have we seen in our days, that have not done every thing which they condemned in their predecessors; though by doing so they undermined the ground upon which they stood and played the game into their enemies' hands again, who did the same before into theirs? How often have we seen them decline any means of raising money, though ever so fatal to trade or their country? Or when have we seen them expend it afterwards with frugality and prudence, to prevent the necessity of raising it over again? And yet, by acting thus, they lessened their own interest with the people, and in consequence too with their prince; who generally will find it necessary to discard them when they become odious and contemptible; and sometimes will think it prudent to recommend himself to his people by delivering them up as sacrifices to publick vengeance: whereas if they acted a faithful and just part, they might grow old in power, and be double blessings to their prince and to their fellow-subjects.

Who does not see the benefit of navigable rivers, which makes the carrying out our own commodities, and the bringing to us what we want, cheap and easy; and consequently increases the price of the former, and lessens the price of the latter? And yet a project of that kind always meets opposition from any people upon trifling motives, without ever considering the advantages on the other side, which most commonly must overbalance their imaginary losses, by computing their whole income and expence.

All private men see the benefit that would accrue to England, and to almost every man in it, by bringing all the materials of navigation, and particularly iron, from our own plantations, which are for the most part bought for money from rival states, who may be, and are often our enemies. Though this would settle our naval power upon a fixed and solid foundation, and leave it no longer to depend upon accidental and precarious supplies liable to the impositions and caprices of those nations, and subject to be intercepted by others who may be in war with us; yet we have seen, oftener than once, that gentlemen of great estates have denied their countries this general good, and preferred the little advantage of selling a particular wood at an advanced price, or the encouragement of a private iron-work, to so great a benefit to themselves and their country; without ever giving themselves leave to balance the much greater augmentation of wealth and security, which would accrue personally to them by keeping so much money in their country, and by bringing in a great deal more from foreign states, by making navigation easy and cheap, by supplying themselves and their tenants with the instruments and utensils of husbandry, building, and house-keeping, at lower rates, and so enabling themselves to make greater profit of their lands, and their tenants to pay them greater rents; and, above all, by increasing the publick safety and power, of which every member will soon find the sensible effects in his own private affairs.

I confess it to be generally true, that the interest of any country is to make all sorts of manufactures themselves, rather than fetch them from neighbouring countries, or even from their own plantations; but it is always an exception to that truth, when those manufactures are necessary to carry on other trades which will return much greater benefit; and more so when they are necessary to carry on all trade in general, as iron and shipping undoubtedly are, upon the cheapness of which all the trade in the world in a great measure depends.

T   *I am, &c.*

NO. 90. SATURDAY, AUGUST 18, 1722.

❧ *Monopolies and exclusive Companies, how pernicious to Trade.*

SIR,

I have in my last letter given some instances of men, who, separating themselves from the publick, act against their own interest, by being too partial to it; but I confess it sometimes happens, that private persons may receive personal advantages from publick losses; and then, considering the depravity of human nature, we are not to hope, and less to presume upon their acting against themselves for other advantages. The chief inducement which men have to act for the interest of one state before another, is, because they are members of it, and that their own interest is involved in the general interest; and the same motives which for the most part engage them to promote the advantage of that peculiar society of which they are a part, before all others, will also engage them to prefer themselves and their own family before the interests of every member, or all the members together, of the same society, whatever becomes of conscience, honour, and generosity, men will be men, in spite of all the lectures of philosophy, virtue, and religion.

This will be often the interest of particular men, but can never be the interest of the whole society, or the major part of them; whose interest must ever be the general interest, that is, the diffusive advantage of the whole, which must suffer in proportion to what any man gets irregularly, and therefore it is their common duty to prevent the unfair gains and depredations of one another; which indeed is the business of the government; *viz.* to secure to every one his own, and to prevent the crafty, strong, and rapacious, from pressing upon or circumventing the weak, industrious, and unwary.

I have often wondered how whole societies (every one of which intends most religiously himself and his own benefit) can yet, all together, so easily be made the dupes of one another, or of lesser societies among themselves, not only in such matters as do not fall within vulgar observation, but in instances which are obvious to the meanest capacities. All the gentlemen through England have their estates ransacked, and are deprived of whatever makes their tables elegant and curious, to put fishmongers and poulterers' wives, at London, in laces and jewels, without adding to the plenty there, much of it being destroyed, or suffered to rot or stink, by those miscreants, to keep up the price: Their cattle sell for little in the country, and will not pay the grazier, who must pay them their rents; and yet, by the jugglings and combinations of butchers and salesmen, the markets are not cheaper supplied; but those insects swallow up the rents of the landlord, and the labour of the husbandmen; as some of the factors do that of the manufacturer: The old useful laws against regraters, forestallers,[1] &c. all lie fast asleep, and no new ones are thought on to enforce them; yet the nobility and gentry of England spend many months every year in Parliament, see all this, buy their own productions at a price by many times greater than they sell them; but are so wholly taken up with other much less views, that they suffer this great mischief to go on, and every day to increase, upon no other pretence than the privileges of particular societies of tradesmen, who pretend a right to oppression; as if any man could have a right or privilege inconsistent with the publick good, and were not ever to be subservient to it. It is true, that no government ought to take away men's natural rights, the business and design of government itself being to defend them; but sure such partial and adventitious advantages as they receive to the detriment of others by ill laws may be taken away by good ones: But no sooner any attempt is made to remedy these universal grievances, but the clamour and solicitation of these humble and inferior oppressors puts an end to the remedy.

I do not wonder, that those who subsist by oppression themselves should countenance all other sorts of it; it is their com-

1. Regrators were those who, in contravention of old English law, bought provisions at a fair or market with the intention of selling them at a higher price within a radius of four miles. The law against forestalling, an indictable offense until its repeal in 1844, prohibited securing the control of commodities that were on their way to market for the purpose of selling them at a higher price.

mon interest to protect one another. But that the country gentlemen, who suffer by all kinds of it, and who have the means in their
hands to prevent them, should suffer themselves to be plundered
and impoverished, to enrich harpies and pick-pockets, and enable
them to live in pride and luxury, is so stupendous, that it could not
be believed, if we did not constantly see it.

But these are petty abuses, when compared to the much
greater grievances of uniting great numbers of artful and wealthy
merchants into conspiracies and combinations against general
trade; and by that means giving or selling the industry and
acquirements of a whole nation to satiate and glut a few overgrown plunderers, and in the end to destroy the trade itself; which
must ever be the case, when trade is committed to the management of exclusive companies. The success and improvements of
trade depend wholly upon supplying the commodities cheap at
market; and whoever can afford those of equal goodness at but
half per cent cheaper than his neighbour, will command any sale.
Now it is impossible that any company can do this upon equal
terms with a private merchant, nor would they if they could. Private men will think of every way to come at their goods cheap, will
make it their whole business to work up the manufactures themselves, or buy them at the best hand, will search narrowly into their
excellencies or defects, will procure carriage at the lowest prices,
see them shipped themselves, and sometimes sell them in person,
and as they find proper and advantageous opportunities; and the
mutual emulation and contention with one another for the preference of markets, obliges them to sell often for little profit, and
sometimes to loss, in expectation of better fortune at other times;
but nothing of this is ever done by companies.

Those who have the direction of their affairs, have often
but small part of their fortunes embarked in their stock, and always
have an interest separate from that of the company, and commonly if not always, raise vast estates at their expence; the materials of their ships, and the commodities which they carry, are
generally sold by themselves, or bought of their friends and relations by confederacy, at exorbitant prices: Favourite shipwrights
are employed for presents; their relations or creatures are made

captains or masters of their vessels, to carry on private commerce, to the detriment of the company; governors of forts, factors, and agents, are sent abroad to get great estates upon the publick, and perhaps share them with their patrons at home; their goods shall be set in such lots, and sold at such times as shall be most for the private interest of the governing directors, who will have them often bought up in trust for themselves or friends; and by these means, as the company oppresses the rest of the nation, the governors and directors cheat the company. But if these trustees be ever so honest, they will not take the same pains for others as for themselves; nor can it be expected that men of their fortunes will employ their whole time for such allowances as are or can be afforded by the society who employs them.

Besides, it is the interest of the nation to sell their commodities at as good a price as the markets abroad can afford to buy them, and to bring in foreign commodities as cheap as they can afford to sell them; especially such as do not interfere with our own (which ought to be prohibited when it can be done without greater inconvenience) and the interest of companies is directly contrary to all this: for other people being prohibited to deal in the same commodities, they can put what price they please upon both, and ever will put what is most for their advantage, and so starve the manufacturer at home, at the same time that their agents charge great prices to the company, and sell the commodities which they bring in return of them at extravagant advantages, often to the discouragement of our own manufactures, which depend upon their cheapness; their business being always to increase the price of stock, without increasing trade.

Besides all this, they keep forts abroad at a great expence, to colour the necessity of such monopolies, and to oppress and rob the natives there with security; for it is a jest to imagine that they can any ways conduce to fair trade. Every nation in the world that has any thing to buy or sell, will see their account in doing so, and will find it their interest to encourage a fair commerce, which will be ever for their own advantage; and if they do not, there is no trading with them against their own consents, though their country be encompassed with forts, which will only provoke and make them enemies; and, in fact, the private traders to Africa pay the Company[2] ten per cent towards their forts, and seldom or never come near them, or receive any benefit by them, and yet have broke the Company, whilst they thrive themselves. The same was true of the interlopers to India formerly, who neither desired nor were suffered to take any advantage of the Company's forts, and always were oppressed by their governors, or agents, and captains of ships,[3] and yet would soon have undone them, if they had been suffered to go on.

The Dutch make other advantages of their forts and garrisons, which is to keep great conquered realms and powerful kings in subjection, and secure to themselves the whole commerce of their countries, by which means they have almost the monopoly of the spices of the world; of which, it is said, they every year burn mountains to keep up the price, as all exclusive companies will ever do: But we have scarce any trade to some of those places, where we are at the charge of keeping forts, which stand there no mortal can tell why. But supposing that forts were necessary to carry on any particular trade, what colour is there to deny that they ought to be kept at the publick expence, or by the contributions of all the merchants, who are to receive advantage from them in proportion to the trade which they carry on; or what pretence is there to confine an advantageous trade to one town alone, and to but few men in that town?

So that, upon the whole, if we consider these companies only as they regard trade, which is the only pretence for establishing them, they are the bane of all fair commerce, the discouragement of our manufactures, the ruin of private and industrious traders, and must end in the ruin of themselves, and all trade whatever; and no one receives advantages from them, but the governors, directors, commanders, or agents, at home and abroad, who have ever raised immense estates, whilst the kingdom has been impoverished, and the company undone. But there are other

2. The Royal African Company. In 1672, this company succeeded the African Company, whose major assets (after 1662) were the forts on the Gambia and Gold Coast and the Company's *Asiento*, its monopoly of the slave trade.

3. The reference is to the East India Company.

mischiefs still behind, which strike yet much deeper; namely, the influence and violence that they bring upon our constitution; which shall be the subject of my next letter.

T   *I am, &c.*

NO. 91. SATURDAY, AUGUST 25, 1722.

How exclusive Companies influence and hurt our Government.

SIR,

In my last letter I have considered exclusive companies as they affect the trade and commerce of the kingdom: In this I shall view them in relation to our constitution; and shew, that they alter the balance of our government, too much influence our legislature, and are ever the confederates or tools of ambitious and designing statesmen.

Very great riches in private men are always dangerous to states, because they create greater dependence than can be consistent with the security of any sort of government whatsoever; they place subjects upon too near a level with their sovereigns; make the nobility stand upon too great an inequality in respect of one another; destroy, amongst the Commons, that balance of property and power, which is necessary to a democracy, or the democratic part of any government, overthrow the poise of it, and indeed alter its nature, though not its name: For this reason, states who have not an agrarian law, have used other means of violence or policy to answer the same ends. Princes often, either by extraordinary acts of power, by feigned plots and conspiracies, and sometimes by the help of real ones, have cut off these excrescent members and rivals of their authority, or must have run the hazard of being cut off by them. Aristocracies put them upon expensive embassies, or load them with honorary and chargeable employments at home, to drain and exhaust their superfluous and dangerous wealth; and democracies provide against this evil, by the division of the estates of particulars after their death amongst their children or relations in equal degree.

We have instances of the first in all arbitrary monarchies, as well as in all the Gothic governments formerly, and in Poland at present, which are constant states of war or conspiracy between their kings and nobles; and which side soever gets the better, the others are for the most part undone. By doing the second, the nobles of Venice keep up their equality; and Holland, Switzerland, and the free states of Germany, make the provision last named; which, as I have said, answers in some measure the purposes of an agrarian law: But by waiting for the division of overgrown substance in private hands, other states have been undone; and particularly Florence was enslaved by the overgrown power of the house of Medici.

And as great riches in private men is dangerous to all states, so great and sudden poverty produces equal mischiefs in free governments; because it makes those who by their birth and station must be concerned in the administration, necessitous and desperate; which will leave them the means, and give them the will, to destroy their country: for the political power will remain some time in their hands after their natural power and riches are gone; and they will ever make use of it to acquire that wealth by violence and fraud which they have lost by folly and extravagance. And as both of these extremes are certainly true of particular men, so they are more dangerous in numbers of men joined together in a political union; who, as they have more wealth than any particular man ever had or can have, so they will have the separate interest of every individual to assist them, arising from the dependence of friendship, relation, acquaintance, or creatures, without that emulation and envy which will always be raised by the sudden and exorbitant riches of private men. It is certain, that they both make too violent an alteration in property, and almost always produce violent convulsions in government.

Now companies bring all these mischiefs upon us; they give great and sudden estates to the managers and directors, upon the ruins of trade in general, and for the most part, if not always, bring ruin upon thousands of families, who are embarked in the society itself. Those who are in the direction and the secret of the management besides all their other advantages, draw out and divide all their principal, and what they can borrow upon their credit; persuade innocent and unwary people to believe that they divide only the profits of their trade, and, by a thousand other artifices heightening their advantages, draw them in to share in them; and when they have wound up the cheat to the highest pitch that it can go, then like rats leave a falling house, and multitudes of people to be crushed by it. This was the case of the East-India and African Companies formerly, whose stock sold for 300 per cent[1] when it was not worth a groat;[2] and how far it is the case of the present East-India Company, their members are concerned to enquire.

What ruin, devastation, and havock of estates! What public misery, and destruction of thousands, I may say millions, have we seen by the establishment and wicked intrigues of the present South-Sea Company, only to make a few unshapely and monstrous members in the body politick! What has that Company done for the benefit of trade, which they were established, forsooth, to promote? They have suffered numbers of our manufactures to rot in their ships, hindered private traders from carrying on an advantageous commerce to the lower parts of America and the South-Sea; and, like the dog in the manger, will neither eat themselves, nor let any one else eat; and, it is said, by their wise conduct, have lost a million or two of the Company's principal.

The benefits arising by these companies, generally, and almost always fall to the share of the stock-jobbers, brokers, and those who cabal with them; or else are the rewards of clerks, thimble-men, and men of nothing; who neglect their honest industry to embark in those cheats, and so either undo themselves and families, or acquire sudden and great riches; then turn awkward statesmen, corrupt boroughs, where they have not, nor can have, any natural interests; bring themselves into the legislature with their pedling and jobbing talents about them, and so become brokers in

1. Of the par value of the stock.
2. Groat: a four-penny coin.

politicks as well as stock, wanting every qualification which ought to give them a place there.

It is a strange and unnatural transition from a fishmonger or pedlar to a legislator: However, as such doughty statesmen, by their single abilities, can do no good, so they can do but little harm; but when united in a body under the direction of artful managers combining with great men, they can turn all things into confusion, and generally do so. When men have great sums of money to give, and will give it, they will ever find people to take it; and there can be no standing against them in a body, how contemptible soever they are in particulars. How often have the cries of the whole kingdom of England been able to prevail against the interest of the East-India Company? What by proper application in former reigns made to our courts, to ministers and favourites, and to the members of each House of Parliament, they have been able to contend and get the better of the tears and complaints of the whole kingdom besides, and to lay asleep the true and real interest of those who assisted them; and if ever hereafter our three great companies should unite together (as it is to be feared they will always do when their interests do not clash), what power is there in being to oppose them, that will be able and willing to do it? In Holland, which is a more jealous government than ours, the East-India Company governs the state,[3] and is in effect the state itself; and I pray God that we may never see the like elsewhere!

What have we been able to do to redress the ravages brought upon us by the South-Sea project? Which yet must have produced much greater, if we had not suffered these. When it was in its meridian,[4] I have heard some persons argue the reasonableness of their having a monopoly of the trade of England, since they were possessed of most of the property of England; and I do not see by what means it could have been prevented. They would have filled the legislature with their own members, all our great men must have been their pensioners, and the crown itself been obliged

3. The Dutch East India Company, founded in 1602, was given extensive political and military authority in the areas under its control. It was given a monopoly of trade with the East Indies and was allowed to import into Holland free of all customs duties.

4. In its meridian: at its highest point.

to have kept measures with them; they would have been the only shop to have gone to for money, would not have parted with it but upon their own terms, and would have been ever lying upon the catch,[5] to purchase more privileges and advantages: so that the nobility and gentry of England must either have embarked their fortunes and expectations in this monopoly, or have been humbly contented to have been governed by a faction composed for the most part of pedlars, grocers, and brokers, or such as lately were so; and the constitution itself had been gone, and changed into a stock-jobbing cabal.

We have seen but few instances where the private traders of England, and the interests of general trade, have been able to dispute with the interests of little companies or particular societies of tradesmen, or the peculiar privileges of corporations; though they are burdens and a dead weight on the estates of every person in both Houses, lessen their income, and increase their expences: Such is the fascination and witchcraft of political confederacy! What will be the event of these combinations no man can foresee, and every wise man must dread. Indeed, I do not see how we can prevent their dismal consequences, but by paying off our debts; and, by dissipating those factious combinations, dissolve the enchantment.

After all that I have said, I must confess that the East-India Company is liable to less objections than any other trading monopoly, but not for the reasons which they give, but for a reason which is worth an hundred of theirs: for as all beneficial trades are most successfully carried on by free and open commerce, so all losing ones do less mischief when monopolized; and as the first ought to receive all possible encouragement, so the other ought to be put under suitable discouragements: And since we can have no prospect at present of that trade's being put upon an advantageous foot, the next best thing that we can desire, is to let it go on upon the present establishment; which in all probability will soon destroy it, and perhaps put it upon a good one, if that can be: for it is certain, that if it could be carried on with its full swing, it would ease us of every penny of our money, and destroy every manufac-

5. Lying upon the catch: on the watch.

ture in the kingdom, as well as every man in it; which in a proper time may be shewn at large.

In fine, monopolies are equally dangerous in trade, in politicks, in religion: A free trade, a free government, and a free liberty of conscience, are the rights and the blessings of mankind.

T   *I am, &c.*

NO. 92. SATURDAY, SEPTEMBER 1, 1722.

❦ *Against the Petition of the South-Sea Company, for a Remittance of Two Millions of their Debt to the Publick.*

SIR,

It has been justly observed of corporations, or political combinations of men, that they have bodies, but no souls, nor consequently consciences. What calls this observation to my mind, is an *Address to his Majesty from the South-Sea Company,*[1] which I have lately seen in print, most modestly requesting, that in this great profusion of money, general affluence, and overflowing of trade, the nation will give them two millions: and the reasons which they give for it are, 1st, that they want the money; next, that they have agreed with the Bank;[2] and 3dly, that they will do what without doubt is the interest of all their members, except directors and brokers, to do; that is, they will consent that a considerable part of their stock shall be turned into annuities (and they had been the wiser if they had said all, for then no more of it could have been lost by management): And to wind up their whole oratory, they add a fourth reason, which is, the benefit that the publick has received already by their interest being reducible in a few years to

1. No copy of this address appears to have survived.
2. In June 1722, the South Sea Company arrived at an agreement with the Bank of England, known as the Bank Treaty, whereby the Bank agreed to buy five-percent Exchequer annuities (yielding £200,000 per annum) held by the South Sea Company for £4,200,000, which the Bank was to finance through a sale of new Bank stock.

four per cent, which reduction was part of their original bargain that was purchased for the seven millions, of which five have been remitted already, and now it is to be a consideration for remitting the other two.[3]

I can never give myself leave to believe (whatever may be furnished by others) that any person (employed by his Majesty) in the present great exigencies of the kingdom, the almost universal poverty in the country, the want of trading stocks and credit in cities, and in great as well as little towns, the prodigious load of debt under which the nation groans, and the general uneasiness conspicuous in the faces, and too observable in the discourses, of people of all sects and denominations; I say, I cannot think that, under such circumstances of publick affairs, any minister can countenance so wild a proposition, as wantonly to desire us to give away two millions of the nation's money, only to bind a bargain between two stock-jobbing societies; which could not be obtained from a late assembly, who I presume will not be disobliged if I say no more of them.[4]

I must therefore believe, if any person in power has been concerned in this negotiation, that he has effectually taken care of the publick, and has comprehended its interest in the agreement; and I am the rather induced to believe this, because of an expression in the address itself, to wit, *that the company will be ready to do any thing for the publick service, &c.* with a caution notwithstanding, *that it be consistent with the security of their present fund:* I hope that this sentence has an allusion to some project intended to be proposed to buy off the two millions, and that they design to offer to sink

3. By the terms of the original agreement between the government and the South Sea Company, the government agreed to pay interest on the debt assumed by and owed the Company in part at five percent and in part at four percent, the whole amount reducible to four percent after 1727. The Company, in turn, agreed to pay the government a fee of approximately £7,000,000. By the terms of a resolution in the House of Commons in May 1721, however, £5,000,000 of this amount was remitted while the remaining £2,000,000 was to be reserved toward the liquidation of the national debt.

4. The bargain referred to is the Bank Treaty of June 1722 between the South Sea Company and the Bank of England. The "late assembly" is the House of Commons, which originally rejected the South Sea Company's request that all £7,000,000 of its debt be remitted. In fact, the remaining £2,000,000 owed the government was indeed remitted by subsequent acts of Parliament.

one hundred thousand pounds *per annum* of their annuities, which is the interest of two millions:[5] And this will answer all honest purposes, will indemnify the publick, ease them of the difficulty of raising so great a sum, and lessen the income of particular members, not above six or seven shillings per cent yearly.[6]

It is impossible to suspect that those gentlemen, who for some years together opposed wild schemes and wilder expences in carrying them on, and who (if they are to be believed themselves) rather chose to throw up their then advantages and expectations, than comply with such gallantries, should at last lose the merit of so much virtue, by wantonly and unnecessarily discharging one company from their contract, only to prevent another from performing theirs, and this at two millions loss to their country: Sure England is not in a condition to discharge all reckonings at home and amongst foreign states too; if so, every man ought to bring in his bill, and then we shall all be upon the square.[7]

On the contrary, I persuade myself that the gentlemen, whose deserts have now set them at the helm, have, during their retirement from business, observed the miscarriages of their predecessors, design to avoid the rocks upon which the others have split, and consequently have put on steady resolutions to extricate the kingdom out of its present calamities; and, possessed with this opinion, I am determined (as I believe many others are) to give them my hearty assistance to attain those good ends, and to forget past errors if new ones do not rub up our memories: I neither envy their preferments, nor I believe shall court them; but shall ever esteem my services to be overpaid, if I can contribute to save my country.

We all know what a noble project has been lately authorized;[8] what ends were designed to be, and have been, served by it; how many thousands were directly ruined by it, and how many more by the fatal consequences which have ensued: but all the arts

5. That is, to set up a sinking fund composed of five-percent annuities (yielding £100,000 per year) for the purpose of paying back the £2,000,000 owed.

6. That is, six or seven shillings per £100 annually.

7. Be upon the square: be honest and straightforward.

8. That is, the South Sea Company's assumption of a good portion of the national debt in 1720.

of the projectors could never have succeeded, if many well-meaning people had not been drawn in to consent to this iniquity, by the prospect of seeing the publick debts put in a method of being paid off; which they thought would atone for many evils that were foreseen by wise men, who yet did not foresee the hundredth part of the mischief which has since happened; and after we had suffered more than words can express, the greatest part of the consideration which drew us into these sufferings has been remitted, I will not say by any of those, but, to those, who brought all our misfortunes upon us; and now the poor remainder is modestly called for; and, if obtained, the wretched people, and, amongst the rest, all who vigorously opposed this vile project, must bear the loss, and the contrivers of the wickedness must carry off the plunder.

Sure such a proceeding sounds very odd, and ought to be supported by obvious reasons! It is a very singular sort of generosity, to punish the innocent, in order to reward the guilty; to fine or tax those who did their utmost to oppose the progress of publick mischiefs, to repair the losses of those who, through guilt, covetousness, or folly, contributed to it. In great publick calamities there must be many sufferers, and some who do not deserve to be so; yet I never heard that they called for reprisals upon their countrymen. Provinces are laid waste, cities and towns burnt, in war, and ships taken by pirates; and yet no bills brought in, or demands made, upon the publick: In pestilential distempers, families are shut up in their houses, and whole cities within their walls, where thousands die for want of food or proper necessaries, and those who are left alive are mostly undone; and yet no nations think themselves obliged to make good their losses: In such cases every one must bear his own misfortunes, even when they come from the hand of God, and he himself does not contribute to them; and all that wise states can do, is to take care of the whole, relieve particulars as far as is consistent with the publick safety, and leave the rest to providence.

But, besides the shrewd reasons which are in print, and are above repeated, let us hear what others are offered to load the publick with this loss. First, we are told that the people's representatives have drawn the subscribers into it; and therefore the people are bound in conscience to repair them: A very notable way of arguing indeed! and which, if carried to its extent, would provide admirably well for the security of nations. Suppose the States of any country should make a foolish law, or engage it in a foolish war, by which a third part of the people are undone, must the rest make them amends, who perhaps are half undone themselves? The Pensioner Parliament, in King Charles II's time, were chosen by the people to act for the common benefit of the kingdom, and they betrayed their principals, and took money from the court to act against it; and was that a good reason for the next Parliament to give a sanction to all the mischief that their predecessors did, or to pray for it? Sure the last Parliament were as much the representatives of the South-Sea Company as of the rest of the kingdom, and acted as agreeably to their inclinations and their desires, or else their acknowledgments were much misplaced.

They tell us, that the publick is better able to bear the loss than private men; which certainly is not true at present; for the publick is much poorer than most private men in England, if regard be had to their occasions and their debts: But if it were so, are they therefore to take the ill bargains of all private men to themselves, and protect them in their good ones? Must every man who has suffered by playing the fool, or playing the knave, call upon the nation for reprisals? But supposing only innocent and unwary people (as all the members of the present South-Sea Company undoubtedly are) ought to be objects of publick compassion; who shall make recompence to the millions of others who have suffered in their estates, by the universal confusion occasioned by this worthy project? Who shall repair the many bankrupts, the many creditors who have lost their debts, the many young ladies who have lost their fortunes, the mechanicks and shopkeepers who have lost their business, spent their stocks, and yet have run in debt to subsist their families; and the gentlemen, merchants, and farmers, who can get little for their commodities and products of their estates, farms, and trades? And must all these contribute at last, out of what remains, to repair the misfortunes of those who brought all these evils upon them?

But because I would avoid giving offence to tender ears, by seeming to take too much part with the inconsiderable interests of men who are vulgarly called the mob, I shall represent the case of persons who much better deserve some people's consideration; I mean brokers, stock-jobbers, dealers in funds, and such who, for many years together, have supported the government, by making twice or thrice the advantage of their money that they could do any where else. Who shall repair the losses of the contractors for stock or subscriptions, or of those who lent them money at five, ten, and twenty per cent *per mensem*,[9] and cannot be paid again? Who pay the many sums lost in the hands of goldsmiths, and by their pretended subscriptions of effects without the owner's consent? Who the losses of those who bought in the East-India Company and Bank at two or three hundred per cent[10] all occasioned by this worthy project; or of those who bought in this Company at eight or nine hundred, and sold at one or two? Who those who bought, or were hindered from selling out of the stocks of all companies by that honest and serviceable bargain to the publick made between the Bank and the South-Sea?[11] Who shall pay the losses in the bubbles, some of which were established or countenanced by Parliament, and others by patents, all which have equal right to put in their claims? And lastly, who shall make satisfaction to the whole kingdom, who must be reduced by such means to an incapacity of paying its debts, and consequently of defending itself? I have heard of no project yet for lessening the public expences, or of the courtiers lessening their own stated incomes, or occasional gains.

And what, after all, are the particular merits of these gentlemen to whom so much favor is to be shewn; and who will receive the benefit of it? Those who remain of the original company have no pretence to it; and at present their capital, with the addition which they have received by the division of the fictitious stock, is more valuable than at first; I believe much more so: Those who have bought in since the fall, have as little pretence to be considered, because they knew the terms upon which they bought: Such

9. *Per mensem*: per month.

10. That is, those who bought stock in either of the two companies at two or three hundred percent of their par values.

11. The "bargain" refers to the agreement reached by the South Sea Company with the Bank in June 1722 to purchase Exchequer annuities held by the Company in return for a payment of £4,200,000.

as have raised fortunes by dabbling in the publick, ought not to complain if they have lost by one project what they got by another; and those who have great or plentiful offices in other respects, must be very immodest if they expect to repair their follies out of the estates of those who are more necessitous than themselves. So that the few that can hope for relief are the poor and helpless, who were trepanned by the rest to buy in at a great price, and could not sell out again before the fall; and I dare appeal to all mankind, whether such could get relief, if their interests were separated from their oppressors: If it be so, we have reason to sing *Te Deum*, for the world is finely mended; but till I can find some other instances of this tender regard to mercy and innocence, I must beg leave to suppose, that there is already, or is to be, some other consideration for the remitting these two millions, if ever they are remitted.

There is another reason left behind, and a shrewd one it is; namely, that we must support publick credit, by enabling the Bank to support the South-Sea, and in consequence enabling them both to sell their stocks for twice as much as they are worth (and so leave a new loss upon other people, who with equal reason must be again repaired); for it is certain, that all or most of the company-stocks fell at present above their real value. Now, with all due submission to the gentlemen of the Alley,[12] it seems to me to be a very odd way of supporting credit, to render the publick incapable of paying its debts: But it is no new thing amongst some sort of people, to endeavour to support credit by the means which destroy all credit. My head has been ever so ill turned, as to think that nations must preserve the opinion of their integrity by the same rules and maxims that private men find necessary; that is, always by selling good merchandise, and not stuffing their bales and casks with counterfeit wares, and covering them at top with those which look well. But we have heard of those times when moonshine and shadows have sold for silver and gold, for lands and tenements; and the wisdom of states has been employed to keep up the imaginary, fraudulent value of this sort of airy merchandise; when thousands and thousands of unwary people have been undone by

12. Exchange Alley.

such purchases, new projects have been formed and countenanced by authority to do as many more: I mean, this has been lately done in France, whose example should not be followed by any who design not to introduce the government of France.[13]

All wise and honest governments ought to protect their innocent, industrious, and unguarded, subjects, against the snares of cheats and frauds of pickpockets; and not combine with such wretches, and be perpetually forming schemes to ruin multitudes for the enriching a few, and to prostitute their power, and their publick honour, to patronize and establish combinations of oppression; and when one sort of it can be supported no longer, to set their wits to work to find out another. It puts me in mind of a story told of Dr. Barebone,[14] who had once drawn an eminent merchant into a building project at Mile-End, whereby he lost many thousand pounds; and when he complained of it, the doctor promised to make him reparation, by letting him share in another which he had just begun at the farther end of Westminster, whereby he lost as much more; and when his Bubble,[15] justly provoked, drew his sword upon the doctor, and bid him draw too, he, like a true stoick, with great calmness, and wholly unconcerned, asked, whither he would be drawn; for that he had drawn him from one end of the town to the other already? Whatever has been done in neighbouring countries, I am persuaded we are in no danger of any such attempts here.

And now having, as I conceive, fully answered the pretences of the South-Sea Company for getting the two millions remitted to them, which pretences they are pleased to call reasons; I shall offer them one of my own why they should not desire it, for

13. The reference is apparently to John Law's Mississippi Company, which rested on a grant of monopoly in three areas, a note-issuing central bank (the Banque Royale, established in December 1718); a trading company with a practical monopoly of the foreign trade of France (the Compagnie des Indes, May 1719, popularly known as the Mississippi Company), and the lease of the collection of taxes (the General Farms, August 1719). Although Law was forced to leave France in late 1720, the French Regent seems to have remained enthralled by Law's schemes; in 1723, he wrote Law that he continued to trust in Law's financial abilities and would like to arrange his return to France.

14. Nicholas Barbon, M.D. (d. 1698), one of the major builders in London following the great fire of 1666.

15. Trenchard is clearly being droll by using "his Bubble" as a title.

that they will be losers upon the whole by it. As I remember, the price of their stock rather decreased than increased upon the remitting the five millions; and it is fallen now upon the expectation of having the rest remitted: and the reason is obvious; for nothing can keep up the credit of publick or private men, but an opinion that they are able to pay their debts, and are willing to do so; and no man in his wits will believe either, if he do not see them endeavour to pay off their old debts, and avoid all occasions of contracting new ones. When a man owes more than he can pay, he must compound with his creditors, lie in gaol, or run away, unless he has privilege; and then they have nothing left to do, for the most part, but to shake their ears, rail, and run away too. People must be very weak not to know, if ever a question should arise, whether a nation will be undone, or undo a small part of it? which it will choose; and therefore every wise man, whose fortune lies in publick securities, will think himself concerned to make the payment of them practicable, and therefore will consider whether it is not his interest to lose a small part of his income, to secure the whole; and every man would consider this over and over, if he did not design at all adventures to save one, and leave the storm to fall upon others: And how well all hitherto have succeeded in this honest intention, we have had as many instances as we have had publick calamities, and lately a very pregnant one, when every man designed to sell, and no one could do so but managers and brokers.

T   *I am, &c.*

NO. 93. SATURDAY, SEPTEMBER 8, 1722.

An Essay upon Heroes.

SIR,

I design this letter as a dissertation upon heroes, who were at first a sort of brave disinterested men, that having more courage and prowess than others, went about doing good to others, and to all, at their own expence and danger. They established and reformed communities, and taught them laws, and punished those who violated justice and law: They destroyed publick robbers and monsters, and the greatest of all publick robbers and monsters, tyrants; and lived the patterns of virtue and useful valour. Hence they were called heroes, a sort of middle beings, superior to other men, and akin to the gods.

But so wild is the nature of man, and so impudent the nature of ambition, that whereas the primitive heroes were the bulwarks of society, and the preservers of men, those who pretended to succeed them, were the disturbers of society, and the destroyers of men; and such tyrants and monsters as the old heroes had destroyed, did themselves (impudently) set up for heroes. With the same modesty, superstition, which destroys religion, has, in the greatest part of the world, usurped the place of religion; tyranny, which is the extirpation of government, calls itself government: And thus arose persecuting priests and lawless kings. But so are words and the world abused; and with so much safety, and even applause, is mischief committed, when it has but a good name.

Alexander deified himself, and Caesar was deified by others, for being universal murderers; and Coke of Bury was hanged for attempting one murder:[1] Had he been at the head of a hundred thousand cut-throats, and murdered a million, he might have been recorded for a hero, his name been handed down to after-ages with elogiums, and publick declamations made in the schools upon his conduct and virtues.

Child, the highwayman, robbed the mail, and was put to death;[2] but, instead of the mail, had he robbed a nation (I mean any nation but this) he might probably have governed it; and, instead of hanging in chains, led a whole people in chains, and been dubbed an able statesman, and a faithful minister.

Mischief is inseparable from the profession of a present hero, whose business and ambition is to multiply conquests, and

1. In March 1722, Arundel Coke was tried at Bury St. Edmonds for abetting an attempt to murder his brother-in-law. He was found guilty and hanged several weeks later.

2. The reference appears to be to John Hawkins who, while still a boy, was engaged in robbing the mails. In Apr. 1722, he and his gang robbed the Bristol mail, which led to his being caught, tried, and executed in the following month.

consequently miseries, upon those whom he conquers. What a wild and inhuman spirit! to plague the world, in order to make a figure in it; to commit great villainies, for a good name; to destroy the peace and prosperity of mankind, to gain their esteem; and to shed their blood, to shew themselves fit to govern them! For none gain by such accomplishments of theirs, but their soldiers, whose lives too they throw away as wantonly as these take away the lives of others. The chief gainers therefore are only a few officers, servants and strumpets, who are about their persons, and execute their will and rage for their own ends: And so, to glut a restless tyrant and his instruments, men and nations must be slaughtered or enslaved. This is the heroism, this the glory, of conquering!

Such is the difference between the old original heroes and these their apes, who, by fraud, violence, perjury, and restless cruelty, make war upon their subjects and neighbours; and, by sacrificing the virtuous and the brave, or, by making them their instruments to sacrifice others, and by distressing, exhausting, plundering, and chaining, all, push human misery as far as it can go. These are the wolves and tigers of [the] human race; imperial beasts of prey who if the world would preserve itself, ought to be driven out of the world, or hung up in it *in terrorem*;[3] or, like these their more innocent brethren, who only kill for food, be locked up in dens, and shewn, as they are, for monsters: Or perhaps it would be still a more equitable punishment, if they could be caught, to shut up a number of them in a madhouse with their beloved arms about them, there to fight and tear one another's flesh, and spill their own detestable blood, till they had no more to spill. This would be giving a sort of satisfaction to mankind, for so much human blood outrageously and wantonly spilt.

But this is not the only mock-heroism in the world; there is yet another sort as mischievous, but still more ridiculous; and that is, a violent appetite for war, and victory, and conquest, without engaging personally in the danger, or coming near it; but being very valorous by proxy, and fond of fighting without drawing a sword. This was the prudent bravery of a late aged conqueror, who

3. "As a warning."

was never tired of war, yet never tired his own person in it:[4] In the heat of a battle fought for his glory, he ran no risk, but sat securely at a great distance with the wise old woman his mistress,[5] waiting for laurels of other people's winning. When his agents had bought a town for him treacherously, or his generals stolen a province as treacherously, still it was victory, still fair conquest; and the glory was his at three hundred leagues' distance: for every thing that he did was glorious, the meanest and the basest things; and by these means he became immortal, immortal in conquest without a scar.

The primitive heroes ventured their lives for the good of others: These mock-heroes expose others to danger and death for the good of themselves, and their own personal renown; and all the time stay at home, and wait for fame in a whole skin. They slaughter thousands who obey them, and undo millions who ought not to obey them; and all to enslave others, who neither wish nor do them any harm, and with whom they have nothing at all to do. Even most of the instruments which they make use of, are made as miserable as they make those whom they oppress; and few or none share the benefit of the plunder, but such as, wanting merit of their own to gain an honest subsistence, prey upon the industry of those that do. So strongly does misery thrive under their influence, and nothing else!

They keep themselves poor, suspicious, and in a state of war with their own subjects, whom they justly suspect for their worst enemies, because they supply them with constant reasons to be so; and therefore they live in a perpetual state of rapine and enmity towards them, and in a continued dread of violence and revolts from them; instead of giving them fatherly protection on one side, and receiving from them dutiful and sincere allegiance on the other; and all for the fruitless and imaginary glory of conquest, and of dominion over their fellow creatures against their will; or, in other words, of being skillful pillagers and oppressors, and successful murderers.

4. Louis XIV.

5. Madame de Maintenon, who was in reality Louis's wife, although this was never officially declared.

It is, however, not to be wondered at, that whilst so many princes are beset with sycophants, always ready to applaud at a venture, their wildest sallies and designs; or with traitors, who, finding their own vile advantages in them, are ever determined to abet and execute them: I say, it is not strange, that princes in these circumstances should run frequently into wild freaks, and pernicious enterprises, to the ruin of themselves and their subjects. But it is stupendous, that these their baneful instruments and worst foes should be able, in any instance, to persuade nations to dance after their destructive maggots, and be contented to be undone, to make some of the worst of men amongst themselves rich and saucy.

What have the people in any monarchical government ever gained by the conquests made by their prince, but to be made slaves; or if they were slaves before, worse slaves, and to have their chains rivetted yet faster? For, besides that these conquests give him a pretence and an ability to keep more troops, and consequently increase his power over them; the conquered nation will find a sort of a revenge in joining to reduce their new masters to the same wretched condition with themselves, and perhaps find an opportunity of conquering the conquerors. One nation will be played upon another, and neither will be trusted to the guard of their own countrymen; but the soldiers of one country will be quartered upon the other, and kept at a great distance from home, lest by constant conversation with their relations, friends, and neighbours, they should, contrary to their duty, warp towards the love and interest of their country: And indeed in most countries where troops are kept, they are always removed from place to place, to prevent their friendship and correspondence with the natives.

What did England gain formerly by their conquests upon the Continent, but constant wars, slaughter, and poverty to themselves, and to their princes precarious foreign provinces at an English expence; and had standing armies been then the fashion of the world, England would doubtless have conquered itself into slavery. The Romans, when they had extended their conquests so far and wide, that they were forced to keep provincial armies to awe and preserve the conquered countries, became a prey to those armies; and their emperors afterwards durst no longer trust to Roman troops, but increased their slavery by the help of those nations whom they had conquered, and who became, in their turns, masters of those who had mastered them.

When Alexander had ventured his own army of Macedonians, and the best men in Greece, to ruin Persia, and a great part of the world, which had given him no provocation; what advantages did Greece and Macedon reap from his mighty victories and conquests; but to become a little province of a great barbarous empire, which by their arms and prowess he conquered, and exhausted them of all their bravest men to preserve? Their condition would still have been worse, if he had left a successor behind him to have preserved his whole empire entire, who would have made Persia, or some other province, the seat of it, and governed Greece at a distance by bashaws: As it was, he left it in a state of constant war and depredation, and they were tossed and tumbled from one oppression to another, till they found a sort of relief in being conquered by the Romans.

What did the French gain by the long wars and many conquests of their late great monarch, but extreme poverty, straiter servitude, great depopulation, and general bankruptcy? So much did they suffer by his acquisitions, and so dear did they pay for his pernicious glory.

What did the Swedes gain by the conquests of the late king, but to lose them again, as they got them, at a vast expence of blood and treasure;[6] and to be reduced to such weakness, as to want the assistance of their neighbours to preserve them from falling under the power of a prince, whom, by conquering him, they taught to conquer them?

And if the conquering countries are such miserable losers by conquest, what must be the doleful condition of the conquered,

6. Gustavus Adolphus, who reigned from 1611 to 1632, was successful in raising Sweden to the status of a first-rank power by force of arms, but this status was short-lived. The costly attempts of his successors to maintain Sweden's pre-eminent position in the Baltic, and particularly Charles XII's defeat in the Great Northern War (1700–1721), soon reduced the nation to the position of a second-class European state.

which are considered only as the sources of plunder, and the professed objects of oppression? Almost all Europe are witnesses of the brutish havock which the conquerors make, and of the dismal scenes of ruin that they leave behind them. If the late French king could have conquered, or bought, or surprized the United Provinces (which by all these generous means he endeavoured) from the richest and most populous republick upon earth, they would have been now a nest of beggarly fishermen, and in a lower condition, if possible, than any of the fine French provinces, which had the honour of being governed by that paternal prince. Never was such mockery, as for a prince to publish reasons to a people, with whom he had nothing to do, why they should be conquered by him; when, let their condition be as ill as it will, it is an hundred to one, nay it is almost certain, that he will make it ten times worse.

"Alas! for that nation whose prince is a hero!" says an excellent and amiable French writer,[7] who saw, with sorrow, the woeful condition of his own nation, from the merciless and unnatural affectation of heroism in the then king.

The same admirable author, in another place, gives us a lively image of heroes and conquests in these words, which he makes Telemachus speak, as he views the field of battle filled with carcases, and drenched with blood:

> Such are the heavy evils that follow wars! What blind fury urges unhappy mortals! So few are the days that they have to live upon this earth, and so miserable do they make these few days! Why will they run thus headlong into the jaws of death, which is of itself making hasty approaches to devour them? Why add so many frightful desolations to a short and bitter life, made so by heaven already? Men are all brethren, and they tear and butcher one another, more unnaturally fierce and cruel than the wild beasts of the desert! Lions make not war upon lions, nor tigers upon tigers: They attack only animals of a different species. Man! Man alone, in spite of his reason, does things that creatures without reason would never do.

7. François de Fénelon, *Dialogues des morts, anciens et modernes* (Second ed.; Paris: Chez Jacques Estienne, 1725). The sentiment can be found in Louis XII's remarks to Francis I in dialogue 10, II:70–77.

But why these consuming wars? Is there not land enough in the universe to satisfy all men with more than they can cultivate? Are there not vast tracts of desert lands, so vast that mankind is not sufficient to fill them? How then! A false glory, a vain title of Conqueror, which a prince is fond of, kindles a war far and wide; and one single man, thrown by heaven into the world, in wrath, sacrifices brutally so many others to his vanity! His glory requires it, and all must perish before him: Countries swim in blood, towns and cities suffer devouring flames; and what escapes from the sword and the fire, famine, more cruel than both, must consume; and all that this man, who thus sports himself with throwing all human nature into pangs, may find in this general destruction his pleasure and his glory. What monstrous glory! Can we too much despise, too much abhor, these monstrous men who have thus forgot humanity? Without being men, they set up for demi-gods; and earn the curses, instead of, what they aim at, the admiration of ages to come.

Oh! with what tenderness should princes undertake wars! That they ought to be strictly just, is not enough; they must be strictly necessary, necessary for the publick good. The blood of the people ought never to be shed but to save the people; and the occasion ought to be extreme. But flattering counsels, false ideas of glory, vain jealousies, boundless rapaciousness under specious disguises, and rash engagements, draw almost all princes precipitately or insensibly into wars which prove fatal to them. In them they hazard all without necessity, and do as much mischief to their subjects as to their enemies.[8]

Thus the divine late archbishop of Cambray, from whom I have translated this affecting passage. It is a book that has ten thousand excellencies, and ought to be read by all mankind.

I will conclude with wishing, that all nations would learn the wisdom of the prudent Sancho, who, when the hero his master madly attacked the wind-mills and the lions, stood at a safe dis-

8. *The adventures of Telemachus, the son of Ulysses* (2 vols.; London: Printed for William Churchill, 1719). The quotation appears in bk. XVII (II:116–18).

tance in a whole skin. If their governing Don Quixotes will fight, right or wrong, let them fight by themselves, and not sit at home and wantonly sacrifice their people against wind-mills and fulling-mills.[9]

G   *I am, &c.*

NO. 94. SATURDAY, SEPTEMBER 15, 1722.

Against Standing Armies.

SIR,

When, in King William's reign, the question was in debate, Whether England should be ruled by standing armies? the argument commonly used by some, who had the presumption to call themselves Whigs, and owned in the *Ballancing Letter*[1] (supposed to be written by one who gave the word to all the rest), was, that all governments must have their periods one time or other, and when that time came, all endeavours to preserve liberty were fruitless; and shrewd hints were given in that letter, that England was reduced to such a condition; that our corruptions were so great, and the dissatisfaction of the people was so general, that the publick safety could not be preserved, but by increasing the power of the crown: And this argument was used by those shameless men, who had caused all that corruption, and all that dissatisfaction.

But that gentleman and his followers were soon taught to speak other language: They were removed from the capacity of perplexing publick affairs any more: The nation shewed a spirit that would not submit to slavery; and their unhappy and betrayed master, from being the most popular prince who ever sat upon the

9. Fulling-mills: mills in which cloth is processed.

1. *A letter ballancing the necessity of keeping a land-force in times of peace: with the dangers that may follow on it* ([London], 1697). The letter, defending a standing army, was written by John, Baron Somers, and published anonymously. Later in the same year Trenchard replied anonymously in *A letter from the Author of the Argument against a Standing Army, to the Author of the Ballancing Letter* ([London], 1697).

English throne, became, through the treachery of his servants, suspected by many of his best subjects, and was rendered unable by their jealousies, to defend himself and them; and so considerable a faction was formed against his administration, that no good man can recollect, without concern and horror, on the difficulties which that great and good King was reduced to grapple with during the remainder of his troublesome reign.[2]

I have lately met with some creatures and tools of power, who speak the same language now: They tell us that matters are come to that pass, that we must either receive the Pretender, or keep him out with bribes and standing armies; that the nation is so corrupt, that there is no governing it by any other means; and, in short, that we must submit to this great evil, to prevent a greater: As if any mischief could be more terrible than the highest and most terrible of all mischiefs, universal corruption, and a military government. It is indeed impossible for the subtlety of traitors, the malice of devils, or for the cunning and cruelty of our most implacable enemies, to suggest stronger motives for the undermining and overthrow of our excellent establishment, which is built upon the destruction of tyranny, and can stand upon no other bottom. It is madness in extremity, to hope that a government founded upon liberty, and the free choice of the assertors of it, can be supported by other principles; and whoever would maintain it by contrary ones, intends to blow it up, let him allege what he will. This gives me every day new reasons to believe what I have long suspected; for if ever a question should arise, whether a nation shall submit to certain rules, or struggle for a remedy? these gentlemen well know which side they will choose, and certainly intend that which they must choose.

I am willing to think, that these impotent babblers speak not the sense of their superiors, but would make servile court to them from topics which they abhor. Their superiors must know,

2. In late 1697 King William urged that England continue to maintain a large standing army despite the recent signing of the Treaty of Ryswick with Louis XIV. The Commons, who by virtue of these recommendatons lost confidence in the King and his Whig ministers, resolutely opposed the King's recommendations. The animosity between William and the Commons engendered by this conflict was to mark the remainder of the King's reign.

that it is raving and frenzy to affirm, that a free people can be long governed by impotent terrors; that millions will consent to be ruined by the corruptions of a few; or that those few will join in their ruin any longer than the corruption lasts: That every day new and greater demands will rise upon the corrupters; that no revenue, how great soever, will feed the voraciousness of the corrupted; and that every disappointment will make them turn upon the oppressors of their country, and fall into its true interest and their own: That there is no way in nature to preserve a revolution in government, but by making the people easy under it, and shewing them their interest in it, and that corruption, bribery, and terrors, will make no lasting friends, but infinite and implacable enemies; and that the best security of a prince amongst a free people, is the affections of his people; which he can always gain, by making their interest his own, and by shewing that all his views tend to their good. They will then, as they love themselves, love him, and defend him who defends them. Upon this faithful basis his safety will be better established than upon the ambitious and variable leaders of a few legions, who may be corrupted, disobliged, or surprised, and often have been so; and hence great revolutions have been brought about, and great nations undone, only by the revolt of single regiments.

Shew a nation their interest, and they will certainly fall into it: A whole people can have no ambition but to be governed justly; and when they are so, the intrigues and dissatisfactions of particulars will fall upon their own heads. What has any of our former courts ever got by corruption, but to disaffect the people, and weaken themselves? Let us now think of other methods, if it be only for the sake of the experiment. The ways of corruption have been tried long enough in past administrations: Let us try in this what publick honesty will do; and not condemn it before we have fully proved it, and found it ineffectual; and it will be time enough to try other methods when this fails.

That we must either receive the Pretender, or keep up great armies to keep him out, is frightful and unnatural language to English ears. It is an odd way of dealing with us, that of offering us, or forcing upon us, an alternative, where the side which they would recommend is full as formidable as the side from which they would terrify us. If we [are] to be governed by armies, it is all one to us, whether they be Protestant or popish armies; the distinction is ridiculous, like that between a good and a bad tyranny. We see, in effect, that it is the power and arms of a country that form and direct the religion of a country; and I have before shewn, that true religion cannot subsist where true liberty does not.[3] It was chiefly, if not wholly, King James's usurped power, and his many forces, and not his being a papist, that rendered him dreadful to his people. Military governments are all alike; nor does the liberty and property of the subject fare a bit the better or the worse for the faith and opinion of the soldiery. Nor does an arbitrary Protestant prince use his people better than an arbitrary popish prince; and we have seen both sorts of them changing the religion of their country according to their lust.

They are therefore stupid politicians, who would derive advantages from a distinction which is manifestly without a difference: It is like, however, that they may improve in their subtleties, and come, in time, to distinguish between corrupt corruption and uncorrupt corruption, between a good ill administration and an ill good administration, between oppressive oppression and unoppressive oppression, and between French dragooning, and English dragooning; for there is scarce any other new pitch of nonsense and contradiction left to such men in their reasonings upon publick affairs, and in the part which they act in them.

Of a piece with the rest is the stupid cunning of some sort of statesmen, and practised by most foreign courts, to blame the poor people for the misery which they bring upon them. They say, that they are extremely corrupt; and so keep them starving and enslaved by way of protection. They corrupt them by all manner of ways and inventions, and then reproach them for being corrupt. A whole nation cannot be bribed; and if its representatives are, it is not the fault, but the misfortune, of the nation: And if the corrupt save themselves by corrupting others, the people, who suffer by the corruptions of both, are to be pitied, and not abused. Nothing can be more shameless and provoking, than to bring a nation, by

3. See Letter No. 66 (Feb. 17, 1721).

execrable frauds and extortions, against its daily protestations and remonstrances, into a miserable pass, and then father all those villainies upon the people, who would have gladly hanged the authors of them. At Rome the whole people could be entertained, feasted, and bribed; but it is not so elsewhere, where the people are too numerous, and too far spread, to be debauched, cajoled, and purchased; and if any of their leaders are, it is without the people's consent.

There is scarce such a thing under the sun as a corrupt people, where the government is uncorrupt: it is that, and that alone, which makes them so; and to calumniate them for what they do not seek, but suffer by, is as great impudence as it would be to knock a man down and then rail at him for hurting himself. In what instances do the people of any country in the world throw away their money by millions, unless by trusting it to those who do so? Where do the people send great fleets, at a great charge, to be frozen up in one climate, or to be eaten out by worms in another, unless for their trade and advantage? Where do the people enter into mad wars against their interest, or, after victorious ones, make peace without stipulating for one new advantage to themselves; but, on the contrary, pay the enemy for having beaten them? Where do the people plant colonies, or purchase provinces, at a vast expence, without reaping, or expecting to reap, one farthing from them; and yet still defend them at a farther expence? Where do the people make distracted bargains, to get imaginary millions; and, after having lost by such bargains almost all the real millions which they had, yet give more millions to get rid of them? What wise or dutiful people consent to be without the influence of the presence of their prince, and of his virtues; or of those of his family, who are to come after him? No, these things are never done by any people; but whereever they are done, they are done without their consent; and yet all these things have been done in former ages, and in neighbouring kingdoms.

For such guilty and corrupt men, therefore, to charge the people with corruption, whom either they have corrupted, or cannot corrupt, and, having brought great misery upon them, to threaten them with more; is in effect, to tell them plainly, "Gentlemen, we have used you very ill, for which you, who are innocent of it, are to blame; we therefore find it necessary, for your good, to use you no better, or rather worse: And, if you will not accept of this our kindness, which, however, we will force upon you, if we can, we will give you up into the terrible hands of raw-head and bloody-bones; who, being your enemy, may do you as much mischief as we, who are your friends, have done you." I appeal to common sense, whether this be not the sum of such threats and reasonings in their native colours.

The partizans of Oliver Cromwell, when he was meditating tyranny over the three nations, gave out, that it was the only expedient to balance factions, and to keep out Charles Stuart; and so they did worse things to keep him out, than he could have done if they had let him in. And, after the king's restoration, when there was an attempt made to make him absolute, by enabling him to raise money without Parliament (an attempt which every courtier, except Lord Clarendon, came into), it was alleged to be the only expedient to keep the nation from falling back into a commonwealth:[4] as if any commonwealth upon earth were not better than any absolute monarchy. His courtiers foresaw, that by their mad and extravagant measures they should make the nation mad, and were willing to save themselves by the final destruction of the nation: They therefore employed their creatures to whisper abroad stupid and villainous reasons, why people should be content to be finally undone, lest something not near so bad should befall them.

Those who have, by abusing a nation, forfeited its affections, will never be for trusting a people, who, they know, justly detest them; but, having procured their aversion and enmity, will be for fortifying themselves against it by all proper ways: and the ways of corruption, depredation, and force, being the only proper ones, they will not fail to be practised; and those who practise them, when they can no longer deny them, will be finding reasons to justify them; and, because they dare not avow the true reasons,

4. In 1662, Charles II's first Parliament enacted legislation (13 Car. II, c. 10) granting the King and his successors a duty of two shillings on every hearth. The authority to levy this tax was granted in perpetuity.

they must find such false ones as are most likely to amuse and terrify. And hence so much nonsense and improbability uttered in
that reign, and sometimes since, to vindicate guilty men, and vilify
an innocent people, who were so extravagantly fond of that prince,
that their liberties were almost gone, before they would believe
them in danger.

It is as certain, that King James II wanted no army to help
him to preserve the constitution, nor to reconcile the people to
their own interest: But, as he intended to invade and destroy both,
nothing but corruption and a standing army could enable him to
do it; and (thank God) even his army failed him, when he brought
in Irish troops to help them. This therefore was his true design,
but his pretences were very different: He pleaded the necessity of
his affairs, nay, of publick affairs; and of keeping up a good standing force to preserve his kingdoms, forsooth, from insults at home
and from abroad. This was the bait; but his people, who had no
longer any faith in him, and to whom the hook appeared threatening and bare, would not believe him, nor swallow it; and if they
were jealous of him, restless under him, and ready to rise against
him, he gave them sufficient cause. He was under no hardship nor
necessity, but what he created to himself; nor did his people with-
draw their affections from him, till he had withdrawn his right to
those affections. Those who have used you ill will never forgive
you; and it is no new thing wantonly to make an enemy, and then
calumniate and destroy him for being so.

When people, through continual ill usage, grow weary
with their present ill condition, they will be so far from being
frightened with a change, that they will wish for one; and, instead
of terrifying them, by threatening them with one, you do but
please them, even in instances where they have no reason to be
pleased. Make them happy, and they will dread any change; but
while they are ill used, they will not fear the worst. The authors of
publick misery and plunder may seek their own safety in general
desolation; but to the people nothing can be worse than ruin, from
what hand soever it comes: A Protestant musket kills as sure as a
popish one; and an oppressor is an oppressor, to whatever church
he belongs: The sword and the gun are of every church, and so are

the instruments of oppression. The late directors[5] were all staunch Protestants; and Cromwell had a violent aversion to popery.

We are, doubtless, under great necessities in our present circumstances; but to increase them, in order to cure them, would be a preposterous remedy, worthy only of them who brought them upon us; and who, if they had common shame in them, would conceal, as far as they could, under silence, the heavy evils, which, though they lie upon every man's shoulders, yet lie only at the doors of a few. The plea of necessity, if it can be taken, will justify any mischief, and the worst mischiefs. Private necessity makes men thieves and robbers; but publick necessity requires that robbers of all sizes should be hanged. Publick necessity therefore, and the necessity of such pedant politicians, are different and opposite things. There is no doubt, but men guilty of great crimes would be glad of an enormous power to protect them in the greatest; and then tell us that there is a necessity for it. Those against whom justice is armed will ever talk thus, and ever think it necessary to disarm her. But whatever sincere services they may mean to themselves by it, they can mean none to his Majesty, who would be undone with his subjects by such treacherous and ruinous services: And therefore it is fit that mankind should know, and they themselves should know, that his Majesty can and will be defended against them and their Pretender, without standing armies; which would make him formidable only to his people, and contemptible to his foes, who take justly the measure of his power from his credit with his subjects.

But I shall consider what present occasion there is of keeping up more troops than the usual guards and garrisons; and shall a little further animadvert[6] upon the arts and frivolous pretences made use of, in former reigns, to reduce this government to the condition and model of the pretended *jure divino* monarchies,[7] where millions must be miserable and undone, to make one and a few of his creatures lawless, rampant, and unsafe.

T *and* G   *I am, &c.*

5. The directors of the South Sea Company.
6. See Letter No. 95 (Sept. 22, 1722).
7. Divine-right monarchies.

NO. 95. SATURDAY, SEPTEMBER 22, 1722.

Further Reasonings against Standing Armies.

SIR,

It is certain, that liberty is never so much in danger, as upon a deliverance from slavery. The remaining dread of the mischiefs escaped, generally drives or decoys men into the same or greater: for then the passions and expectations of some run high; the fears of others make them submit to any misfortunes, to avoid an evil that is over; and both sides concur in giving a deliverer all that they are delivered from. In the transports of a restoration, or victory, or upon a plot discovered, or a rebellion quelled, nothing is thought too much for the benefactor, nor any power too great to be left to his discretion, though there can never be less reason for giving it him than at those times; because, for the most part, the danger is past, his enemies are defeated and intimidated, and consequently that is a proper juncture for the people to settle themselves, and to secure their liberties, since no one is likely to disturb them in doing so.

However, I confess, that custom, from time immemorial, is against me, and the same custom has made most of mankind slaves. Agathocles saved the Syracusans, and afterwards destroyed them: Pisistratus, pretending to be wounded for protecting the people, prevailed with them to allow him a guard for the defence of his person; and by the help of that guard usurped the sovereignty: Caesar and Marius delivered the commons of Rome from the tyranny of the nobles, and made themselves masters of both commons and nobles: Sulla delivered the Senate from the insolence of the people, and did them more mischief than the rabble could have done in a thousand years: Gustavus Ericson delivered the Swedes from the oppression of the Danes, and made large steps towards enslaving them himself:[1] The Antwerpians called in the Duke of Alençon to defend them against the Spaniards; but he

1. Gustavus Ericksson Vasa, King of Sweden until 1560, led a successful revolt against Danish supremacy in 1523 and proceeded to consolidate the power of the monarchy.

was no sooner got, as he thought, in full possession of their town, but he fell upon them himself with the forces which he brought for their defence:[2] but the townsmen happened to be too many for him, and drove these their new protectors home again: Which disappointment, and just disgrace, broke that good duke's heart. Oliver Cromwell headed an army which pretended to fight for liberty; and by that army became a bloody tyrant: As I once saw a hawk very generously rescue a turtle dove from the persecution of two crows, and then eat him up himself.

Almost all men desire power, and few lose any opportunity to get it; and all who are like to suffer under it ought to be strictly upon their guard, in such conjunctures as are most likely to increase and make it uncontrollable. There are but two ways in nature to enslave a people, and to continue that slavery over them; the first is superstition, and the last is force: By the one we are persuaded that it is our duty to be undone; and the other undoes us whether we will or no. I take it, that we are pretty much out of danger of the first, at present; and, I think, we cannot be too much upon our guard against the other: for, though we have nothing to fear from the best prince in the world; yet we have every thing to fear from those who would give him a power inconsistent with liberty, and with a constitution which has lasted almost a thousand years without such a power, which will never be asked with an intention to make no use of it.

The nation was so mad upon the restoration of King Charles II that they gave him all that he asked, and more than he asked: They complimented him with a vast revenue for life, and almost with our liberties and religion too; and if unforeseen accidents had not happened to prevent it, without doubt we had lost both; and if his successor could have had a little patience, and had used no rogues but his old rogues, he might have accomplished the business, and popery and arbitrary power had been of divine institution at this day: But he made too much haste to be at the end of his journey, and his priests were in too much haste to be on horseback too; and so the beast grew skittish, and overthrew them both.

2. The reference is to Francis, Duke of Alençon and Anjou and brother of King Henry III of France. The incident described occurred in 1583.

Then a new set of deliverers arose, who had saved us from King James's army, and would have given us a bigger in the room of it, and some of them foreigners. They told us that the King[3] longed for them, and it was a pity that so good a prince should lose his longing, and miscarry: but he did lose it, and miscarried no otherwise than by losing a great part of the confidence which many of his best subjects before had in his moderation; which loss made the remainder of his reign uneasy to him, and to every good man who saw it. I remember that all men then declared against a standing army, and the courtiers amongst the rest, who were only for a land force, to be kept up no longer than till the King of France disbanded his, and till the kingdom was settled, and the people better satisfied with the administration; and then there was nothing left to do, in order to perpetuate them, but to take care that the people should never be satisfied: An art often practised with an amazing success!

The reasons then given for keeping up an army were, the great number of Jacobites, the disaffection of the clergy and universities, the power and enmity of France, and the necessity of preserving so excellent a body of troops to maintain the Treaty of Partition,[4] which they had newly and wisely made. But notwithstanding that the army was disbanded, no plot, conspiracy, or rebellion, happened by their disbanding. The Partition Treaty was broke; a new army was raised, which won ten times as many victories as the former; and Europe, at last, is settled upon a much better foot than it would have been by the Partition Treaty. The Emperor is as strong as he ought to be. The Dutch have a good barrier.[5] Another power is raised in Europe to keep the balance even, which neither can nor will be formidable to us without our own fault; France is undone, and the Regent must be our friend,

3. William III.

4. The treaties—there were in fact two—determining the disposition of the Spanish empire on the death of Charles II of Spain, who was childless. The first was signed in 1698, the second in 1700. William III of England felt it necessary to keep his armies mobilized during negotiations, especially since he viewed war with France as inevitable should negotiations fail.

5. Under the terms of the Barrier Treaty of 1715, the Emperor ceded to the Dutch the right to garrison a number of fortresses on the French frontier of the Austrian Netherlands as protection against an attack from France.

and have dependence upon our protection: So that some few of these reasons are to do now, what all together could not do then, though we are not the tenth part so well able to maintain them as we were then.

I should be glad to know in what situation of our affairs it can be safe to reduce our troops to the usual guards and garrisons, if it cannot be done now. There is no power in Europe considerable enough to threaten us, who can have any motives to do so, if we pursue the old maxims and natural interest of Great Britain; which is, to meddle no farther with foreign squabbles, than to keep the balance even between France and Spain. And this is less necessary too for us to do now than formerly; because the Emperor and Holland are able to do it, and must and will do it, without us, or at least with but little of our assistance; but if we unnecessarily engage against the interests of either, we must thank ourselves, if they endeavour to prevent the effects of it, by finding us work at home.

When the army was disbanding in King William's reign, a prince was in being[6] who was personally known to many of his former subjects, had obliged great numbers of them, was supported by one of the most powerful monarchs in the world,[7] that had won numerous victories, and had almost always defeated his enemies, and who still preserved his power and his animosity: His pretended son[8] was then an infant, and, for any thing that then appeared, might have proved an active and a dangerous enemy; and it was to be feared, that his tutors might have educated him a half Protestant, or at least have taught him to have disguised his true religion. At that time the Revolution and revolution principles were in their infancy; and most of the bishops and dignified clergy, as well as many others in employment, owed their preferments and principles to the abdicated family; and the reverse of this is our case now.

6. James II.
7. The King of France.
8. It was a tenet of Whig doctrine at the time that James Stuart, the Old Pretender, was a suppositious child.

France has been torn to pieces by numerous defeats, its people and manufactures destroyed by war, famine, the plague, and their Mississippi Company; and they are so divided at home, that they will find enough to do to save themselves, without troubling their neighbours, especially a neighbour from whom the governing powers there hope for protection.[9] The prince who pretended to the thrones of these kingdoms is dead; and he who calls himself his heir is a bigoted papist, and has given but little cause to fear any thing from his abilities or his prowess. The principles of liberty are now well understood, and few people in this age are romantick enough to venture their lives and estates for the personal interests of one whom they knew nothing of, or nothing to his advantage; and we ought to take care that they shall not find their own interest in doing it; and, I conceive, nothing is necessary to effect this, but to resolve upon it. Almost all the dignified clergy, and all the civil and military officers in the kingdom, owe their preferments to the Revolution, and are as loyal to his Majesty as he himself can wish. A very great part of the property of the kingdom stands upon the same bottom with the Revolution. Every day's experience shews us how devoted the nobility are to gratify their King's just desires and inclinations; and nothing can be more certain, than that the present House of Commons are most dutifully and affectionately inclined to the true interest of the crown, and to the principles to which his Majesty owes it. And besides all this security, a new conspiracy has been discovered and defeated;[10] which gives all occasion and opportunity to prevent any such attempts for the future; which can never be done, but by punishing the present conspirators, and giving no provocation to new ones: In both which, I hope, we shall have the hearty concurrence of those who have the honour to be employed by his Majesty; by which they will shew, that they are as zealous to prevent the necessity of standing armies, as I doubt not but the Parliament will be.

I presume, no man will be audacious enough to propose, that we should make a standing army part of our constitution; and if not, when can we reduce them to a competent number better

9. Spain.
10. The Atterbury Plot of May 1722.

than at this time? Shall we wait till France has recovered its present difficulties; till its king is grown to full age and ripeness of judgment;[11] till he has dissipated all factions and discontents at home, and is fallen into the natural interests of his kingdom, or perhaps aspires to empire again? Or, shall we wait till the Emperor and King of Spain have divided the bear's skin,[12] and possibly become good friends, as their predecessors have been for the greatest part of two centuries; and perhaps cement that friendship, by uniting for the common interests of their religion? Or, till Madam Sobiesky's heir is at age,[13] who may have wit enough to think, that the popish religion is dearly bought at the price of three kingdoms? Or, are we never to disband, till Europe is settled according to some modern schemes? Or, till there are no malcontents in England, and no people out of employments who desire to be in them?

It is certain, that all parts of Europe which are enslaved, have been enslaved by armies; and it is absolutely impossible, that any nation which keeps them amongst themselves can long preserve their liberties; nor can any nation perfectly lose their liberties who are without such guests: And yet, though all men see this, and at times confess it, yet all have joined in their turns, to bring this heavy evil upon themselves and their country. Charles II formed his guards into a little army, and his successor increased them to three or four times their number; and without doubt these kingdoms had been enslaved, if known events had not prevented it. We had no sooner escaped these dangers, than King William's ministry formed designs for an army again, and neglected Ireland (which might have been reduced by a message) till the enemy was so

11. Louis XV, who ascended the French throne on the death of his great-grandfather Louis XIV in 1715, was, at the time of the publication of this letter, twelve years old.

12. The exact meaning of the phrase is unclear. The term "selling the bear's skin" was used among stock jobbers to denote selling stock for future delivery that one did not yet possess, that is, selling short. In the context in which it is here used, the phrase appears to refer to the benefits from an alliance between the Emperor and the King of Spain, which are likely to be reaped before they are even paid for.

13. Marie Clementina Sobieski, daughter of King John of Poland, was the wife of James Edward Stuart, the Old Pretender. "Madame Sobieski's heir" is thus the Young Pretender, Charles Edward, who was born in late Dec. 1720.

strong, that a great army was necessary to recover it; and when all was done abroad that an army was wanted for, they thought it convenient to find some employment for them at home. However, the nation happened not to be of their mind, and disbanded the greatest part of them, without finding any of these dangers which they were threatened with from their disbanding. A new army was raised again when it became necessary, and disbanded again when there was no more need of them; and his present Majesty came peaceably to his crown, by the laws alone, notwithstanding all his endeavours to keep him out, by long measures concerted to that purpose.

It could not be expected, from the nature of human affairs, that those who had formed a design for restoring the Pretender, had taken such large steps towards it, and were sure to be supported in it by so powerful an assistance as France was then capable of giving, should immediately lose sight of so agreeable a prospect of wealth and power, as they had before enjoyed in imagination: Yet it seems very plain to me, that all the disturbance which afterwards happened might have been prevented by a few timely remedies; and when at last it was defeated with a vast charge and hazard, we had the means in our hands of rooting out all seeds of faction and future rebellions, without doing any thing to provoke them; and it is certain, that his Majesty was ready to do every thing on his part for that purpose, which others over and over promised us; and what they have done, besides obliging the nation with a Septennial Parliament,[14] increasing the publick debts a great many millions, and by the South-Sea project paying them off, I leave to themselves to declare.

However, I confess, an army at last became necessary; and an army was raised time enough to beat all who opposed it: Some of them have been knocked on the head, many carried in triumph, some hanged, and others confiscated, as they well deserved. And, I presume, the nation would scarce have been in the humour to have kept up an army to fight their ghosts, if a terrible invasion

14. The first Parliament of George I, 1715 to 1722, whose enactments included the Septennial Act, which extended the term of each Parliament to a maximum of seven years instead of the previous three.

had not threatned from Sweden;[15] which, however, was at last frightened into a fleet of colliers, or naval stores, indeed I have forgot which. This danger being over, another succeeded, and had like to have stole upon us from Cadiz, notwithstanding all the intelligence that we could possibly get from Gibraltar, which lies just by it; and this shews, by the way, the little use of that place: But we have miraculously escaped that danger too; the greatest part of their fleet was dispersed in a storm, and our troops have actually defeated in the highlands some hundreds of the enemy,[16] before many people would believe they were there. Since this we have been in great fear of the Czar; and last year one reason given by many for continuing the army was, to preserve us against the plague.

But now the King of Sweden is dead, the Czar is gone a Sophi-hunting,[17] the plague is ceased, and the King of Spain's best troops have taken up their quarters in Italy, where (if I guess right) they will have employment enough; and what are we to keep up the army now to do, unless to keep out the small-pox? Oh! but there is a better reason than that, namely, a plot is discovered, and we cannot find out yet all who are concerned in it; but we have pretty good assurance, that all the Jacobites are for the Pretender; and therefore we ought to keep in readiness a great number of troops (which are to sleep on horseback, or lie in their jack-boots) which may be sufficient to beat them all together, if they had a twelve-month's time given them to beat up for volunteers, to buy horses and arms, to form themselves into regiments, and exercise them; lest, instead of lurking in corners, and prating in taverns, and at cock-matches, they should surprize ten or twelve thousand

15. In early 1717 a complex conspiracy involving the Swedish minister in England was uncovered. The plot to restore the Pretender included an invasion of Scotland by Sweden, with whom George I, as Elector of Hanover, was already at war. During the period that information regarding the plot was published, numerous rumors circulated that a Swedish invasion fleet had been sighted off the British coast.

16. The Jacobite invasion of Scotland under the Duke of Ormonde in 1719 was in fact launched from Cadiz, using Spanish ships of the line. This fleet was scattered by squalls off the coast of Scotland while the small Jacobite army that was to meet it was defeated by royalist troops at Glenshiel.

17. That is, "the Czar is occupied in a war with Persia."

armed men in their quarters. I dare appeal to any unprejudiced person, whether this be not the sum of some men's reasonings upon this subject.

But I desire to know of these sagacious gentlemen, in what respect shall we be in a worse state of defence than we are now, if the army were reduced to the same number as in King William's time, and in the latter end of the Queen's reign;[18] and that it consisted of the same proportion of horse and foot, that every regiment had its complete number of troops and companies, and every troop and company had its complement of private men. It is certain, that, upon any sudden exigency, his Majesty would have as many men at command as he has now, and, I presume, more common soldiers, who are most difficult to be got upon such occasions; for officers will never be wanting, and all that are now regimented will be in half-pay, and ready at call to beat up and raise new regiments, and fast as the others could be filled up, and they may change any of the old men into them, which reduces it to the same thing. By this we shall save the charge of double or treble officering our troops, and the terror of keeping up the corps of thirty or forty thousand men, though they are called only thirteen or fourteen; and sure it is high time to save all which can be saved, and, by removing all causes of jealousy, to unite all, who, for the cause of liberty, are zealous for the present establishment, in order to oppose effectually those who would destroy it.

I will suppose, for once, what I will not grant, that those called Whigs are the only men amongst us who are heartily attached to his Majesty's interest; for I believe the greatest part of the Tories, and the clergy too, would tremble at the thought of popery and arbitrary power, which must come in with the Pretender: But taking it to be otherwise, it is certain that the body of the Whigs, and indeed I may say almost all, except the possessors and candidates for employments or pensions, have as terrible apprehensions of a standing army, as the Tories themselves. And dare any man lay his hand upon his heart, and say, that his Majesty will find greater security in a few thousand more men already regimented, than in the steady affections of so many hundred

18. That is, the reign of Queen Anne.

thousands who will be always ready to be regimented? When the people are easy and satisfied, the whole kingdom is his army; and King James found what dependence there was upon his troops, when his people deserted him. Would not any wise and honest minister desire, during his administration, that the publick affairs should run glibly, and find the hearty concurrence of the states of the kingdom, rather than to carry their measures by perpetual struggles and intrigues, to waste the Civil List by constant and needless pensions and gratuities, be always asking for new supplies, and rendering themselves, and all who assist them, odious to their countrymen?

In short, there can be but two ways in nature to govern a nation: One is by their own consent; the other by force: One gains their hearts; the other holds their hands. The first is always chosen by those who design to govern the people for the people's interest; the other by those who design to oppress them for their own: for, whoever desires only to protect them, will covet no useless power to injure them. There is no fear of a people's acting against their own interest, when they know what it is; and when, through ill conduct, or unfortunate accidents, they become dissatisfied with their present condition, the only effectual way to avoid the threatening evil is, to remove their grievances.

When Charles, Duke of Burgundy, with most of the princes of France, at the head of an hundred thousand men, took up arms against Lewis XI[19] this prince sent an embassy to Sforza, Duke of Milan, desiring that he would lend him some of his veteran troops; and the duke returned him for answer, that he could not be content to have them cut to pieces (as they would assuredly have been) but told him at the same time, that he would send him some advice which would be worth ten times as many troops as he had; namely, that he should give satisfaction to the princes, and then they would disperse of course. The King improved so well upon the advice, that he diverted the storm, by giving but little satisfaction to the princes, and none at all to those who followed

19. Angered by the attempts of Louis XI to consolidate and centralize political authority in France at the expense of its barons, the French nobility formed a League of Public Welfare and, allied with Charles the Bold of Burgundy, declared war on Louis in 1465.

them. The body of the people in all countries are so desirous to live in quiet, that a few good words, and a little good usage from their governors, will at any time pacify them, and make them very often turn upon those benefactors, who, by their pains, expence, and hazard, have obtained those advantages for them. Indeed, when they are not outrageously oppressed and starved, they are almost as ready to part with their liberties as others are to ask for them.

By what I have before said I would not be understood to declare absolutely against continuing our present forces, or increasing them, if the importance of the occasion requires either, and the evils threatened be not yet dissipated: But I could wish, that if such an occasion appear, those who think them at this time necessary, would declare effectually, and in the fullest manner, that they design to keep them no longer than during the present emergency; and that, when it is over, they will be as ready to break them, as I believe the nation will be to give them, when just reasons offer themselves for doing so.

T   *I am, &c.*

NO. 96. SATURDAY, SEPTEMBER 29, 1722.

Of Parties in England; how they vary, and interchange Characters, just as they are in Power, or out of it, yet still keep their former Names.

SIR,

The English climate, famous for variable weather, is not less famous for variable parties; which fall insensibly into an exchange of principles, and yet go on to hate and curse one another for these principles. A Tory under oppression, or out of a place, is a Whig; a Whig with power to oppress, is a Tory. The Tory damns the Whig, for maintaining a resistance, which he himself never fails to practice; and the Whig reproaches the Tory with slavish principles, yet calls him rebel if he do not practice them.

The truth is, all men dread the power of oppression out of their own hands, and almost all men wish it irresistible when it is there.

We change sides every day, yet keep the same names for ever. I have known a man a staunch Whig for a year together, yet thought and called a Tory by all the Whigs, and by the Tories themselves. I have known him afterwards fall in with the Whigs, and act another year like a Tory; that is, do blindly what he was bid, and serve the interest of power, right or wrong: And then all the Tories have agreed to call him a Whig; whereas all the while he was called a Tory, he was a Whig: Afterwards, by joining with the Whigs, he became an apostate from Whiggism, and turned Tory.

So wildly do men run on to confound names and things: We call men opprobriously Tories, for practicing the best part of Whiggism; and honourably christen ourselves Whigs, when we are openly acting the vilest parts of Toryism, such parts as the Tories never attempted to act.

To know fully the signification of words, we must go to their source. The original principle of a Tory was, to let the crown do what it pleased; and yet no people opposed and restrained the crown more, when they themselves did not serve and direct the crown. The original principle of a Whig was, to be no farther for the interest of the crown, than the crown was for the interest of the people. A principle founded upon everlasting reason, and which the Tories have come into as often as temptations were taken out of their way; and a principle which the Whigs, whenever they have had temptations, have as vilely renounced in practice. No men upon earth have been more servile, crouching, and abandoned creatures of power than the Whigs sometimes have been; I mean some former Whigs.

The Tories therefore are often Whigs without knowing it; and the Whigs are Tories without owning it. To prove this, it is enough to reflect upon times and instances, when the asserting of liberty, the legal and undoubted liberties of England, has been called libelling by those professed patrons of liberty, the Whigs; and they have taken extravagant, arbitrary, and violent methods to suppress the very sound of it; whilst the Tories have maintained and defended it, and put checks upon those, who, though they had risen by its name, were eager to suppress the spirit, and had appointed for that worthy end an inquisition, new to the constitution, and threatning its overthrow: An inquisition, where men were used as criminals without a crime, charged with crimes without a name, and treated in some respects as if they had been guilty of the highest.

Parties like or dislike our constitution, just as they are out of power, or in it: Those who are out of power like it, because it gives them the best protection against those who are in power; and those who have been in power have blamed it, for not giving them power enough to oppress all whom they would oppress. No power cares to be restrained, or to have its hands tied up, though it would tie up all hands but its own: Like sects in religion, who all abhor persecution, and disclaim its spirit, while it is over them, but fall almost all into it when they are uppermost. The papists among us make a great outcry against persecution and oppression; because, though they be protected in their lives and estates, their mass-houses are taken from them, and they are taxed double,[1] though they do not pay double: Yet it is most certain, that their religion makes it a sin to tolerate any other religion, and obliges its votaries, on pain of damnation, to burn and destroy all who will not blindly, and against conscience, submit to its absurd and contradictory opinions, and to its impious and inhuman spirit.

The golden rule prevails little in the world; and no man scarce will bear, if he can avoid it, what almost all men will make others bear, if they can. Men who have the government on their side, or are in the government, will never see its excesses while they do not feel them; nay, they will be very apt to complain, that the government wants more power; and some, in those circumstances, have said, and called in God Almighty for a witness and a voucher, that it ought to be irresistible: But when they dislike the government, and the government is jealous of them, their tone is quickly and entirely changed, they are loud with the first against

1. The land-tax bill, first passed by the Long Parliament and reenacted annually, provided that the estates of Roman Catholics and nonjurors be taxed double. In addition, by virtue of a tax imposed by Parliament in 1722 (9 Geo. I, c. 18), an additional tax of £100,000 was levied on the real and personal property of the two groups.

the long hands of power, and its encroachments and oppressions, and often make faults as well as find them.

In King Charles II's reign, at the trial of Mead and Penn, for preaching (a great crime, in those days, out of a church) one of the King's Counsel declared, that he now saw the wisdom, necessity, and equitableness of the Spanish Inquisition, and thought that it would never be well with the church and monarchy, till one was established here; or words to that effect.[2] Now, can any one think that this wicked and impudent man, with all his malice against his country, would not have hated and dreaded the Inquisition as much as any other man, but that he was determined to be of the same side?

I never yet met with one honest and reasonable man out of power who was not heartily against all standing armies, as threatening and pernicious, and the ready instruments of certain ruin: And I scarce ever met with a man in power, or even the meanest creature of power, who was not for defending and keeping them up: So much are the opinions of men guided by their circumstances! Men, when they are angry with one another, will come into any measures for revenge, without considering that the same power which destroys an enemy, may destroy themselves; and he to whom I lend my sword to kill my foe, may with it kill me.

Men are catched, and ruled, and ruined, by a present appetite; and, for present gratification, give up even self-preservation. So weak is reason, when passion is strong! Most of the instruments of arbitrary power have been sacrificed to it as wantonly as they had sacrificed others; and were justly crushed under a barbarous Babel of their own raising. But that has been no lesson to others, who have been for complimenting their prince with a power which made all men, and themselves amongst the rest, depend for their life and property upon his breath; for no other reason, than that it made many others depend at the same time upon theirs.

2. The comments appear in the account of the trial, which occurred in 1670, written by the defendants themselves and published under the title *The People's Ancient and Just Liberties Asserted, in the Trial of William Penn and William Mead at the Sessions held at the Old Bailey in London . . . against the Most Arbitrary Procedure of that Court* (London, 1670).

Nothing is more wild, fickle, and giddy, than the nature of man; not the clouds, nor the winds. We swallow greedily to day what we loathed yesterday, and will loathe again to-morrow; and would hang at night those whom we hugged in the morning. We love men for being of our opinion, when we are in the wrong; and hate them afterwards, if they be in the right. We are enraged at those who will not renounce their sense, to follow us in our anger; and are angry at them for being angry, when we have made them so. We boast of being guided by our own sentiments; but will allow no body to be directed by theirs, if theirs thwart ours. We are governed by our own interest, and rail at those that are. We oppose those who will not purchase our friendship; and when they do, we oppose all that oppose them. Those who are for us with reason on their side, provoke us, if they are not so without reason. We commend human reason, and mean only our own folly. And our religion, however ridiculous, is always the best for all men, who are in a dangerous way, if they be not in our absurd one. If we adhere to our opinions, and will not alter our conduct, we cannot forgive those who will join with us; and if they do, we do not forgive them when we change, if they do not change too.

Thus inconsistent, foolish, and shameless, is the nature of men; selfish and prone to error. Methinks those who were once in our circumstances and sentiments, might, at least, forgive us, if, when they leave us and their own principles for a very bad reason, we still adhere to ours for a very good one: But this piece of plain equity is not to be expected. Men are so partial to themselves, that almost every man, if he could, would set up the arbitrary standard of his own will, and oblige all men blindly to follow it. The story of Procrustes is full of excellent instruction, and a lively emblem of human nature: That tyrant had an iron bed, which he seemed to intend for the standard of human stature; those who were too long for it, had their legs chopped off; those who were too short, had their bodies extended by a rack; and both the long and the short were made to fit the tyrant's bed. What is the Inquisition, what is tyranny, and what is any extravagant power, but Procrustes's bed? And who would not be Procrustes, if he had his will, in some respect or other?

The very name of France used to be an abomination to the Whigs: They hated the country for the sake of its government; and were eternally upbraiding the Tories with a fondness for that government. Who would have expected, after all this, that ever the Whigs, or any of them, could have spoken with patience, much less with approbation, of the French government? Any the least hint of this kind was shameful and unpardonable in a Whig. But there are Whigs, who, not content to shew their dislike and resentment of every thing said or done in behalf of liberty, and the English constitution, have boldly told people how such things would be rewarded in France: That is to say, the government of France is defended by galleys, wheels, racks, and dragoons, and we want the same methods here; for, if they dislike such methods, how come they to mention them? If men commit crimes against the English government, there are English laws to punish them; but if they be guilty of no crime against the laws of England, why are they thought worthy of the arbitrary punishments of France, unless those who think that they are, thirst after the arbitrary power of France? Or, if they mean not thus, why do they talk thus; and, shewing rage without provocation, scatter words without a meaning? I know no sort of Englishmen worthy of French chains, and French cruelty, but such apostate Englishmen as wish for the power and opportunity of inflicting them upon their countrymen, and of governing those by terrors and tortures, who despise weak capacities, and detest vile measures.

And have Whigs at last the face to tell us how they rule in France? Here is an instance of Toryism which every modern Tory, of any sense, disclaims and abhors; and which some modern Whigs have modestly avowed, and are therefore become old Tories. Thus do parties chop and change. One party, by railing with great justice at another, gets into its place; and loses it as justly, by doing the very things against which it railed.

By these means, and by thus acting every one of them contrary to their professions, all parties play the game into one another's hands, though far from intending it; and no party has ever yet found their account in it, whatever their leaders may have done: For the most part, a revolution of five or six years subjects them to oppressions of their own inventing. Others get into their seat, and turn their own hard measures upon them; nor can they complain, with a good grace, that they suffer those evils which they have made others to suffer; and their own conduct having been as bad as that of which they complain, they have not sufficient reputation to oppose the progress of publick mischief and miscarriages, which perhaps they began.

It is therefore high time for all parties to consider what is best for the whole; and to establish such rules of commutative justice and indulgence, as may prevent oppression from any party. And this can only be done by restraining the hands of power, and fixing it within certain bounds as to its limits and expence. Under every power that is exorbitant, millions must suffer to aggrandize a few, and men must be strangely partial to themselves and their own expectations, if, in the almost eternal changes and revolutions of ministries they can hope to continue long to be any part of those few.

G   *I am, &c.*

NO. 97. SATURDAY, OCTOBER 6, 1722.

How much it is the Interest of Governors to use the Governed well; with an Enquiry into the Causes of Disaffection in England.

SIR,

No man, or small number of men, can support themselves in power upon their own proper strength, without taking in the assistance of a great many others; and they can never have that assistance, unless they take in their interests too, and unless the latter can find their own account in giving it: for men will laugh at bare arguments brought to prove that they must labour, be robbed of that labour, and want, that others may be idle, riot and plunder them. Those governments therefore, which are founded upon oppression, always find it necessary to engage interests enough in

their tyranny to overcome all opposition from those who are tyran-
nized over, by giving separate and unequal privileges to the instruments and accomplices of their oppression, by letting them share
the advantages of it, by putting arms in their hands, and by taking
away all the means of self-defence from those who have more right
to use them.

But when a government is founded upon liberty and equal
laws, it is ridiculous for those in the administration to have any
hopes of preserving themselves long there, but by just actions, or
the appearance of just actions; and by letting the people find, or
fancy that they find, their own happiness in their submission. It is
certain, that people have so just a dread of publick disturbances,
that they will bear a great deal before they will involve themselves
in tumults and wars; and mankind are so prone to emulation and
ambition, and to pursue their separate interests, that it is easy to
form them into parties, and to play those parties in their turns
upon one another; but all parties will at last confer notes, and find
out, that they are made use of only as cudgels in the hands of
wicked men, to assault each other by turns, till they are both
undone. It is downright madness, to hope long to govern all
against the interests of all; and such knight-errants have qualifications only to be sent to Bedlam, or to be shut up in some other
mad-house.

People will for some time be dallied with, and amused with
false reasonings, misrepresentations, and promises, wild expectations, vain terrors, and imaginary fears; but all these hopes and
apprehensions will vanish by degrees, will produce a quite contrary
effect, and no wise man will think it prudent to provoke a whole
people. What could the late King James do against his whole people? His ministers betrayed him, his family deserted him, his
soldiers revolted from him: And it was foolish to expect any thing
else; for how could he hope, that those who could have no motive
to stand by him, besides their own personal interest, and every
motive to oppose him arising from conscience and honour, would
not leave him when that interest changed, and when they could
serve themselves better by serving their country?

I laugh at the stupid notions of those, who think that more
is due from them to their patrons, who are trusted to dispose of

employments for the publick benefit, than to their country, for whose sake, and by whose direction, those employments were first instituted, out of whose pockets the profits of them arise, and from whose confidence or credulity their pretended benefactors derive all their power to give them. Those who receive them, accept the gift upon the terms of the constitution; that is, to execute them faithfully for the publick good, and not to take the people's money to destroy the people.

What did the whole power of Spain do against a few revolted provinces, when all the people were enraged by oppression?[1] How many armies were lost, how many millions foolishly squandered, to recover by force what a few just concessions would have done at once? Her generals no sooner took one town, but two revolted; and they sometimes lost ten without striking a stroke, for one that they gained by the sword: What by the mutinies of her own soldiers, and other common events, which usually happen in such cases, they twice lost all together, and were forced to begin their game anew; and so destroyed a mighty empire, to oppress a little part of it, whose affections might have been regained by doing them but common justice.

It is senseless to hope to overcome some sorts of convulsive distempers, by holding the patient's hands, and tying him with ropes, which will only increase the malady; whereas the softest remedies ought to be used: Violent methods may stop the distemper for a little time; but the cause of the grief remains behind, and will break out again the more furiously. What did King James get by all his bloody executions in the west,[2] by his manacling us with chains, and keeping up a military force, to lock them on, but to frighten his friends, still more to provoke his enemies, and at last to unite them all against himself? And yet, I believe, I may venture to assert, that if, instead of throwing his broad seal into the Thames, and deserting his people, he had suffered his Parliament

1. The reference is to the rebellion in the Netherlands.
2. Trenchard is here alluding to the Bloody Assizes, the court circuit of the west country led by Lord Chief Justice Jeffreys following Monmouth's Rebellion in 1685. Jeffreys dealt ruthlessly with all those implicated in the rebellion, punishing hundreds by having them hanged, drawn, and quartered. He was rewarded with the Lord Chancellorship by James II.

to sit, and given up some of the instruments of his tyranny, and had permitted them to have taken a few proper precautions to have hindered it for the future, he need not have been a fugitive through the world.

It is certain, that if King Charles had made at first, and with a good grace, but half of those concessions which were extorted from him afterwards, that bloody war, so fatal to himself and his family, had been prevented, and the ambition or malice of his personal enemies had been suppressed, or turned to their own confusion, and he himself might have reigned a happy prince, with as much power as he had right to by the constitution: Whereas, if my Lord Clarendon [is] to be believed, the whole kingdom (very few excepted) took part against the court at first, and continued to do so, till some leading men in the House of Commons discovered intentions to overturn the monarchy itself.[3] And I will add further, that if some men, whom I could name, had set themselves at the head of these prosecutions against the South-Sea directors, and their directors, agents, and accomplices, and had proposed, or shewn an inclination to have come into effectual methods to have paid off the publick debts, and to have lessened the publick expences, the name of a Jacobite had been as contemptible as it is now dreadful; and a few constables might possibly have saved the charge of a great many camps.

It is foolish therefore to be frightened with apprehensions which may be removed at pleasure: The way to cure people of their fears, is, not to frighten them further, but to remove the causes of their fears. If the kingdom be disaffected (as its enemies of all sorts would make us believe), let enquiry be made into the motives of that disaffection. It cannot be personally to his Majesty, who is a most excellent prince; and his greatest opponents neither do nor can object to him those vices, which too often accompany and are allied to crowns: Nor is there the least pretence to accuse him of any designs of enlarging his prerogative beyond its due bounds; but on the contrary it is said, that he was content by the Peerage Bill to have parted with a considerable branch of it in

3. Edward, Earl of Clarendon, *The history of the rebellion and civil wars in England begun in the year 1641*, bk. II, sects. 93 and 94 (I.1.139–40).

favour of his people, whatever use others intended to make of that concession. It is certain, that when he came to the crown, he had a large share in the affections of his people, and he himself has done nothing to make it less.

It cannot be to his title, which is the best upon earth, even the positive consent of a great and free nation, and not the presumptive consent of succession: Besides, all his subjects of any degree have sworn and subscribed to his title, and the ink is yet wet upon their fingers; nor can any formidable number of them (whilst they are governed justly and prudently) have any motives to call in a popish pretender, educated in principles diametrically opposite to their civil and religious interests.

Whence therefore should such disaffection arise, if there be any such, as I hope there is not? And it appears plainly, that there is not, or that it is not general, by the dutiful reception which his Majesty met with in all places throughout his late progress in the west. And the same loyal disposition would appear more and more every day, if those who have the honour to be admitted to his more immediate confidence would represent honestly to him, how acceptable his presence would always be to his people.

It is childish to say, that a few flies and insects can raise a great dust; or, that a small number of disappointed and unpreferred men can shake a great kingdom, with a wise prince at the head of it, supported with such powers and dependences. A great fire cannot be raised without fuel, and the materials which make it must have been combustible before. And if this be our case, we ought to ask, how they came to be so? and, who made them inflammable? Who laid the gunpowder? as well as, who fired, or intended to fire, it? When we have done this, we ought to remove the causes of the distemper, allay the heat of the fever by gentle lenitives, throw in no more fiery spirits to inflame the constitution, but do all that we can to soften and cool it.

Every country in the world will have many malcontents; some through want and necessity; others through ambition and restlessness of temper; many from disappointments and personal resentment; more from the fear of just punishment for crimes: But all these together can never be dangerous to any state, which knows how to separate the people's resentments from theirs. Make the former easy, and the others are disarmed at once. When the causes of general discontent are removed, particular discontents will signify nothing.

The first care which wise governors will always take, is, to prevent their subjects from wanting, and to secure to them the possession of their property, upon which every thing else depends. They will raise no taxes but what the people shall see a necessity for raising; and no longer than that necessity continues: And such taxes ought to be levied cautiously, and laid out frugally. No projects ought to be formed to enrich a few, and to ruin thousands: for when men of fortune come to lose their fortunes, they will try by all means to get new ones; and when they cannot do it fairly, they will do it as they are able; and if they cannot do it at all, will throw all things into confusion, to make others as miserable as themselves. If people are poor, they will be desperate, and catch at every occasion, and join with every faction, to make publick disturbances, to shuffle the cards anew, and to make their own condition better, when they find it cannot be worse.

Wise statesmen will see all this at a distance; will use the best precautions, and most prudent measures, to procure general plenty, increase trade and manufactures, and keep the people usefully employed at home, instead of starving, and prating sedition in the streets. They will not be perpetually provoking them with constant injuries, giving them eternal occasions and reasons for dissatisfaction, and then quarrel with them for shewing it, and be still increasing their discontents, by preposterously endeavouring to put a stop to them by new shackles, armed bands, bribery and corruption, and by laying on them fresh burdens and impositions to maintain such oppressions; and so when they have raised resentment to the highest pitch, vainly hope to stop the tide with their thumbs. This is what the King of Spain did formerly in the Dutch provinces, and King James II lately in England, but what, I hope, will never be seen here again.

But it will be said, that people will be sometimes dissatisfied without any just provocations given to them by their governors: The necessities of all states will sometimes subject them to greater taxes and other seeming oppressions, than they can well bear; and then, like sick men, they will quarrel with their physicians, their best friends, and their remedies, and reproach all who have the direction of their affairs; as a countryman once cursed Cardinal Mazarine,[4] when his ass stumbled (perhaps justly, for the oppressions of that minister might have rendered him unable to feed his ass, and to keep him in good heart).

When this happens to be the case, there ought to be double diligence used to prevent any ill consequences from such disaffection: No war ought to be continued longer than is absolutely necessary to the publick security; nor any new one to be entered into out of wantonness, ambition, or, indeed, out of any other motive than self-defence: No more money ought to be raised than is strictly necessary for the people's protection; and they are to be shewn that necessity, and are to see from time to time, the accounts of what they give, that it is disbursed frugally and honestly, and not engrossed by private men, lavished upon minions, or squandered away in useless pensions to undeservers; and that the product of the whole people's labour and substance is not suffered to be devoured by a few of the worst of the people. For (as it is said elsewhere)

> What can be more invidious, than for a nation, staggering under the weight and oppression of its debts, eaten up with usury, and exhausted with payments, to have the additional mortification to see private and worthless men riot in their calamities, and grow rich, whilst they grow poor; to see the town every day glittering with new and pompous equipages, whilst they are mortgaging and selling their estates, without having spent them; to see blazing meteors suddenly exhaled out of their jakes, and their mud, as in Egypt, warmed into monsters?[*]

T   *I am &c.*

4. Jules Mazarin (1602–1661) was made cardinal in 1641 and succeeded Richelieu as prime minister of France in the following year, a position he retained until his death.

* Considerations upon the state of the nation, and of the civil list; written by Mr. Trenchard. [The correct title is: *Some Considerations upon the State of our Publick Debts in general, and of the Civil List in Particular*, p. 10. "Their mud, as in Egypt, warmed into monsters" refers to Moses' second plague (Exodus 8:1–15).]

NO. 98. SATURDAY, OCTOBER 13, 1722.

⅋ Address to the Members of the House of Commons.

SIR,

I have hitherto directed my letters to yourself; but I desire you will direct the enclosed to the illustrious deputies of the whole people of England. Not that I presume to think myself capable to inform them of their duty, or that they want such information, or would accept it from me; but I intend to shew my good wishes to my countrymen, and to prepare them to expect the blessed effects of their discreet choice; not in the least doubting but their worthy representatives will speak aloud the almost unanimous sentiments of the whole nation; and by so doing, preserve the dignity of the crown, and the liberty of the people whom they represent.

TO THE HONOURABLE MEMBERS OF THE PRESENT
HOUSE OF COMMONS

GENTLEMEN,

You have now the political power of all the commons of Great Britain delegated to you; and, as I doubt not but you will make an honest use of it, so will you have their natural power too at your command; that is, you will have their thanks, their wishes, their prayers, and their persons, as well as their purses, to serve your king and country. This is the greatest trust that can be committed by men to one another; and contains in it all that is valuable here on earth, the lives, the properties, the liberties, of your countrymen, and in a great measure of all Europe, and your own present and eternal happiness too. This great trust, Gentlemen, is not committed to you for your own sakes, but for the protection, security and happiness of those whom you represent. And you are accountable to your own consciences, and to the high tribunal of heaven, for the just execution of this great authority: Not to mention the applauses and blessings of millions of people, which will attend the faithful discharge of your duty; and the detestation, reproaches, and curses, with their other worse consequences, which ought to pursue corruption and bribery, and which I am sure you will never deserve.

You have, Gentlemen, the purest religion in the world to cherish and support; the interests, reputation, and security, of the best of princes to guard and defend: You have a great and populous nation, abounding with men of understanding, integrity and courage, imploring your assistance; whom you are obliged, by all the ties of gratitude, justice, and generosity, by all the laws of God and man, to protect and preserve: A people loaded with debts, enervated by war, and in former reigns plundered by miscreants, and just ready to sink under those burdens, unless they can receive sudden help from your healing hands. Here is a scene of glory, an opportunity put by gracious heaven into your hands, to exercise your virtues, and to obtain a reputation far above the tinsel triumphs of fabulous and imaginary heroes. Virtuous men could not ask more of providence; nor could providence bestow more upon mortal men, than to set them at the head of a corrupted and almost undone people, and to give them the honour of restoring their power, and reforming their manners. I cannot doubt, but these strong and forcible motives will call up all your virtue, generosity, and publick spirit; and inspire you with resolutions to assist our gracious sovereign in redressing all our grievances, and in making us once more a great and happy people. It is in your power to do so; and from your endeavours we hope and expect it.

Every man whom you represent has a right to apply to and to petition you for protection and redress, and with modesty and humility to complain of his own or his country's sufferings; and, by virtue of this undoubted right, I address to you in my own behalf, and in the behalf of millions of my fellow-subjects, who, next to God and our gracious sovereign, are to receive their preservation and whole happiness from your breath. Your own personal security too is nearly linked and blended with theirs; for you can make no laws, countenance no corruptions, nor bring or suffer any mischiefs upon your country, but what must fall upon yourselves and your posterity; and for these reasons, as well as from your known principles of honour and virtue, I assure myself that you will act for your own and the publick interest.

The most notorious conspirators, and chief instruments of power, who headed that detestable Parliament that gave up the liberties of a neighbouring nation, involved themselves in the general ruin, and were amongst the first who lost their estates.[1] Even the Pensionary Parliament in King Charles II's time stopped short, and turned upon that corrupt ministry, when the last stroke was levelled against our liberties: They well saw that when they should become no longer necessary, they would be no more regarded, but be treated as traitors always are by those who take advantage of their treason: for it is a steady maxim always with oppressors, to court and gratify the people whom they enslave, by sacrificing the instruments which they make use of, when they can be no longer serviceable; a maxim which discharges all obligations to them, and gives some recompence to their unhappy and undone subjects, by shewing them the grateful sight of their worst and most implacable enemies caught in their own snare.

View, Gentlemen, the dismal and melancholy scene before your eyes: Behold, not above thirty years since, a powerful nation engaged in an expensive, but successful war, for defence of their own liberties, and of all Europe; which might have been equally carried on with less money than is now paid for interest, without leaving us one penny in debt; but a nation in late reigns almost undone by the vile and despicable arts of stock-jobbers, combining with others, from whom we expected preservation, and now loaded with numerous taxes: Their finances discomposed; their trade loaded with various and burdensome duties, or manacled with exclusive companies; and in debt almost sixty millions; and by that means (as we have lately experienced) unable to contend with small powers, without every year increasing our debts and burdens; and no effectual method ever yet taken to pay them off, or lessen them, but always new methods found out to enhance the account.

1. The reference is to the regicides and leaders of the Commonwealth who controlled the Rump Parliament, which had fought and defeated the armies of Scotland. By the Act of Indemnity, enacted at the Restoration, some fifty of these regicides were sentenced to death, their estates reverting to the crown.

Sure, Gentlemen, none of you can hope that neighbouring nations will sit still, and not take advantage of our weakness; even those nations for whose sakes we are brought into this forlorn condition. The vicissitude of human affairs must bring new wars among us, though none among ourselves could find their accounts in courting them; and how think you, in such a circumstance, we shall defend our country? For my own part, I can see but one remedy at hand, and that is a dreadful one; unless we take speedy and effectual methods to lessen the publick expences, to cut off all exorbitant fees, pensions, and unnecessary salaries, to encourage trade, regulate our finances, and all defects in the administration; and by such means save all which can be saved, and apply it to the discharge of the publick burdens.

I wish that our dabblers in corruption would count their gains, and balance their losses with their wicked advantages. Let them set down in one column their mercenary gifts, and precarious dependences; sometimes half purchased with money, sometimes by dividing the profits with parasites, and always with the loss of their integrity and reputation; and on the other side, let them write down expensive contentions, and constant attendance in town to the neglect of their families and affairs, and a manner of living often unsuitable to their fortunes, and destructive to their health, and at least one fourth part of their estates mortgaged, and liable to the discharge of the publick debts; and, above all the rest, the insecurity of what remains, which must be involved in every species of publick misery: And then let them cast up the account, and see where the balance lies. This is not a fictitious and imaginary computation, like South-Sea stock, but a real and true state of the unhappy case of twenty dealers in corruption, for one who has been a gainer by it; without mentioning the just losses which many of them have suffered by the last detestable project.

Consider too, what a figure they make in their several countries amongst their neighbours, their acquaintance, their former friends, and often even amongst their own relations. See how they have been hunted and pursued from place to place, with reproaches and curses from every honest man in England; how they have been rejected in countries, and populous and rich boroughs, and indeed only hoped for success any where by the mere force of exorbitant corruption, which has swallowed up a great part of their unjust extortions. Then let them set against all these evils a good conscience, a clear reputation, a disengaged estate, and being the happy members of a free, powerful, and safe kingdom; all which was once their case, and might have continued so, if they had acted with integrity. Sure it is worth no man's time to change an estate of inheritance, secured to him by steady and impartial laws, for a precarious title to the greatest advantages at the will of any man whatsoever.

But even these corrupt advantages are no longer to be had upon the same terms. The bow is stretched so far, that it must break if it goes farther. Corruption, like all other things, has its bounds, and must at last destroy itself, or destroy every thing else. We are already almost mortgaged from head to foot. There is scarce any thing which can be taxed, that is not taxed. Our veins have been opened and drained so long, that there is nothing left but our heart's blood; and yet every day new occasions arise upon us; which must be supplied out of exhausted channels, or cannot be supplied at all. How think you, Gentlemen, this can be done? What has been raised within the year, has not been found sufficient to defray the expences of the year: And will any one amongst you, in times of full peace, consent to new mortgage the kingdom to supply the current service? And if you could be prevailed upon to consent to it, how long do you believe it can last, or you find creditors? And what can be the consequence of such credit? Sure it must make the payment desperate; and if ever that grows to be the case, what think you will be the event? Who do you imagine will have the sweeping of the stakes? Do you believe that those who brought your misfortunes upon you will pay the reckoning at last, or save themselves, by endeavouring to complete their wickedness? There is no way, Gentlemen, to prevent all these evils which lower over and threaten you and us, but by preventing or removing the causes of them; and I hope, that you will think it worthy of your best considerations, and most vigorous endeavours, to do so, rather than to suffer under, and be undone by, them.

By doing this great service to your country, you will not only consult your reputation, your own interests, and the interests of those whom you repesent; but in the most effectual manner will serve your prince, by making him a glorious king, over an happy, satisfied, dutiful, and grateful, people. A great and rich people can alone make a great king; their diffusive and accumulative wealth is his wealth, and always at his command, when employed for his true glory, which is ever their happiness and security; and the figure which he does or can make among foreign states, bears exact proportion to the affections which he has amongst his own people: If his people be disaffected, his neighbours and his enemies will despise him; and the latter will insult him, if they think his subjects will not defend him. And therefore, since nothing is wanting on his Majesty's part, to make him beloved, honoured, I had almost said, adored, by his people; it lies upon you, Gentlemen, to remove all those causes, which at any time hereafter, by the fault of others, may sully and blemish his high character. It is your duty and your interest too, to acquaint him with all miscarriages in the inferior administration, which you have frequent opportunities of knowing, and which is next to impossible he should otherwise know. Princes are seated aloft in the upper regions, and can only view the whole of things, but must leave the detail and execution of them to inferior agents.

T   *I am, &c.*

NO. 99. SATURDAY, OCTOBER 20, 1722.

The important Duty of Attendance in Parliament, recommended to the Members.

SIR,

I know not a more laudable ambition in any man, than that of procuring, by his credit with the people, a place in the legislature; and when it is procured this way, it is a testimony given by his country to his uprightness, and to his capacity to serve it. This is as high an honour as an Englishman can arrive at, and few but Englishmen can arrive at it; and the trust is still as high as the honour, and increases it. The liberty, the property, nay the virtue, credit, and religion of his country, are in his hands. Can heaven or earth afford stronger motives for diligence, probity, and attendance? When the happiness or misery, the security or bankruptcy, the freedom or servitude, of a nation, and all the good or evil which this life affords, depend upon his behaviour, he will find sufficient cause, from virtue, tenderness, and duty, to call up all his care, industry, and zeal.

But so it has often happened in the world, that all the activity and attendance, or most of it, have been on the wrong side; and as the evil that is in the world does infinitely over-balance the good, they who pull down are vastly more numerous, as well as more busy, than they who build up. Vice reigns amongst men, while virtue scarce subsists; and in many countries the publick has been as vigorously assaulted, as it has been slowly and faintly defended. Thus it is that liberty is almost every where lost: Her foes are artful, united, and diligent: Her defenders are few, disunited, and unactive. And therefore we have seen great nations, free, happy, and in love with their own conditions, first made slaves by a handful of traitors, and then kept so by a handful of soldiers: I mean a handful in comparison of the people, but still enough to keep them in chains.

So that in most nations, for want of this particular zeal in every man for his country, in which all men are comprised, the publick, which is every man's business, becomes almost any man's prey. It was thus under the first triumvirate, when Pompey, Crassus, and Caesar, three citizens of Rome, were, by the assistance of Roman armies, sharing out the Roman world among themselves: Nay, they procured the authority of the Senate, and the sanction of the people, for this monstrous three-headed tyranny over Senate and people; and procured it by means that will always procure it: Some they bought, others they terrified, and all they deceived, corrupted, and oppressed. The tribunes of the people, who were the people's representatives, and should have been their protectors, they bribed; and the people were betrayed and sold by their tribunes.

Such is the misfortune of mankind, and so uncertain is the condition of human affairs, that the very power given for protection contains in it a sufficient power to destroy; and so readily does government slide, and often start into oppression! And only by watching and restraining power, is this monstrous and dreadful transition prevented. For this good purpose we have Parliaments, to whom our ministers are accountable; and by whom the administration is supported, and its limits and power fixed. And to our having Parliaments, it is owing that we are not groaning under the same vile vassalage with the nations round about us. They had once their parliaments as well as we; but in the room[1] of parliaments their governors have substituted armies, and consequently formed a military government, without calling it so: but, whatever it be called, that government is certainly and necessarily a military government, where the army is the strongest power in the country: And it is eternally true, that a free Parliament and a standing army are absolutely incompatible, and can never subsist together.

By parliaments therefore liberty is preserved; and whoever has the honour to sit in those assemblies, accepts of a most sacred and important trust; to the discharge of which all his vigilance, all his application, all his virtue, and all his faculties, are necessary; and he is bound, by all the considerations that can affect a worthy mind, by all the ties that can bind a human soul, to attend faithfully and carefully upon this great and comprehensive duty: A duty, which, as it is honestly or faithfully executed, determines the fate of millions, and brings prosperity or misery upon nations.

Whatever has happened in former reigns, we have reason to hope, that none come now into Parliament, with an execrable intention to carry to market a country which has trusted them with its all; and it would be ridiculous to throw away reason upon such banditti, upon publick enemies to human society. Such men would be worse than cannibals, who only eat their enemies to satisfy their hunger, and do not sell and betray into servitude their own countrymen, who trust them with the protection of their property and persons. But, as I have heard that some men formerly, to whom this important trust has been committed, have been treacherous enough, through negligence, to sacrifice their duty to laziness or pleasure, I shall endeavour to shew the deformity of such conduct.

1. Room: place.

The name of a Member of Parliament has a great and respectful sound; his situation is attended with many privileges, and an eminent figure! All which make men ambitious of acquiring a seat there; though I am told that some of them have scarce ever appeared there. The glory and terror of the name was enough for them; which glory they tarnished, and converted into their crime and their shame, by neglecting the duty which was annexed to it, and alone produced it. Small and ridiculous must be the glory of that general, who never attends the duties of war, and is always absent upon the day of battle; or of a minister, who, while he should be making dispatches, or concerting schemes for the publick, is wasting his time at ombre,[2] at chess, or with a mistress.

It would scarce be believed, if it had not been felt, that the insensibility of men, as to all that is good and honourable, should go so far as to carry the directors and guardians of the publick to a cock-match, a race, or a drunken bout, when a question has been upon the stage which has concerned the very being of the publick. This passion for pleasure is strangely preposterous upon such occasions, and to follow it is cruel; cruel and disloyal to our country, and ever to ourselves. All our happiness, and consequently all our reasonable pleasures, are contained in the general happiness; and when that is gone, or lessened, through our neglect, we need not be surprised, but may thank ourselves, if in the publick misfortunes and curse we find our own.

When a pernicious question has been carried, it is a poor apology to allege, and had better be left unalleged, that *I was not there*. Why were you not there? Was it not your duty to be there? And were you not bound, by the solemn and awful trust which you undertook, to have been there? Had you been there, perhaps it would not have been carried, perhaps not attempted; or if both, you would have acquitted your own soul, and had the honourable testimony of your country, and of a good conscience.

Every body knows, that in the pensionary Parliaments, in Charles II's time, the session was almost always drawn out into a tedious length, on purpose to tire the members, and drive them all out of town, except the trusty creatures of the court, who were in

2. Ombre: a card game.

Parliament with no other view than to make a penny of their betrayed principles, and to pick the publick purse, for the promise of having shares with those who set them on. Were not the absent members answerable, in a great degree, for the treachery of those staunch and patient parricides, by leaving them an opportunity to commit it, when they knew that they would commit it? When a man leaves his wife with a known ravisher, and his money in the hands of a noted thief, he may blame himself if he suffer loss and dishonour.

Members of Parliament are set in a high place, as publick stewards and guards (the best and only sure guards that a free country can have) to watch for the publick welfare, to settle the publick expences, and to defend publick and private property from the unclean and ravenous hands of harpies; and they are obliged, by every motive that can oblige, to adhere to their station and trust: When the major part neglect or desert it, who knows but in times to come there may be always enough remaining to give it up, and be remaining for that very end? He who does not prevent evil when he may, does in effect commit it, by leaving others to do so, who he cannot be sure will not do it.

I have heard that some of these truants from Parliament have boasted that they never voted wrong: But how often have they been out of the way when they should have voted right, and opposed voting wrong? And is not this omission of voting well the next crime to voting ill? And where it is habitual, is it not worse than even now and then voting ill? He who commits but two murders is less guilty, as to the community, than he who robs ten thousand pounds from the publick, is a more innocent man than he who suffers it to be robbed of an hundred thousand: Or, if he who does not prevent a great evil, be less guilty in his own eyes than he who actually commits a less; the publick, which feels the difference between ten and twenty, must judge far otherwise, and consider him as the more pernicious criminal of the two, as they who are traitors within the law are the most dangerous traitors of all.

How ridiculous is it to take a great deal of pains, and to spend a great deal of money, to come into Parliament, and afterwards come seldom or never there, but keep others out, who would perhaps give constant attendance? It is foolish to allege, that the adversary is so strong, that your attendance will be useless; for it has rarely happened, that any dreadful mischief has been carried in a full house, or indeed attempted; but opportunities have always been taken from the absence of the country members. Besides, how often has it happened, that one extravagant attempt has given a steady majority to the other side? The Pensionary Parliament itself, in King Charles II's time, turned upon that corrupt court: King James's first loyal and passive obedience Parliament did the same, when he declared for governing by armies;[3] and in King William's time, the anti-court party, who for many years together could scarce ever divide above eighty or ninety, yet grew so very considerable, upon the attempt for a standing army, that the court, for several years after, could not boast of a much greater number of followers;[4] and though I confess that this produced many real mischiefs to the publick, yet the courtiers had no one to blame but themselves for it. How absurd is it for men to bring themselves into such a dilemma, as either to submit to certain ruin, or, in some instances, to hazard their lives and estates to get rid of it, by an unequal struggle; when both may be easily prevented, by doing what they have promised to do, what is their duty, and ought to be their pleasure, to do, and what may be done without further expence, than making an honest use of two monosyllables?

The notions of honour generally entertained, are strangely wild, unjust, and absurd. A man that would die rather than pick a private pocket, will without blushing, pick the pockets of a million: And he who would venture his life to defend a friend, or the reputation of a harlot who has none, will not lose a dinner, or a merry meeting, to maintain the wealth and honour of his country. There have been gentlemen of this sort of honour, who really wished well to the publick; yet, rather than attend to a debate of the utmost consequence to the publick, would with infinite punctualness meet

3. In 1686, James II requested and received funds for a standing army, one in which Roman Catholics would be permitted to obtain commissions. The demand, however, created a nucleus around which an intractable opposition to the crown developed.

4. William's regular requests for funds to underwrite a standing army finally helped cement opposition to the crown. The result was that after 1698 he was regularly confronted with a hostile House of Commons.

a company of sharpers, to throw away their estates at seven or eleven.[5] So much stronger is pernicious custom than publick virtue and eternal reason, which alone ought to create and govern custom; and so much to the publick shame and misfortune are such wicked customs, from the influence of which even wise men are not entirely exempted! So weak and wild a thing is the nature of man!

It is observed of Cato the Younger, that he always came first to the Senate, and left it last. Pompey and his faction, finding that he would never be persuaded nor frightened into their execrable designs against their country, contrived a thousand treacherous devices to keep him out of the way: But he saw their ill arts, and disappointed them. He said, that he entered upon the business of the state, as the business of every honest man; that he considered the publick as the proper object of his care, zeal, and attendance, and not as a bank for his own private wealth, or a source of personal honours; that it was a hideous reproach for men who are guided by reason, and by it superior to all other creatures, to take less care of the society to which they belong, than such insects as bees and ants take of their hives and common stores; that he would never prefer private interest or pleasure to that of the publick, and that none of those considerations should ever with-hold him from attending faithfully in the Senate.[6]

Here is a virtuous and illustrious example, which I would leave upon the minds of my readers, and particularly recommend to those who may most want it. When Caesar had, by all manner of wicked ways, by violence, by fraud, and by bribery, procured the government of Gaul and Illyricum for five years, with an army of four legions, with which he afterwards enslaved Rome itself; Cato could not reproach his own heart, that he had been absent when that fatal law passed: He opposed it with all his zeal and eloquence, and with the hazard of his life; and told those who made it, what they afterwards sadly felt, that they were placing an armed tyrant in their citadel.[7]

5. Seven or eleven: craps.
6. These observations appear in Plutarch, *Cato Minor*, 19.
7. The incident is reported in Plutarch, *Cato Minor*, 33.3–4.

Consider, for God's sake, Gentlemen, the extent and sacredness of your trust: Your country and constitution are in your hands: One unjust, one rash law, may overturn both at once, and you with them, and cancel all law and all property for ever; and one good and wise law may secure them to your latest posterity. Can it be indifferent to you, whether the one or the other of these laws pass? And if it be not indifferent, will you avoid attending? Be but as assiduous against evil as others have been for it, and you have a fair chance to prevent it for ages. Why should not honour, virtue, and good conscience, be as active and zealous as falsehood, corruption, and guilty minds? Consider the injustice, the barbarity, the treachery, and the terrible consequences, of sloth and absence. Liberty, when once lost, is scarce ever recovered, almost as rarely as human life, when it is once extinguished.

G   *I am, &c.*

NO. 100. SATURDAY, OCTOBER 27, 1722.

Discourse upon Libels.

SIR,

I intend in this, and my next letter, to write a dissertation upon libels, which are liberties assumed by private men, to judge of and censure the actions of their superiors, or such as have possession of power and dignities. When persons, formerly of no superior merit to the rest of their fellow-subjects, came to be possessed of advantages, by means which, for the most part, they condemned in another situation of fortune, they often have grown, on a sudden, to think themselves a different species of mankind; they took it into their heads to call themselves the government, and thought that others had nothing to do but to sit still, to act as they bade them, and to follow their motions; were unwilling to be interrupted in the progress of their ambition, and of making their private fortunes by such ways as they could best and soonest make them; and consequently have called every opposition to their wild and ravenous schemes, and every attempt to preserve the people's right, by the odious names of sedition and faction, and charged them with principles and practices inconsistent with the safety of all government.

This liberty has been approved or condemned by all men, and all parties, in proportion as they were advantaged or annoyed by it. When they were in power, they were unwilling to have their actions scanned and censured, and cried out, that such licence ought not to be borne and tolerated in any well-constituted commonwealth; and when they suffered under the weight of power, they thought it very hard not to be allowed the liberty to utter their groans, and to alleviate their pain, by venting some part of it in complaints; and it is certain, that there are benefits and mischiefs on both sides the question.

What are usually called libels, undoubtedly keep great men in awe, and are some check upon their behaviour, by shewing them the deformity of their actions, as well as warning other people to be upon their guard against oppression; and if there were no further harm in them, than in personally attacking those who too often deserve it, I think the advantages which such persons receive will fully atone for the mischiefs which they suffer. But I confess, that libels may sometimes though very rarely, foment popular and perhaps causeless discontents, blast and obstruct the best measures, and now and then promote insurrections and rebellions; but these latter mischiefs are much seldomer produced than the former benefits; for power has so many advantages, so many gifts and allurements to bribe those who bow to it, and so many terrors to frighten those who oppose it; besides the constant reverence and superstition ever paid to greatness, splendor, equipage, and the shew of wisdom, as well as the natural desire which all or most men have to live in quiet, and the dread which they have of publick disturbances, that I think I may safely affirm, that much more is to be feared from flattering great men, than detracting from them.

However, it is to be wished, that both could be prevented; but since that is not in the nature of things, whilst men have desires or resentments, we are next to consider how to prevent the great abuse of it, and, as far as human prudence can direct, preserve the advantages of liberty of speech, and liberty of writing (which secures all other liberties) without giving more indulgence to detraction than is necessary to secure the other: For it is certainly of much less consequence to mankind, that an innocent man should be now and then aspersed, than that all men should be enslaved.

Many methods have been tried to remedy this evil: In Turkey, and in the eastern monarchies, all printing is forbidden; which does it with a witness: for if there can be no printing at all, there can be no libels printed; and by the same reason there ought to be no talking, lest people should talk treason, blasphemy, or nonsense; and, for a stronger reason yet, no preaching ought to be allowed, because the orator has an opportunity of haranguing often to a larger auditory[1] than he can persuade to read his lucubrations: but I desire it may be remembered, that there is neither liberty, property, true religion, art, sciences, learning, or knowledge, in these countries.

But another method has been thought on, in these western parts of the world, much less effectual, yet more mischievous, than the former; namely, to put the press under the direction of the prevailing party; to authorize libels to one side only, and to deny the other side the opportunity of defending themselves. Whilst all opinions are equally indulged, and all parties equally allowed to speak their minds, the truth will come out; even, if they be all restrained, common sense will often get the better: but to give one side liberty to say what they will, and not suffer the other to say any thing, even in their own defence, is comprehensive of all the evils that any nation can groan under, and must soon extinguish every seed of religion, liberty, virtue, or knowledge.

It is ridiculous to argue from the abuse of a thing to the destruction of it. Great mischiefs have happened to nations from their kings and their magistrates; ought therefore all kings and magistrates to be extinguished? A thousand enthusiastick sects have pretended to deduce themselves from scripture; ought therefore the holy writings to be destroyed? Are men's hands to be cut off, because they may and sometimes do steal and murder with

1. Auditory: audience.

them? Or their tongues to be pulled out, because they may tell lies, swear, or talk sedition?

There is scarce a virtue but borders upon a vice, and, carried beyond a certain degree, becomes one. Corruption is the next state to perfection: Courage soon grows into rashness; generosity into extravagancy; Frugality into avarice; justice into severity; religion into superstition; zeal into bigotry and censoriousness; and the desire of esteem into vainglory. Nor is there a convenience or advantage to be proposed in human affairs, but what has some inconvenience attending it. The most flaming state of health is nearest to a plethory:[2] There can be no protection, without hazarding oppression; no going to sea, without some danger of being drowned; no engaging in the most necessary battle, without venturing the loss of it, or being killed; nor purchasing an estate, going to law, or taking physick, without hazarding ill titles, spending your money, and perhaps losing your suit, or being poisoned. Since therefore every good is, for the most part, if not always, accompanied by some evil, and cannot be separated from it, we are to consider which does predominate; and accordingly determine our choice by taking both, or leaving both.

To apply this to libels: If men be suffered to preach or reason publickly and freely upon certain subjects, as for instance, upon philosophy, religion, or government, they may reason wrongly, irreligiously, or seditiously, and sometimes will do so; and by such means may possibly now and then pervert and mislead an ignorant and unwary person; and if they be suffered to write their thoughts, the mischief may be still more diffusive; but if they be not permitted, by any or all these ways, to communicate their opinions or improvements to one another, the world must soon be over-run with barbarism, superstition, injustice, tyranny, and the most stupid ignorance. They will know nothing of the nature of government beyond a servile submission to power; nor of religion, more than a blind adherence to unintelligible speculations, and a furious and implacable animosity to all whose mouths are not formed to the same sounds; nor will they have the liberty or means to search nature, and investigate her works; which employment

2. Plethory: a morbid condition due to an excess of blood.

may break in upon received and gainful opinions, and discover hidden and darling secrets. Particular societies shall be established and endowed to teach them backwards, and to share in their plunder; which societies, by degrees, from the want of opposition, shall grow as ignorant as themselves: Armed bands shall rivet their chains, and their haughty governors assume to be gods, and be treated as such in proportion as they cease to have human compassion, knowledge, and virtue. In short, their capacities will not be beyond the beasts in the field, and their condition worse; which is universally true in those governments where they lie under those restraints.

On the other side, what mischief is done by libels to balance all these evils? They seldom or never annoy an innocent man, or promote any considerable error. Wise and honest men laugh at them and despise them, and such arrows always fly over their heads, or fall at their feet. If King James had acted according to his coronation oath, and kept to the law, Lilly-Bulero[3] might have been tuned long enough before he had been sung out of his kingdoms. And if there had been no South-Sea scheme, or if it had been justly executed, there had been no libels upon that head, or very harmless ones. Most of the world take part with a virtuous man, and punish calumny by the detestation of it. The best way to prevent libels, is not to deserve them, and to despise them, and then they always lose their force; for certain experience shews us, that the more notice is taken of them, the more they are published. Guilty men alone fear them, or are hurt by them, whose actions will not bear examination, and therefore must not be examined. It is fact alone which annoys them; for if you will tell no truth, I dare say you may have their leave to tell as many lies as you please.

The same is true in speculative opinions. You may write nonsense and folly as long as you think fit, and no one complains of it but the bookseller: But if a bold, honest, and wise book sallies forth, and attacks those who think themselves secure in their trenches, then their camp is in danger, they call out all hands to

---

3. "Lilli-Bulero" was the title of a British marching song ridiculing the Irish and James II. The tune was immensely popular during the Revolution of 1688.

arms, and their enemy is to be destroyed by fire, sword, or fraud. But it is senseless to think that any truth can suffer by being thoroughly searched, or examined into; or that the discovery of it can prejudice true religion, equal government, or the happiness of society, in any respect: Truth has so many advantages above error, that she wants only to be shewn, to gain admiration and esteem; and we see every day that she breaks the bonds of tyranny and fraud, and shines through the mists of superstition and ignorance: and what then would she do, if these barriers were removed, and her fetters taken off?

Notwithstanding all this, I would not be understood, by what I have said, to argue, that men should have an uncontrolled liberty to calumniate their superiors, or one another; decency, good manners, and the peace of society, forbid it: But I would not destroy this liberty by methods which will inevitably destroy all liberty. We have very good laws to punish any abuses of this kind already, and I well approve them, whilst they are prudently and honestly executed, which I really believe they have for the most part been since the Revolution: But as it cannot be denied, that they have been formerly made the stales of ambition and tyranny, to oppress any man who durst assert the laws of his country, or the true Christian religion; so I hope that the gentlemen skilled in the profession of the law will forgive me, if I entrench a little upon their province, and endeavour to fix stated bounds for the interpretation and execution of them; which shall be the subject of my next letter.

T   *I am, &c.*

NO. 101. SATURDAY, NOVEMBER 3, 1722.

꣸   *Second Discourse upon Libels.*

SIR,

I have been told that in some former reigns, when the attorney-general took it in his head to make innocent or doubtful expressions criminal by the help of forced innuendos, the method of proceeding was as follows: If the counsel for the prisoner insisted, that the words carried no seditious meaning, but might and ought to be understood in a reasonable sense; he was answered, that his exception would be saved to him upon arrest of judgment;[1] in the mean time the information was tried, and the malign intention of the words was aggravated and left to a willing jury; and then, upon a motion in behalf of the prisoner, to arrest judgment, because the words were not criminal in law, he was told, that the jury were judges of the intention; and having found it an ill one, it was too late to take the exception. Whether this was ever the truth, I have not lived long enough to affirm from my own knowledge; or, whether this method of proceeding be law now, I have not skill enough in that science to determine: But I think I may justly say, that if it be law, it is worth the consideration of our legislature whether it ought to continue so.

It is certain, that there is no middle in nature, between judging by fixed and steady rules, and judging according to discretion, which is another word for fancy, avarice, resentment, or ambition, when supported by power, or freed from fear. And I have said in my former letter,[2] that as there can be no convenience but has an inconvenience attending it, so both these methods of judging are liable to objections. There is a constant war between the legislature and the pleader; and no law was ever enacted with so much circumspection, but flaws were found out afterwards in it, and it did not answer all the purposes intended by the law-makers; nor can any positive law be framed with so much contrivance, but artful men will slip out of it, and particularly in relation to libels. There are so many equivoques[3] in language, so many sneers in expression, which naturally carry one meaning, and yet may intend another, that it is impossible by any fixed and stated rules to determine the intention, and punish all who deserve to be punished. But to get rid of this inconvenience at the expence of giving any man, or number of men, a discretionary power to judge

1. That is, that the defendant's objection to the ruling of the court should be reserved to requesting a stay of the court's final judgment.
2. See Letter No. 100 (Oct. 27, 1722).
3. Equivoques: expressions capable of more than one meaning.

another's intentions to be criminal, when his words do not plainly denote them to be so, is subverting all liberty, and subjecting all men to the caprices, to the arbitrary and wild will, of those in power. A text in scripture cannot be quoted, without being said to reflect on those who break it; nor the ten commandments read, without abusing all princes and great men, who often act against them all.

I must therefore beg leave to think, that it is a strange assertion, which, as I have heard, has been advanced by lawyers in Westminster-Hall;[4] *viz.* That it is an absurdity to affirm, that a judge and jury are the only people in England who are not to understand an author's meaning; which, I think, may be true in many instances, when they act judicially, and the words which he uses, candidly construed, do not import that meaning, Tiberius put many Senators to death, for looking melancholy or dissatisfied, or enviously at his power; and Nero many others, for not laughing at his play, or laughing in the wrong place, or sneering instead of laughing; and very probably both judged right in their intentions; but sure no body will think amongst us, that such examples ought to be copied. A man, by not pulling off his hat, or not low enough, by a turn upon his heel, by a frowning countenance, or an over-pleasant one, may induce his spectators to believe that he intends a disrespect to one to whom it is criminal to own it; yet it would be a strange act of power to punish him for this unobservance. So words may be certainly chosen with such art, or want of it, that they may naturally carry a compliment, and perhaps may mean it; and yet other people, by knowing that the person intended does not deserve one, may think him abused. And if this way of judging may be indulged in Westminster-Hall, the Lord have mercy upon poets, and the writers of dedications, and of the epitaphs too upon great men. Surely it is of less consequence to mankind, that a witty author should now and then escape unpunished, than that all men should hold their tongues, or not learn to write, or cease writing.

I do agree, when the natural and genuine meaning and purport of words and expressions in libelous writings carry a crimi-

4. During the eighteenth century, the courts of common law sat at Westminster.

nal intention, that the writer ought not to escape punishment by subterfuge or evasion, or by a sly interpretation hid in a corner, and intended only for a court of justice, nor by annexing new names to known things, or by using circumlocutions instead of single sounds and expressions; for words are only arbitrary signs of ideas; and if any man will coin new words to old ideas, or annex new ideas to old words, and let this meaning be fully understood, without doubt he is answerable for it. But when words used in their true and proper sense, and understood in their literal and natural meaning, import nothing that is criminal; then to strain their genuine signification to make them intend sedition (which possibly the author might intend too) is such a stretch of discretionary power, as must subvert all the principles of free government, and overturn every species of liberty. I own, that with such a power, some men may escape censure who deserve censure, but with it no man can be safe; and it is certain, that few men or states will be aggrieved by this indulgence, but such as deserve much worse usage.

It is a maxim of politicks in despotick governments, that twenty innocent persons ought to be punished, rather than one guilty man escape; but the reverse of this is true in free states,[5] in the ordinary course of justice: For since no law can be invented which can give power enough to their magistrates to reach every criminal, without giving them, by the abuse of the same law, a power to punish innocence and virtue, the greater evil ought to be avoided: And therefore when an innocent or criminal sense can be put upon words or actions, the meaning of which is not fully determined by other words or actions, the most beneficent construction ought to be made in favour of the person accused. The cause of liberty, and the good of the whole, ought to prevail, and to get the better of the just resentment otherwise due to the impertinence of a factious scribbler, or the impotent malice of a turbulent babbler.

This truth every man acknowledges, when it becomes his own case, or the case of his friends or party; and almost every man complains of it when he suffers by it: So great is the difference of

5. This maxim later appears in William Blackstone's *Commentaries on the Laws of England*, bk. 4, chap. 27 (IV:322 of the 1765–69 edition).

men's having power in their hands or upon their shoulders! But at present, I think that no party amongst us can find their account either in the suppression or in the restraint of the press, or in being very severe in their animadversion upon the liberties taken by it. The independent Whigs think all liberty to depend upon freedom of speech, and freedom of writing, within the bounds of manners and discretion, as conceiving that there is often no other way left to be heard by their superiors, nor to apprize their countrymen of designs and conspiracies against their safety; which they think ought to be done boldly, though in respect to authority, as modestly as can be consistent with the making themselves understood; and such among them as have lately quitted their independence, think themselves obliged to handle a subject tenderly, upon which they have exerted themselves very strenuously in another circumstance of fortune.

Very many of the Tories, who may be at present ranked amongst the former sort of men, and who every day see more and more the advantages of liberty, and forget their former prejudices, will not be contented hereafter to receive their religion and politicks from an ignorant licenser, under the direction of those who have often neither religion nor politicks. And even the Jacobites themselves are so charmed with their own doughty performances, that they would not lose the pleasure of scolding at or abusing those whom they cannot hurt. Many of our spiritual guides will not be deprived of doing honour to themselves, and advantage to their flocks, from informing the world what they ought to believe by their particular systems; and the dissenting preachers are willing to keep their own flocks, and would not have the reasonableness of their separation judged of alone by those who differ from them, and have an interest in suppressing them. And I believe that all our world would be willing to have some other news besides what they find in the *Gazette*;[6] and I hope that I may venture to say, that there is no number of men amongst us so very popular, as by their single credit and authority to get the better of all these interests.

6. The *London Gazette*, the official organ for announcements by the government.

But, besides the reasons that I have already given, there is another left behind, which is worth them all; namely, that all the methods hitherto taken to prevent real libels have proved ineffectual; and probably any method which can be taken, will only prevent the world from being informed of what they ought to know, and will increase the others. The subjecting the press to the regulation and inspection of any man whatsoever, can only hinder the publication of such books, as authors are willing to own, and are ready to defend; but can never restrain such as they apprehend to be criminal, which always come out by stealth. There is no hindering printers from having presses, unless all printing be forbidden, and scarce then: And dangerous and forbidden libels are more effectually dispersed, enquired after, and do more mischief, than libels openly published; which generally raise indignation against the author and his party. It is certain, that there were more published in King Charles II's and King James's times, when they were severely punished, and the press was restrained, than have ever been since. The beginning of Augustus's reign swarmed with libels, and continued to do so, whilst informers were encouraged; but when that prince despised them, they lost their force, and soon after died. And, I dare say, when the governors of any country give no occasion to just reflexions upon their ill conduct, they have nothing to fear but calumny and falsehood.

Whilst Tiberius, in the beginning of his reign, would preserve the appearance of governing the Romans worthily, he answered a parasite, who informed him in the Senate, of libels published against his person and authority, in these words; *Si quidem locutus aliter fuerit, dabo operam ut rationem factorum meorum dictorumque reddam; si perseveraverit, invicem eum odero:*[7] "If any man reflect upon my words or actions, I will let him know my motives and reasons for them; but if he still go on to asperse and hate me, I will hate him again." But afterwards, when that emperor became a bloody tyrant, words, silence, and even looks, were capital.

T   *I am, &c.*

7. "If someone were to criticize me, I would be prepared to render an account of my words and deeds; if he persists, however, our enmity would be mutual." Suetonius, *Tiberius*, 28.

NO. 102. SATURDAY, NOVEMBER 10, 1722.

The Contemptibleness of Grandeur without Virtue.

SIR,

The first reasonable desire which men have, is, to be in easy circumstances, and as free from pain and dangers as human condition will permit; and then all their views and actions are directed to acquire homage and respect from others; and, indeed, in a larger sense, the latter are included in the former. Different ways are taken to attain this end; arts, arms, learning, power, but most of all, riches, are sought after; and when just and proper means are used to acquire them, the pursuit is reasonable, and always to be commended. But when they are gained by injustice, the end is frustrated for which alone they are valuable; that is, the respect is lost which they are intended to procure: For, who does not value an honest man in moderate circumstances, before another grown rich by oppression? Who does not esteem a steady patriot, who despises threats, bribes, and dignities, when they stand between him and his duty to his country, before an over-grown plunderer, who has sacrificed a nation to his ambition? Men will indeed bow down in the House of Rimmon,[1] but they detest the idol in their heart. It is all false homage. Such men are adored publickly, and cursed privately; and most of those who seem to adore them, would with much more pleasure follow them to the scaffold.

How many have we seen in our days, who are thought to have died martyrs to their pride and covetousness, hooted with the reproaches and detestation of every honest man in England, and, I doubt not, with the private curses of many of their own followers? And how many are there in all countries, who are never seen or spoken of but with contempt and indignation, even in the midst of greatness?

1. The temple of the Babylonian god of thunder in which the Syrian general Naaman felt he should bow down, despite having accepted the God of Israel as all-powerful (2 Kings 5:18).

What is there in this world worth being a knave for; especially a man's being so, who already enjoys all the conveniencies of life? Who would lose the just applause of honest men, wise men, and free men, for the servile incense of flatterers? How much more preferable is it, to make millions of people happy, and receive the grateful acknowledgments of a thankful nation, than to purchase their hatred and resentments, by making them abject, poor, and miserable, and themselves and their families so too in consequence? And what is all this for? To create false dependents, who flatter them, in order to cheat them, or otherwise make their advantages of them, instead of steady and true friends: For a certain degree of familiarity is necessary to friendship, or free conversation; without which no conversation is agreeable, or worth having. Few men take pleasure in the company of those who are much their superiors, who always strike them with awe, and most commonly with emulation; and what is got amongst them is generally spent among equals.

I have seen many supple and bowing guests at the table of a great man, whom, for his vanity, he treated magnificently, and at a great expence; none of which he would have kept company with in any other place, nor perhaps they with him. Men of virtue and understanding are conscious of their own worth: They will be sought after, and can be brought rarely to contribute to the pride, grandeur, and ostentation of those whom they privately hate, fear, or contemn: And therefore the latter, in their own defence, are obliged to associate with the most worthless part of mankind, with flatterers and parasites, hunters of good tables, sharpers, and pickpockets; which are the usual attendants and ornaments of their greatness. Their domestick followers are generally made up of insolent and debauched beggars, who fancy themselves to be gentlemen; and as they cheat their master to be so, so depending upon his protection, they insult his neighbours, ride over the country people, and are perpetually annoying the peaceable and industrious farmers and labourers, and giving examples of prodigality and lewdness; insomuch that an estate is some years' purchase less valuable that lies within the influence of such malignant constellations.

Their sons are educated in idleness, debauchery, and igno-rance; taught to believe, that greatness consists in pride, insolence, and extravagance; and so, for the most part, want every qualifica-tion proper to adorn their characters, to serve their prince or coun-try, or to direct their own conduct, govern their families, or manage their own estates; which generally become the property of their stewards, bailiffs, or debauched followers, whilst they them-selves often pay large interest to them for their own money, run in debt to tradesmen and mechanicks for the common conveniences of life, whom they either pay not at all, or pay treble values to; till at last their necessities make them submit to a paltry pension; and, instead of being the generous asserters of publick liberty, they become the mean and humble instruments of power.

Their daughters partake of this happy education; they are bred up to be above looking to their own families, or to know any thing of their own affairs; and, indeed, it is become a qualification now, to be good for no one thing in the world, but to dance, dress, play upon the guitar, to prate in a visiting-room, or to play amongst sharpers at cards and dice: And when they cannot be exercising these laudable accomplishments, they are always in the vapours and the spleen; and so they can get no husbands, or ruin those who are indiscreet enough to marry them. The necessities of their parents, arising from their profusion in all other respects, will not afford fortunes great enough to marry them to men of their own quality, who run into the city for grocers' and mercers'[2] daughters, to repair their shattered affairs, and generally use them as such. For all private gentlemen (whose alliance is worth court-ing) are ever afraid of her ladyship, and think themselves not wor-thy of so much honour; very few instances excepted of vain and inconsiderate young gallants, who are caught with outside shew and pageantry, and drawn in to make great settlements, and repent it all their lives after.

I do not say that this is always the case: For virtue and good sense is not confined to any order of men or women; and without doubt there are excellent men and ladies amongst the quality. But I appeal to general experience, whether what I have

2. Mercer: textile dealer.

said be not most commonly the real truth. And who dares be so sanguine, as to hope that it will not be the case of his own posterity, if something be not done to mend the present education of youth; which never can be done, without mending that which must mend every thing else? For those who have an interest in keeping the nobility and gentry ignorant, debauched, and extravagant, and consequently necessitous and dependent, will never voluntarily endeavour to lessen their own power and influence.

This is indeed a melancholy, but true, scene of modern greatness. And is this a condition to be envied or courted by any who have plentiful (though not great and exorbitant) fortunes? who have all the means of enjoying private happiness, and of educating their children in virtue, knowledge, and publick principles, and can make a modest provision for them after their death; and, by leaving them examples of frugality, and prudent oeconomy, enable them to abound in the true necessaries and conveniencies of life; which the other (like Tantalus) want in the midst of profusion?

Nature is easily contented, and with few things. The most luxurious palate may be gratified by what moderate circumstances can afford. Those who have the most magnificent palaces, choose to live in the least and meanest apartments of them; and such as have the richest and most expensive clothes, and other personal ornaments, wear the worst when by themselves; so that all the rest are only pride and ostentation, and often procure emulation and ill-will from neighbours and acquaintance, but seldom true and real respect. However, since the mind of man, like every thing else in nature, is in constant progression, and in perpetual pursuit of one thing or other, I do not condemn the moderate pursuit of wealth, if we do not buy it too dear, and at the price of our health or integrity; for riches in a wise man's hands are certainly conducive to happiness, though they are more often the causes of misery to others.

Men, for the most part, are not so solicitous to acquire them for the real pleasure that they give, and to satiate personal appetites, as in compliance with the custom of the world. We seldom examine ourselves, but enquire of others, whether we are happy or not; and provided we can make those whom we do not value, and who do not value us, envy and admire our felicity, are contented to know that we have none. Such is the force of prejudice, flowing from foolish vanity, pride, or custom! True happiness resides alone in the mind; and whoever hunts after it elsewhere, will never find it. All the hurry and tumults of faction, most of the eager pursuits after vice under the name of pleasure, and the vain and noisy chases of ambition, are but so many disguises to cover internal uneasiness, and stratagems to fly from ourselves; but *haeret lateri lethalis arundo:*[3] The deer is struck, and where-ever he flies, must carry his griefs about him.

Nothing can fill the mind of a truly great man, but the love of God, of virtue, and of his country. All other pleasures ought to be but amusements, and subservient to these, and very often turn to misfortunes; but here is an inexhaustible source of inward satisfaction, which is the only true happiness, which wicked men never feel; and consequently they are the most unhappy of all men.

T   *I am, &c.*

NO. 103.   SATURDAY,   NOVEMBER 17,   1722.

Of Eloquence, considered politically.

SIR,

In free states, where publick affairs are transacted in popular assemblies, eloquence is always of great use and esteem; and, next to money and an armed force, is the only way of being considerable in these assemblies. This talent therefore has been ever cultivated and admired in commonwealths, where men were dealt with by reason and persuasion, and at liberty to ratify or reject propositions offered, and measures taken, by their magistrates, to examine their conduct, and to distinguish them with honours or punishments as they deserved. But in single monarchies, where reason is turned into command, and remonstrances and debating

3. "The lethal shaft clings fast to her side." Virgil, *Aeneid*, 4.73.

into servile submission, eloquence is either lost, or perverted to sanctify publick violence, and to deify the authors of it.

In the free states of Greece and Rome this popular eloquence was of such force and consequence, that the best speakers generally governed them; and their greatest orators were often not only their chief magistrates, but their principal commanders. Rhetoric was the first and great study, because the first and great offices of the state were the sure price of rhetoric. By it Cicero came to be the first man in Rome, and Pericles the first man in Athens. Themistocles, Thucydides, Xenophon, and Alcibiades,[1] could speak as well as they could fight: so could Sulla, Pompey, Caesar, Cato, Brutus, M. Antony, and many more; who were not only great orators, as well as great soldiers, but for the most part owed their military power to their powerful speaking. Not that eloquence is necessary to a soldier, no more than skill in war to a civil officer: But both were necessary parts, and indeed the principal parts of the Roman education; and the candidates for preferments were either good speakers, or supported by such. Pompey, though he principally derived his fame and credit from military glory, had been far from neglecting the other accomplishments of the gown and the bar. We have the testimony of Cicero, that he was a graceful and engaging speaker.[2] His great employments, and many wars, had with-held him long from the exercise of declaiming, and his eminent authority in the state had made it for some time unnecessary: But he resumed it with great application in the latter years of his life; when Curio, a young tribune of vast spirit and eloquence, being gained by an immense sum of money, to the interest of Caesar, was by publick and perpetual harangues misleading the people into his party. Cicero continued this exercise till near his death; and Mark Antony and Augustus in the midst of their wars.

The chief power of the state being in the people, and all the great offices in their gifts, made eloquence a necessary qualification in every one who courted their favour, and sought their suf-

1. *Themistocles*, Athenian democratic statesman and military leader of the early fifth century B.C.; *Thucydides*, Athenian military commander and the author of *The Peloponnesian War*; *Xenophon*, Athenian general and author; *Alcibiades*, Athenian general and statesman of the late fifth century B.C.

2. Cicero, *Pro lege Manilia*, 14.42.

frages. And a candidate thus qualified, rarely missed gaining them; till money, more prevailing than eloquence, and every other accomplishment, corrupted their hearts, abolished their integrity, and finding their souls and their voices saleable, made them first the market, then the slaves, of ambition. But in the times of their purity, before their virtue was vanquished by irresistible gold, which has been ever an over-match for the probity of the sons of men, it must be owned, to their honour, that in almost all the questions and debates in the Roman state, the justest side was the strongest; and he who spoke best, that is, with most reason and truth, had the most voices. Such was the equity and good sense of the Roman people! Even in the days of their degeneracy they gave many proofs, that it was with shame and pain they had departed from their ancient integrity and publick spirit: They continued to prefer many worthy citizens, merely for their worth: They carried Cicero, particularly, through all the considerable offices of the state, only because he deserved them. Cato they created their tribune, in spite of violence and opposition; and would have chosen him praetor, when he first stood for it, notwithstanding the influence and bribery of the faction of the first triumvirate, had they not been cheated and terrified by a religious lie of Pompey's, who by it broke up the assembly. Cato was however chosen next year; and, by the usual power of his eloquence and credit with the people, frustrated many of the pernicious designs of the triumvirate against his country, and consequently prevented, for a time, many public mischiefs, as he foretold them all.

The credit of eloquence among the Greeks was at least equally high, and its force as visible. However, in Greece itself it was differently esteemed and practised, according to the difference of the forms of government in the several Greek cities. In Sparta, where little riches were to be acquired, and the acting power of the state was chiefly in the Senate, the faculty of haranguing was less studied, in proportion to the smaller power of the people, who had only a negative vote, and the bare right of confirming or refuting the laws proposed to them, and none to debate about them, nor to explain them, much less to offer new laws. Their laws therefore, and their publick deliberations, being carried, as far as regarded the people, without popular speeches and cabals, that city was no proper scene for popular speakers; and, doubtless, it was the most perfect and best established state then in the world; but not being formed for conquest, nor indeed for trade, or increase of people, it was undone by an endeavour to enlarge it.

At Athens it was far otherwise: The multitude, the unrepresented multitude, being the legislature, governed all things, and were themselves governed by their orators; who therefore swarmed in that city, and filled all the great offices in it, as they always will do in such a state. They would never suffer any thing to remain fixed and quiet; but, to make themselves considerable, were for ever starting new projects, new treaties, and new wars; which, at last, ruined the state, as I shall shew in another letter.[3] Aristotle finds just fault with their demagogues, who were making them continually drunk with torrents of inflammatory eloquence. There wanted a proper power to check and balance that of the people;[4] the court of Areopagus being only a court of justice, and its credit and authority broken by Ephialtes and Pericles, two of the chief orators, who hated to see any authority in Athens but their own.

As eloquence itself is necessary, or checked, or quite discouraged, in different forms of government; so the manner of eloquence must vary, even where it is useful, according to the various classes of men to whom it is addressed. There is a considerable difference between the speeches spoken by Cicero in the Senate, and those which he spoke to the people. In an assembly of gentlemen, he who speaks with brevity and clearness, and strong sense, speaks best. The chief court is to be paid to the understanding; and silence is better than a rote of good words, that carry with them no conviction. I do not deny, but in the most polite assembly, the manner of speaking, the voice, and the choice of words, will considerably recommend the speech and the speaker: But it is equally true, that a theatrical action, and an ostentation of language, prejudice both, as they break in upon propriety; and, instead of adorning good sense, disguise it with shew and sound.

3. Although no subsequent letter is explicitly devoted to this topic, the theme is taken up in several (e.g., Letter No. 112 [Jan. 19, 1722]).

4. *Politica*, 2.12.4 (1274a).

But in speeches to assemblies of the people, much greater latitude is allowed; and vehemence of tone and action, a hurry and pomp of words, strong figures, tours of fancy, ardent expression, and throwing fire into their imaginations, have always been reckoned proper ways to gain their assent and affections. I think Valerius Maximus says of Pericles, that whenever he spoke to the people, he always left a sting in their souls: And hence, *sine armis tyrannidem gessit,*[5] he was a tyrant without an army. Demosthenes gave many proofs of the same dictatorial force of speaking, not only at Athens, but all over Greece; which, in spite of all King Philip's arts, and power, and ambassadors, and bribes, he worked up into a general insurrection and confederacy against him. The Thebans, particularly, though terrified by Philip's name and conquests, and dreading to risk again the calamities of war which they had lately felt, no sooner heard Demosthenes, but they were subdued by the dint of his words; and, losing all terror of the Macedonians, ran headlong into the war. "He inflamed their minds," says the historian,

> with a passion for glory and liberty, and covered all their wary considerations in the magical mist of his eloquence; so that, inspired by it, like men possessed, they took sudden, bold, and honourable resolutions.[6]

The substance and reasoning part of this potent speech might have been comprised in a few plain and short propositions, more proper than a copious harangue for a cool council of wise men, taught by experience to weigh every step which they took, and to examine the soundness of the sense divested of deceitful words: But such a summary and dry representation of the orator's meaning would probably not have moved a fifth part of his auditory; or had the oration itself been read by a clerk, or uttered by one of our pleaders in Westminster-Hall, in an unaffecting tone, and with an unanimated gesture, I doubt it would have had the same or no effect: But it was an oration, and an oration pronounced by an orator, with all the lightning of figures, and thun-

5. "He conducted a tyranny without arms." Valerius Maximus, 8.9.2.
6. Plutarch, *Demosthenes*, 18.3.1–3.

der of expression: He poured forth persuasion like a torrent; and in his voice, when he cried to war, they heard the sound of a trumpet.

By what I have said of our own pleaders, I mean no sort of reflections upon the gentlemen of the long robe, or upon their manner of speaking, which I think is the only proper manner for our bar; where the rules of proceeding being strict and ascertained, there is no room for haranguing. The judge is tied to the rigid letter of the law, and not to be moved from it by pity or resentment; and therefore an address to his passions would be ridiculous and offensive. In a speech to an assembly that acts by discretion, or to an absolute prince who has life and death in his hands, it is the business of the speaker, by flattering insinuations, to steal into the affections of his judges, and, by a hurricane of tropes and impetuous words, to animate their passions in his behalf: But a speech of this sort would be waste language in Westminster-Hall, and the author of it would be thought fit for Moorfields, where the imagination has more scope. At our bar many excellent pleaders have been very bad orators; and some good speakers, very bad pleaders. To know law, and to speak to the point, is the only rhetoric approved, or indeed allowed, there; and therefore the jokes which witty men have made upon the cold and plain manner of speaking there return upon the makers.

In the pulpit there is much more latitude for oratory, and the preacher has the affections and imaginations of his hearers much more in his power; and, by distracting them with terrors, or elevating them with joys, may awaken and enkindle their passions almost as much as he will. He has a vast field, and full scope for decorations, fine phrases, lively descriptions, and all the pompous array of language; and if he has a fine tuneable voice and his audience a good ear, I know no wonders which he may not work. But as the plainest sermons have generally the best sense and most piety in them, I am almost amazed that the very fine figurative ones do no more harm.

If we enquire into the use and purposes of eloquence, and into the good and evil which it has done, we must distinguish between eloquence and eloquence. That which consists of good sense, put into good words, is every-where useful and commendable: But as to that which consists of fine figures and beautiful sounds, artfully and warmly applied to the passions, and may disguise and banish sense, embellish falsehood as well as truth, and recommend virtue as well as vice; it has done some good, and infinite mischief. It is the art of flattering and deceiving, as one of the ancients calls it: It fills the mind with false ideas; and, by raising a tempest in the heart, misleads the judgment: It confounds good and evil, by throwing false colours over them; and deceives men with their own approbation: And it has in many instances unsettled all good order, and thrown flourishing states into pangs and desolation. But though rhetoric in this sense be but a bad art, yet I do not think it possible to destroy it, without destroying with it most other good arts; for it almost always flourishes and decays with them: And where-ever politeness, liberty, and learning subsist, rhetoric will be cultivated as part of them. It is an evil growing out of much good; and nothing but the abolishing of all liberty and learning can absolutely cure it. In this cure the Turks have succeeded best; and they who would be like them in this, must be like them in all things. Besides, as the several states of Europe are now constituted, they do not seem to have much, or any thing to apprehend from the power of rhetoric, except that which comes from the popish ecclesiasticks, who in the midst of monarchies form a democracy every-where; and every village has one of many popular orators, who have but too successful a talent at turning the heads of the multitude, and inflaming their hearts; a misfortune which has cost many countries very dear: Insomuch that preaching monks have been reckoned publick plagues; as it would be, no doubt, a sort of a publick blessing, if they were all alike idle and dumb. Even the Lutheran monks at Hamburgh are every day preaching that free city into strife and confusion; and will at last, if they are not better controlled, preach it out of its liberty, as more than once they have well nigh done.[7]

T   *I am, &c.*

7. From the late seventeenth century, Hamburg was the scene of bitter strife between pietists and orthodox Lutherans on the one hand, and aristocratic and democratic elements on the other; by 1708 the city had degenerated into chaos and mob rule.

NO. 104. SATURDAY, NOVEMBER 24, 1722.

Of Eloquence, considered philosophically.

SIR,

If we now enquire how eloquence operates upon the minds of men, we must consider three things or causes: The sense, the sound, and the action. The first is addressed to the understanding; and the other two to the passions, and have consequently the greatest force.

Nothing is too hard for sound, which subdues every thing, and raises the highest and most opposite perturbations. One sound lulls men to sleep; another rouses them from it: one sort sets them a fighting, another to embracing; and a third sets them a weeping: It makes them groan or rage; it melts them into compassion, or animates them to resentment. And as to action, in which I also comprehend the motions of the countenance, and of the eyes, it is of such force, that Demosthenes being asked, which was the first excellency of an orator? answered, *Action*; that the second was *Action*; and the third was *Action*.[1] Here is a testimony of a great and experienced judge.

Now the power of action seems to arise chiefly from hence: As it is a sign that the speaker is in earnest, and vehemently means what he speaks, it begets an opinion, that what he says is just, and reasonable, and important: And so his hearers adopt his passions and opinions, and are equally animated with him who animates them, and often more. Hence it is possible for a man, who thus carries his spirit in his gestures, and his meaning in his face, to look another into his sentiments and out of his senses, only by shewing, in the energy of his countenance, that he himself is strongly affected with that passion which he would convey to another, and that his external motions are but the result of his internal. Men have been converted into Quakerism at the silent-meetings of Quakers; and solemn looks, dumb shew, and ghostly groans, have had all the most prevailing effects of eloquence.

1. This appears in *De oratore*, 3.56.

Nothing is so catching and communicative as the passions. The cast of an angry or a pleasant eye will beget anger, or pleasure: One man's anger, or sorrow, or joy, can make a whole assembly outrageous, or dejected, or merry; and the same men are provoked or pleased by the same words spoken in different tones; because they who hear them, take them just as he who speaks them seems to mean them. I have seen a preacher of mean sense and language set a whole congregation a howling, merely because he himself howled. By repeating the words *heaven* and *hell*, with distortion and clamour, he possessed their imaginations with all the joys of the blessed, and all the torments and terrors of the damned; and, by making them feel both by turns, raised their passions higher than the reading of our blessed Saviour's crucifixion, or his Sermon upon the Mount, could have raised them.

The fancy when once it is heated, quickly improves the first spark into a flame; which being an assemblage of strong and glowing images, is, while it lasts, the strongest motion, and consequently the greatest power, in a man; for all animal power is motion. And when a man has thus got a fire in his head, his reason, which is the gradual and deliberate weighing of things, and the cool comparing of one inward pulse with another, must shift its quarters till his brains grow cool again. I dare say, that many men, and still more women, who have without emotion heard the great Dr. Tillotson talk excellent sense and morality for half an hour, would have been powerfully edified, that is, violently transported, with the tuneful and humble reveries of John Bunyan, of Bishop Beveridge, or Daniel Burgess.[2]

This aptness to be moved by sounds is natural, but improvable by education and the use of words. There are in the brain certain fibres, or strings, which naturally stretch and exert themselves as soon as certain sounds strike upon them; but without being able to annex to them any determinate idea, only, in general, that they feel pleasure or pain. It is like rubbing the hand of a man born deaf and blind with a file, or a flesh-brush: He feels the skin

2. John Bunyan (1628–1688), English religious writer, preacher, and author of *The Pilgrim's Progress*. William Beveridge (1637–1708), Bishop of St. Asaph. Daniel Burgess (1645–1713), Presbyterian ecclesiastic. All three were known for the power of their sermons.

irritated, or soothed, but knows not with what. When these fibres are touched, they disperse the motion to the whole animal spirits, and create in them motions and agitations according to the force and quality of that sound which was the first mover. Hence people are said to be cured of the bite of the tarantula by musick; which, by quickening the motions of the animal spirits, raises in the blood such a ferment, as drives out the poison.

But when description is added to those sounds, when they convey particular and distinct images, when scenes of horror or of joy are represented in sounds proper to convey them; then the sense and the sound heightening vastly each other, their united power over the soul is infinite and uncontrollable. The word *hell*, for example, is, without doubt, capable of being pronounced in such a hideous tone and action, as to affect and affright even a Hottentot, who knows nothing of hell: But if, with the sound of *hell*, the description of hell be likewise conveyed; that it is a dark, immense, and baleful dungeon, guarded by frightful and implacable furies, armed with whips and torches; that it is filled with suffocating and burning sulphur, and unintermitting fire; that it is inhabited by the damned, whose incessant shrieks, hideous roarings, and dismal yells, are the chief entertainments there; and by devils, who by their endless insults add, if possible, to their intense tortures and horrible burning, which are never, never, to end. . . .

> ————Sights of woe,
> Regions of sorrow, doleful shades, where peace
> And rest can never dwell, hope never comes,
> That comes to all; but torture without end
> Still urges, and a fiery deluge, fed
> With ever-burning sulphur unconsum'd————[3]

I say, this idea of hell, added to the sound of *hell*, would dreadfully aggravate the horror even in a Hottentot. He might likewise be charmed with a soft and melodious sound of *heaven*, well pronounced, without having any conception of heaven; but still much more charmed, if the idea of it accompanied the sound,

3. John Milton, *Paradise Lost*, I.64–69.

and all the celestial scenery of delight, a blessed immortality, God, and glory, were set, as it were, before his eyes.

Such force has sound over the human soul, to animate and calm its passions; and when proper action is added to proper sound, which two parts constitute the mechanical power of eloquence, the effects of it are as certain as the effects of wine, and its strength as irresistible. In this respect men resemble musical instruments, and may be wound up, or let down, to any pitch, by touching skillfully the stops and chords of the animal spirits. An expert hand can make a violin rage as violently, weep as bitterly, beg as heartily, and complain as mournfully, as words can express those several passions; and more than words, without proper modulation, can express them. Timotheus the musician played before Alexander the Great an air so martial and animating, that he started from the table in a warlike fury, and called for his horse and his arms; and by another soft air so quelled the hostile tumult in his mind, that he sat down quietly to meat again.[4] Thus was the conqueror of the world himself conquered by sound! Drums and trumpets make men bold: And the Marquis de Biron, one of the bravest men that ever lived, died like a coward for want of them.[5]

In a day of battle, when the onset is animated by all the awakening military sounds of a camp, the eager neighing of the horses, and even the busy and hollow treading of their feet; a general and warlike murmur of every man preparing to fight; the clattering of arms, calling into the imagination the sudden use that is to be made of them; the hasty thunder and vehement rattling of drums, inspiring an impatience for battle; the dead and sullen dubbing of the kettle-drums, creating a steady and obstinate bravery; and, above all, the loud and shrill clangor of the trumpet, rousing a cheerful and lively boldness: All these hostile sounds, each of them destructive of coldness and fear, must occupy and

4. The Timotheus to whom Gordon is here referring was a musician and poet from Boeotia who was reputed to have been a great favorite of Alexander. The events are recounted in Dio Chrysostom's *First Discourse on Kingship*.

5. Armand de Goutant, Baron de Biron, marshal of France. He was killed by cannon shot while on a reconnaissance mission at the battle of Epernay in 1592.

incense every spirit that a man has in him, set his soul in a flame, and make even cowards resolute and brave.

I have seen a beggar gain an alms by a heavy and affecting groan, when a speech of Cicero's composing, spoken without Cicero's art, would not have gained it. That groan struck the animal spirits sympathetically; and, being continued to the imagination, raised up there a thousand sudden conjectures and preoccupations in his favour, and a thousand circumstances of distress, which he who uttered it perhaps never felt, nor thought of. Looks and appearances have the like efficacy: Another beggar, shivering and naked in a cold wet day, with humble, pale, and hungry looks, or despairing ones, shall be as eloquent, without uttering a word, as the other by uttering a groan. The human sympathy in our souls raises a party for him within us, and our fancy immediately represents us to ourselves in the same doleful circumstances; and, for that time, we feel all that the beggar feels, probably much more; for he is used to it, and can bear it better. If to the above melancholy sound and miserable sight, we add the grievous symptoms of pain, sickness, and anguish (as one often meets with objects under all these terrible classes of misery), there is no pitch of human pity and horror, that such a group of human woes cannot raise.

Now, if single sound be thus bewitching, and gesture alone thus persuasive, and still greatly more when united; how vastly prevailing must be their force, when it comes arrayed and heightened by a swelling and irresistible tide of words, enlivened by the most forcible and rapid ideas, and bears down all before it? When the orator attracts your eyes, charms your ears, and forces your attention; brings heaven and earth into his cause, and seems but to represent them, to speak their sense, and to contend for their interest? When he carries your passions in his hands, suspends or controls all your faculties, and yet persuades you that your own faculties guide you? When he lessens great things, magnifies little things, and disguises all; his very gesture is animated, and every muscle persuades; his words lighten, and his breath is on fire; every word glows, and every image flames; he fills, delights, kindles, and astonishes, your imagination; raises a storm in your heart, and governs you in that storm; rouses all that is human in you, and makes your own heart conspire against you! In this magical and outrageous tempest, you are at the entire mercy of him who raised it.

Caesar was resolved to punish Q. Ligarius;[6] but Cicero had a mind to save him, and undertook his defence. Caesar admitted him to speak, only out of the gaiety of his heart, and for the mere pleasure of hearing him; for he was determined not to be shaken from his purpose. But he was deceived: Cicero in the very beginning of his speech wonderfully moved him, and proceeded in it with such a variety of pathos, and such an amazing grace, that Caesar often changed countenance; and it was plain that his soul was in a hurricane, and that all his passions were agitated. But the orator touching artfully upon the battle of Pharsalia,[7] so transported him, that he trembled all over; the papers which he held dropped out of his hands; and, being quite overcome, he acquitted Ligarius.[8]

What an amazing instance of the power of speaking! Behold the great and conquering Caesar, the absolute master of Rome, and of all the Roman world, provoked at a man who had borne arms against him, fixed upon his doom, and life and death in his hands! Behold this great and arbitrary man, this angry, awful, and prepossessed, judge, overpowered by the force of eloquence, disarmed of his wrath, his designs wrested from him, his inclinations, when he thought himself best fortified in them, entirely changed, and himself, from being terrible, brought to tremble! Caesar too was a great orator, and had often tried upon others, with success, the power of his own rhetoric; but was not then aware how much it could do upon himself. It was Cicero, it was the orator, and not the cause, that triumphed here. The bare sense of that fine speech would not have suspended Caesar's displeasure for a moment: But the speaker was not to be resisted: All opposition fled, and every spark of resentment vanished, before

6. Quintus *Ligarius*, Roman proconsul who had fought with Pompey's forces in Africa.
7. A plain in Thessaly, famous as the site of the battle in 48 B.C. where Julius Caesar's armies inflicted a decisive defeat on Pompey's forces.
8. Plutarch, *Cicero*, 39.5–6.

him. The emperor was enchanted by the orator; and Caesar was, as it were, possessed of Cicero.

I am, &c.

P.S. I have in these two letters comprised all that I purposed to say upon eloquence: In my last I have considered it politically, in this philosophically; and in both I have shewn its force. I have likewise examined the several kinds of it, as far as it affects my present purpose; and shewn, how it affects government and human nature, and from what sources in both it proceeds. Those who would study it as an art, and know the many accomplishments necessary to excel in it, must read Cicero *de Oratore* and Quintilian.[9]

G

NO. 105. SATURDAY, DECEMBER 1, 1722.

Of the Weakness of the human Mind; how easily it is misled.

SIR,

Things of the greatest seeming difficulty appear the easiest to us when found out. There was no wit necessary to set an egg on one end, when Columbus had shewn the way. Jugglers do many things by slight of hand, which to a gaping beholder appear to be witchcraft; and when he knows how they are done, he wonders at himself for wondering at them. A ship as big as a castle is sailed by a rudder and a puff of wind; and a weight, which a thousand men cannot move, may be easily managed by one, by the help of wheels and pullies. The same is true in the direction of mankind, who will be always caught by a skillful application to their passions and weaknesses, and be easily drawn into what they will be very difficultly driven. The fiercest horses are subdued by the right management of the bit; the most furious wild beasts tamed by

9. Marcus Fabius *Quintilianus* (c. A.D. 30–c. 95): together with Cicero, the greatest rhetorician Rome produced. His *Institutio Oratoria* is regarded as a masterpiece.

gratifying their appetites, or working upon their fears; and the most savage tempers are made tractable by soothing their foibles, or knowing how to manage their panicks.

This is what is called the knowledge of mankind, which very few of them know any thing of. Pedants hope to govern them by distinctions and grave faces; tyrants by force and terror; philosophers by solemn lectures of morality and virtue. And all these have certainly a share in influencing their minds, and determining their actions; but, all together, not half so much as applying to their reigning appetites, appearing interests, and predominant foibles, and taking artful advantages of favourable opportunities, and catching at lucky conjectures, to effect at once what a long series of wise counsels, and the best concerted measures, cannot bring about.

Wise statesmen will understand this foible in human nature, and often take advantage from a plot discovered, or a rebellion quelled; from the transports of a restoration, or a victory obtained; or during the terrors of a pestilential distemper, or the rage of a prevailing faction, or the fears of a desponding one, to accomplish what neither threats nor armies could extort, nor bribes nor allurements persuade.

The same advantages have been as luckily taken by the leaders of popular parties, upon sudden discontents and unsuccessful acts of power, to obtain concessions and privileges which they durst not think of, much less hope for, at other times. My Lord Clarendon furnishes us with many instances of such concessions, which neither the crown would have granted, nor the people been prevailed upon to ask, nor perhaps accept, before, or possibly after.[1] Whereas a preposterous and ill-timed attempt, on either side, would have increased the power which they designed to lessen, or take away. The greatest secret in politicks is, to drive the nail that will go.

If a solemn soothsayer, a poet, or philosopher, talk of the dignity of human nature, man is lifted up to a resemblance with his great Creator: He is lord of the universe; all things are made for

1. Edward, Earl of Clarendon, *The history of the rebellion and civil wars in England begun in the year 1641*, passim.

his use, even such as are of no use to him, but do him mischief. The sun is placed in the firmament to ripen his cabbage, and dry his linen; and infinite millions of stars are stuck there, many thousand times bigger than the earth, to supply the want of farthing candles, though vastly many of them are not to be seen but by glasses, and, without doubt, infinite others not to be seen with them. He is made wise, discerning, formed for virtue, mutual help and assistance; and probably it was all true before the fall: But as he is now degenerated, I fear that the reverse of all this is true. It is plain that he is foolish, helpless, perfidious, impotent, easily misled and trepanned, and, for the most part, caught by as thin snares and little wiles as his fellow-creatures, which, we are told, are made for his use; and his boasted faculty of reason betrays him to some from which the others are exempt.

True reason has little to do in his speculations or his actions. Enthusiasm or panick fear often supplies the place of religion in him: Obstinacy is called constancy; and indifference, moderation: His passions, which direct and govern all the motions of his mind, seem to me to be purely mechanical; which perhaps I may shew more at large hereafter: and whoever would govern him, and lead him, must apply to those passions; that is, pull the proper ropes, and turn the wheels which will put the machine in motion. When Chrysippus was introduced into the presence of Dionysius, and, according to the custom of the court, fell upon his face, and kissed the oppressor's feet; he was asked by Plato, how he, who was a Greek, a free man, and a philosopher, could fall prostrate before a tyrant, and adore him? He answered merrily, "That he had business with the tyrant; and if his ears were in his feet, he must speak to him where his ears lay."[2]

Now most people's ears lie in the wrong place; and whoever will be heard, must apply accordingly: We rarely see a wise man, who does not carry a half-fool about him; one who, by soothing his vanities, flattering his passions, and taking advantages of his other weaknesses, can do more with him than all the world

2. Gordon is in error in imputing the incident to Chrysippus. Diogenes Laertius notes that it was the Cyrenaic philosopher (and close friend of Socrates) Aristippus who is reputed to have fallen at the feet of Dionysius (*Aristippus*, 2.78).

besides. Indeed most men are governed by those who have less wit than themselves, or by what ought least to influence them. Men, like other animals, are caught by springs, wires, or subtleties: Foxes are trepanned by traces, pheasants by a red rag, and other birds by a whistle; and the same is true of mankind.

A lucky thought, a jest, a fortunate accident, or a jovial debauch, shall bring about designs and revolutions in human affairs, which twenty legions in the field could not bring about. A filthy strumpet made Alexander, for a kiss, burn Persepolis, the august seat of the Persian empire;[3] and I have heard, somewhere or other, of a great prince, who being prevailed upon to swear by his mistress's bum, that he would dissolve the States of his kingdom, religiously kept that oath against his interest, though he never valued all the rest that he took upon the evangelists. How often hath a merry story in our days turned a debate, when the most grave and solemn arguments, and the most obvious representations of publick advantage, could not prevail? And how many a fair and accomplished lady has been won by bribing her chambermaid, when perhaps all the solicitations of her parents and relations, and all the motives of self-interest, would have proved ineffectual?

The lucky adjusting of times and seasons, taking advantage of prevailing prejudices and panicks, and knowing how to humour and lay hold of the predominant enthusiasm of human nature, has given birth to most of the revolutions in religion and politicks which ever happened in the world. A juggler swallowing bibles and hour-glasses, shall do more with a modern mob than a philosopher; and a scarecrow prater, with distorted limbs and understanding, shall make thousands of them weep and wring their hands, when the oratory of Demosthenes, or the reasonings of Mr. Locke,[4] would make them laugh or hoot. There is a certain assimilation of passions and faculties in men, which attract one another when they meet, and always strike together. As when two

3. Despite the absence of evidence, some commentators have claimed that Persepolis was set ablaze by Alexander's own hand in 331 B.C. at the instigation of Thaïs, one of his courtesans, after a day of debauchery.

4. John Locke.

fiddles are tuned up to the same pitch, if you hit the one, the other sounds; so men are easiest operated upon by those of like under-standings with their own, or those who the best know how to dally and play with their foibles, and can do the same thing with design as the others do naturally.

I doubt not but I shall be censured for making thus bold with the Lord of the Creation, by those who make much more bold with Him on other occasions, and who would have the monopoly of enjoying all the scandal to themselves. But, by the leave of those solemn gentlemen, I shall take the liberty of considering man as he is, since it is out of our power to give a model to have him new made by.

Since then, by the sins of our first parents, we are fallen into this unhappy and forlorn condition, all wise and honest men are obliged, in prudence and duty, not only by lectures of philos-ophy, religion, and morals, to fashion this sovereign of the uni-verse into his true interest, but to make use of his weaknesses to render him happy, as wicked men do to make him miserable; in which I shall be more particular hereafter.

T   *I am, &c.*

The End of the Third Volume.

CATO's LETTERS:

OR,

ESSAYS *on* LIBERTY,

CIVIL and RELIGIOUS,

And other important SUBJECTS.

In FOUR VOLUMES.

VOL. IV.

The SIXTH EDITION, *corrected.*

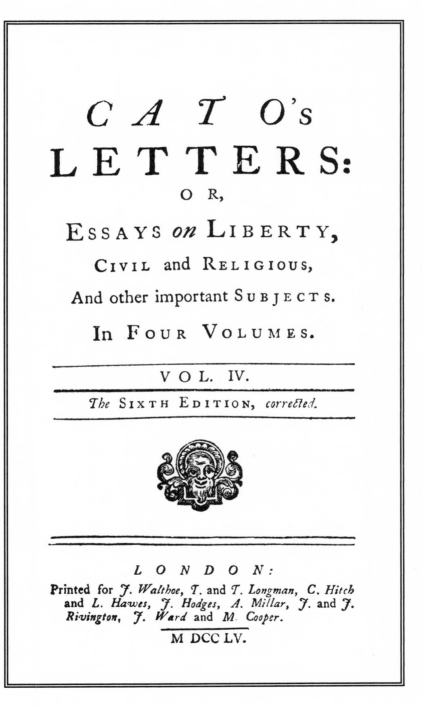

LONDON:

Printed for *J. Walthoe*, *T.* and *T. Longman*, *C. Hitch*
and *L. Hawes*, *J. Hodges*, *A. Millar*, *J.* and *J.*
Rivington, *J. Ward* and *M. Cooper*.

M DCC LV.

❧ *Of Plantations and Colonies.*

SIR,

I intend, in this letter, to give my opinion about plantations; a subject which seems to me to be understood but by few, and little use is made of it where it is. It is most certain, that the riches of a nation consist in the number of its inhabitants, when those inhabitants are usually employed, and no more of them live upon the industry of others (like drones in a hive) than are necessary to preserve the oeconomy of the whole: For the rest, such as gamesters, cheats, thieves, sharpers, and abbey-lubbers,[1] with some of their betters, waste and destroy the publick wealth, without adding any thing to it. Therefore, if any nation drive either by violence, or by ill usage and distress, any of its subjects out of their country, or send any of them out in foolish wars, or useless expeditions, or for any other causes, which do not return more advantage than bring loss, they so far enervate their state, and let out part of their best heart's blood.

Now, in many instances, men add more to the publick stock by being out of their country, than in it; as ambassadors, publick ministers, and their retinues, who transact the affairs of a nation; merchants and tradesmen, who carry on its traffick; soldiers, in necessary wars; and sometimes travellers, who teach us the customs, manners and policies, of distant countries, whereby we may regulate

1. Abbey-lubbers: lazy monks, that is, do-nothings.

747

and improve our own. All, or most of these, return to us again with advantage. But, in other instances, a man leaves his country, never, or very rarely to return again; and then the state will suffer loss, if the person so leaving it be not employed abroad in such industry, in raising such commodities, or in performing such services, as will return more benefit to his native country, than they suffer prejudice by losing an useful member.

This is often done by planting colonies, which are of two sorts: One to keep conquered countries in subjection, and to prevent the necessity of constant standing armies: a policy which the Romans practised, till their conquests grew too numerous, the conquered countries too distant, and their empire too unwieldy to be managed by their native force only; and then they became the slaves of those whom they conquered. This policy for many ages, we ourselves used in Ireland, till the fashion of our neighbours, and the wisdom of modern ages, taught us the use of armies: And I wish that those who come after us may never learn all their uses. I must confess, that I am not wise enough to enter into all the policy made use of formerly in governing that country; and shall in proper time communicate my doubts, in hopes to receive better information. In the mean time, I cannot but persuade myself, that when our superiors are at leisure from greater affairs, it may be possible to offer them a proposition more honourable to the crown, more advantageous to each kingdom, and to the particular members of them, and vastly more conducive to the power of the whole British empire, than the doubtful state which they are now in. But as this is not the purpose of my present letter, I shall proceed to consider the nature of the other sort of colonies.

The other sort of colonies are for trade, and intended to increase the wealth and power of the native kingdom; which they will abundantly do if managed prudently, and put and kept under a proper regulation. No nation has, or ever had, all the materials of commerce within itself: No climate produces all commodities; and yet it is the interest, pleasure, or convenience, of every people, to use or trade in most or all of them; and rather to raise them themselves, than to purchase them from others, unless in some instances, when they change their own commodities for them, and employ as many or more people at home in that exchange, such as would lose their employment by purchasing them from abroad. Now, colonies planted in proper climates, and kept to their proper business, undoubtedly do this; and particularly many of our own colonies in the West Indies employ ten times their own number in Old England, by sending them from hence provisions, manufactures, utensils for themselves and their slaves, by navigation, working up the commodities that they send us, by retaining and exporting them afterwards, and in returning again to us silver and gold, and materials for new manufactures; and our northern colonies do, or may if encouraged, supply us with timber, hemp, iron, and other metals, and indeed with most or all the materials of navigation, and our neighbours too, through our hands; and by that means settle a solid naval power in Great Britain, not precarious, and subject to disappointments, and the caprices of our neighbours; which management would make us soon masters of most of the trade of the world.

I would not suggest so distant a thought, as that any of our colonies, when they grow stronger, should ever attempt to wean themselves from us; however, I think too much care cannot be taken to prevent it, and to preserve their dependences upon their mother-country. It is not to be hoped, in the corrupt state of human nature, that any nation will be subject to another any longer than it finds its own account in it, and cannot help itself. Every man's first thought will be for himself, and his own interest; and he will not be long to seek for arguments to justify his being so, when he knows how to attain what he proposes. Men will think it hard to work, toil, and run hazards, for the advantage of others, any longer than they find their own interest in it, and especially for those who use them ill: All nature points out that course. No creatures suck the teats of their dams longer than they can draw milk from thence, or can provide themselves with better food: Nor will any country continue their subjection to another only because their great-grandmothers were acquainted.

This is the course of human affairs: and all wise states will always have it before their eyes. They will well consider therefore how to preserve the advantages arising from colonies, and avoid the evils. And I conceive, that there can be but two ways in nature to hinder them from throwing off their dependence; one to keep it out of their power, and the other out of their will. The first must be by force; and the latter by using them well, and keeping them employed in such productions, and making such manufactures, as will support themselves and families comfortably, and procure them wealth too, or at least not prejudice their mother-country.

Force can never be used effectually to answer the end, without destroying the colonies themselves. Liberty and encouragement are necessary to carry people thither, and to keep them together when they are there; and violence will hinder both. Any body of troops considerable enough to awe them, and keep them in subjection, under the direction too of a needy governor, often sent thither to make his fortune, and at such a distance from any application for redress, will soon put an end to all planting, and leave the country to the soldiers alone; and if it did not, would eat up all the profit of the colony. For this reason, arbitrary countries have not been equally successful in planting colonies with free ones; and what they have done in that kind has, either been by force, at a vast expence, or by departing from the nature of their government, and giving such privileges to planters as were denied to their other subjects. And I dare say, that a few prudent laws, and a little prudent conduct, would soon give us far the greatest share of the riches of all America, perhaps drive many of other nations out of it, or into our colonies, for shelter.

If violence, or methods tending to violence, be not used to prevent it, our northern colonies must constantly increase in people, wealth, and power. Men living in healthy climates, paying easy or no taxes, not molested with wars, must vastly increase by natural generation; besides that vast numbers every day flow thither from our own dominions, and from other parts of Europe, because they have there ready employment, and lands given to them for tilling; insomuch that I am told they have doubled their inhabitants since the Revolution, and in less than a century must become powerful states; and the more powerful they grow still the more people will flock thither. And there are so many exigencies in all states, so many foreign wars, and domestick disturbances, that these colonies can never want opportunities, if they watch for them, to do what they shall find their interest to do; and therefore we ought to take all the precautions in our power, that it shall never be their interest to act against that of their native country; an evil which can no otherwise be averted than by keeping them fully employed in such trades as will increase their own, as well as our wealth; for it is much to be feared, if we do not find employment for them, they may find it for us.

No two nations, no two bodies of men, or scarce two single men, can long continue in friendship, without having some cement of their union; and where relation, acquaintance, or mutual pleasures are wanting, mutual interests alone can bind it: But when those interests separate, each side must assuredly pursue their own. The interest of colonies is often to gain independency; and is always so when they no longer want protection, and when they can employ themselves more advantageously than in supplying materials of traffick to others: And the interest of the mother-country is always to keep them dependent, and so employed; and it requires all their address to do it; and it is certainly more easily and effectually done by gentle and insensible methods than by power alone.

Men will always think that they have a right to air, earth, and water, a right to employ themselves for their own support, to live by their own labours, to apply the gifts of God to their own benefit; and, in order to it, to make the best of their soil, and to work up their own product: And when this cannot be done without detriment to their mother-country, there can be but one fair, honest, and indeed effectual way to prevent it; which is, to divert them upon other employments as advantageous to themselves, and more so to their employers; that is, in raising such growth, and making such manufactures, as will not prejudice their own, or at least in no degree equal to the advantage which they bring: And when such commodities are raised or made, they ought to be taken off their hands, and the people ought not to be forced to find out other markets by stealth, or to throw themselves upon new protectors. Whilst people have full employment, and can maintain themselves comfortably in a way which they have been used to, they will never seek after a new one, especially when they meet encouragement in one, and are discountenanced in the other.

As without this conduct colonies must be mischievous to their mother-country, for the reasons before given, so with it the greatest part of the wealth which they acquire centers there; for all their productions are so many augmentations of our power and riches, as they are returns of the peoples's labour, the rewards of merchants, or increase of navigation; without which all who are sent abroad are a dead loss to their country, and as useless as if really dead; and worse than so, if they become enemies: for we can send no commodities to them, unless they have others to exchange for them, and such as we find our interest in taking.

As to our southern plantations, we are in this respect upon a tolerable foot already; for the productions there are of so different a nature from our own, that they can never interfere with us; and the climates are so unhealthy, that no more people will go or continue there than are necessary to raise the commodities which we want; and consequently they can never be dangerous to us: But our northern colonies are healthy climates, and can raise all or most of the commodities, which our own country produces. They constantly increase in people, and will constantly increase; and, without the former precautions, must, by the natural course of human affairs, interfere with most branches of our trade, work up our best manufactures, and at last grow too powerful and unruly to be governed for our interest only: And therefore, since the way lies open to us to prevent so much mischief, to do so much good, and add so much wealth and power to Great Britain, by making those countries the magazines of our naval stores, I hope we shall not lose all these advantages, in compliment to the interests of a few private gentlemen, or even to a few countries.

We have had a specimen of this wise conduct in prohibiting the Irish cattle, which were formerly brought to England lean, in exchange for our commodities, and fatted here; but are now killed and sent abroad directly from Ireland:[2] And so we lose the whole carriage and merchants' advantage, and the vent of the com-

2. In 1667 Parliament enacted legislation prohibiting the export of Irish cattle to England, thus protecting English farmers from competition in the home market.

modities sent to purchase them. And lately we have made such another prudent law, to prevent the importing their woollen manufacture;[3] which has put them upon wearing none of ours, making all or most of their own cloth themselves; exporting great quantities of all sorts by stealth, and the greater part of their wool to rival nations; and, by such means it is that we are beholden to the plague in France, to their Mississippi Company, and their total loss of credit, that we have not lost a great part of that manufacture. It is true, we have made some notable provision to hedge in the cuckoo, and to make all the people of that kingdom execute a law, which it is every man's interest there not to execute; and it is executed accordingly.

I shall sometime hereafter consider that kingdom in relation to the interest of Great Britain;[4] and shall say at present only, that it is too powerful to be treated only as a colony; and that if we design to continue them friends, the best way to do it is, to imitate the example of merchants and shopkeepers; that is, when their apprentices are acquainted with their trade and their customers, and are out of their time, to take them into partnership, rather than let them set up for themselves in their neighbourhood.

T   *I am, &c.*

NO. 107. SATURDAY, DECEMBER 15, 1722.

֍   *Of publick Credit and Stocks.*

SIR,

I have in a former letter[1] observed, that men ever have been, and I doubt ever will be, cheated by sounds, without having any just ideas annexed to them. When words have obtained an

---

3. By an act of 1698, all Irish wool and woollen manufactures were prohibited from being exported except to England and Wales. The law destroyed a flourishing industry in Ireland and contributed substantially to the economic decline of the country.

4. In fact, Cato does not address the topic again.

---

1. See Letter No. 103 (Nov. 17, 1722).

esteem, and sort of veneration, their meanings will be varied as often as those in possession of reverence and popular applause have occasion to make different uses of them. It seems to me, that no word has suffered more from this abuse than the word *credit*; nor in any instance has the publick suffered more mischief than by the abuse of it.

A merchant, or tradesman, is said to be in good credit, when his visible gains appear to be greater than his expences; when he is industrious, and takes care of his affairs; when he makes punctual payments, and the wares which he sells may be depended upon as to their goodness and value; and when those who deal with him can have a reasonable assurance that he will make a profit by his care from the commodities that they entrust him with; and, if it should happen otherwise, that he has a remaining substance sufficient at last to answer all demands. A private gentleman is said to have great credit who lives within his income, has regard to his character and his honour, is just to his word and his promises, and is known to have an unencumbered estate, or one superior to all his supposed engagements; from whence his creditors form a reasonable expectation that they shall be paid again without a law-suit, and a certainty that they can be paid with one: And therefore all these will be trusted for as much as they are worth, and sometimes more, at the lowest price for the goods which they buy, and at the lowest interest for the money which they borrow.

But if a merchant be observed to live in riot and profusion, to leave his estate to the direction of servants, who cheat him, or neglect his business; if he turn projector, do not pay his bills, and shuffle in his bargains, and sell faulty goods which are bought upon his word: Or, if a gentleman be known to spend more than his income, to mortgage his lands to take no care of his estate, or how his stewards or bailiffs manage it; if he run in debt to tradesmen and mechanicks, and be perpetually borrowing money, without any thoughts how to pay it: I say, under such management, no fair dealer will have any thing to do with them; and of course they fall into the hands of scriveners, knavish attorneys, and griping usurers; will be fed from hand to mouth, pay double and treble interest for what they receive, till their creditors watch their opportunity, and sweep all.

Credit is said to run high in a nation, when there are great numbers of wealthy subjects in the former circumstances, which will always be produced by an affluent trade; and when the commodities of a country, and the production of the people's labour, find a ready vent, and at a good price: for then they will see their account in punctuality of payment and fair dealing, and will not run the hazard of losing a regular sustenance for their families, or a constant profit arising from an open trade, for the present and occasional advantage which they may hope to receive from a knavish bargain, or a fraudulent circumvention: And those who do otherwise, are generally undone, and sell a constant and a yearly income to themselves, and possibly to their families after them, for a year or two's purchase, and often for much less.

But if any of these be above or without the reach of the laws, or by reason of their station and figure, it be difficult to get the benefit of the laws, their credit will proportionably abate, because a great part of the security which they can give fails, and they must consequently pay greater interest and procuration for the money that they borrow, and a greater price for the goods that they buy: for, those who deal with them, will always propose to be gainers by the whole, upon computing their delays and hazards.

The credit of a state, or what we call publick credit, must be preserved by the same means as private men preserve theirs; namely, by doing strict justice to particulars; by being exact in their payments, not chicaning in their bargains, nor frightening and tricking people into them, or out of them; by letting them know what they buy, and not altering the nature or property of it, to serve after-purposes, and without the free-consent of the persons interested: And they are always to take especial care to sell nothing but what is valuable; to coin silver and gold, and not put the stamp of public authority upon base and counterfeit metals.

Indeed, states are much more concerned to keep up the opinion of their integrity than private men; because those that trust them have, in effect, only their honour and their interest to depend upon for payment; and therefore will well consider whether it be their interest to maintain their honour. I doubt private men would have little credit, and upon very ill terms too, if they could not be used, or could vacate their own securities; for, when it becomes more a man's interest not to pay, than to pay, his debts, and he can choose which he pleases, no one would care to have any part of his fortune depend upon those resolutions. It is certainly the interest of all men to keep up the reputation of their honesty as long as it can be kept, in order to be trusted for the future; but when they can be trusted no longer, nor are able to pay what they are already trusted with, and can decline paying it when they see apparent ruin in being honest, it is easy to guess what course will be taken.

What nation besides our own has explained publick honour, by any other maxims than those of publick interest? Or have kept their treaties or agreements with foreign states, or one another, any longer than it was their interest upon the whole to keep them? And indeed very few have kept them so long. I am sure that no wise state will depend upon the observance of leagues and national contracts any longer. What country has not made frequent acts of resumption, when the folly and knavery of their predecessors has embezzled the publick revenues, and rendered the state unable to defend itself? Whence private men have been deprived of estates to which they had undoubted titles by the laws of their country, estates which perhaps had passed many descents and many purchases; and yet the losers sometimes have no other reason to complain, than that they want the consolation of seeing their country undone with them; which must have been the case, if they had not been undone alone. Sweden did this in the last age; Spain lately; and another country, in our time, has not only in effect cancelled all its engagements, but by various stratagems drawn the wealth of the whole into its coffers, and seized it when it was there.[2] Which puts me in mind of a story of a butcher, who

2. In 1680 the Swedish Estates charged those who had been active in the regency government of Charles XI (from 1660 to 1675) with maladministration and gross corruption, and ordered them to refund large sums to the state. Philip V of Spain was confronted by the defection of a substantial number of the aristocracy to the Hapsburg cause during the War of the Spanish Succes-

thought himself happy in the possession of a sagacious, diligent, and seemingly faithful dog, to whom, by long experience of his service, he thought he might safely trust the custody of his shambles in his absence: But Hector one day observing, against a great festival, the shop to be much fuller of meat than usual, thought it was high time to set up for himself, and so very resolutely denied his master entrance; who had then no remedy left but to shoot him.

I have above endeavoured to shew what, and what alone, ought to be called credit. But there has lately risen up, in our age, a new-fangled and fantastical credulity, which has usurped the same name, and came in with the word *Bite*,[3] which has been made free of a neighbouring court;[4] whereby the poor, innocent, industrious, and unwary, people, have been delivered into the ravenous and polluted jaws of vultures and tigers; and thousands, I had almost said millions, have been sacrificed, to satiate the gluttony of a few. This has inverted the oeconomy and policy of nations; made a great kingdom turn all gamesters; and men have acquired the reputation of wisdom, from their skill in picking pockets: It has entered into the cabinets of courts; has guided the counsels of senates, and employed their whole wisdom; nay, most of their time has been employed in keeping up this wild and airy traffick; as if the business of government was not to protect people in their property, but to cheat them out of it.

This is eminently true in a neighbouring country; I wish I could say, that nothing like it had ever happened amongst us. But as no men now in power are answerable for this great mischief, so I hope and believe, that we shall have their hearty assistance to extricate us out of all these evils. And as I please myself with believing, that I speak the sense of my superiors, so I shall take the liberty to

---

sion. As a consequence, the government confiscated the property of the nobility who had abandoned the Bourbon cause in 1706 and again in 1710. The reference to "another country" is probably to France, which, under the regency of the Duc d'Orléans, had recently repudiated a substantial portion of its enormous national debt.

3. Bite: a slang term for "Tricked you!"

4. This, and the following allusion to a "neighbouring country," refer to France and to the Mississippi Company.

say, that neither publick nor private credit can consist in selling any thing for more than it is worth, or for any thing but what it is worth. It is certainly the interest of a country, that its commodities should sell at a good price, and find a ready vent; that private men should be able safely to trust one another; that lands should find ready purchasers, good securities, money at low interest; and that mortgages should be easily transferable. And the way to bring these good purposes to pass, is to ascertain titles; to give ready remedies to the injured; to procure general plenty by prudent laws, and by giving all encouragement to industry and honesty. But it will never be effected by authorizing or countenancing frauds; by enabling artful men to circumvent the unwary; by stamping the public seal upon counterfeit wares; or by constantly coining a new sort of property, of a precarious, uncertain, and transitory, value; and, by constant juggles and combinations, conspiring to make it more so: Which conduct, whenever practiced, must soon put an end to all publick and private credit.

In what country soever these practices meet with encouragement, all fair and honest dealing will be turned into juggling. There will quickly grow a sort of cabalistical learning: And there will be a secret and vulgar knowledge; one to be trusted only to the trusty adepts and managers; and the other to be divulged to the people, who will be told nothing but what is for the interest of their betters to communicate; and pretty advantages may be made by being in the secret. As for example: Just before any publick misfortune is to make its appearance, those who know of it may sell out; and in the height of the danger buy again; and when it is over, by taking another opportunity, they may sell a second time. And when these evils are averted, they may go to market once more; and so, *toties quoties*,[5] till the greatest part of the property of a kingdom be got into the hands of but a few persons, who will then undoubtedly govern all the rest. Nor can these mischiefs be possibly prevented, but by wholly destroying this sort of traffick, or by appointing skillful pilots to set up occasional buoys and sea-marks, according to the shifting of the winds and the tides; that is, by ascertaining and publishing the real value of all publick securities,

5. "So often and as often."

as often as there is an alteration made in them by new provisions, or by wholly preventing the abuses occasioned by the vile trade of stock-jobbing; which I conceive is not difficult to do, when stock-jobbers have no hand in directing the remedy.

Till something of this kind be done, it is foolish to think, and worse to pretend to think, that any effectual methods can be taken to discharge and pay off the national engagements: For, in whatever country it happens, that the publick funds become the markets and standing revenues of those who can best cure the evil; where great and sudden estates may be more easily raised by knavery and juggling, than small ones by virtue and merit; where plumbs may be got at once, and vast societies may be made the accomplices of power, in order to be indulged with separate advantages; it is not to be hoped that effectual methods will be taken to dam and choke up such inexhaustible sources of wealth and dominion: On the contrary, it is to be feared, that new projects will be yearly invented, new schemes coloured with popular pretences, to toss and tumble the publick securities, and to change them into as many shapes as Proteus knew. One year shall metamorphose the schemes of another; and the next shall undo both. The leaders of one faction shall unravel the projects of their predecessors; shall charge their designs with corruption and rapine, and be more rapacious themselves; and all in their turns shall raise vast estates upon the publick ruins; and the last spirit shall be always the worst. Artful and conspiring men shall buy up desperate debts, and then use intrigues and corruption to load their country with them; and the business of nations shall stand still, or rather, it shall become their business to fish in these troubled streams, till, by long experience of the loss of their fellows, the fish will bite no longer; and then it is easy to guess what is next to be done. There is but one method which can be taken; and that will be taken.

I would gladly know what advantage ever has, or even can, accrue to the publick, by raising stocks to an imaginary value, beyond what they are really worth to an honest man, who purchases them for a regular support to himself and family, and designs not to sell them again, till he has occasion for the money that they will produce. It can most assuredly serve no honest purpose, and will promote a thousand knavish ones. Besides those before-mentioned, it turns most of the current coin of England out of the channels of trade, and the heads of all its merchants and traders off their proper business: It enriches the worst men, and ruins the innocent: It taints men's morals, and defaces all the principles of virtue and fair dealing, and introduces combination and fraud in all sorts of traffick. It has changed honest commerce into bubbling; our traders into projectors; industry into tricking; and applause is earned, when the pillory is deserved: It has created all the dissatisfaction so much complained of, and all the mischiefs attending it, which daily threaten us, and which furnish reasons for standing or occasional troops: It has caused all the confusion in our publick finances: It has set up monstrous members and societies in the body politick, which are grown, I had almost said, too big for the whole kingdom: It has multiplied offices and dependencies in the power of the court, which in time may fill the legislature, and alter the balance of government: It has overwhelmed the nation with debts and burdens, under which it is almost ready to sink; and has hindered those debts from being paid off. For if stocks fell for more, or much more upon the Exchange, than the prices at which they are redeemable; or more can be got by jobbing them than by discharging them, than all arts will be used to prevent a redemption. But as this is not at present our case, so it is every man's interest, concerned in our funds, to secure their principal, and to promote every means which will enable their country to pay them.

I doubt not but I shall incur the censure of many, by thus laying open our nakedness, and probing our wounds; and I cannot deny but I found some reluctance in doing it: But it must be done before they can be cured. The patient cannot now bear quacking; and if effectual remedies be not speedily taken, the case is desperate. The security and interest of the crown, the power and reputation of the kingdom, the credit and honour of the ministry, depend upon doing this great work: And I really believe that the latter have inclinations and resolutions to do it. It can never be done effectually without their assistance; and if they give it, and set themselves at the head of so publick a good, they will justly obtain a reputation far beyond any who have ever appeared before them, and will enjoy unenvied all the wealth and advantages which attend greatness and power. It is folly in any one, who is the least acquainted with the affairs of nations, to pretend not to see, that if we do not soon put our publick debts in a method of being paid, they can never be paid; and all will certainly do their utmost to prevent so fatal a mischief to their country; I mean, all who do not intend it. But if there be any such, which I hope and believe there are not, they will then undoubtedly take early care to save themselves out of the general wreck; which very few will be able to do, tho' all will intend it. Those in the secret will have the advantage; for when selling becomes the word, no one can sell, unless he sells for little or nothing. All will be waiting for a rise; and if that happen, all or most will endeavour to sell, and then all selling is at an end: The managers and brokers will engross the books, as they did lately, and command the first sale; and by the time that they are got out, no one else will be able to get out.

There is nothing therefore left to be done, but for all honest men to join heads, hearts, and hands, to find all means to discharge the publick burdens, and to add no more to them; to search every measure how we can lessen the national expences; to avoid all occasions of engaging in new ones; and to do all in our power to increase trade and the publick wealth, without sacrificing it to any jobs or private views. Which conduct alone will enable us honestly to pay off what we owe, and to become once more a free, rich, happy, and flourishing people.

T   *I am, &c.*

Inquiry into the Source of moral Virtues.

SIR,

Morality, or moral virtues, are certain rules of mutual convenience or indulgence, conducive or necessary to the well-being of society. Most of these are obvious; for every man knows what he desires himself; which is, to be free from oppression, and the insults of others, and to enjoy the fruits of his own acquisitions, arising from his labour or invention. And since he can have no reason to expect this indulgence to himself, unless he allow it to others, who have equal reason to expect it from him, it is the common interest of all, who unite together in the same society, to establish such rules and maxims for their mutual preservation, that no man can oppress or injure another, without suffering by it himself. As far as these rules are discoverable by the light of reason, or that portion of understanding, which most, or all men have, they are called morality: But when they are the productions of deeper thought, or the inventions only of men of greater sagacity, they are called political knowledge. But as men are often in such a situation in respect of one another, that the stronger can oppress the weaker, without any fear of having the injury returned; and most men will pursue their own personal advantage independently of all other men; therefore Almighty God, in compassion to mankind has annexed rewards and punishments to the observance or non-observance of these rules: The belief of which, and a practice pursuant to it, is called religion.

I have often read, with pleasure, pretty speculative discourses upon the intrinsick excellence of virtue, and of its having a real existence independent of human considerations, or worldly relations: But when I have been able to forget, or lay aside the dalliances and amusements of fancy, and the beautiful turns of expression, I could consider it philosophically, only as an empty sound, when detached and separated from natural, national, or religious politicks; unless in some few instances, where constitution, and innate tenderness, engage men to pity others in ease to themselves, which is called humanity.

All cardinal and private virtues are branches of these general politicks. Fortitude enables us to defend ourselves and others. Compassion is a fellow feeling of calamities which we may suffer ourselves; and it is evident that people feel them in proportion, as they are likely to suffer the same or the like calamities. Charity obliges us to give that relief to others, which we, our friends, or relations, may want for ourselves. And temperance and frugality are necessary to the preservation of our bodies and estates, and being useful members of society. I freely confess, that for my part I can find out no other motives in myself, or others, for these affections, or actions, except constitution, ostentation, or temporal or religious politicks, which are, in other words, our present or eternal interests; and I shall own myself beholden to any else who can find out any other; for there cannot be too many motives for a virtuous life.

How far the systematical gentlemen[1] will agree with me in this speculative philosophy, I do not know, nor shall think myself much concerned to enquire; but it is certain that their practice, and many of the doctrines which they teach, confirm what I have said. I think that all mankind, except the Brahmins, and transmigrators of souls in the East, agree, that we may destroy other animals for food and convenience, and sometimes for pleasure, or to prevent but any trifling prejudice, to ourselves; though they have the same, or very near the same, organizations as we have, equal or greater sensations of pleasure and pain, and many of them sagacity and reasoning enough to over-reach and circumvent us; nor are they guilty of any other crime, than that of acting according to their natures, and preserving their beings by such food as is necessary to their existence.

Indeed, as things stand at present, though we had not revelation for it, we may be very sure that God Almighty has given us dominion over other creatures, because he has actually given us the power, in a good measure, to destroy and preserve them, as far as they may be hurtful or useless to us; and therefore we think them not objects of moral duties, because we can hurt them and they cannot make reprisals, or equal reprisals, upon us; But if Almighty God had thought fit to have given to lions and tigers the use of speech, length of life to have gained more experience, and had formed their claws and hands to write and communicate that experience, and by such means had enabled them to have formed themselves into societies for mutual defence against mankind (whom they could quickly have destroyed, though only by confining and starving them in enclosures and fortifications) I say, in

1. Systematical gentlemen: philosophers.

such a circumstance of affairs, will any man affirm, that it would not have been our interest and duty to have treated them with morality and social offices? I doubt, in such a case, they would have told us, and have made us feel too, that they were not made only for our use.

I will suppose, for once, a dialogue between his Holiness and a lion, since poets and some others have informed us, that beasts have spoken formerly; and I am sure that they were never more concerned to speak than upon the present occasion.

Pope. Thou art an ugly four-footed monster, and thou livest upon the destruction of thy fellow-animals.

Lion. I am as nature has made me, which has given me many faculties beyond yourself. I have more courage, more strength, more activity, and better senses of seeing, hearing, &c. than you have: Nor do I destroy the hundredth part of my fellow-animals in comparison with those that you destroy. I never destroy my own species, unless I am provoked; but you destroy yours for pride, vanity, luxury, envy, covetousness, and ambition.

Pope. But thou art a great gormandizer, and eatest up all our victuals, which was designed for the use of men only; and therefore thou oughtest to be exterminated.

Lion. Nature, which gave me life, designed me the means of living; and she has given me claws and teeth for that purpose, namely, to defend myself against some animals, and to kill and eat others for my sustenance; and, amongst the rest, your reverence, if I cannot get younger and better food. You men, indeed, may eat and live comfortably upon the fruits of trees, and the herbs and corn of the field; but we are so formed, as to receive support and nourishment only from the flesh of other animals.

Pope. Sirrah, thou hast no soul.

Lion. The greater is my misfortune. However, I have a mind and body, and have the more reason to take care of them, having nothing else to take care of; and you ought the less to deprive and rob me of the little advantages which nature has given me, you who enjoy so much greater yourself.

Pope. The earth was given to the saints; for (as St. Austin very judiciously observes) the wicked have right to nothing, and the godly to all things; and thou art certainly a very wicked animal, and no true believer.

Lion. I have heard indeed before, that such reasonings will pass amongst you men, who have faculties to reason yourselves out of reason; but we beasts know better things: For having nothing but our senses to trust to, and wanting the capacities to distinguish ourselves out of them, we cannot be persuaded to believe, that those who have no more honesty, and less understanding than their neighbours, have a right to their goods, and to starve them, by pretending to believe what the others do not understand; therefore, worthy Doctor, you shall catch no gudgeons[2] here: You may brew as you bake amongst one another, but you will find no such bubbles amongst us.

Pope. Thou art a sniveling saucy jackanapes, and a great rogue and murderer, and I wish thou hadst a soul that I might damn it, and send thee to the Devil.

Lion. Not half so great a rogue as yourself, good Doctor, nor so great a murderer. You do more mischief in a year than all the lions in the world did since the Creation. We kill only with our teeth and claws; you use a thousand instruments of death and destruction. We kill single animals; you kill by wholesale, and destroy hecatombs[3] at once. We kill for food and necessity; you kill for sport and pastime, out of wantonness, and to do yourselves no good. In fine, you murder or oppress all other animals, and one another too.

Pope. Rascal, thou art made for my use, and I will make thee know it, and order thee to be immediately knocked on the head for thy skin, thou varlet, and beast for Satan.

Lion. I will try that presently.

Pope, (crossing himself.) Jesu! Maria! *(Exit in haste.)*

Lion. Farewell, thou lord of the Creation, and sovereign of the universe.

2. Gudgeons: gullible people.
3. Hecatombs: massive sacrifices.

I believe I may venture to say, if lions could speak, that they would talk at this rate, and his Holiness but little better. But to return to my subject.

I have said, that all, or most of mankind, act upon the former principles, and, without the motives of religion, can find out no reason to hope'that they should ever act otherwise; and I am sorry to say, that religion itself has yet wanted power enough to influence them (for the most part) to contrary sentiments or actions. What nation or society does not oppress another, when they can do it with security, without fear of retaliation, or of being affected by it in their own interests, and their correspondence with other states? It is plain that all social duties are here at an end; for what is called the law of nations, are only rules of mutual intercourse with one another, without which they could have no intercourse at all, but must be in constant course of war and depredation; and therefore whenever any state is in no condition to repel injuries, nor can have protection from any other, who are concerned to preserve them, constant experience shews us, that they become the prey of a greater, who think themselves obliged to keep no measures with them, nor want pretences from religion or their own interests to oppress them. Father Austin's distinction is always at hand when they can get no better; and for the most part (if not always) they find men of reverence to thank God for their roguery.

Since therefore men ever have, and, I doubt, ever will act upon these motives, they ought not to be amused by the play of words, and the sallies of imagination, whilst designing men pick their pockets; but ought to establish their happiness, by wise precautions, and upon solid maxims, and, by prudent and fixed laws, make it all men's interest to be honest; without which, I doubt, few men will be so.

T   *I am, &c.*

NO. 109. SATURDAY, DECEMBER 29, 1722.

Inquiry into the Origin of Good and Evil.

SIR,

W e have been long confounded about the origin of good and evil, or, in other words, of virtue and vice. The opinion of some is, that virtue is a sort of real being, and subsists in its own nature. Others make it to consist in rules and cautions, given us by the Supreme Being for our conduct here on earth and either implanted in our natures, or conveyed to us by revelation. A late philosopher searches it from the will and commands of the civil magistrate.[1] But, for my own part, I must conceive it only as a compound of the two last; namely, a relation of men's actions to one another, either dictated by reason, by the precepts of heaven, or the commands of the sovereign, acting according to his duty.

It is the misfortune of those publick-spirited and acute gentlemen, who have obliged the world with systems, that they always make common sense truckle to them; and when they are bewildered, and entangled amongst briars and thorns, never go back the way that they got in, but resolve to scramble through the brake, leap over hedge and ditch, to get into their old road, and so for the most part scratch themselves from head to foot, and sometimes break their necks into the bargain. They never look back, and examine whether their system be true or false, but set themselves to work to prove it at all adventures: They are determined to solve all contradictions, and grow very angry with all who are not so clear-sighted as themselves.

This seems to me to be the case in the present question. The common light of reason has told all mankind, that there cannot be an effect without a cause; and that every cause must be an effect of some superior cause; till they come to the last of all, which can be no otherwise than self-existent, that is, must have existed from all eternity. Some sects of philosophers have thought this first cause to be only pure matter, not being able to conceive that any

1. Thomas Hobbes.

thing can be made out of nothing, or can be annihilated again afterwards; and they suppose that matter has been in eternal motion, and has the seeds of animals, vegetables, and of every thing else within itself, and by its constant motion and revolutions gives them life, duration, and at last death; and throws them into the womb of nature again to rise up in new shapes.

But others, by far the greatest part of mankind, are not able by this dark system to account for the exquisite contrivance and consummate wisdom shewn in the formation of animals and vegetables, in the regular and stupendous structure and circulation of the heavenly bodies, and of the earth, no more than for the operations of our own minds. They therefore most reasonably judged, that when so much contrivance is necessary to bring about our own little designs; the great machine of heaven and earth, and the infinite and admirable systems in it, could not be the spontaneous or necessary productions of blind matter. Thence they determine, that the First Being must have suitable wisdom to contrive and execute these great and amazing works.

But these latter are not so well agreed amongst themselves about the manner of acting, or the operations of this being. For some think that he must act from the necessity of his own nature: For, since his being is necessary, they think that his will and attributes (which are parts of his being, essential to it, and inseparable from it) and consequently his actions, which are results of that will, and of those attributes, must be necessary too. They cannot conceive how a being, who has the principles and causes of all things within itself, could exist without having seen every thing intuitively from all eternity; a consideration which must exclude from his actions all choice and preference, as these imply doubt and deliberation.

They cannot apprehend how reason and wisdom can be analagous in him to what are called by the same names in men: For judgment in them, as far as it regards their own voluntary operations, is only the balance of the conveniences or inconveniences which will result from their own or other's thoughts or actions, as they have relation to beings or events out of their power, and which depend upon other causes: But if a being can have no causes without itself, but produces every thing by its own energy and power, sees all things at once, and cannot err, as men may, nor consequently deliberate and debate with itself, they think that it must act singly, and in one way only; and where there is no choice, or, which is the same thing, but one choice, they conceive that there is always necessity.

But the contrary is much the more orthodox and religious opinion, and has been held by far the greatest and best part of mankind in all ages, before and without revelation: They have thought that this last opinion bordered too much upon the material system, as being able to see but little difference in the operations of a being acting necessarily, and the productions of blind matter constantly in action, and acting mechanically; since the effect is supposed to be the same, though wisdom and contrivance, or what we are forced to call by those names for want of another, be the first spring, or chief wheel of the machine, or one link of the chain of causes: And therefore men have condemned this opinion as impious and atheistical.

Indeed the other speculations have been only the wild and babbling notions of fairy philosophers, or of enthusiastick and visionary madmen; for all prudent and modest men pretend to know no more of this being, without revelation, than that he is wise, good, and powerful, and made all things; and do not presume farther to enquire into the *modus*[2] of his existence and operations. However, their own interest and curiosity were so much concerned to guess at his designs and motives in placing them here, that it was impossible they could be otherwise than solicitous and inquisitive about it; and finding, or fancying themselves to be the most valuable part of the whole, it was very natural for them to believe, that all was made for their sakes; and that their happiness was the only or chief view of the Supreme Being.

With these thoughts about him, every man knowing what he had a mind to have himself, and what he believed would constitute his own happiness, and not being able to attain it without

2. *Modus:* manner.

making the same allowance to other people; men agreed upon
equal rules of mutual convenience and protection, and finding
these rules dictated to them by impartial reason, they justly
believed that they were implanted within them by the deity; and as
they expected themselves returns of gratitude or applause for benefits conferred by them upon others, they thought the same were
due to the original being who gave them life, and every thing else
which they enjoyed: and this is called natural religion.

But as the motive which men had to enter into this equal
agreement, was their own pleasure and security, which most or all
men prefer before the advantage of others, so they often found
themselves in a condition, by superior power, will, and abilities, to
circumvent those who had less than themselves, and either by artful confederacies, impostures, or by downright force, to oppress
them; and in order to it, have invented systems or partial schemes
of separate advantage, and have annexed suitable promises or
menace to them: All which they have pretended to receive from
this divine being. They assumed to have communication with him,
and to know his will, and denounced his anger against all who
would not take their word, and let them do by his authority what
they would never have been permitted to do by any other; and the
herd not daring to oppose them, or not knowing how, have acqui-
esced to their tales, and come in time to believe them. From hence
sprang all the follies and roguery of the heathen and Jewish
priests, and all the false religions in the world; with all the persecutions, devastations, and massacres caused by them; which were all
heterogeneous engraftments upon natural religion.

Almighty God thought it proper therefore at last to communicate himself again to man, and by immediate revelation to
confirm what he at first implanted in all men's minds, and what
was eradicated thence by delusion and imposture; but though he
thought it not necessary to tell us more than we were concerned to
know, namely, to do our duty to himself and to one another, yet
we will still be prying into his secrets, and sifting into the causes of
his original and external decrees, which are certainly just and reasonable, though we neither know his reasons, nor could judge of
them, if we did.

From hence arises this dispute concerning the origin of good and evil, amongst a thousand others. For, our vanity inducing us to fancy ourselves the sole objects of his providence, and being sure that we receive our beings from him, and consequently our sensations, affections, and appetites, which are parts of them, and which evidently depend either mediately or immediately, upon causes without us, and seeing at the same time, that many things happen in the world seemingly against his revealed will, which he could prevent if he thought fit; we either recur to the intrigues of a contrary being, whose business is to thwart his designs, and disappoint his providence, or else account for it by a malignity in human nature, more prone to do evil than good, without considering from whence we had that nature; for if the malignity in it be greater than precepts, examples, or exhortations can remove, the heavier scale must weigh down.

How much more modest and reasonable would it be to argue, that moral good and evil in this world, are only relations of our actions to the Supreme Being, and to one another, and would be nothing here below, if there were no men? That no event can happen in the universe but what must have causes strong enough to produce it? That all causes must first or last center in the supreme cause; who, from the existence of his own nature, must always do what is best, and all his actions must be instantaneous emanations of himself? He sees all things at one view, and nothing can happen without his leave and permission, and without his giving power enough to have it effected: When therefore we see any thing which seems to contradict the images which we have presumed to form about his essence, or the attributes which we bestow upon him (which images and attributes are, for the most part, borrowed from what we think most valuable amongst ourselves), we ought to suspect our own ignorance, to know that we want appetites to fathom infinite wisdom, and to rest assured that all things conduce to the ends and designs of his providence, who always chooses the best means to bring them about.

T   *I am, &c.*

NO. 110. SATURDAY, JANUARY 5, 1722.

Of Liberty and Necessity.

SIR,

I have already said, that I could consider good and evil only as in relation to men's actions to one another, or to the Supreme Being; in which actions they can have for their end their own interest alone, in present or futurity. But when I consider these ideas in regard to God, I must consider them as objects of his will, which can alone constitute right or wrong, though they may sometimes not quadrate[1] with the notions that we form of justice amongst one another, and which are only prudent rules for our own separate convenience, and take in no part of the creation but ourselves. We cannot enter into the rationale of God's punishing all mankind for the sin of their first parents, which they could not help; nor for his punishing all Israel with a pestilence for the private sin of David,[2] which, without doubt, many of them condemned; nor for his bringing plagues upon the Egyptians, because he had hardened Pharaoh's heart; no more than for his destroying all mankind at the Deluge, for crimes which he could have prevented; and multitudes of the like instances in Holy Writ besides, which we cannot account for by our weak reasonings (which have for their object only our own advantage). But we are very sure that these things were done, and rightly done; and all conduced to some superior, wise, and just end. Almighty God judges of the whole of things, and we only of them as they regard ourselves: The whole system of the universe is his care; and all other inferior beings must be subordinate to the interests of this great one, must all contribute, in their several stations and actions, to bring about at last the grand purposes of his providence. Infinite millions of animals are born with the morning sun, and probably see old age, and feel the pangs of death, before noon: Great numbers of them by their

1. Quadrate: conform.
2. The reference is to the plague visited on Israel after David had determined to take a census of his kingdom, an act commonly regarded as unholy (2 Sam. 24:1–15).

death preserve life, or give convenience to others who otherwise could not live at all, or must live upon very ill terms. Vegetables rise, grow, decay, die again, and get a new resurrection in other shapes. All nature is in perpetual rotation, and working through a thousand revolutions to its last period, and the consummation of all things, when its great author will know how to make all individuals recompence for the evils which they have suffered here, and perhaps give us faculties to know, admire, and glorify his conduct, in those instances which may seem most mysterious to our narrow capacities in this frail state.

But this general and comprehensive system of the universe, this honourable conception of the deity, acquiescence in, and submission to his will, will not square with the interests of particular societies of men, who think themselves concerned to find out a system for themselves alone; and therefore, to avoid those consequences (which I can see no purposes of religion served in avoiding) they compliment away his power, prescience and general providence, to do respect to the notions which they have pleased to conceive of his justice, which they have thought fit to measure by their own interests, or what they think best for themselves. They first determine what they desire to have; then call it just, and immediately interest heaven to bring it about; and finding that it contradicts the experience of mankind, and all the notions that they can conceive of the workings of providence, and the nature of things themselves (which always operate from cause to effect) they set themselves to work to form a new scheme at the expence of denying all that they see or can know.

In order to this, they have made man the *primum mobile,* and his mind the first principle or spring of all his actions, independent of the author of his being, and of all the second causes which evidently influence and concur to determine his resolutions and his actions. They say, that Almighty God (who has infinite justice and power) having given to mankind a rule to act by, and annexed rewards or menaces to the observance or non-observance of this rule, has given a free uncontrolled, and impartial liberty to him to determine, without being coerced or restrained by any other power to do, or not to do an action, or to choose good or evil to himself: His justice, they say, obliges him to this conduct, and his power enables him to execute and bring it to pass; and so by affecting to do right to one attribute of his, which they cannot understand, and which they may possibly mistake, by supposing it to be different from his will (which alone, as has been said, can constitute right or wrong) they take away and rob him of all or most of the rest.

His prescience or knowledge (from all eternity) of every event which does or can happen in the universe, is denied at once; for whatever is contingent in its own nature, and may or may not happen, cannot be foreseen: for when any being sees that a thing will be, it must be; for it is impossible to know that any event will come to pass, that may not come to pass; and it is equally impossible to foresee an effect, without knowing the causes which produce it. It is no irreverence to the Supreme Being, to say, that he cannot do impossibilities, and know things which cannot be known; and it is certain he must know all things that can be known, because they depend upon his will.

It reflects upon his wisdom or power: Upon the first, as supposing that he desires or intends to bring any designs or purposes to pass, and yet that he has not chosen the proper methods to attain them; or upon the latter, that he cannot attain them if he would: It entrenches upon his providence and government of the universe, by giving part of his power out of his own hands, and by leaving it to the discretion of inferior and weak beings, to contradict himself, and disappoint his intentions: And even his justice itself, to which all the rest are so freely sacrificed, is attacked upon such reasons, in charging Almighty God with severity in punishing crimes committed through weakness, want, or predominant appetites, and which he could have prevented by giving others. I do not see what has been, or can be said to these objections more, than that we are not to reason upon the proceedings of providence, which acts upon motives and maxims far above us, and which are not to be scanned[3] by our little rules and scanty capacities; and if these gentlemen could but be persuaded to reason thus at first,

3. Scanned: judged.

they would save themselves the trouble of solving perpetual contradictions.

For what can be more evident, than that the actions of man, which seem most spontaneous and free, depend upon his will to do them; and that that will is directed by his reasoning faculties, which depend again upon the good or ill organizations of his body, upon his complexion, the nature of his education, imbibed prejudices, state of health, predominant passions, manner of life, fortuitous reasonings with others, different kinds of diet, and upon the thousands of events, seeming accidents, and the perpetual objects which encompass him, and which every day vary and offer themselves differently to him; all or most of which causes, and many more which probably determine him, must be confessed to be out of his power? Constant experience shews us, that men differently constituted, or differently educated, will reason differently, and the same men in different circumstances. A man will have different sentiments about the same things, in youth, in middle age, and in dotage, in sickness and in health, in liquor and sobriety, in wealth and in poverty, in power and out of it; and the faculties of the mind are visibly altered by physick, exercise, or diet.

The same reason which is convincing to one man, appears ridiculous to another, and to the same man at different times; and consequently, his or their actions, which are results of those reasonings, will be different: And we not only all confess this, by endeavouring to work upon one another by these mediums, but heaven thinks fit to choose the same; for what else can be meant by offering rewards and denouncing punishments, but as causes to produce the effects designed, that is, to save those whom Almighty God in his deep wisdom has preordained to bliss, and to be influenced by those motives? We all confess, that no man can do his duty without the grace of God, and whoever has the grace of God will do his duty. It is undoubtedly to be obtained by prayer, but we must have grace to pray for it; and I am not insensible that Almighty God does any other way give his grace, but by offering to us, or by laying in our way sufficient inducements to obey his will: I am sure that I can find none else in myself, or discover them in others, whatever the enthusiastick and visionary gentlemen may do. I doubt much, that what they call grace, is what I call enthusiasm, or a strong conceit or persuasion of their own godliness and communication with the deity.

What sort of reasoning then is this, to say, that heaven gives every man sufficient power and motives to choose the best, which yet prove insufficient; that he has made every man free to act or not to act by a rule, and yet has placed him in such a situation as to find a thousand obstacles in his way to that freedom; and that he has given him a judgment capable to determine right, and opportunities rightly to exercise that judgment; yet by making use of that judgment and those opportunities, he often judges directly contrary: And all this is to make good a system, as yet owned but by a very small part of mankind, and for which I can find no foundation in reason and scripture?

I must beg leave to think it very audacious in a small number of men, to determine the workings of providence by their own narrow schemes, at the expence too of the opinions and reasonings of the greatest part of the world in all ages. All or most of the sects of philosophers in Greece and Rome, held fate or necessity, as the several sects among the Jews did, except the Essenes, a very small sect indeed, not exceeding some few thousands.[4] The Mahometans, thro' the world, hold predestination: The Calvinists, and some other Protestant sects, hold it now; and I do not understand the articles of the Church of England, if it be not the orthodox opinion amongst us; and it certainly was held to be so, till a few doctors in King James' and Charles I's time advanced the contrary system, and who, in the addresses of Parliament, were always, in those reigns, ranked with the papists for doing so; and it is yet undoubtedly the opinion of the common people through the world. However, I do not condemn any one who may think that this is derogatory to the attributes of God, for offering in a modest manner, his reasons against any dogma ever so well established (which I think is the right of all mankind); yet I could wish that he would shew the same modesty, in

4. A Jewish ascetic sect originating in the second century B.C., the Essenes shared with the Pharisees a belief in free will and divine providence.

giving other people their liberty of defending the contrary opinion with the same good intentions.

The most pregnant and usual objection against this doctrine is, that if men are predestinated to eternal bliss or misery, their own endeavours are useless, and they can have no motives to prefer good before evil; which I confess, will always be the reasonings of men who are predestinated to the latter (if it be possible to suppose that there can be any such); but those who are determined to the first, will always believe, that God takes proper means to attain his ends, and that he designs to save men by the medium of good works, and of obeying his will; and this conviction will be an adequate cause to produce such obedience in those who are destined to happiness. If the end be predestinated, the means must be predestinated too. If a man [is] to die in war, he must meet an enemy; if he [is] to be drowned, he must come within the reach of water; or if he [is] to be starved, he must not know how to come at any victuals, or have no mind to eat them, or stomach to digest them.

For my own part, I dare not believe, that the all-good, all-wise, and most merciful God, has determined any of his creatures to endless misery, by creating and forming them with such appetites and passions as naturally and necessarily produce it; though I think it to be fully consistent with his power, goodness, and justice, to give inclinations which may lead and entitle us to happiness. And, as I conceive that there is nothing in the holy scriptures which expressly decides this difficulty, as I may possibly shew hereafter;[5] so I shall not presume to search too narrowly into the secret dispensations of providence, or to pronounce any thing dogmatically concerning his manner of governing the universe, more than that he cannot make his creatures miserable without just and adequate reasons. And therefore, since we find in fact, that many of them are so in this state, we must account for this, but mediums agreeable to his indisputed attributes, or own that we cannot account for it at all, though it be unquestionably just in itself. All means will probably conduce in the end to impartial and universal good; and whatever, or how many states soever of probation we

5. In fact, Cato does not deal with the topic again.

may pass through, yet I hope, that the mercies of God, and the merits of Jesus Christ, will at last exceed and preponderate the frailties, mistakes, and temporary trangressions of weak and mortal men; all which I shall endeavour, in time, to shew from scripture and reason:[6] The former of which, in my opinion, is too generally mistaken or perverted, to signify what it does not intend; by straining some passages beyond their literal and genuine signification, by explaining others too literally, and by not making due allowances to the manner of speaking used amongst the eastern nations, which was very often, if not most commonly, in hyperboles, and other figures and allegories. But more of this hereafter; when I dare promise to deserve the pardon of every candid person, whom I cannot convince.

T   *I am, &c.*

NO. 111. SATURDAY, JANUARY 12, 1722.

The same Subject continued.

SIR,

As all the ideas or images of the brain must be caused originally by impressions of objects without us, so we can reason upon no other. A man born blind can have no image of light or colours; nor one who has been always deaf, of sounds; whatever descriptions are given him of them. There are many creatures in the world who want some organs of sense which we have, and probably there are others in the universe which have many that we want: and such beings, if there be any such, must know many things of which we have no conception; and must judge of other things, of which we have a more partial conception, in different lights from what we are capable of judging. It is not certain that any two men see colours in the same lights; and it is most certain, that the same men at different times, according to the good or evil disposition of their organs, see them in various ones, and conse-

6. The subject is again touched upon in Letter No. 124 (Apr. 13, 1723).

quently their ratiocinations upon them will be different; which experience shews us to be true in distempered, enthusiastick, or melancholy men.

Our senses are evidently adapted to take in only finite or limited beings; nor are we capable of conceiving their existence, otherwise than by mediums of extension and solidity. The mind finds that it sees, hears, tastes, smells, and feels, which is its manner of first conceiving things, or in other words, is the modus in which objects affect it; and it can reason no farther upon them, than according to those impressions: So that it is conversant only about the film or outside of bodies, and knows nothing of their internal contexture, or how they perform their operations; and consequently can affirm or deny nothing about them; but according to the perceptions which it has. When it goes further, or attempts to go further, it rambles in the dark, wades out of its depth, and must rave about non-entities, or, which is the same thing to us, about what we do or can know nothing of, or nothing to the purpose; and yet these things, or these nothings, have employed the leisure, speculations, and pens of many very learned men, as if true wisdom consisted in knowing what we want faculties to know.

All that we can know of infinity, eternity, &c. is, that we can know little or nothing about them. We must understand what we mean by the terms, or else we could not use them, or must use them impertinently. We perfectly apprehend what we mean by duration, which is our conception of the continuance of things, and contains in it a *terminus a quo* to a *terminus ad quem*,[1] that is, it has certain boundaries in our imaginations, and we can multiply this conception backwards and forwards, without ever being able to come to the end of it, and so may be sure that it is without end; and then the imagination is lost, and can go no further. We know that all extended bodies are divisible and can never be divided so often, but they may be divided farther; and therefore say justly, they are infinitely divisible; nor can any body be so large or long, as to come to the end of extension. And therefore we may safely affirm, that extension or space (which is our conception of the existence and immensity of bodies) is infinite. But then we know no

1. "The limit from which" and "the limit to which."

other properties of infinity or eternity, but by the help of these conceptions, which being limited and finite, cannot measure what is infinite and eternal; that is, we cannot comprehend what is incomprehensible to any being which is not infinite and eternal too, and whose existence is not as unmeasurable by time and place as those images are.

All the disputes, seeming contradictions, and absurdities, which offer themselves when we think or talk of infinity or eternity, arise from our applying our thoughts, which are confined to finite beings, and our words, which are coined to convey finite conceptions, to subjects which are infinite, and of which we can have no adequate ideas that can be expressed by sounds. Nothing is more true in finite beings, than that the whole must consist of all its parts; but in infinity there is no whole, nor consequently parts. Where there is no beginning, nor any end, there can be no middle; and where there is no whole, there can be no half. Time or space in theory are not divisible, because nothing but time or space can divide them, and then they are not divided; yet we know that time or space, as they have relation to finite beings, and our existence of duration, may be divided, and are so; and therefore the riddles made about them are owing to the narrowness of our capacities, and to our endeavouring to apply such conceptions as we have, to objects of which we can have no conception; which is, in effect, to attempt to hear sights, and see sounds.

It is the same thing to pretend to define eternity, or comprehend infinity; which is, to put limits and ends to what has no limits and ends, and to comprehend what is incomprehensible; which conceptions contradict one another, and cannot stand together in a proposition. It is the same to talk of infinite number, for all number must be finite.

How vain therefore is it to form any propositions or reasonings beyond our images, or to make positive deductions from premises wholly negative! From hence I conceive proceed all the fairy disputes about the modus of God's existing; what are his attributes and manner of acting; whether space is a real being, or only the order of things amongst themselves; whether it is the sensorium of God; or what is the meaning of the word *sensorium*:

Which controversies have taken up great part of the time of two very learned men,[2] that has been spent, as I think, mostly in shewing that they know nothing of the matter, or next to nothing. I am sure that I have learned nothing from their elucidations, whatever others may have done.

All that God Almighty has thought fit to tell us about the modus of his existence, is, *I am that I am*. And this we should have known, if he had not told it to us; and I believe it is all that we ever shall know, till he gives us other faculties. We are very sure that God *is*; that some being must have existed before any limitation of time, and independent of every other being; and consequently must have existed necessarily, or what we call eternally. It is exceeding probable, and, I think, certain, that there cannot be two or more such beings as are necessary and self-existing; and if but one, then that must be the cause of all the rest; or, which is the same thing, must produce all the rest; which mediately or immediately must derive their existence, faculties, sensations, capacities, powers of action, and consequently their actions themselves, from him.

But by what energy or power he effects this, we are wholly ignorant; and though the wits of learned men have been employed in solving this intricate question for many thousand years, yet the world is now just as wise as when they are first set out; and therefore I humbly think it high time to give over, and to content ourselves with knowing all that we can know, that is, that we can know nothing about it; and, consequently, ought not to form propositions about God's essence, or his attributes, concerning his eternity, his infinity, the modus or the sensorium of his existence, or concerning his ways or motives for making or governing the universe: For I conceive that in these questions we must walk wholly in the dark; like travellers who are out of their way, the farther they go, the greater is their journey home again.

2. Samuel Clarke and Anthony Collins. Both Clarke (1675–1729) and Collins (1676–1729) were eminent theologians and metaphysicians; Clarke was a disciple of Isaac Newton and a staunch opponent of deism, materialism, and empiricism, while Collins, an intimate of John Locke, wrote extensively defending deism and necessitarianism.

However, I think that we are left at liberty to reason about things which we do know; and therefore may with great assurance say, that God made all things, and that every thing depends immediately, or, by second causes, mediately, upon him; and that it is absolutely impossible that they can do otherwise.

I do not see how a greater absurdity can be put together in words, than that one being shall make another, create the matter of which it was made, give it all the faculties that it has, all its capacities of reasoning, powers of action, means of thinking, and present it with all its objects for thinking, yet leave it at liberty to act against them all; which I conceive is a downright impossibility. A pair of scales perfectly poised cannot ponderate on either side; and a man who has no motives to act, will not act at all. Every thing must be at rest which has no force to impel it: but as the last straw breaks the horse's back, or a single sand will turn the beam of scales which hold weights as heavy as the world; so, without doubt, as minute causes may determine the actions of men, which neither others nor they themselves are sensible of. But certainly something must determine them, or else they could not be determined; and it is nothing to the purpose to say, that their choice determines them, if something else must determine that choice: for, let it be what it will, the effect must be necessary. To say, that a man has a power to act, without any motives or impulse to act, seems to me to be a direct blunder. A man cannot have a will to act against his will; and if he has a will to do it, something must determine that will; and, whatever it is, must be his cause of action, and will produce the action; and that can only be the appearance of advantage arising from it; and those appearances must arise from the seeming relations of objects to one another, or to himself; which relations are not in his disposal, nor consequently are his actions, in the sense contended for.

If a man can do a voluntary action without a design to do it, and without any reason or motive for doing it, then matter without understanding has a self-moving power; which is atheism with a witness: though I will not, according to laudable custom, call the asserters of it atheists, because they may not see the consequence; for, take away understanding, and there can be nothing left but matter: And understanding is certainly taken away, when a being has no reason for acting; but when he has a reason, that reason is the cause, or co-cause of the action.

The question therefore is not, whether a man can do what he has a mind to do? but, whether he can do what he has no mind to do? That is, if his inclinations concur with his reasonings, his appearing interests, and his predominant passions, whether all together will not form his resolutions, and make him act pursuant to them, whilst those motives continue? One may as well say, that a man can avoid seeing, when an object strikes the eye, or hearing, when it hits the ear, as to believe that he can decline thinking, when the motion caused by the object reaches the brain, or where-ever else the seat of thinking is, unless some other more powerful object obstruct or divert it in its journey, or afterwards; and when he does think, he must think as he can, that is, according as objects from without are represented by their images to him within; or, in other words, as they act upon the animal spirits, or whatever else it is which sets the machine in motion. A man cannot avoid feeling pain or sickness, which are sensations of the mind, nor choose whether he will feel them or not; nor can he avoid desiring to get rid of them, unless some stronger motives determine him, which promise him greater advantages than he suffers inconveniences.

But here the metaphysical gentlemen distinguish between the motions of the body and those of the mind: They own that the pulse will beat, the nerves, arteries, muscles, and blood, will move, whether we will or not; and is it not as evident, that, according as they move or beat, the mind receives alteration, is enlarged or less-ened, improved or impaired, and determined in many of its reso-lutions? A man sick, or in pain, will send for or go to a physician or surgeon, which draws after it a train of other resolutions or actions; and, according to the success which he meets with, may alter the whole scheme of his life, and of his after-thinking, and very often of his capacity of thinking. As our bodies are healthy or disordered, we are courageous, jealous, fearful, enthusiastick, or melancholy, and reason differently, and act differently: And is it not then choice philosophy, to say, that the contexture and disposi-tion of our bodies (which were not of our own making) often direct or influence the resolutions of our mind, and yet are not the causes of those resolutions; and to go on to suppose, that our minds act independently of them, as well as of all other causes? For it is ridiculous to say, that though the mind has a principle of self-motion, yet other causes co-operate to produce the action; for if any other cause make it do what it would not otherwise do, that is the cause, or co-cause of the action produced, to all the purposes of this argument; nor can I guess at any other argument (that can be made use of to shew, that second causes can produce part of the action, or co-operate in producing it) which can prove them incapable to produce the whole. The most that can be pretended is, that there is a possibility that it may be so; but I conceive that no reason can be assigned why it may not be otherwise. But whether it be so or not, I think I have shewn, that the mind of man can be only a secondary cause, must be acted upon by other causes; that God alone is the first cause or principle of all motion; and that the actions of all other beings are necessarily dependent upon him.

A very great and justly celebrated author, who supposes that a man has a self-moving power, and, I think, only supposes it, endeavours to determine the question, by reducing his opponents to account for what no man yet has accounted for, and yet every man sees to be true: He says,[*]

> If the reasons and motives upon which a man acts be the immediate and efficient cause of the action, then either abstract notions (as all reasons and motives are) are in themselves substances, or else that which has no real subsistence can put a body in motion.

Now the force of this reasoning consists in putting his adversary upon shewing how the mind acts upon the body, or the body upon the mind: and he would have done kindly to have let us into that secret himself. When he is so obliging to inform the world, how the eye sees, the ear hears, or the palate tastes, I dare

---

[*] Dr. Clarke's remarks upon a philosophical enquiry concerning human liberty. Page 43. [The complete title of Samuel Clarke's work is *Remarks Upon a book, entitled A Philosophical Enquiry Concerning Human Liberty*, published in London by J. Knapton (1717). Clarke's work was a commentary on Anthony Collins's earlier work entitled *A Philosophical Enquiry Concerning Human Liberty*.]

undertake to solve any other difficulty which he proposes. We find, by experience, that when an object strikes the eye, it causes that sensation which we call seeing; and a man cannot then avoid seeing, no more than in other circumstances he can avoid feeling pain and sickness, which are undoubtedly actions of the mind, or, if he choose another manner of expression, we will call them passions (and indeed they are both; *viz.* the latter as they are impelled by other causes; and the former, as they produce future events: And it seems very trifling to me, in so great a man, to spend so many pages about the propriety of a word, when the meaning intended to be conveyed by it was fully understood): but certainly they are species of thinking, or, if he pleases, abstract notions, which often put a body in motion, as all thinking undoubtedly does: But how these effects are produced, we are wholly in the dark.

We see and feel, that desires and fears, that abstract notions or images of the brain, alter the disposition of the whole fabrick, and often destroy the contexture of it. We see that the longings of women with child will stamp impressions upon the fetus, which longings are certainly abstract notions; and if these are not corporeal, then we must confess, that what is not so will affect what is: For as to his words *substance* and *subsistence*, I shall not pretend to understand them without a farther explanation, if he mean any thing by them besides body. Methinks this truly worthy and learned author should not call upon another to solve what no man is more capable of solving than himself. I freely own my ignorance; and, since, as I conceive, revelation is silent in the matter, am contented to continue in that ignorance.

The other argument is as follows:

If insensible matter, or any other being or substance continually acting upon a man, be the immediate and efficient cause of his actions, then the motion of that subtle matter or substance must be caused by some other substance, I would choose to call it some other being, and the motion of that by some other, till at last we arrive at a free being.[3]

3. *Remarks Upon a Philosophical Enquiry Concerning Human Liberty*, p. 43.

Now, if, instead of the words *free being*, he had said a self-existent being, which I call God, his conclusion had been inevitable; nor do I oppose it in the words which he uses: But as we may possibly differ, and I doubt shall do, in the meaning of the words *free being*, so I neither assent to, nor dissent from, his proposition. I mean by a *free being*, one who has nothing, without itself, to determine or control its actions; which God has not, and I think man has. His conclusion therefore from such premises are nothing to me.

T   *I am &c.*

NO. 112. SATURDAY, JANUARY 19, 1722.

*Fondness for Posterity nothing else but Self-love.
Such as are Friends to publick Liberty, are the only
true Lovers of Posterity.*

SIR,

Men, for the sake of their posterity, do many things, which, they tell us, they would not do for their own sakes. The wealth which they do not spend, they lay up for posterity; and their care for posterity is made a pretence, to justify all the acquisitions that they make of fortune and dominion. But this is false reasoning, though by it they often deceive themselves and others. They find that they have greater appetites to acquire wealth, than they have to enjoy it; and, not being able to deny, that wealth is only so far useful as it is enjoyed, and no farther, they cannot justify their conduct, but by furnishing themselves with a false excuse from their regard for posterity: As if the affections of men could be stronger for others, and for a future race, of whom they know nothing, or for such as perhaps may never exist, than for themselves. Doubtless, men are in no circumstances to be separated from themselves: They are ever the chief objects of their own tenderness and good wishes; and the love of posterity is only self-love continued beyond the grave. We see those who have no posterity, nor the prospect of any, engaged in the same passionate and greedy pursuits as those who have; and they often leave their estates, when they die, to those for whom, while they lived, they shewed no concern.

This ambition therefore amongst men, of leaving an illustrious posterity, is mere self-love; a passion to survive themselves, and to make a figure after they are dead. To gratify this passion, men in all stations often take wild and unaccountable courses: They employ great pains for that which they can never enjoy, and run many dangers for what they will never reap: They drudge, and laboriously contrive ways to wear themselves out, they deny themselves rest and ease, and the comforts of life, that some future men, whom they know not, may live in idleness and abundance, and perhaps despise these their careful and penurious ancestors, who painfully provided for them the means of luxury, and enabled them to be insolent, or debauched, or insignificant to society. They are indeed generally but even with one another: The descendent receives, without gratitude, an estate which his ancestor left him without affection. People would take it greatly amiss, if you supposed that they wanted honour for their ancestors, or regard to their posterity; and that they themselves were the only real objects of all this regard, and of that honour. But let them ask themselves, whether they would restore to their grandfather again the estate which he left them, were he to rise from the dead, and demand it? or, whether they are willing to part with it to their children before their own death? or, if they sometimes do, whether they have not other motives besides paternal affection? and, whether their own credit and vanity be not the strongest?

Thus men gratify their own tempers, and invent fine false reasons and specious names for what they do. A passion for posterity, is a passion for fame; and he who raises a family, considers his race as hereditary trustees for his name and grandeur, and as the proper means and channel for perpetuating himself. Nor does he carry about him an appetite more selfish and personal than this. So that all the wicked things which a man does to raise a posterity, are but so many infamous steps to acquire personal fame, which he will never arrive at; and does therefore but labour against the very end which he labours for. If his posterity prove good, it will be remembered to their praise, and his shame, what a vile ancestor they had: If they prove bad, it will not be forgot how much they resemble him; and he will become still more odious in his odious descendents. Even the wisest men do a foolish thing, when they employ great assiduity and care to leave a great estate to a random heir, whom nature, or chance, or the law, gives them. How many immense estates, gathered in a long course of years and application, have we seen thrown away suddenly upon harlots and sharpers! The acquisitions of half a century have disappeared, as it were, in a moment; and the chief remaining monuments of the founder's name were jests made upon his memory.

But of all the foolish and wicked ways of raising families, none equals that of raising them upon the ruins of publick liberty. The general security is the only certain security of particulars; and though desperate men often find safety in publick destruction, yet they cannot ensure the same safety to their children, who must suffer with the rest in the misery of all. If great wicked men would consider this, the world would not be plagued with their ambition. Their posterity scarce ever miss to reap the bitter fruits of their actions; and the curse of their iniquities rarely fails to follow them to the third and fourth generation.

The instruments of public ruin have generally at once entailed misery upon their country and upon their own race. Those who were the instruments and ministers of Caesar and Augustus, and put the commonwealth under their feet, and them above the laws, did not consider, that they were not only forging chains for their country, but whetting swords against their own families, who were all cut off under succeeding tyrants: Nay, most of their children fell early and bloody sacrifices to the cruel and suspicious spirit of Tiberius. He began his reign with the murder of young Agrippa,[1] whose father had, by his courage and conduct in war, established the tyranny in that house. What availed to Agrippa all his great riches, his sumptuous buildings, and even his near alliance with the prince, whose daughter he married, but to hasten and magnify the fall and destruction of his own house?

1. Marcus Vipsanius *Agrippa* Postumus (12 B.C.–A.D. 14), whose father was a lifelong friend and supporter of Augustus. He was executed by order of Tiberius immediately following the death of Augustus.

There was not one Roman family wickedly enriched by their base subserviency to Augustus, but was slaughtered and confiscated under his successors, and most of them under his immediate successor: Nay, their riches and splendor were reasons for destroying them. The freed slaves of the emperors grew afterwards the first men in Rome, and had at their mercy the heads and estates of the patricians; nor could any of the great Roman lords come into any post or office in their own empire, but by the pleasure and permission of those slaves, and by servile court paid to them.

Would their illustrious ancestors, who were the friends and abettors of Caesar, have done as they did, had they foreseen this vile subserviency of their posterity to slaves and pathicks, and the daily and wanton sacrifices made of their boasted blood? And yet was not all this easily to be foreseen? While they were arming him with a power over their country, they stripped themselves of all title to their lives and estates. By laying up riches for their families, they did but lay snares for the ruin of their families. It grew a crime under these tyrants, to be conspicuous for any thing; and riches, virtue, eloquence, courage, reputation, nay, names and accidents, became crimes. Men, and even women, were put to death, for having had illustrious ancestors; and some, for bearing the fortuitous surnames of great men dead an hundred years before.

So that these men, who, from the bait of present wealth and place, helped to overthrow the constitution of that great state, were not only the parricides of their country, but the murderers of their own children and families, by putting a lawless dagger into the hands of these tyrants to execute these murders. They sold their own blood and posterity to these imperial butchers, whose chief employment it was to shed it. These mistaken men might flatter and blind themselves with a conceit, that they were laying up riches for ages, and entailing honours upon their latest race: For what is so blind as ambition and avarice? But to their unhappy descendents it proved a terrible inheritance of servitude, exile, tortures, and massacre. What they meant to perpetuate, their fortune and race, were the first things seized and extirpated. They had been real traitors to make their children great; and their children were put to death for false treason, merely for being great. So nearly are punishments allied to crimes, and so naturally do they rise from them!

Thus rash and unadvised, even as to themselves and their own families, are those wicked men, who raise up an enormous power in their country, because they were its livery, and are for some time indulged by it in their own pride and oppressions! And so ungrateful is that power when it is raised, even to the props and instruments that raised it! They themselves are often crushed to death by it, and their posterity certainly are.

This may serve among other arguments, to prove, that men ought to be virtuous, just, and good, for their own sake, and that of their families; and especially great men, whose lasting security is best found in the general security. Pericles had long and arbitrarily lavished away the publick money to buy creatures, and perpetuate his power; and, dreading to give up his accounts, which the Athenians began to call for, thought that he had no other way to avoid doing this justice to his country, but by adding another great crime to his past crimes. He would venture the ruin of the commonwealth, rather than be accountable to it: He therefore threw all things into confusion, raised armies, and entered precipitately into a war with Lacedaemon; which, after much blood, misery, and desolation, ended in the captivity of his country. During that war, he died of the plague, which the war was thought to occasion; and to his pride and guilt alone were owing the plague, war, and the taking of Athens, with the desolation of the city and territory. Before he died he felt the loss of his whole family, and of all his friends and relations; and, doubtless foresaw the downfall of his country. What huge and complicated ruin! He would see the state sink, rather than lose his authority in it: But in the destruction of his country, his own was justly and naturally involved. Where was now the great, the politick, the eloquent, Pericles? Where was the proud state which he had long and haughtily swayed? Where was his family and race? Where were all his mighty future views? Why, the sword, the pestilence, and foreign conquest, had, by his own management, put an end to them all; and his wisdom and profound foresight proved miserable and ruinous folly.

T   *I am, &c.*

NO. 113. SATURDAY, JANUARY 26, 1722.

ℛ *Letter to Cato, concerning his many Adversaries and Answerers.*

HORATIUS TO CATO

SIR,

I have had a long ambition to say something about you one way or other; but I doubted whether I had best write to you, or against you. That doubt is now decided; and lo! I who might have been your adversary, am become your correspondent and advocate. I send you your apology, and shew you the good that you do.

You have, sir, opened a new source of provision for the poor, by finding employment for all the wits mendicant about town: And though they ought to reverence your name, as that of another Sutton,[1] by whose alms they are sustained, yet they vilely fly in your face, and pollute, by their matchless ingratitude, the very bread which you generously put into their mouths; like maggots, who prey upon the flesh that they are bred in, till they turn flies, which are vermin with wings. Thus reprobates serve heaven; they affront and blaspheme it, and receive their existence from it. You scarce had appeared in the world, but you recalled superannuated authors to life again; and, toothless as they were, set them a biting, biting at the hand that brought them back from oblivion. Obsolete and despairing authors once more violently grasped their pen: The lean and ill fed candidates for weekly work from the booksellers brightened up, and began to be clothed; and puny poets, and the humble composers of ditties, left their tags and ballads, to live upon Cato; even those who had got some reputation, thought that they had now a lucky opportunity to improve it, by breaking a lance with a champion who drew all eyes upon him, and was yet invincible: And Cato became at once the butt of the

---

1. Thomas Sutton (*c.* 1532–1611), founder of Charterhouse school and hospital and probably the richest commoner in England at the time of his death. His entire fortune was left to charitable purposes.

envious, the mark of the ambitious, and the stay and support of the needy.

It is the lot of grandeur: A great man must have his poor and impertinent dependents, as well as his useful and agreeable: They will serve to make up his train. A troop of beggars besetting his coach, or following it in the street, do, notwithstanding their rags, and ill-favoured looks, and dismal style, but add to the lustre of his figure. Jesters and buffoons, cynics and declaimers, are likewise of the same use, to swell his pomp, and divert him, though they be often too free with him. Your retinue, sir, of this kind is infinite: From the Cockpit[2] to Moorfields you maintain a wag, an orator, a critick, a poet, a journalist, in every street, and whole swarms in the alleys: Nor would I desire a surer patent for fame than such a shoal of calumniators. Their scolding is compliment; and while they aim blows at you, they only cudgel themselves on your behalf: *Offendent solido;*[3] you know the fable of the viper biting the file.[4]

Envy always praises those whom it rails at. It is indeed the only way that foul mouths can make your panegyric, or that of any man. Were they to extol you in earnest, it would be downright scandal and railing; a foul conspiracy against your reputation; like the fawning of a whelp, who, to express his fondness, pisses upon you. If therefore they meant their scurrilities and satyrical non-sense in love, you would have ground for provocation: But to mean them as they do the contrary way, is their only genuine way of thanking you for their food. There are many sorts of folks whose calumnies I would be proud of for the same reason why I would be ashamed of their praise. A great man at Athens was fol-lowed from a publick assembly, all the way home, by a very compe-tent reviler, with a world of panegyrical ill names and acceptable abuses. That great man took all these kind volleys of defamation for so many huzzas; and calling to his servant, "Go," says he, "take

2. The colloquial term for a block of buildings opposite Whitehall Palace, housing additional palace apartments and later used as offices by the Privy Council.

3. "They knock against a solid object."

4. An Aesopian fable: A viper tried to bite a file, thinking it edible, whereupon the file remarked that its province was to bite, not to be bitten.

a light, and conduct that worthy gentleman, who has honoured me with all those civil acclamations, home to his lodging."[5]

Now, if this ill-tongued Athenian had not been in earnest, his courtesy would have been half lost. I hope that your numerous answerers and revilers mean what they say, else the obligation is but small; and the smaller, because these their panegyricks upon you are not at all encouraged. The town is still profoundly ignorant what a swarm of retailers, what loud and vehement flatterers, you have in it. They have filled, and do weekly fill, mighty reams of paper in extolling you, as great a secret as the world would make of it, to use the words of a witty author.

Love, they say, is blind; and perhaps from hence may be fetched a proof, that these your pretended adversaries are your real friends, since in their writings against you, that is, for you (for it is all one) they are guided by no other rule of right and wrong, than whether Cato affirms a thing, or denies it; and are always sure to take the contrary side: Nay, some of them contradict Cato, at the expence of their constant and favourite opinions. Does not this look like playing booty?[6] By their works one would think that you had the licensing of your opponents, and, but for their hideous bulk, the overlooking of them: At least by your profound silence, and great meekness towards them, you seem well pleased with their labours. I dare say, you would not change them for any set of defamers that could be pick'd up for you.

A lady of my acquaintance is fond of dogs. She has at present two or three little curs, that are very noisy at every visitant who is taller than ordinary. The puny vermin have a spite at elevation. They once particularly, made an incessant and slanderous clamour at a noble lord, well known for his fine person, and graceful mien; nor could they be stilled. The lady was out of countenance: She told him that she would have them knocked on the head, or given away: "By no means, Madam," says his lordship, sagely enough, "I know you cannot be without dogs, and perhaps the next may bite me."

5. The "great man" is Pericles, and the incident is reported in Plutarch, *Pericles*, 5.

6. The term denotes joining with accomplices to bilk another player and carries the sense of pretending to win while deliberately losing.

I think that I have read you impartially, and cannot say that I have found in you any knavish reasoning, any base or dishonest principles. You need not therefore be concerned who writes against you. However, as I would trust no body, in any circumstances, with any sort of absolute power, methinks I should not be displeased to see you checked and watched a little in that great authority which you have acquired over the minds of men. No body has shewn us better than yourself, that all discretionary power is liable to be abused, and ought not to be trusted, or cautiously trusted, to mortal and frail men. For this reason, though you be a monarch of the press, I would have you a limited monarch: As such it becomes you to bear with, and receive kindly, the admonitions and remonstrances of men of honour and sense, when such differ with you; and it is agreeable to your sense and character, to laugh at the profane contumelies of slaves. Your calumniators do your business. The viper carries within it a remedy for its own poison. You are secure, by the baseness of their fears, against the baseness of their malice; and their malice is harmless, by being obvious.

There is something diverting in the number and variety of your adversaries, and in their different views. Some are old stagers; and, being used to spill ink for pay in the quarrel of parties, made an offer of themselves to enter the lists again, and scold for wages at Cato. The finances were not in Cato's disposal: This was a good and conscientious reason to them for being against him. But these volunteers are not suitably encouraged. One of them has in two years writ near a dozen pamphlets against you; but with ill success every way. The town will not buy them; the other end of the town will not reward the author; nor will you take any notice of them. A melancholy case; that learned Oxonian is at present in the slough of despond.

Others, who had not been used to receive pay, and I doubt never will, thought themselves qualified to earn it: For, alas! what is so deceiving as self-love? So upon Cato they fell; and, by way of answer, cracked jests, and called him names. Fraught with this merit, away they footed sweating to the office; where, after many petitions, and much waiting, they were admitted to the audience of one of the clerks. They begged to be considered as humble auxiliaries, and to have an acknowledgment, the smallest acknowledgment. These gentlemen had better luck than the above ancient author: They were fully rewarded; that is to say, they were civilly thanked by the aforesaid clerk, and owned to be well-meaning persons. And yet they are ungrateful, and make heavy complaints, as if they had nothing. They still hope for more another time.

A bookseller of my acquaintance tells me, that he has refused within this year, five and fifty pamphlets written against you; and that the authors, one and all, offered to write for him by the year. They were all of opinion, that they could carry through a weekly paper with as much reputation and success as any yet written against you: Which he did not deny; and yet dismissed them. He told me, it was but this winter, that a man in a livery came to him, and asked him, what he would give for a sermon to be preached by his master the doctor on a publick occasion? He answered, "Nothing." "Oh, sir," says the valet, "my master's will sell like wild-fire. You cannot think, sir, how purely he claws off Cato: And you will see he'll soon be made a . . ."* You may see, sir, that you are a useful man to many, and even considered as a scale to great preferment. This sermon is since out, and it has neither hurt you nor exalted the preacher, though he has there laboured the point very hard. The doctor wanted no good will, whatever else he wants. Unluckily for him, there is not an argument (I should have said assertion) used by him against writing, but what will bear fifty times as strongly against preaching. I will, however, acquit him from meaning this consequence, or any other but that which his man meant; and which seems a consequence at least extremely remote. The doctor is, indeed, admirable: While he thought himself haranging and scattering words against libelling, he was actually inveighing virulently against himself, and preaching an angry libel against preaching. May the press and liberty be ever blessed with such foes! The doctor does not want words; it is pity but he knew the use of them.

* Here he mentioned one of the highest dignities in the church.

Says Mr. Bayes, in *The Rehearsal*,[7]

I bring out my bull and my bear; and what do you think I make them do, Mr. Johnson?

Johnson. Do! why fight, I suppose.

Bayes. See how you are mistaken now! I would as soon make them dance: No, igad, sir, I make them do no earthly thing.

There is this difference between the doctor's bull and Mr. Bayes's bull: The doctor's bull bellows; besides this he does no earthly thing neither.

Pray, sir, be not so proud and lazy; read some of your adversaries, and their bulls will divert you.

Methinks, as great a man as the world takes you to be, and as you may think yourself, you treat your intended adversaries, but real friends, too superciliously, and, I conceive, with too much contempt. I am told by some of your intimate friends, that you have never read any of their works; and yet, to my knowledge, several of them please themselves with having mortified you, and do themselves no small credit amongst their acquaintance by bragging of it. Give your poor retainers this consolation, since they are like to have no other: Consider them as brats of your own begetting; and, since you have brought them into the world, that you ought to support them. Your taking but the least notice of them, and their performances, will give them food and raiment: But I will beg leave to say, that it is very unnatural, when you have given birth to so many innocent and harmless creatures, to leave them afterwards to starve. You see that they want no industry and application; and it is not their fault if they want success. Take, generous Cato, a little notice of them; and I am sure they will gratefully acknowledge your indulgence. Read their labours, and condescend to throw away a few leisure hours in contemplating the imbecility of human nature. It becomes the greatest men to know the weak sides

7. The author of plotless dramas in *The Rehearsal* (1671) by George Villiers, second Duke of Buckingham. The lines quoted by Gordon do not appear in the published version of the play.

of it as well as the strong; at least you will learn this lesson by it, that

Man differs more from man, than man from beast.

Give me leave to conclude with a story: Once upon a time, I saw a large brave bull, of great comeliness and dignity, brought out upon a green near a country village to be baited. Among the bull-dogs fetched to bait him, were seen several dirty, deformed curs, called house dogs, that vented their choler in filthy noise. They barked aloud and bitterly, and disturbed every body but the bull, who, at all their snapping, snivelling, and snarling, never turned his head, nor moved a foot or horn. At last the squire of the place, who presided at the entertainment, shewed himself a man of taste and equity. "Take away," says he, with a voice of authority, "take away these yelping mongrels: We do not use to bait bulls with turnspits."[8]

G

> *I am, Sir,*
> *Your humble servant,*
> HORATIUS.

NO. 114. SATURDAY, FEBRUARY 2, 1722.

The necessary Decay of Popish States shewn from the Nature of the Popish Religion.

SIR,

As I do not pretend to be inspired myself, nor have received any personal revelation concerning the Whore of Babylon,[1] nor to have skill enough in the Apocalypse to discover the exact time of the fall of Antichrist; so I shall leave that charge to the profound persons who are learned in prophetick knowledge; but would humbly advise them to use a little of their own endeavours

8. Turnspits: curs.

1. The papacy.

to demolish the harlot, and not to expect the whole from providence. And to encourage them in this undertaking, I shall attempt to shew in this paper, what is told in the *Homilies*, that she is old and withered, and would have long since fallen to pieces, if she had not been patched with searcloths,[2] and kept alive by cordials, administered by the charity of those who were, or ought to have been, her enemies;[3] and that as soon as they leave off their complaisance, give her no more physick, nor adopt her trumpery, her end will be certain: And this I shall attempt to prove from natural causes, leaving the supernatural ones to those who understand them better.

It has been more than once said in these letters, that population, labour, riches, and power, mutually procure one another, and always go together; that where there are but few people, and those few are not employed, there will be little wealth, and as little power; and consequently, those governments, which provide least for the increase of their people, and for the employment of those that they have, are less capable of annoying their enemies, or of preserving themselves.[4] Now, if we try the power of Protestant and popish states by this test, it will appear absolutely impossible that the latter can long subsist, if the former do not lose their natural advantages by political blunders.

In the popish states of Europe, there are a million or more of male ecclesiasticks, and almost as many of the other sex, who by their religion are hindered from marriage, and consequently from procreation, unless by stealth, spurious births, which rarely produce living children; and all, or most of these, subsist upon the plunder of the people, without contributing any thing to the publick wealth, either by their labour, or out of their immense revenues, which are

2. Searcloth: winding sheets.

3. Although this precise language is not used in the *Homilies*, the sermons contain numerous examples of similar sentiments. See *Certain Sermons or Homilies Appointed to be Read in Churches in the Time of Queen Elizabeth of Famous Memory* (London: Printed for George Well, etc., 1687), passim, and especially "The Third Part of A Sermon of Good Works Annexed Unto Faith," pp. 55–58, and "The Fifth Part of An Homily Against Disobedience and Wilful Rebellion," pp. 626–31.

4. The theme is touched on throughout, but see especially Letters 10, 87, and 106 (Jan. 3, 1720, and July 28 and Dec. 8, 1722).

usually exempted from taxes, as are their persons from wars; on the contrary, they have no other business, but to fascinate and turn the brains of weak and enthusiastick people, to make them loiter after masses and useless harangues, and to fill their heads with senseless speculations and wild chimeras, which make them either useless or dangerous to their governors, and the ready tools and instruments of turbulent and seditious pedants; which evil is, or should be, better provided against in all Protestant states.

In popish countries, one third part of the year, or more is spent in most religiously worshipping dead men and women under the name of saints; in all which time the people dare not work to support their families, but must contribute, out of the little which remains, to pay their oppressors for preaching them out of their wits; and, by consequence, the publick loses all that the people would earn in those days; whereas, in Protestant states, all, or most of this trumpery is laid aside, and they most reasonably judge, that Almighty God is not worshipped by his creatures starving themselves, and weakening their country.

In popish countries the power of the ecclesiasticks is so great, and their revenues so large, that the civil authority is often not able to protect its subjects. The priests, by the Inquisition and various cruelties, seize their estates, drive away their merchants and people, or starve them at home, and frighten others from coming in their room; so that their princes are forced to keep measures with them, connive at, submit to, and support their tyranny, in order to be protected in their own power; and, by so doing, their unhappy and undone subjects are reduced to the condition of their great Master, to be crucified between two thieves. On the contrary, in Protestant states the ecclesiasticks are equally subject with the rest of the people to the civil power; are not so numerous, nor have so large revenues, and those revenues are taxable; nor have they so much power and influence to mislead their hearers, and consequently cannot do so much mischief, and if kept to their proper business, may do much good by their pious examples, and by their godly precepts.

In popish countries a great part of the year is spent in keeping Lent, and in fasting-days, when the people, by their poverty, are reduced to live upon stinking or unwholesome food, whence many of them perish, and the rest are weakened and enervated, and rendered unfit either for labour or procreation; and then succeeds a riotous carnival, during which they are idle and debauched; and both these extremes, in their turns, produce diseases, poverty, and misery; whereas in Protestant countries the people live in regular plenty, according to their condition, keep themselves in constant labour and exercise, and by such means preserve their bodies in health, and their minds within their bodies, without sending them abroad a vision hunting.

In popish countries great quantities of gold, silver, and jewels, which ought to circulate, and be used in commerce, are buried as uselessly as when in the mine; are applied to adorn images and churches, or are locked up in caverns, and rendered unserviceable to mankind. This, forsooth, is called devotion, and giving to God what he before gave to men for their use; and their way of obeying him, is to make no use of it, and to lodge it only where there can be an ill use made of it. But, I thank God, this superstition is pretty well over in Protestant countries, where the people (a few old women and dotards excepted) think that their riches are better employed to maintain their families, relations, and friends, than to support idlers and cynics.

In popish countries, their ecclesiasticks, living in idleness and riot, must be more lascivious than if otherwise employed; and by the means of confessions, and other secret communications with women, have better and frequenter opportunities to debauch them themselves, and to carry on intrigues for others, whereby they break in upon the peace of families, and interrupt the harmony which ought to accompany a married estate. To prevent in a good measure which mischiefs (since they are forbid to marry), their states are necessitated to tolerate established courtezans under a regulation; an institution which hinders many others from marrying, debauches their minds, ruins their estates, and enervates their bodies, and yet gives few children to the commonwealth: Which mischief is well provided against in Protestant countries; for there no man is obliged to trust his wife with a priest, and, for the most part, the clergy find it convenient to marry themselves; and a blessing visibly attends their endeavours, no rank of people being more observed to multiply their species.

In popish countries many foreign wars are raised and stirred up by the pride and ambition of the ecclesiasticks to increase their power; and many domestick ones fomented for the same reason, about the power of the Pope, the investiture of princes, the immunities of the clergy; and endless contentions arise with the states which they live under, about their peculiar privileges, as well as constant persecutions against all who oppose their pretences: All which wars and quarrels exhaust the people, perplex the publick affairs, and either divide them into factions, or, which is much worse, make them all of their own. But in Protestant countries these evils are less enormous: The people begin to see with their own eyes, and will not undo one another to gratify the ambition of any who would oppress them all; nor force or drive out of their country useful inhabitants, for dry chimeras and useless notions, and for the shape of their thoughts and imaginations; and many of their clergy do not desire it.

In popish countries, great numbers of idle and useless members of society are employed to support the luxury of the ecclesiasticks, or to contribute to their superstition; as organists, fidlers, singers, scholars, as they are called, numerous officers of various kinds, and many lazy beggars, who feed upon their scraps, or are supported by their means out of the charity of others, who are persuaded that they serve God in keeping them idle and necessitous, and without labouring for a subsistence: All these are a dead weight upon society, live like drones in a hive, and eat honey without making any. This grievance is not so great in Protestant countries, the clergy amongst them not being used to throw away their money without having something for it.

In popish countries there is an asylum and sanctuary in every parish, where robbers, murderers, and all sorts of criminals, are defended against their sovereigns and their laws; by which means banditti and assassins are become a sort of establishment, and are the Swiss and guards of the papacy, depend upon the priests for protection, and are always at hand to execute their bloody designs, and to partake of the spoil, as well as to be hired by others; by which means there are numerous and nightly murders in those countries, and the people there dare not go about their necessary affairs; and therefore cannot have the same security and encouragement as in Protestant countries, where this enormous wickedness is not allowed and practised, and where the priests cannot protect assassins; and the worst that can be said of any of them is, that they will not find fault with them afterwards, but are ready to absolve them at the gallows, if they have been doing their work: And in one instance, in a certain jurisdiction* where a certain high-priest, or those who act under him, compound with delinquents by the great for crimes which they have committed, or are to commit for the year ensuing; *à la mode* of his Holiness at Rome.

These, and other infinite evils, are produced by the popish religion, which depopulates nations, destroys industry, overturns law and justice, the cements of society, discourages trade, drives out merchants, enervates states, and renders the race of mankind feeble, lazy, and miserable. Nor can I see a bare possibility how these wretched people can extricate themselves out of their doleful condition, which must still go on from bad to worse, till they become so weak as to be the prey of foreign enemies, or to expire by an internal consumption; for the power of the ecclesiasticks is so great, and depends so much upon keeping the laity poor, ignorant, idle, and helpless, that they cannot have the will or power to recover themselves.

This wicked policy has turned the Campania of Rome, and all the populous and fertile provinces of Italy, into bogs, morasses, and deserts, and would have long since extinguished popery, if some of the Protestant states had not forgot the principles upon which they had reformed, and others had submitted to domestick slavery, but little worse than ecclesiastical, as both flowing from the same root, and producing the same evils, though not in the same degree; however, I think that the catastrophe of popery is but a

---

* Westminster, in the time of Dr. Atterbury, whose protection, or that of his high bailiff, some bawdy-houses claimed against the authority of the justices of peace. [Francis Atterbury was a Tory High Churchman and Jacobite sympathizer, who, in 1713, was made Bishop of Rochester and Dean of Westminster.]

little farther removed, for the few states amongst the Protestants, with prudent laws, and a wise conduct alone, may be in a condition, if they can keep their liberty, without striking a stroke but in their own defence, to demolish and overturn this monstrous Babel, or make or suffer it to destroy itself.

T   *I am, &c.*

NO. 115. SATURDAY, FEBRUARY 9, 1722.

The encroaching Nature of Power, ever to be watched and checked.

SIR,

Only the checks put upon magistrates make nations free; and only the want of such checks makes them slaves. They are free, where their magistrates are confined within certain bounds set them by the people, and act by rules prescribed them by the people: And they are slaves, where their magistrates choose their own rules, and follow their lust and humours; than which a more dreadful curse can befall no people; nor did ever any magistrate do what he pleased, but the people were undone by his pleasure; and therefore most nations in the world are undone, and those nations only who bridle their governors do not wear chains.

Unlimited power is so wild and monstrous a thing, that however natural it be to desire it, it is as natural to oppose it; nor ought it to be trusted with any mortal man, be his intentions ever so upright: For, besides that he will never care to part with it, he will rarely dare. In spite of himself he will make many enemies, against whom he will be protected only by his power, or at least think himself best protected by it. The frequent and unforeseen necessities of his affairs, and frequent difficulties and opposition, will force him for his own preservation, or for the preservation of his power, to try expedients, to tempt dangers, and to do things which he did not foresee, nor intend, and perhaps, in the beginning, abhorred.

We know, by infinite examples and experience, that men possessed of power, rather than part with it, will do any thing, even the worst and the blackest, to keep it; and scarce ever any man upon earth went out of it as long as he could carry every thing his own way in it; and when he could not, he resigned. I doubt that there is not one exception in the world to this rule; and that Dioclesian, Charles V, and even Sulla, laid down their power out of pique and discontent, and from opposition and disappointment.[1] This seems certain, that the good of the world, or of their people, was not one of their motives either for continuing in power, or for quitting it.

It is the nature of power to be ever encroaching, and converting every extraordinary power, granted at particular times, and upon particular occasions, into an ordinary power, to be used at all times, and when there is no occasion; nor does it ever part willingly with any advantage. From this spirit it is, that occasional commissions have grown sometimes perpetual; that three years have been improved into seven, and one into twenty;[2] and that when the people have done with their magistrates, their magistrates will not have done with the people.

The Romans, who knew this evil, having suffered by it, provided wise remedies against it; and when one ordinary power grew too great, checked it with another. Thus the office and power of the tribunes was set up to balance that of the consuls, and to

1. The emperor Diocletian resigned his office in A.D. 305, purportedly because his health had collapsed the previous year. In 1558, Charles V, in whose person the thrones of Spain and the Holy Roman Empire were united, relinquished his various kingdoms and retired to a monastery in Spain. Sulla, the Roman dictator, convinced of the truth of a prophecy that he had but a short time to live, divested himself of his dictatorial powers, restored constitutional government, and returned to private life in 80 B.C.

2. A reference to the extension of Parliamentary terms. In 1716, fearful of a Jacobite rising, Parliament enacted the Septennial Act, prolonging its own life from three to seven years and making seven years the new legal term for future Parliaments. The Long Parliament was summoned by Charles I in 1640 and early in its sitting passed a bill preventing its dissolution without its consent. It dissolved itself in 1660.

protect the populace against the insolence, pride, and intrench-
ments of the nobility: And when the authority of the tribunes grew
too formidable, a good expedient was found out to restrain it; for
in any turbulent or factious design of the tribunes, the protest or
dissent of any one of them made void the purposes and proceedings of all the rest. And both the consuls and tribunes were chosen
only for a year.

Thus the Romans preserved their liberty by limiting the
time and power of their magistrates, and by making them answerable afterwards for their behaviour in it: And besides all this, there
lay from the magistrates an appeal to the people; a power which,
however great, they generally used with eminent modesty and
mercy; and, like the people of other nations, sinned much
seldomer than their governors. Indeed, in any publick disorder, or
misfortune, the people are scarce ever in the fault; but far on the
other side, suffer often, with a criminal patience, the sore evils
brought wantonly or foolishly upon them by others, whom they
pay dear to prevent them.

This sacred right of appealing to the people, was secured
to them by a very good and very severe law, which is found in Livy
in these words:

> Aliam deinde consularem legem de provocatione, unicum
> praesidium libertatis, decemvirali potestate eversam, non
> restituunt modo, sed etiam muniunt, sanciendo novam legem, ne
> quis ullum magistratum sine provocatione crearet: Qui creasset,
> eum jus fasque esset occidi: Neve caedes capitalis noxae
> haberetur.[3]

The former consular law for appealing to the people (the
first and only great support of liberty), having been overturned by the usurpation of the Decemviri, was now not

---

3. "Next they not only restored the consular law concerning appeal, liberty's
unique protection, which had been overturned by the power of the decemvirs,
but they also secured it for the future by enacting a new law whereby no one
could declare the election of any magistrate without appeal. Should such an
election be declared, whosoever announced it might be killed without offense
to law or custom, and the homicide would not be regarded as a capital crime."
Livy, 3.55.4–5.

only restored, but fortified by a new law, which forbad the creating of any magistrate without appeal, and made it lawful to kill any man that did so, without subjecting the killer to a capital penalty.

The Romans had but too good reason for these laws; for the Decemviri, from whom there was no appeal, had enslaved them.

And because the being frequently chosen into power, might have effects as bad as the long continuance in it, Cicero, in his book *De Legibus*, tells us, that there was an express law, *Eundem magistratum, ni interfuerint decem anni, ne quis capito;*[4] "That no man should bear the same magistracy which he had borne before, but after an interval of ten years." This law was afterwards strengthened with severe penalties. Hence Rutilius Censorius[5] blamed the people in a publick speech for creating him twice censor: And Fabius Maximus[6] would have hindered them from choosing his son consul, though possessed of every virtue proper for one, because the chief magistracies had been too long and too often in the Fabian family. And there are many instances in the Roman history, of magistrates, chief magistrates, being degraded for their pride, avarice, and maladministration; and those who were thus degraded, were by law disabled, like our late directors,[7] from ever enjoying again any post or power. Nor were the Romans less careful to oblige their magistrates as soon as they came out of their offices and governments, to make up their accounts, and to give a strict account of their good behaviour; and for an ill one they were often condemned, and their estates confiscated. Besides all which, to be a Senator, or a magistrate, a certain qualification in point of fortune was required; and those who had run through their fortunes were degraded from the dignity of Senators. A reasonable

---

4. "No one shall hold the same office unless ten years intervene between terms." Cicero, *De legibus*, 3.3.9.

5. Gaius Marcius Rutilus *Censorinus* served as censor in 294 B.C. and again in 265 B.C., the only Roman to hold the office twice.

6. Quintus *Fabius* Maximus Verrucosus (d. 203 B.C.), Roman general and five times consul.

7. The directors of the South Sea Company responsible for the Bubble.

precaution, that they who were entrusted with the interest of their country, should have some interest of their own in it.

In this manner did the Roman people check power, and those who had it; and when any power was grown quite ungovernable, they abolished it. Thus they expelled Tarquin, and the kingly government, having first suffered much by it; and they prospered as eminently without it. That government too had been extremely limited: The first Roman kings were little more than generals for life: They had no negative vote in the Senate, and could neither make war nor peace; and even in the execution of justice, an appeal lay from them to the people, as is manifest in the case of the surviving Horatius, who slew his sister.[8] Servius Tullius[9] made laws, says Tacitus, which even the kings were to obey.[10] By confining the power of the crown within proper bounds, he gained power without bounds in the affections of the people. But the insolent Tarquin broke through all bounds, and acted so openly against law, and the people of Rome, that they had no remedy left but to expel him and his race; which they did with glorious success.

The dictatorial power was afterwards given occasionally, and found of great use; but still it was limited to so many months; and there are instances where even the dictator could not do what he pleased, but was over-ruled by the judgment of the people. Besides, when the Romans came to have great and distant territories, and great armies, they thought the dictatorial power too great and too dangerous to be trusted with any subject, and laid it quite aside; nor was it ever afterwards used, till it was violently usurped, first by Sulla, afterwards by Caesar, and then Rome lost its liberty.

T   *I am, &c.*

8. "The surviving Horatius" is the last of the three Horatii; his two brothers were killed in combat, and he was acquitted on appeal for the murder of his sister Horatia.

9. The sixth King of Rome, *Servius* Tullius is purported to have been the author of a series of constitutional reforms.

10. *Annales*, 3.26.

NO. 116. SATURDAY, FEBRUARY 16, 1722.

That whatever moves and acts, does so mechanically and necessarily.

SIR,

It is justly observed by Mr. Locke, and by Mr. Hobbes and others before him, that we have no innate ideas, nor can reflect upon them before we have them; that is, we cannot think before we have something to think upon. All objects and materials for thinking must be let in upon the mind through the organs of sense; and when they are there, we reflect or reason upon them; or, to speak philosophically, when the action of exterior bodies strikes upon us, it must cause a second action or motion, and continue it *in infinitum,* unless it meets obstruction. This first action causes sensation, and the second reflection; and the first seems to me as necessarily to produce the latter, as wind sails a ship, or the winding up of a clock sets it in motion.

Every system of matter has peculiar organizations, and can perform only peculiar functions. A cow cannot perform the offices of a horse, nor a man of a monkey; nor indeed, in many instances, can one man perform those of another. As some machines or systems of matter consist of vastly finer and more numerous parts than others, so they are capable of more operations. A watch which points to minutes or seconds, has more wheels, than one which only shews hours; and a striking or repeating watch has more than both, though all are wound up by the same key. Animals who consist of infinite tubes, veins, arteries, muscles, and juices, which also consist of infinite globular, and other figured particles of matter, must have suitable and very surprizing operations, though all their actions must be confined within the circle of their machine; but they will be multiplied in equal or greater degree than the chances upon dies.[1] Two dies have six times as many chances as one, and three as two, and so on *in infinitum;* and therefore there seems to be no difficulty in accounting for the great variety of actions in

1. Dies: dice.

animals, more than in inferior machines: And as mankind never have, nor, I presume, ever will discover all the powers of mechanical experiments; so with greater reason one may venture to assert, that no animal ever yet has exerted all the faculties which it was endued with: A thousand dies may turn up all sixes; but I believe this has never happened, nor I believe ever will.

Vegetables seem to me to be analogous in many respects to animals: Their generation appears to be much alike: They both rise from seeds, or eggs, and continue their kinds by the same: Their life is continued alike, and their nourishment conveyed through veins or other tubes; and when that nourishment ceases, they die; and as the action of the sun, and other bodies, set the former in motion, and causes that sort of sensation which we call vegetation, so the same power, or some other like it, seems to rouze animal life, and sets it in like motion; and all motion must be progressive in the same system till it be destroyed, or that system become another, or part of another; which shall be more fully shewn hereafter.

This action is called by different names, as it affects the different parts of the machine. When it affects the eye, it is called seeing; the ear, hearing; the palate, tasting; the nose, smelling; which indeed are but different sorts of feeling: But when the motion is continued further, and gets to the brain, or other internal parts of the system, it causes that effect which we call thinking; which again operates within the animal, and drives it to farther action, which is always analogous to the disposition of the fabrick, and regular, or irregular, according to the present formation of the machine, and of the powers which impel it. And here we cannot enough admire the exquisite skill of the Supreme Architect, who has formed such stupendous and amazing works of his omnipotence; and in many instances, I conceive we should judge right if we only admired them, and not vainly attempted to find out what we can never know. We want faculties to search the causes of most things in nature, and know nothing of their internal contexture, and but little of the *modus* of their operations. We see only some sensible effects of the actions of bodies upon one another; but how they produce these effects, we are utterly ignorant, and I believe ever shall be whilst we are in this state: We cannot tell why the fire burns, the grass grows, the eye sees, the ear hears, or the mind thinks, only we find in fact, that they do so; and here is our *ne plus ultra*.

It is exceedingly imprudent therefore for men to pretend to determine the powers of matter and motion, when they know not what matter is, of what parts it consists, or indeed any thing about it, but by a few outward effects; nor can we form any notions of it but from those effects, which yet probably do not exhaust the millionth part of its powers: And it is still more ridiculous to use the word *spirit* (of which we have no sort of idea), to account for other things, of which we have very little or no idea neither; and in many instances, deny what we see, to pretend to believe what we do not understand. Words are only the signs of images, as figures are of numbers; and what use is there of a sound, or scrawl, which signifies nothing, or, which is the same thing, which stands for what we know nothing of?

Now if a man should ask a modern philosopher, what he meant by the word *spirit?* he possibly will answer, that it is something which wants extension and solidity. If it be asked again what conception he has of any thing which has neither extension or solidity? and he answer, that he has none at all; but that there may be beings in nature of which he neither has, nor can have any idea: If then he be asked, why he uses a word which has no conception annexed to it, to explain another thing about which he is wholly in the dark? his reply, I presume will be, that he cannot account for some operations of that being by the images which he had before conceived of it, and the definitions about it which he had been used to; and therefore he was forced to recur to negative ideas. If he be asked again, how he knows that his definitions are right, and take in all the powers of that being? he must acknowledge that he knows not the thousandth part of its powers; but yet perhaps will say, that he is very sure that it has not powers inconsistent with the nature of body. It will be asked of him, how he, who knows little or nothing of the nature of body, can know what is against the nature of body? which difficulty I shall leave to wiser men to unriddle.

Now it appears to me, that there are many mechanical operations of the minds and bodies of animals, which result only from their peculiar systems of matter; or, in other words, compounded bodies, peculiarly systematized, attain new qualities and powers which they had not before, and which influence their own actions, and the actions of other bodies, as necessarily as the loadstone draws iron, or the root and fibres of a tree or plant attract the juices of the earth, and convey them on till they are transmuted into wood, leaves, and fruit. A chick or a young pheasant, hatched in an oven, as soon as it is out of the shell, will eat bread, or emmet eggs,[2] and soon after shew signs of love or fear, and shrink from danger (like the sensitive plant from the touch) before it has gained any experience, has any sense of injuries, or can know how it can be hurt. Birds hatched in a cage will not only generate together, but will build their nest in the same manner, and of the same materials with those of the same kind, if they can come at them, without having seen any of the same sort before. Infant animals immediately seek after the teats of their dams, without being taught to do so; and all animals and vegetables seek or attract the peculiar nourishment that is proper to their species, without any direction but from nature; and have the same affections and passions, with but little variation: which I think plainly shews, that their particular organizations, or systems of matter, by a natural sort of gravitation or attraction direct their operations; and though every particular of the same species differ in some respects from another, and consequently their actions will vary, yet they are confined within the limits prescribed to the whole species. And this observation runs through all nature.

Now I conceive that this must be accounted for as above, or we must recur to constant miracle, or else suppose that God Almighty has given to every species of animals peculiar minds different from all other kinds, and to every particular a mind different from all the rest of the same kind; which mind guides and directs all our actions; and makes all the specifick as well as identical differences that we see: For which supposition I can find no foundation in reason, or from observation; nor can I perceive what

2. Emmet eggs: ants' eggs.

use can be made of such a concession; for whether the actions of animals are directed by the disposition of the materials which form them, or they were originally constituted with such appetites, they must act the same way; and this farther raises our admiration of the power and providence of God, who has formed all his creatures in such a manner as to answer his intentions in creating them; and has so disposed the mechanism and juices of every living species, as well as of every individual, as will best conduce to its preservation, and to perform the function intended.

But here a notable distinction arises between the operations of the mind, and those in the body, or, in other words, between sensations and reflections, between appetites and reasonings; which I must beg leave to think in this regard, has no foundation in nature, and only exists in metaphysical brains. There can be no sensations, inclinations, or appetites, without the cooperation of that faculty, capacity, energy, or whatever else it is that we call the mind. Dead men can no more hear, see, feel, &c. than a lump of earth, because their organization is destroyed, or the animal spirits which set them in motion can no longer continue that motion, or the separate principle, called the mind, can no longer keep its habitation; but whatever it be, or by what name soever called, it is certainly the *causa sine qua non* of the actions of the animal, and is one link of the chain of causes which direct and govern his voluntary motions.

It is the mind which sees, hears, tastes, smells, feels, desires, or fears; and herein consists the difference between animals and vegetables: They have both life, and both have organizations proper to preserve and continue that life, by suitable nourishment conveyed through veins and tubes: Both have surprising operations, unsearchable by our capacities; and both must have a long train of causes from nature to enable them to produce those operations: but besides many other possible causes linked together in those chains, and many of them existing within animals themselves which we do not know, there is one which we do, namely, the will or desire to do a thing; and this certainly, in a thousand instances, depends upon causes without us, and which are undoubtedly out of our power; which causes without set the other causes within us at work, and produce the will, and consequently the action.

A chick, or a young pheasant, would no more peck, or a lamb suck, than if it was dead, if it did not intend to do it: It feels uneasiness by hunger, and strives to help itself: It certainly shews thought and choice, in preferring one sort of food before another, and in shrinking or running away from danger: And these are all actions of the mind. It is true, as it grows older, and its contexture stronger, its experience increases, and its capacity grows with it; but the faculty is the same, and, for any thing which appears to the contrary, results from the formation of the system; nor can I conceive how all birds, beasts, and fishes of the same species should have the same, or very near the same sensations, desires, and fears, and chuse the same kinds of food and means of preservation, and always use the same, or very near the same address, cunning, or artifice, unless their contexture, the disposition of materials and juices, of which they are compounded by a natural mechanism, produced these effects, either by constituting or acting upon that energy, called their minds, and then directing and coercing those minds to exert the faculty, called the will, which produces the action, if it may be lawful to distinguish an operation of the same power from its self.

I am not aware of any other objection to this reasoning, but that we can have no conception how matter can produce an act or operation of the mind in brute animals; and therefore other systems have been invented, equally unconceivable, to avoid this, and which apparently contradict fact. It is plain, that their minds are affected, altered, and receive addition and diminution by diet, physick, and exercise, and partake, in many respects, of the fate of their material system; and their faculties are greater or less, according to the disposition of that system, as shall be more fully shewn in future papers.[3] And since the whole must consist of the several parts, what reasons can be assigned to prove, that material causes may create or produce the parts, and not the whole, I mean of their minds; for as to the soul of man, I shall consider it separately hereafter. For my own part, I have had always so unfortu-

3. See Letters 122 and 123 (Mar. 30 and Apr. 6, 1723).

nate a turn of thinking, that I could never subscribe to opinions, because others held them before me; nor will I send into the clouds for solutions, which lie under my nose, or refuse the benefit of my eyes to amuse my understanding; neither shall I regard the calumnies and uncharitable censures of those who dare not peep out of their dark dungeons, and would measure all truth by imbibed prejudices: but shall ever think, that I shall do more honour to Almighty God, in believing that he has so formed at once the whole fabrick of heaven and earth, as to produce all the events which he intended, than to suppose that he has often found cause to mend and alter his first resolutions; though I confess that it may consist with his wisdom, and conduce to the ends of his providence, to suffer matters, in some respects, and at some times, to appear to us in other lights.

He certainly is a more skilful artificer, who can make a watch which will go for a thousand years, and then break to pieces at a stated time, than another who makes one which must be wound up every day, and mended every month.

T   *I am, &c.*

NO. 117. SATURDAY, FEBRUARY 23, 1722.

Of the Abuse of Words, applied more particularly to the covetous Man and the Bigot.

SIR,

I have often thought, that most of the mischiefs under which mankind suffers, and almost all their polemick disputes are owing to the abuse of words. If men would define what they mean by the sounds which they make use of to express their thoughts, and then keep to those definitions, that is, annex always the same ideas to the same sounds, most of the disputes in the world would be at an end: But this would not answer the purposes of those who derive power and wealth from imposing upon the ignorance and credulity of others. And therefore, till the world can agree to be honest, and to buy and sell by the same measure (which they do not seem in haste to do), I doubt this evil is likely to go on.

There are no words in language which seem to me to be more misapplied than the word *self-interest*, by divines, orators, philosophers, or poets: All have exerted themselves with great efforts of exhortation, reason, eloquence, and wit, against this reigning vice; but I conceive, that they have all missed the mark. Indeed, in the larger sense of the word, I think it impossible for any man to act upon any other motive than his own interest: For every pursuit that we make must have for its end the gratification of some appetite, or the avoiding of some evil which we fear; and, in truth, when we say that any man is self-interested, we mean only, that he is not enough in his own interest.

A good-humoured man, when he pities another, gratifies a natural passion, in having a fellow-feeling of the calamities of others, and a desire to see all men out of pain or trouble. A generous man pleases his vanity, ostentation, or temper, in doing good to others; or by it intends to gain friends or dependents. An indulgent parent takes pleasure to see that his children (whom he esteems parts of himself) live happy, contented, and make a figure in the world; and derives credit and reputation to himself from their doing so. A beneficent patron, or a man in love, reaps great personal satisfaction in obliging the objects of his kindness, and by making them more devoted to himself. And all these pity or contemn one who wants these agreeable appetites, and most reasonably judge, that he wants many pleasures which they themselves enjoy; as well knowing, that, next to the preservation of their beings by wholesome food, and warm raiment, and the enjoying the common necessaries and usual diversions of life, all that can be added to their happiness is, to obtain respect, love, and esteem, from others.

Even all the worst passions flow from the same source. For, what is hatred, malice, and revenge, but gratifying vicious appetites? And fear and cowardice are only struggles in nature to avoid evils to ourselves. Of all men, the covetous man is the most unhappy: For, as every pleasure is the gratification of some appetite or desire, the man who has least desires and appetites, must have the least pleasures, and he must lose many agreeable sensations which other men enjoy. I laugh at the foolish philosophy of some sects in old Greece, who placed the *summum bonum,* or chief happiness, in the absence of all passions or desires; which can be only a state of death, or perfect stupidity, whilst we are alive. Men exceed vegetables no otherwise than as they think; and when they cease to think (if that can be) they are in a temporary state of death; and the objects of all thinking must be something which we desire to attain, or fear to lose: And as thought itself is only a motion of the mind, so one motion must produce another, as every thought must do, and be perpetually progressive, till death puts an end to all thoughts. Here covetousness therefore can only proceed from a poorness and dejection of soul, which always fears want and misery, and must ever be bereft of all lively and sparkling imaginations, be in a constant state of diffidence and despondency, and lose all the gay, cheerful and generous sensations, which flow from a free, active, happy, and beneficent mind.

I must take the liberty therefore to think, that *self-interest,* in the ill sense of the word, ought to be new-defined, and made applicable only to those who prefer a small interest to a great one, or to such who take a wrong way to attain that great one: And in this latter sense the bigot is the most self-interested person in the world: His whole thoughts are so wound up in himself, and his own personal views, that he is wholly regardless of what becomes of the rest of the world, unless he can find his own benefit in it. Indeed he will give some loose pence to beggars or vagabonds, and perhaps sums to maintain idlers and cynicks, not out of humanity and generous principles, but in order to put it out to large interest: I do not mean for five or six per cent but for more than sixty times sixty thousand; though, if a nation [is] to be saved, or a great people protected from slavery, he is wholly unconcerned about the event, as esteeming the little affairs of this world much below his notice and consideration.

He is the same in respect of the other world, as the covetous man is in respect of this; and both their good qualities proceed from the same principles and appetites in nature. He is covetous for the good things in the kingdom of heaven, as the other is for them here; and both take much the same way to get them. They both contemn wise men, because wise men contemn them; their despising the vanities of the world, saves money; their condemning the modest pleasures of life, gratifies their sour and censorious temper; their living cloistered and retired lives, feeds natural melancholy; and the former hopes to carry heaven (which the other does not trouble himself about) by singing songs upon earth, by being perfectly useless to society, and good for no one thing in the world.

This sort of creature is the tool for knaves to work with, and made use of to serve their interests, whilst he intends only to pursue his own. He is made to believe that kingdoms, infinitely preferable to those of this world, are to be gained by the manner of cutting his corns, or by forms, fashions, habits, postures, cringes and grimaces; by using a rote of words, or by useless speculations, and dancing after idle harangues, and always by being an implacable enemy and a furious adversary to all who have generous and beneficent affections towards their own species. He values opinions like rotten cheese, in proportion as they are old: and is more concerned for people's believing right, than for their doing right. He thinks that the way to shew our gratitude to God, is to refuse his gifts; and believes truth the more sacred, the less it is understood; and nothing worthy to be called faith, but what is absurd to reason, and contradicts all the principles of science. He is a fast friend to every thing that looks like a mystery; thinks common sense too common, and sublime nonsense to be always a proof of inspiration. He measures virtue and vice, right and wrong not by the interests of mankind, but by scanty and partial rules, invented by pedants and hypocrites, and calculated chiefly for their own benefit. He is a friend to no man, and all his thoughts and speculations are above humanity and social pleasures, and all the frail things of this world; and so he keeps all his money to himself, and, at last, perhaps, starves his friends and family, to leave it to such wretches as he is, not out of kindness to them, but to receive ample payment again where he is going.

I have often wondered how this stupid animal could ever be in repute; how the most insignificant and worst being in the universe could be thought the most acceptable to the best; and how any one can be supposed to merit heaven, by being useless upon earth. Castruccio Castracani said well, that he would never believe that Friar Hieronymo had more interest above than he himself had.[1] Surely he judged right; yet the world ever has run, and, I doubt, ever will run, madding after hermits, cynicks, dreamers of dreams, venders of prophecy, and after recluse and sequestered persons, who are supposed to know heavenly things in proportion as they know nothing here. They call their solemn folly, divine wisdom; their spleen and melancholy, godly contemplation; their envious, sullen, and morose tempers, strict and rigid virtue, and detestation of vice: Covetousness in frugality, and the contempt of things below. Whereas a truly virtuous and godly man is the most candid, amiable, and best natured creature upon earth: He spends his life in doing all the good that he can, and to all the men that he can: He takes pleasure in seeing all men happy, and will endeavour to make them all happy: He has large and comprehensive notions of the deity; and as he finds in himself kind and beneficent affections towards the whole creation, believes that the Supreme Being has the same; and, consequently, will not make our happiness or misery to depend upon what is out of our power, or upon such speculations or actions as can produce no moral good, but often destroy it, and promote evil.

T

God wants nothing; and if we have any gifts to bestow, his creatures are our only proper objects: But those who crave in his name largesses and endowments, which they apply to their own use and luxury, and call their own luxury and pomp the serving of him, make the Almighty as greedy as they are, and the giver of all things to want almost every thing; and confining all their bounty and charity to their own dear persons, think that he does so too, and that they are as dear to him as they are to themselves; and so hate and despise, distress and destroy, in the name of God, all

---

1. Castruccio Castracani degli Antelminelli (1281–1328), soldier and a leader of the Ghibelline forces in Italy. In 1327 he was created Duke of Lucca. "Friar Hieronymo" refers to Girolamo Savonarola (1452–1498), the Dominican monk and religious zealot.

whom they hate for their own sakes: So that, excepting a very few men (the most ridiculous and the worst of the whole) all the human species are esteemed by them as outcasts, whom the wise Creator and Governor of the World has sent into it only to abhor and to damn them; and though his favours are infinite, yet they think that he bestows them all upon a little island, or a poor desert, or on a small and contemptible corner of the earth, purely because the inhabitants wear blue, or black, or broad bonnets, quaint doublets, or long petticoats; and eat, or refuse to eat fish or flesh, and other food given for the general use of all men; or make selfish and partial speeches to him, and use crazy distinctions about him, which he commands not, which wise men understand not, and which the weakest men alone are governed by.

With bigots almost every thing that is truth is blasphemy. With them a sour face, and a bitter and implacable heart, are qualifications so acceptable to the wise, merciful, and forgiving God, that he hates all who want these qualifications: So that, in great detestation of blasphemy, they blasphemously make the God and father of mercies, and of man, a party-man too; or, at best, the head of the most senseless, useless, inhuman, and mischievous party in the universe, the party of bigots; who, being blindly and obstinately addicted to their own incurable follies, are furiously bent against all the wise and sober men in the world: they improve the world by defacing it; and their way of building up, is to destroy and pull down. This they call edification.

But religion is another and a contrary thing; and whoever would entertain a just idea of the divine being, must conceive of him in direct opposition to the bigot's conceptions; namely, that the God of Truth is not the author of contradictions; that when he speaks to men, he speaks not above the capacities of men, but to their capacities, which is the end of speaking; that he who makes the hearts of men, is the best and only judge of men's hearts, who cannot see into one another's, that being the only province and privilege of omniscience; that his perfect goodness cannot punish men, whom he has created naturally subject to errors, for involuntary errors; that having not made man perfect, he cannot be offended with him for natural and inevitable imperfections.

That we cannot provoke him, when we intend to adore him; that the best way to serve him, is to be serviceable to one another; he himself, who is omnipotent, wanting none of our impotent assistance and benefits, which must come from him, but cannot go from us to him; that to hurt men, or betray them, for his sake, is to mock him, and impiously to father upon the God of Wisdom and Peace our own rage and folly; that to him neither sounds, nor gestures, nor actions, are good or bad, pleasing or displeasing, but as the intentions from whence they spring are sincere or insincere, of which he alone can be judge.

That he who made the world has not restrained his gifts, favours, and mercies, to a nook of it; nor picks out from among men, who are all his, a few particular minions and favourites, or gives these authority to domineer over the rest, and to oppress them in the name of that God who is not the god of a nation, or of a sect, but of all nations, tongues, and persuasions, and is heard of all that call upon him and fear him: That the only way to please and resemble him, is to do, as he does, good to all impartially, and to restrain men from hurting or persecuting one another: And, in fine, that anger, revenge, and ambition, are not religion; nor the author and object of it an angry, partial, whimsical, and cruel being; but that religion is as different from bigotry, and as far above it, as the wise, great, and good God is above weak, little, ill, and angry men.

G   *I am, &c.*

NO. 118. SATURDAY, MARCH 2, 1722.

🪰 *Free states vindicated from the common Imputation of Ingratitude.*

SIR,

It is a common objection against free states, that they are ungrateful: But I think that I shall be able to shew the contrary, that they are much more grateful than arbitrary princes; and are rarely ungrateful but to those who use them ungratefully, and forfeit by it any obligation which they had laid upon them.

It is the chief and first ambition of free states, to preserve themselves; and such as contribute most to that end amongst them, are generally placed by them in the first stations of figure and power. But as men generally over-rate their own merit, publick rewards, however great, are rarely so great as are the expectations and pretensions of men to these rewards. So that such as are preferred for serving, or for a capacity of serving, the publick, are seldom preferred so high as they think they deserve; and, being neither pleased with the measure nor duration of their power, where it is not boundless and perpetual, are apt to be struggling to make it so, though to the ruin of those who gave it for their own preservation, and to the overthrowing of every purpose for which it was given. When this is the aim, as it too often is, the people grow presently very ungrateful, because they will not become slaves to their own servants. And here is the source of most of the contentions in the world between the governors and governed. The people provoke their rulers by a very heinous and ill-bred crime, that of distinguishing between protection and oppression: For this they are ungrateful. They are ready enough almost everywhere to give their governors too much; but that will not do. Nero, after he put off the hypocrite, never conferred any office upon any man, but he always gave him these short instructions: "You know what I have occasion for: let it be your care and mine that nobody else have any thing."[1] Nor was Nero the last that made a power to protect property a warrant for seizing it.

Gratitude is, doubtless, due from the obliged to those who oblige them as long as they do not pretend to measure or force their own reward, nor to use the others ill, upon the pure merit of having used them well. There is such a thing as the cancelling an obligation in publick as well as in private life; as when it is turned into an injury, by being made the means of oppression, or a pretence for contempt or calumny. I would rather not be obliged, than ill used for having been obliged; and believe most men are of my mind.

1. Suetonius, *Nero*, 32.

A state may sometimes over-pay a benefactor; but scarce any subject can do more for the state than he owes it. We owe all things to our country, because in our country is contained every thing that is dear to us, our relations, our fortunes, and ourselves: And our labours, our studies, and our lives, are all due, upon occasion, to our country, which protects us in them all. But when we have dedicated all these to the state, it is far from being true, that the state ought to sacrifice itself, or venture any part of its security, to make us recompence. To save it from others, in order to seize it ourselves, is so far from entitling us to any reward but that of resentment and death, that, as it is adding the base crimes of treachery and ingratitude to the cruel crime of usurpation, no foreign foe can be half so wicked and detestable as such an intestine traitor, who calls himself a friend.

Spurius Melius thought himself an unquestionable benefactor to the Roman people, for having bestowed on them *gratis* a large quantity of corn in a time of dearth; by which false bounty he gained the hearts of the many, who saw not into his design of bribing and feeding them, in order to enslave them: but Servilius Ahala,[2] who killed him, was a much greater and real benefactor; because in Melius he slew their most dangerous enemy. T. Manlius[3] defended the Capitol bravely and generously; but when, not content with the many honours that were done him for a worthy action, he would have unworthily oppressed Rome itself for having saved part of it, he was justly thrown headlong from that very Capitol.

Caesar and Marius were the most ungrateful monsters that ever lived: They had done brave things not for the state, as the event shewed, but for themselves; and the state covered them with honours, adorned them with magistracies and triumphs, loaded them with benefits, and pursued them, even to profusion, with all publick and splendid marks of respect. But all this could not satisfy these shameless great men, unless they had a power granted them perpetual and enormous, a power destructive of all liberty, and of

2. Gaius Servilius *Ahala* is reputed to have preserved Roman liberty by killing Spurius Maelius, who, it was thought, was seeking dictatorial powers.
3. Gordon is in fact referring to Marcus *Manlius* Capitolinus.

the state that gave it. And so they barbarously oppressed the state that exalted them.

On what side, in this instance, did the ingratitude lie? Is there a pretence for charging that generous people with this base vice, or for acquitting these parricides from the blackest? If the Prince of Orange, having at the head of the Dutch troops driven the invading French out of the Seven Provinces, had enslaved the States with their own forces, because, perhaps, they had refused to deliver up their government to his will and pleasure, and to give him a power to oppress them, as a reward for having defended them; who would have been ungrateful in this case, the prince or the States? They for refusing to be slaves, or he for making them slaves?

The people lose much more by their generosity to their benefactors, than the benefactors lose by the ingratitude or stinginess of the people, whose fault is almost always on the other side. By giving them too much, they often tempt and enable them to take all; as in the cases of Marius, Sulla, Caesar, Pisistratus, Agathocles, Oliver Cromwell, the late kings of Denmark and Sweden,[4] and many more. But suppose it had happened sometimes (which has rarely happened) that a worthy man should not meet a proper reward from his countrymen, for publick services done them; it is still better that he has too little, or even none, than too much; and a worthy man will never seek revenge upon his country, for a mistake in his merit; a mistake which may be easily committed, and is at worst pardonable. But a man who has served his country, and then turns it upside down, because that it has not, or he thinks that it has not, given him reward enough, shews that he deserved none.

Sometimes a man's ill deeds balance his good, and then he pays himself; or overbalance them, and then he is entitled more to punishment than reward; and both rewards and punishments ought to be faithfully paid: though there is generally more crime

4. In 1660, the King of Denmark, with the support and encouragement of the Danish clergy and burghers, was able to transform the kingdom into a hereditary and absolute monarchy. Twenty years later, in 1680, Charles XI, with the backing of the lower nobility and commoners, established an absolutist regime in Sweden.

and insecurity in not punishing well, than in not paying well; a fault too frequent in free states, who, dazzled with great benefits, are often blind to greater offences, or overlook them, and reward before they enquire.

The dearest and most valuable things are most apt to create jealousies and fears about them; and the dearest of all being liberty, as that which produces and secures all the rest, the people's zeal to preserve it has been ever called ingratitude by such as had designs against it; and others, ignorant of its value, and indifferent about it, have promoted and continued the false charge. Shakespear, in the tragedy of *Timon of Athens*, makes Alcibiades, who was banished by the state, cry out with indignation, "Oh the ungrateful spirit of a commonwealth!"[5] And I have seen a loud and vehement clap raised upon it by those who were angry at the word *commonwealth*, though they lived under a free government: For every free state is, in a large sense, a commonwealth; and I think our own the freest in the world. In my opinion Alcibiades, though a brave man, was justly exiled as an ambitious and dangerous man, who behaved himself turbulently in that city, was perpetually creating or inflaming factions in it, and against it; and shewed too plainly, that he aimed at overturning it for the sake of that uncontrollable power, which he could not have while its government subsisted.[6] The citizens of Athens treated him with great distinction, and gave him great authority and eminent commands; and only banished him, out of fear of him, for which they had too much ground.

States have been often destroyed by being too generous and too grateful; and where they are really ungrateful, they are only so through error; to which, however, they are not so subject as absolute princes, who generally destroy their greatest men, and prefer the vilest, and in their courts pimps often ruin patriots. I think that those who most dislike free governments, do not pre-

5. At no point does Alcibiades utter these exact words, although they are entirely compatible with his indignation at the ingratitude shown by the Senate. See *Timon of Athens* III.v. 95–119.

6. In 415 B.C., Alcibiades was recalled from his position as one of the commanders of the Athenian expedition against Sicily to stand trial for impiety. He escaped arrest and went into voluntary exile, where he was not above offering advice to Athens's enemies.

tend to shew above four or five instances of ingratitude in the Roman people, from the beginning of their commonwealth to the end of it, for several hundred years; and Coriolanus and Camillus are two of those instances.[7]

As to Coriolanus, he was justly banished, as a declared enemy to the equality of the government, and engaged in an open design to oppress the people; which design he executed with all fierceness and contempt, and even outrage, surrounded like a monarch with guards of the young hot-headed nobility: And though the people did him no injustice, yet, to be revenged upon them, he invaded his country at the head of a foreign enemy.

Camillus was guilty of the same partiality, though not in the same degree, towards the nobles, and had broke his word with the people; for both which he was banished: But by saving his country afterwards, he gloriously cancelled all past faults, and was gratefully styled the second founder of Rome, and highly honoured, and even adored, to the end of his life, by that grateful people, in every instance where they could shew it. And indeed all the ingratitude that can be charged upon them, was, their opposing, in their own defence, the encroachments of the nobility; and the excellent laws produced by that opposition shewed its reasonableness and necessity.

Scipio Africanus is likewise mentioned as another great instance of ingratitude of the Romans. He was a great and glorious commander: He had forced Hannibal, the most dangerous foreign foe that the Romans ever had, out of Italy, which he had ravaged successfully many years; he had conquered the same Hannibal in battle, subdued Carthage and Africa, and assisted his brother Asiaticus in conquering the great King Antiochus. For which extraordinary services and merit he was the darling of the people; who were so far from being ungrateful to him, that they violated the laws of Rome, and of their own security, to do him honour;

7. Coriolanus's impeachment and exile were said to have been brought on partially by his arrogant demeanor toward the commons. Marcus Furius *Camillus* was regarded as the savior of Rome after the Gallic invasion of 387/6 B.C. His domestic policies were aimed at reasserting patrician influence in the Republic. Camillus was reputed to have been exiled at one point in his career for appropriating booty to his own personal use.

and not only made a youth their chief magistrate, but renewed the dignity so often, that the precedent proved pernicious to them.[8] The extraordinary steps taken by him and them, and by them for his sake, were of dangerous example and consequence; and, without his intending it, shook the foundations of Rome, and made way for the violent proceedings and usurpations of Marius, and afterwards of Caesar.

Scipio did likewise another thing, which ought by no means to have been suffered in a free state. When he was cited to answer before the people to the crimes with which he was charged, he refused to answer. "Upon this very day, my countrymen," says he, "I vanquished Hannibal"; and tearing the papers that contained the charge, walked haughtily out of the assembly. This was disowning or contemning the supreme authority of Rome; yet the people were so personally fond of the man, that they would decree nothing severe against him. He retired to his own country-house, where he lived peaceably all the rest of his honourable life.[9]

G   *I am, &c.*

NO. 119.   SATURDAY,   MARCH   9,   1722.

The same Subject continued.

SIR,

No people upon earth were more grateful to their good citizens than the Greeks and Romans were, or encouraged virtue more, or rewarded it better: Nor did they scarce ever banish any man till he became terrible to them; and then it was time. Nor is there one great absolute monarchy in the world, or ever was from the beginning of it, but destroyed more innocent men in a

8. Scipio Africanus was elected aedile in 212 B.C., although not having yet reached the legal age for this office; two years later, when he was only twenty-four, he was chosen to take command of all Roman forces in Spain. In 206 B.C., Scipio was elected consul, despite his age—he had just turned thirty—and despite his not first having filled the office of praetor.

9. The events are recounted in Livy, 38.51.4–12.

month, than the commonwealth of Rome did in a hundred years; besides, that a free state produces more great men in fifty years, than an absolute monarchy does in a thousand.

Those who had done any signal service to the state of Athens, were endowed with eminent privileges, and distinguished with all publick marks of honour: They had the first seats at publick entertainments and assemblies; they had publick statues erected to them; they had crowns conferred upon them; they were exempted from duties, taxes, and contributions, they were maintained at the publick charge, and sometimes their families after them: The publick resented the injuries done them; buried them magnificently; made publick orations in their praise; portioned out their daughters; and paid lasting honours to their name. And all this at a time when publick honours were only the rewards of merit, and parsimoniously distributed.

The Athenians had a particular law against ingratitude: And as to the ostracism, which may seem to contradict it, and by which they banished for ten years such great men as they judged formidable to their state, though they had formerly served it; it ought to be considered in its behalf, that the Athenians, like other free states, had suffered so much from their first-rate citizens, who suppressed their liberty under colour of advancing it, that they had great reason to be jealous of such. Whoever would live in a free state, must live upon a foot of equality; which great officers, accustomed to command, care not to do; and if they do not, they are justly removed. It is better that one man, however innocent, should suffer, than a whole people be ruined, or even hurt, if not by him, yet by his example: Nor ought they to shew, in one instance that cannot harm them, an indulgence, which in other and future instances may be their overthrow. Besides, the ostracism took nothing from any man, but a power of hurting every man: It affected not their goods, nor their persons, nor even their good name; and left them their full possessions, and their full liberty, every where but at Athens; whither, after ten years, they had a right to return, and were often recalled much sooner. It was likewise made use of sometimes only to pacify the fury of the envious, and to protect the innocent from it; and when base fellows came at last to be banished by it, it was laid aside.

The first purpose of the ostracism was, to keep publick benefactors from turning publick parricides, great men from being too great, subjects from growing too powerful for the state; a reasonable precaution, and practised some way or other by every state in the world: nor can any state subsist where it is not practised. Even in England, the hanging of two or three great men among the many guilty, once in a reign or two, would have prevented much evil, and many dangers and oppressions, and saved this nation many millions.

If we now consider absolute monarchy, we shall find it grafted upon ingratitude, which is blended with the root of it. Arbitrary princes cannot, dare not, be grateful to elevated merit, which by the tenour of their power they are obliged to dread. They only consider their single selves, and their separate interest; and must cut off, for their own security, every man whose true glory may eclipse their false, and who draws away, in any degree, the thoughts and eyes of the people. If they have no magnanimity of their own, they hate or fear such as have; or if they are brave themselves, they will be jealous of those who are more so, or as much. The same may be said of every other virtue. They may heap wealth upon buffoons, and confer dignities upon parasites; but celebrated virtue, conspicuous abilities, and signal services, are their eye-sores and certain aversion. If they be hated, they will not bear that any one should be esteemed; and if they be valued themselves, they will hate rivals.

Under most of the Roman emperors, popular virtue was certain death; *ob virtutes certissimum exitium*;[1] and those who served them most, were surest of destruction; *nec minus periculum ex magna fama quam ex mala.*[2] Germanicus, who saved the empire of Tiberius, his uncle and father by adoption, by reconciling to him the mutinous and revolted legions, was the first great sacrifice to his jealousy, being poisoned in Asia, whither he was sent under pretence

1. "Virtue brought certain destruction." Tacitus, *Historiae*, 1.2.
2. "No less danger from great fame than from ill repute." Tacitus, *Historiae*, 1.2.

of commanding it.[3] Thus Nero too rewarded Corbulo; and thus Domitian rewarded Agricola;[4] both the greatest officers of their time, and the greatest benefactors to these ungrateful tyrants, who aimed at cutting up virtue by the roots: Nor did Vespasian, the first Roman emperor that changed for the better, prove much more grateful to Antonius Primus, who had signally served him, and paved his way to the imperial diadem.[5]

It were endless to mention other absolute monarchies. They are all animated by the same ungrateful, cruel, and suspicious spirit, and make havock of every thing that is good, destroying fastest those who serve them most. If they be ever grateful, they are only so to the vilest instruments of their tyranny; but for such as serve them against their foreign foes with just and popular glory, they are generally sacrificed to their endless jealousy of every thing that is noble. Belisarius[6] is an affecting instance of this; an illustrious general, who, in the decline of the Roman empire, did, as it were, new conquer the world for his royal master; and for a reward, was stripped of all that he had, and turned off to beg his bread with his eyes put out.

It is a fine observation of Tacitus; *Neque nobilem, neque ingenuum, neque libertinum quidem praeponere armis, regia utilitas est;*[7]

> It is the business and special interest of an arbitrary prince, that his forces be commanded neither by a nobleman, nor by a freeman, nor, indeed, by any man who is two degrees removed from a slave.

3. On the death of Augustus in A.D. 14, Germanicus quelled a mutiny among the legions of Lower Germany who wished to raise him, rather than Tiberius, to the imperial throne. He was poisoned in A.D. 19, possibly under orders from Tiberius.

4. The emperor Domitian, envious of Gnaeus Julius *Agricola*'s skills as governor of Britain, is reputed to have had him poisoned in A.D. 93.

5. Marcus Antonius *Primus*, one of Vespasian's generals, gained a decisive victory over the armies of the emperor Vitellius at Bedriacum in A.D. 69.

6. Belisarius was the emperor Justinian's greatest military general. Found guilty of conspiring against Justinian's life, he was imprisoned for one year in his own palace. The story that he was deprived of his property and had his eyes put out, thus forcing him to wander as a beggar through Constantinople, is apocryphal.

7. "It is useful for a ruler that neither nobles nor free men, nor even freedmen, be placed in command of armies." Tacitus, *Germania*, 44.

Or, if such princes be obliged by the necessity of their affairs to employ an illustrious person in an important command, they always employ him with fear; and when their turn is served, and he has made them safe, dismiss him into obscurity with contempt, if he escape so well; for all their suspicions generally end in blood. Machiavel, who knew this well, says, that a great and successful general, under an arbitrary prince, has but two ways to escape the certain ruin which his glory, services, and renown, will else bring upon him: He must either quit the army, and, retiring from all power, live like a private man; or depose his master, and set up himself: Which last is generally the safer course.[8]

It is well known how the Ottoman monarchs reward their bravest bashaws. The successful and unfortunate have the same fate: As the latter are sacrificed to rage, the other are to jealousy: Even their own sons have been recompensed with death, for deserving esteem. Nor is that cruel ingratitude peculiar to one race or family of princes, but eternally attached to that sort of power where-ever it is found.

But far different is the spirit of the people: They are prone to gratitude, and lavish in their affections and returns for benefits received. Nothing is too much or too high for the benefactor, or for one whom they think so. They are apt to continue blind to his faults, even when he has forfeited their favour; and to remain constant in their zeal to his name and posterity, in instances where they ought to detest both. This is abundantly exemplified and confirmed by the lasting respect and reverence paid by the Romans to those plagues of Rome, and of the earth, the family of the Caesars; by the French, to the stupid and sanguinary posterity of Charlemain; by the Turks, to the bloody family of Ottoman;[9] by the Egyptians, to their luxurious and contemptible Ptolemies; by the Jews, to the cruel race of the Asmonaeans,[10] or Maccabees; by the Parthians, to the barbarous line of the Arsacides;[11] and by almost every instance of every people

8. *Discourses*, I.30.2.
9. That is, Osman, the founder of the Ottoman dynasty.
10. The Asmoneans, the Hebrew family name of the Maccabean royal house.
11. The Arsacids were the ruling house of the Parthian kingdom, corresponding to the province of Khorasan in modern Iran, all of whose kings adopted the name of the dynasty's founder, Arsaces.

in the world. I could mention instances here at home, but they will occur fast enough to every reader who knows any thing of our history. The people are indeed grateful and constant, even to superstition, to persons and names to which they conceive themselves once obliged: Nor do they ever act ungratefully, but where they are first deceived by those whom they trust. The people of Athens, deceived by some of their demagogues, put once to death some of their sea officers, who did not deserve it; but they soon grew apprized of their error, and were severely revenged upon the traitorous calumniators who caused it.[12]

Several instances may, no doubt, be found of the people's ingratitude to their friends, and of the contrary quality in some absolute monarchs. But exceptions do not weaken a rule.

G   *I am, &c.*

NO. 120. SATURDAY, MARCH 16, 1722.

Of the proper Use of Words.

SIR,

As I have in former papers treated of the abuse of words;[1] so I shall, in this, discourse about the use of them. They are the signs of ideas, as figures are of numbers; and are intended to convey the conceptions of men to one another: They have no more meaning in themselves than inarticulate sounds, till men have agreed to put a meaning upon them, which meaning is wholly arbitrary; and therefore unless they mean the same things by the same words, that is annex the same conceptions to the same sounds, they cannot understand one another, or discourse

12. Despite their innocence, several Athenian naval commanders were accused of having abandoned the survivors of the Athenian ships wrecked in the battle at Arginusae in 406 B.C. and, after a largely illegal trial, were executed. Popular opinion against the officers had been inflamed by, among others, the statesman Theramenes, who was successful in shifting the blame for the disaster onto the commanders in the field.

---

1. See especially Letter No. 117 (Feb. 23, 1722) and Trenchard's letter on eloquence, No. 103 (Nov. 17, 1722).

together. If one man annex more or less ideas to the same words than another does whom he reasons with, it is impossible that they should agree in conclusions; when their premises are different, their reasonings will be a game at blindman's-buff: And therefore it is absolutely necessary, in all disputes, to settle the meanings of the terms made use of, before any thing can be affirmed or denied on either side.

A word not standing for any idea, is only a bare sound; and it is no more, to one who knows not what idea it stands for. The agreeing therefore in sounds, and not agreeing in the meaning of them, is no agreement at all; and though this may be a good test of orthodoxy amongst some sets of ecclesiasticks, yet I will presume to say, that it is none in common sense. It appears to me, that most of the polemick quarrels in the world have flowed from this inobservance. Men use the same sounds to express different conceptions, either in whole or in part; that is, one man comprehends more or less ideas in the terms which he makes use of than another, and then makes use of other words equally uncertain to explain that meaning; and so in a few propositions quite loses his argument, and the combatants quarrel about what they have been talking of. But though this manner of scuffling in the dark be a great obstruction, and almost an insurmountable bar to all sorts of useful knowledge, yet it highly conduces to the power and credit of those who derive riches and authority from the ignorance and credulity of others.

It gives them the reputation of learning, for talking unintelligibly: It enables them to discourse upon all subjects alike, and to fetch every thing out of every thing; for by not explaining their words, they make them signify what they please, and vary them as often as they have occasion: so that in the course of a debate they have failed in all the points of the compass. The abuse is yet more observable and mischievous in translations from one language to another; for, as few or no men understand a dead language, in many respects, in the sense which it was spoken in (and indeed few men in the same country, and the same language, speak many words in the same sense that their ancestors spoke them, the meaning of words, like all other things, being in perpetual rotation) and as few words in any language, such as comprehend complex ideas, are exactly answered by correspondent words in any other, that is, do not contain just the same number of ideas; so it is very difficult, if not impossible, in many instances, to make an exact translation; and, consequently, very easy to make a false one: And therefore it is very ridiculous (to call it by no worse a name) in controverted points, to build an hypothesis upon the signification of single words in a dead language (which, perhaps, was translated from another language) when we neither know their manner of speaking, the philosophy and speculations which they were conversant with, nor the customs to which they alluded, and are very sure that they were different from our own, and, in many instances, had not the same common conceptions or images.

But it is not enough that we must have what are often called ideas to our words, but they must be adequate ones; for all inadequate ideas are no ideas; that is, they must be adequate as far as they are ideas: What stands for no conception, stands for nothing; and the word used can only stand for the conception, such as it is, and as far as it goes; and when the conception goes no farther, no word can stand for that which is not. It is certain, that there is no one thing in the universe of which we can have an adequate conception in the strict sense of those words; but we convey by words only such conceptions as we have, which possibly do not exhaust the millionth part of their properties; but then we are in the dark as to all the rest, and neither can affirm nor deny any thing about them: And if one man take any more or less ideas in the term he makes use of than another, he does not talk with him to the same point.

One man has no conception of gold but by the colour, and he will call prince's-metal[2] gold; another knows it by its weight, fineness, and touch; and if a new metal should be discovered, which answers all these marks, and should yet want some medicinal qualities, or, perhaps, the same solubility which gold has, yet he will still call it gold, according to the properties which his imagination has annexed to the word *gold*; and all these three will be called

2. Prince's metal: an alloy consisting of three parts copper to one part zinc and resembling gold.

by the same name, and yet different metals will be meant; and every one of these conceptions, as far as they go, are adequate, though neither of them are so to the subject, which has undoubtedly many properties which no one knows any thing of: but then we do not reason upon those properties, nor do the sounds which we use stand for them.

From what has been said appears the absurdity of being told, that we must believe things which we do not understand; or of believing things above reason, though not contrary to reason. We must have ideas, or images, of all objects of belief, or else we believe in nothing, but that we hear a sound; and it is the same thing to us whether it signify any thing or not, if we do not know what it signifies. If a man make a proposition to me in the Chinese language, and tell me that I must believe it, nothing here can be the object of my faith, but that the man does not tell me a lie, which has nothing to do with the proposition itself; and it would have been the same thing to me, if he had told me that I must believe in his thought, without telling me what that thought was; and there can be no difference, if he use words in a language which I am acquainted with, if I do not understand the meaning in which he uses those words.

From hence appears the ridicule of a late sect in Holland, and of many other visionary madmen at home, who think that the scripture is to be for the most part understood metaphorically, and find meanings in it which the words do not naturally import;[3] which is making the Almighty speak in riddles to his creatures, and obliging them to pay largely out of their substance to those who make them yet greater riddles. What can be more absurd and wicked, than to suppose, that the great and good God should speak to mankind with a design not to be understood? should give them a rule to act by, yet express that rule in words which few can pretend to apprehend, and those few differ about? Certainly, as has

3. The "late sect in Holland" has reference to the Familia Caritatis, an Anabaptist sect founded by Hendrik Niclaes in Amsterdam in 1540. His teachings, pantheistic and Antinomian in nature, won a number of adherents in England, where the sect's members were known as Familists. Although they flourished under Cromwell, the sect disappeared by the end of the seventeenth century, amalgamating with the Quakers and other groups.

been said, words are of no use but to convey ideas; and if they be not used in their common acceptation, to signify those conceptions which custom has annexed to them, or such as men shall agree to put upon them, then they must be perfectly useless, will convey no ideas at all, can give us no rule, nor can communicate any knowledge.

It is certain, as has been said, that no man's perceptions can exhaust the properties of any one thing in the world: All that we know of them is from a few obvious qualities which affect our senses; but without doubt they have thousands of others, of which we know nothing; much less can we know any thing of their *substratum*, or internal essence, or contexture: but then neither can we believe any thing of those hidden essences, or qualities, nor do we mean any thing about them when we talk of any being or substance. As in the instance before given; if a man carry to a goldsmith a solid substance, and ask him what he thinks it to be, and the goldsmith look upon the colour, touch it, weigh it, melt it, and then tell him that he believes it to be gold; it is certain that the goldsmith neither believes nor affirms any thing about it, further than of its colour, its touch, its weight, and its solubility, which are his ideas of gold: But gold has, without question, many other properties which he has never heard of; but then he does not take in those properties in this perception of gold; and he neither does nor can believe any thing about them, till he has formed some idea of those hidden qualities.

This leads me to consider what men mean, when they say that they believe in a mystery. We must understand the meaning of the words connected, and of the verb which connects them, and makes them a proposition, or else we believe in nothing; that is, we must have a perception of all those ideas which the words stand for in our imaginations; and so far it is no mystery. But then we may be told, that the beings, to which we have annexed those ideas, and by which we distinguish them from other beings, may, and undoubtedly have, many other qualities, or properties, that we know nothing of: An assertion which must be granted to be true of every thing in nature. And in this sense every thing is a mystery, and every man will readily believe such a mystery. But then if we be told, that we must believe in the properties, or qualities, of which we know nothing, or have any idea; I think that the mystery will then consist in the nonsense of the proposition; and it is the same thing to tell us, that we must believe in *fe-fa-fum*: For, a man cannot believe without believing something; and he must know what that something is, that is, he must know what he believes, or else his belief is only an abstract word, without any subject to believe in, or any thing of.

Thus when we say, that we believe there are three persons in the Trinity, and but one God, we must have distinct ideas to the words *person*, *Trinity*, and *God*. For if men have no meaning to these words, they mean nothing by the proposition; and if they annex different perceptions to them, then they have a different creed: though they fancy that they subscribe the same. No one can know whether another be orthodox in his sense, till the terms be defined, and stand for the same ideas in both their minds: To say, that they believe in three persons, without telling what they mean by the word *person*, is the same as to say, that they believe in three somethings, or in the word *three*; which indeed is a very mysterious belief, and a pretty center of unity: for no man can believe any thing else, till he has fixed a meaning to the word *person*; and if another do not agree with him in that meaning, they will differ in religion, though they agree in sounds, and perhaps in falling foul upon every one who desires them to explain themselves; which behaviour, amongst too many people, is the main test of orthodoxy.

They must agree also in what they mean by the word *God*. I do not mean, that they must define his essence, have any adequate notion of his infinity, eternity, or of the *sensorium* of his existence; for of these things we neither know, nor can know, any thing: But we must know what we mean by the sound which we make use of; that is, we must have a perception of those images annexed to the word *God* in our minds, and a perception adequate to itself, though in no-wise adequate and correspondent to the subject; which images in different men, I doubt, are very various; and when they are so, these men plainly differ in the object of their worship, and are of a different religion, though they may think themselves to be of the same. This shall be the subject of some other paper hereafter;[4] in which I shall shew, how absurd as well as impious it is, for men to fall together by the ears upon the account of their difference in trifles, when they scarce agree in any one thing in the world, if they explain themselves, not even in the attributes annexed to the object of all worship, though they can know nothing of him but from his attributes.

T   *I am, &c.*

NO. 121. SATURDAY, MARCH 23, 1722.

Of Good Breeding.

SIR,

Good breeding is the art of shewing men, by external signs, the internal regard which we have for them. It arises from good sense, improved by conversing with good company. A well-bred fool is impertinent; and an ill-bred wise man, like a good instrument out of tune, is awkward, harsh, and disagreeable. A courteous blockhead is, however, a more acceptable guest, almost every-where, than a rude sage. Men are naturally so fond of themselves, that they will rather misspend their time with a complaisant ape, than improve it with a surly and thwarting philosopher. Every bow, or good word, whencesoever it comes, is taken by us as a sign of our importance, and a confession of our merit; and the neglect of that complaisance, as a token that we are thought of none: A reproach which, however silent, few care to bear.

Good breeding is never to be learned by study; and therefore they who study it are coxcombs, and formalists and stiff pedants. The best-bred men, as they come to be so by use and observation only, practice it without affectation. You see good breeding in all that they do, without seeing the art of it. It is a habit; and, like all others, acquired by practice. A weak and ignorant man, who has lived in good company, shall enter a room with a better grace, and say common things much more agreeably, than

4. See Letter No. 137 (July 20, 1723).

a profound wise man, who lives by himself, or with only such as himself, and is above the forms of the world, and too important to talk of indifferent things, and to be like other people. A footman employed in *How d'ye's* shall address himself to a person of figure with more decorum, and make a speech with more ease, than a learned serjeant,[1] who lives wholly over briefs; or the deep head of a college, occupied only in a momentous science. I have known a man, who, with the learning of a whole university, had the manners of a clown, and the surliness of a porter; not from the want of sense, though that want be very consistent with a world of learning, but from living long in a college, and dictating to boys and pupils, or with old Fellows, who had no more breeding than himself, and, like himself, were spoiled by living rarely upon the square with any other sort of people.

Good breeding therefore is never to be learned in a college, where the sphere of conversation is so narrow, where the distance between men is so great, and where the old have none to teach the young. Hence you generally see young men come from the universities with a conceited air, and a quaint manner, which often turns them into fops: They are generally either pert or prim: The tone of their voice, and the position of their muscles, shew their accomplishments, before they have spoke two words: Their step, and the manner of using their legs and arms, do the same; and every joint about them, and every action they do, declares the place and way of their education. As to the senior fellows, and heads of houses, they are such starched pedants, such solemn mamamouches, and such kingly old fops, that from their mien you may know their characters, and read their titles and preferments in their hats. They carry the college about them where-ever they go, and talk at a table as they do at a lecture; or, if sometimes they break into gaiety, it is either imperious or insipid, disrespectful or awkward, and always ungraceful: They want a good manner, less conceit, and the appearance, at least, of more humility; all which are only to be acquired by living abroad in the world, and by conversing with all sorts of men. This accustoms one to treat all men as

1. Serjeant: an officer of the court.

they expect to be treated; and such general good treatment given to all is called good breeding.

Hence the breeding of courts is always the easiest and most refined. Courtiers have the constant advantage of living daily with the best-bred men: Besides, having occasion for all sorts of people, they accustom themselves to use all sorts of people civilly. By conversing with all sorts, they can fall readily into all sorts of styles, and please every body by talking to him in his own way. They find too, by daily experience, and promiscuous conversation, that the difference between men and men is not so great, as an unacquaintedness with men would generally make it: They are therefore under no awe, nor shyness, in speaking to the greatest; nor have any general contempt for the meanest: a contempt which too often rises from a wrong judgment, grounded upon pride, and continued by inexperience. They consider, that as the greatest can do them good, so the meanest can hurt them: They are therefore respectful without awe to those above them, and complaisant without disdain to those below them. Courts therefore are the best schools for good breeding; and to be well-bred we must live not only with the best sorts of men, but must be acquainted with all sorts.

The want of this general conversation may be one reason why the country clergy are so often accused of want of breeding. They come from the university full of an opinion, that all that is to be learned is to be learned there; and believing themselves to have already every accomplishment, often remain without any. In their parishes they can learn nothing but an additional pride, from seeing or fancying themselves the biggest men there. If there be a squire in the place, he rarely mends them.[2] If he have a delicate taste, he will not converse with them: But it frequently happens, that his taste is as crude as theirs, and consists in eating much, and drinking more, and talking loud. From this conceited education, and narrow conversation, arises their impatience of contradiction, and their readiness to contradict. I own that I am always cautious of reasoning with the vicar: His first argument is generally an assertion; and his next, an affront.

2. Mends: reforms.

An engaging manner and a genteel address may be out of their power; but it is in their power to be condescending and affable. When people are obliging, they are said to be well-bred. The heart and intention are chiefly considered: When these are found friendly and sincere, the manner of shewing it, however awkward, will be kindly overlooked. Good breeding is artificial good nature; and complaisance is understood to be a copy of the invisible heart. When people are satisfied of one another's good-will and sincerity, the forms they shew them are generally laid aside. Between intimate friends there is little ceremony, and less between man and wife. Some, however, is still necessary, because by signs and actions the affections are shewn. But a courteous behavior, which is known to mean nothing, goes for nothing, and is not necessary when the meaning is known to be good. Expressions of kindness, when they are not thought the marks and effects of kindness, are empty sounds: And yet these unmeaning expressions are necessary in life. We are not to declare to every man whom we dislike, how much we dislike him, nor to shew it by dumb signs. When a man says, that he is my humble servant, he obliges me; not by the words, which in common speech signify scarce any thing, but because by these words he shews that he thinks me worth notice. Good breeding therefore is then just, when the actions which it produces are thought sincere: This is its end and success: It must seem produced by kindness for the person for whom it is shewn.

Good breeding is of so great importance in the world, that an accomplishment this way goes often further than much greater accomplishments without it can do. I have known gentlemen, who with moderate parts and much good breeding have been thought great men; and have actually come to be so. Great abilities alone make no man's person amiable; some have been unpopular with the greatest, and some even ridiculous. But the gay, the easy, the complaisant man, whose chief abilities are in his behaviour, pleases and obliges all, and is amiable to as many as he obliges. To learn this behaviour, people must begin early. One who sets out into the world at twenty, shall make twice as much progress in life, as one who with twice his sense sets out at forty; because he is then less susceptible of the arts of life. Habits are not to be got in a day; and after a certain age, never. Forced complaisance is foppery; and affected easiness is a monster. I have seen a world of tradesmen, and almost as many gentlemen, take such pains to be well-bred, that I have been in pain for them: Native plainness is a thousand times better.

Complaisance is ingenious flattery: It makes those to whom it is paid flatter themselves, while they take every act of complaisance in others as the declaration of merit in themselves: And beyond a certain degree it is not innocent. Courtiers know its efficacy so well, that to it alone no small part of their power is owing. Hence so many people have always been deceived by civil words and kind looks. To know speculatively the delusions of this art, is not sufficient to put you upon your guard against it. A fair and plausible behaviour, with a ready rote of kind expressions, and all the appearances of sincerity, will be apt to mislead you in spite of your foreknowledge. They will catch your senses, and beat you off your theory in politicks. You must find their insincerity some time before you will come to distrust it. Their art and your own self-love will conspire against you, drive away your incredulity, and beget faith, as it is often begot, against evidence and reason. You will still flatter yourself, that you are an exception to the rule, though there were never another exception. The credulity of some is perfectly incurable; many have continued steady believers, in spite of daily proofs and fatal experience for twenty years together. They were always persuaded, that every promise was at least intended to be kept, and always forgave the breaking of it. The great man smiled graciously, bowed courteously, excused himself earnestly; and vowed to God, that you should have the next thing. You miscarried; and then, with a concerned face, he vowed to God, that he could not help it, promised again with the same solemn vow, was again believed and always believed. This wretched credulity is the fruit of self-love, of an opinion that we are as considerable in the eyes of others as we are in our own. Mankind are governed by their weaknesses; and all that statesmen have to do to keep expecting crowds about them, and attached to them, is to promise violently, to seem violently in earnest, and never be so: That is, they must be extremely well-bred.

Good breeding is indeed an amiable and persuasive thing: It beautifies the actions, and even the looks of men. But equally odious is the grimace of good breeding. In comparison with this, bluntness is an accomplishment. The ape of a well-bred man is just as offensive as the well-bred man is agreeable: He is a nuisance to his acquaintance. I am frighted at the affected smile, and the apish shrug. When these foul copies of courtiers throw their civil grin in one's face, it is as much as one can do to avoid spitting in theirs. A starched rogue forcing smiles, is a more hideous sight than a mummy. He is a fugitive from nature; and it is notable impudence in such a creature to pretend to be courteous.

As to ill-breeding, or rudeness, there is something still worse in it than its deformity. It is immoral; it is using others as you would not be used.

G   *I am, &c.*

NO. 122. SATURDAY, MARCH 30, 1723.

Inquiry concerning the Operations of the Mind of Man, and those of other Animals.

SIR,

The world has always run riot after one whimsy or another. Astrology was the madness of the last age: Pretended prophets, fortune-tellers, conjurers, witches, apparitions, and such-like superstitious fooleries, have been in request in all ages. Dreamers of dreams led, misled, and governed mankind, for more than two thousand years together; and they are far from being out of fashion yet: And it is no small comfort, that this sort of divination, and instruction is left to us: for I do not find, that any society of men pretend to any jurisdiction over sleeping dreams, or to have the sole conduct, regulation, or interpretations of them; but every man, when he is asleep, is left at liberty to dream as he can, and to interpret his dreams as he thinks fit; which indulgence is not allowed to our waking dreams. I shall therefore take the advantage of this present toleration of dreaming, to dream too; and though I will not vouch or be answerable for the truth of my dreams, yet I dare compare them with those of the ancient and some modern philosophers.

I conceive, that the divines of all religions have ever agreed, that the soul of man is a being separate from the body, and in its own nature capable of subsisting independent of it. I also conceive, that all Christian divines hold, or ought to hold, that it is a distinct being from what we call the mind, and superadded to it by the divine goodness, to distinguish mankind from the brute creation, to continue his being after the dissolution of the body, and to make him an object of future rewards and punishments. For it is certain, that other animals have minds too; that they reason and resolve, though in an inferior degree to ourselves; and I think also, that it is almost universally agreed, that those minds take the fate of their bodies, and die with them.

The philosophers of all ages have set themselves to work, and employed their wits, to trace the minds of brutes to their first sources or principles, and so to account for their operations; but have differed as widely as they do in other matters about which they know nothing. Some have supposed them to be modifications of matter and motion, and operations resulting from the organization and mechanism of the body, like the striking of a clock, or watch, or musick made by blowing into or striking upon an instrument; for as the percussion of one body against another makes sound, so the instruments or vehicles upon which or through which it hits or passes, modify and determine the species of it.

These endeavour to illustrate the power of voluntary motion (namely, how a sudden impulse of the will can set a great machine in action) by what they think is analogous to it in mechanical obervations: As for instance, a little agitation of the air will turn a windmill, or sail a great ship; and it is demonstrable in mechanicks, that a hair of a man's head, or a puff of his breath, by the help of proper springs, wheels, and pulleys, may have force enough to move a body as big and heavy as the world. Then they reason, that if the little contrivance and trifling experiments which we can make of the powers of matter and motion can convince us of its capacity to produce such surprizing effects and operations, a machine organized by the excellent skill and most wise contrivance of the Supreme Architect, consisting too of such subtle animal spirits, and of such infinite springs, wheels, and tubes, must have suitable operations, some of them such as are not perceivable by our senses, or penetrable by our capacities. They conceive, that there is something in vegetation analogous to animal life; and that the difference of the appearing sensations between the highest vegetable and the lowest animal (as for example, between the sensitive plant and worm or snail) is so very little, that they can account for them both by the same system of reasoning; or rather, they are both equally unaccountable by our reason: And therefore, since the former is undoubtedly only a modus or operation of matter and motion they think that we cannot know but the other may be so too.

Many pretenders to philosophy have thought the mind of a brute animal to be part of the body, originally formed with it, and differing only from the other parts, as it has a finer contexture, and consists of more subtle and volatile particles of matter, that cannot keep together without their case or shell, and consequently cannot exist together in a separate state from the body; but when the organization and mechanism of its inclosure is dissolved or broken to pieces, it must dissipate into the mass of matter again.

But the greater number have thought, that there is an *anima mundi,* or universal spirit, that permeates and actuates all matter, and is the source of vegetable and animal life; which spirit receiving its modification from, and assimilating itself to, the nature and structure of the body through which it passes, or in which it acts, constitutes all the specific effects and operations which we daily see, feel, and admire; as in the instances before given, the same wind, blown into different instruments, makes different kinds of musick.

Many of this latter sort have fancied, that all nature is full of organized bodies, with each a particular and sufficient portion of this universal and vital spirit annexed to or inherent in them; which bodies being in constant motion, fall gradually into peculiar matrixes or wombs, which are necessary to bring them to perfection. They think that the first seeds of all vegetables and animals (which are indeed the vegetables and animals themselves) must have been formed at the creation of the world; that the seeds of the former must make their progression through the veins and tubes of the vegetables of the same kind, to prepare them to become fruit, and to produce that grosser sort of seed which more easily, and by another motion, grows into the same kind of plant or tree again; and that those of the latter must pass through the body of the male to awaken the first life of those who are sent to be nursed in the eggs of the female for increase and expansion; and they conceive, that experience confirms this opinion; for that an egg will not produce an animal, till the male has thrown one into it; but afterwards, by the assistance of that vital warmth which it receives from a living body (or that heat which is equivalent to it, and is necessary to preserve the tender fibres and juices of infant animals) it continues life, nourishes and increases it, till it swell and break out of its first inclosure, and be strong enough to receive grosser nourishment.

It seems to me, that the generation or production of vegetables is analogous to, if not the same with, that of animals, and that they both receive their first nourishment and increase in eggs; and what are vulgarly called the seeds of the former, are eggs, that inclose the minute specks of entity, which are its original seeds or principles, or rather the whole plants or trees in miniature, nourish them for some time, and defend them against the injuries of exterior bodies, when they first expand themselves, and swell out of their native beds, and their tender parts become susceptible of outward violence. It is evident, that if we break up new or maiden ground, many sorts of vegetables will spontaneously arise, which have undoubtedly their proper seeds in the earth, and as undoubtedly none of those gross seeds which produce the same plant again; and it is plain, that the latter are subject to be destroyed by exterior accidents, and to decay and die; which the others are not, but very probably have had an unmolested existence from the beginning of time, and would have continued in their first state, if they had not received a fermentation, and found a proper matrix, by the opening the fibres and bowels of the earth; which matrix must be different from what multiplies the same species afterwards.

There have been other sects of philosophers (if folly may be called by that name) who have distinguished themselves by supposing the mind and soul to be the same being, and consequently enjoyed in common by other animals, as well as men; and they have supposed this being not only to be different too from the body, and capable in its own nature, not only of subsisting independent of it, but believed that it received prejudice, and was restrained from the free use of many of its faculties, by its imprisonment and union with the body; and yet, when it was discharged from its gaol, was at liberty, capable or obliged to enter into some other organized body, to animate it, and to perform the functions of it. This was the opinion of the transmigrators of souls formerly, but is justly rejected by very many Christians; is contrary to revelation, and would put brute animals upon a level with mankind: for it cannot be denied that other living creatures have minds, and as certainly no souls; nor are they capable of just or unjust actions, or of receiving future rewards and punishments due to those actions.

It is certain that they have minds, and consequently thought; reflection upon past actions, or memory; sensations of pleasure and pain; and in many instances they judge well of their own interests, and choose proper means to attain them: And mankind have not only the above qualities in common with them, but possess them in a greater degree; and over and above enjoy, by the bounty of heaven, immortal souls, capable of continuing their duration to all eternity; of which some traces are discoverable in our nature, and the rest are ascertained to us by revelation, which man alone is capable of receiving: But how this superadded being operates upon and controls the actions of the mind and body, we seem to be wholly in the dark; but it is certain that in some respects they are all blended together, co-operate, and act as one being; and therefore are answerable for their joint actions, and are to take the same fate at last, when they come to be united again. However, in this discourse it may be proper to consider them separately, and not to impute the mechanical operations of matter and motion immediately to our immortal part; especially in such instances as are the same, or analogous to the actions of brutes, who are wholly mortal.

Therefore, if we consider this energy, or principle, called *mind*, as separate from an human soul, we shall find, that it mingles with, animates, and informs the bodies of men, and of all animals; and whether it be only a modification of matter and motion, whether subtle, volatile, and elastick particles of matter, called animal spirits; whether it be elementary fire, or what the ancients called *anima mundi*, or *divinae particula aurae*,[1] that is, a particle of the soul of the universe, or a spark or impulse of the divinity; or whatever else it be unknown to us; it is most certain, that its power and action over some sorts of organized bodies is very surprizing, and not to be accounted for by any other system of matter and motion which falls within our comprehensions; nor can I conceive it possible that it ever should be: For how should any being trace its own principles, and the causes which gave it being, know what it was before it was, or be able to think how it came to think, unless by resolving all thinking into the power of its creator? To know the modus of creation is the next step to creation, and to a creature's creating itself, or another being like itself, and rendering the *opus operatum*,[2] or the work performed, equally or near as valuable as the artificer.

The powers of this principle are very stupendous. We seem to owe to this most, if not all our sensations, appetites, affections, and passions, which obviously receive constant alteration by the addition of new and adventitious particles of matter, which must more or less be penetrated and inspired with this spirit, which unites to what is called the mind, as the grosser parts do to the body; for neither can grow but by addition, or be lessened but by subtraction, though their actions may be, and are often clogged by internal and external impediments. Our desires and fears, which appear to direct, and indeed comprehend, all the actions of the mind, are only passions, or perturbations of it, made by the impressions of external and internal causes; and what we call judgment seems to me to be no more than a struggle of those passions, or, in other words, the balance of the conveniences or inconve-

1. "Soul of the universe," or "a small part of the divine spirit."
2. "The work performed."

niences which will result from what we desire or fear, and the heavier scale must weigh down.

When a proper proportion of this active force is duly diffused through the whole machine, it will equally receive or resist the impressions of objects; the passions will be alike balanced, and consequently our thoughts and actions will be regular, and what we call prudent: But if there be too little to animate the mass, or if it meet such obstructions as hinder its energy, it becomes stupidity or folly; but if it abound, and overinform its tenement, or if it be unequally dispersed, or put or kept out of its proper place by natural or accidental obstructions, it causes indiscretion, extravagance, and, in a greater degree, madness. Of which several manners of thinking there are as many kinds and degrees as there are irregularities in man's conduct; and I doubt there are few men so equally tempered, but they have, at different times, more or less of all these qualities by the unequal supplies of this vital spirit, or by the occasional obstructions which it meets with. When we denominate a man mad, or a fool, we mean only that he is more so than most others of his species; for all men at times have a mixture of both, and no men's actions will always bear the test of just reasonings, and if we could enter and look into their private thoughts, I doubt they would much less do so. All sudden passion is temporary madness, as continued passion is continued madness; and all want of apprehension is folly.

Madness too is undoubtedly to be learned and acquired by habit and exercise, as well as covetousness, pride, ambition, love, desire of revenge, and other qualities: All which, carried beyond a certain degree, become madness; as every thing else is, when men's desires or fears, or the means chosen to attain the one, or avoid the other, are extravagant, and above human power or prudence. Nor does madness (as has been said) depend only upon wrong organizations at first, or upon the original ill temperament of the juices, by an undue mixture or superabundance of this active spirit; but often upon the fortuitous alterations which both receive afterwards by diet, physick, action, or accidents: for when those volatile particles have been long diverted, and used to run in wrong and indirect channels, the proper ones will be closed up, and they will have no others but the wrong ones to go in; which unequal distribution must overload some, and starve the rest, and make their operations as heterogeneous and irregular as their causes are; and daily experience shews, that men who have been long used to think or act only in one way, are very difficultly, if ever, put into another.

But of all the several species or kinds of madness in the world, none is so flagrant, catching, and mischievous, as the madness of enthusiasm; which is still the worse, as it adopts and puts on the mask and appearance of zeal, and often passes for sobriety and inspiration; and consequently is incapable of a cure, because it will not seek or accept a remedy. This shall be the subject of my next two papers; and then my dream will be out.

T   *I am, &c.*

NO. 123. SATURDAY, APRIL 6, 1723.

Inquiry concerning Madness, especially religious Madness, called Enthusiasm.

SIR,

I have supposed, in my last, that our desires and fears are passions or impressions made upon us by the actions of other beings; and that a due balance of those passions, or equal impressions made upon the several parts of the machine, duly impregnated with vital spirit, makes it act regularly, and constitutes what we call prudence: but when it is over-informed, or irregularly informed, or when those impressions are too strong for the machine to grapple with, it becomes madness and distraction; for the truth of which we need only appeal to experience. Men of warm constitutions are easily animated into madness by fiery liquors and high food, or by occasional strokes of good or bad fortune; whereas those who have not a sufficient share of vital spirit, are only elevated and raised to a proper pitch by high living, or wholly depressed by afflictions, as wanting vigour to resist their power, whilst nature, in the former, by an unequal struggle and contention with it, over-exerts itself, and disorders and shakes the whole machine.

This hypothesis receives further confirmation from the methods usually taken to cure madness; namely by fasting, bleeding, or purging; which methods can operate only by removing, carrying off, or suffering to exhale or perspire, the superabundant particles of spirituous matter, which overcharge and disorder the fabrick, till it receive a fresh fermentation from the addition of new ones, when the distemper again returns. Since therefore it is evident, that some of our thinking faculties receive addition and diminution from the action of other bodies, and from many internal and external causes, it must be equally evident, that they must be mortal, or perishable in their own nature; for what is mortality but a being changing its form, shape, or state? And what is immortality, but its continuing always the same? And every alteration makes it a different being in some respects from what it was before.

It seems therefore to me, that all the operations of our minds do not flow from our immortal souls; but that many of them have much lower sources: For what can be more absurd, than to suppose that what is immortal, and consequently not perishable, can be bleeded, purged, or starved away, in whole or in part? or that a being independent of matter, that pervades and permeates all matter, and yet (as it is said) has no extension, nor takes up or fills any place, can be acted upon by matter, which we cannot conceive to act otherwise than by contact or impulse, and consequently cannot affect what it cannot touch mediately or immediately; that is to say, either by instant action upon an adjoining body, or by striking or gravitating upon distant ones, by the communication of most or of all which are intermediate. I do not pretend to describe the *modus* of gravitation, or to explain how material substances attract one another, whether by Lucretius's system of hooked atoms, or by an elastick principle that God has given every particle of matter, which keeps it in constant motion, and by impelling all contiguous parts; which motion must force the more dense bodies together, the more subtle and thin ones not being able to resist their power, and interrupt their union.

It is highly probable, if not certain, that every part of matter is affected more or less by all parts of matter; and therefore the greater the quantity is that is united together, the more it must impel some bodies, and resist others; and when any part of matter is kept from having its full influence and operation upon a dense and aggregate substance by the interposition of another, acted upon by the motion of bodies encompassing it, then it seems evident that those two substances must meet together, unless some other power hinders their junction; for all circumambient bodies having their full force upon them, except in those parts which look towards one another, and they still preserving their own force and intrinsick motion, must necessarily gravitate, and more where they meet with the least opposition. But whether this be the true cause of gravitation, or whether we shall ever know the cause of it whilst we are in these frail bodies still I conceive that we are under no necessity to recur immediately to the first cause, when we cannot dive into his manner of governing the universe; nor, since we want faculties to conceive how he has united the soul to the body, are we to determine it to be done in a manner which apparently contradicts the nature of both; but we ought to leave and submit those searches to the secret decrees of providence, and to the time of the last resurrection, when our minds and bodies will be as immortal as our souls, and when possibly all these matters may be revealed to us.

I think therefore it is pretty evident, by what I have said in this paper and the last, as well as from constant observation, that madness is a super-abundance of vital spirits; which must burst their vessel, if they do not overflow, or be let out by tapping; but which way soever they find their evacuation, they generally ferment first, and make a terrible combustion within. This is the devil which haunts us, and often carries away part of an empty house, or blows it up. If he ascend to our garrets, or upper regions, he disorders the brain, and shews visions, airy and romantick images and appearances, carries the hero out of himself, and then sends him armed *cap-a-pee*[1] in wild expeditions, to encounter windmills, and giants of his own making; till at last he return home (if ever he

1. Cap-a-pee: from head to foot.

return home) transported with his victory, and in his own opinion a most consummate knight-errant.

Whenever the mind cannot be confined within its inclosure, but flies like Phaeton[2] into the great abyss, and gives the full reins to imagination, it will quickly be carried out of its knowledge, and ramble about wherever fancy, desire, or vision, leads it. It will quickly rise above humanity, become proper conversation for the celestial beings; and, when once it can persuade itself into such angelical company, will certainly despise all other; and the man who is animated by it will think that he has a right to govern all. If the excess of any passion be madness, the excess of them altogether is exorbitant and outrageous madness; and whoever can get it into his head, that he has secret communications with the deity, must have all his passions at work together. The awe of a divine presence must strike him strongly with fear and reverence: The fancied indulgence and condescension shewn him, must raise the highest love, adoration, and transports of joy: So visible a partiality of the deity to him beyond other men, must create pride, and contempt towards others: Such a support and assistance must inspire the highest courage and resolution to overcome all opposition: Hatred, and revenge, to all who do not believe him, will bring up the rear. At last the jumble of all these passions, with many more, will make an accomplished reformer of mankind.

Religious enthusiasm, therefore, is a flaming conceit that we have great personal interest with the deity, and that the deity is eminently employed about us, or in us; that he warms and solaces our hearts, guides our understandings and our steps, determines our will, and sets us far above those who have less pride and more sense than our selves. The enthusiast heats his own head by extravagant imaginations, then makes the all-wise spirit of God to be the author of his hot head; and having worked up his brains into the clouds, despises and hates all that are below, and if he can, kills them, unless they submit to be as mad as himself; for, because he takes his own frenzy for inspiration, you must be guided by his

2. The son of Helios, whom the Sun permitted to guide the solar chariot for a day. Phaeton was unable to control the chariot's horses, which bolted and threatened to set the world on fire until Zeus killed Phaeton with a thunderbolt.

frenzy; and if you are not, you are a rebel to God, and 'tis ten to one but he has a call to put you to death.

I have but a bad opinion of that devotion which is raised by a crazed head, and can be improved by a dram, and a hot sun, or the assistance of wine, or can be lessened by cold weather, or by letting of blood. It is great madness, mixed with presumption, to pretend to have the spirit of God, unless we can shew it by doing works which only God's spirit can do; that spirit which can do all things, but foolish things. Enthusiasm is doubtless a fever in the head, and, like other fevers, is spreading and infectious; and all the zeal of the enthusiast is only an ambition to propagate his fever.

You never knew a madman of any sort, who was not wiser than all mankind, and did not despise his whole race, who were not blessed with the same obliquity of head. Those in Bedlam think, that they are all mad who are out of it; and the madmen out of Bedlam, pity the madmen in it. The virtuoso, or dealer in butterflies, who lays himself out in the science of blue and brown beetles, thinks all science but his own to be useless or trifling. The collectors of old books are of opinion, that learning, which is intended to improve and enlighten the understanding, is inseparable from dust, and dirt, and obscurity, or contemptible without them. The pedant loads his heavy head with old words, and scorns all those who are not accomplished with the same lumber.

Now all these madmen, and many more who might be added, are harmless enthusiasts; and their pride being part of their madness, is only a jest. But your holy enthusiast is often a mischievous madman, who out of pure zeal for God, destroys his creatures, and plagues, and harasses, and kills them for their good. The Saracens, a barbarous, poor, and desert nation, half-naked, without arts, unskilled in war, and but half-armed, animated by a mad prophet, and a new religion, which made them all mad; overrun and conquered almost all Asia, most part of Africa, and a part of Europe. Such courage, fierceness, and mischief, did their enthusiasm inspire. It is amazing how much they suffered, and what great things they did, without any capacity of doing them, but a religion which was strong in proportion as it wanted charity, probability, and common sense.

They saw rapturous visions in the air, of beautiful damsels richly attired, holding forth their arms, and calling to them for their embraces; and being animated by such powerful deities, no enterprize was too hard for them. They scarce ever departed from any siege, however inferior to it in military arts or numbers. Their constant rule was to fight till they had subdued their enemies, either to their religion, or to pay tribute. They had God and his great apostle on their side, and were obstinately determined to die, or to conquer; and therefore they always did conquer. And their success confirmed their delusion; for finding that they performed greater actions than any other race of mankind ever did, or could do, they believed themselves assisted by heaven; and so esteemed their madness to be inspiration. And then it was very natural to believe, that they were the sole favourites of the Almighty, who interposed thus miraculously in their behalf; that they were employed to do his work; that all the good things of this world were but just rewards of their obedience; and consequently that it was their duty to plunder, distress, kill, and destroy all who resisted the will of God, and denied to give to them their undoubted right.

Now what was able to withstand these inspired savages; who if they lived and conquered, had this world, or, which was better, if they were killed, had the next? They were sure either of empire or paradise; a paradise too, which gratified their carnal appetites. There is no dealing with an armed enthusiast: If you oppose real reason to his wild revelations, you are cursed; if you resist him, you are killed. It signifies nothing to tell him, that you cannot submit to the impulses of a spirit which you have not, and do not believe; and that when you have the same spirit, you will be of the same mind: No, perhaps, that very spirit has told him, that he must kill you for not having it, though you could no more have it, than you could be what you were not.

Don Quixote was a more reasonable madman: He never beat, nor famished, nor tortured the unbelieving Sancho, for having a cooler head than his own, and for not seeing the extraordinary miracles and visions which he himself saw. If a man see battles in the air, or armies rising out of the sea, am I to be persecuted or ill used because I cannot see them too, when they are not to be seen! Or ought not rather their distracted seer to be shut up in a dark room, where no doubt he will have the same sights, and be equally happy in his own imaginations? As there is no reasoning with an enthusiast, there is no way to be secure against him, but by keeping him from all power, with which he will be sure to play the Devil in God's name. I would not hurt him for his ravings; but I would keep him from hurting me for not raving too.

All men who can get it into their own heads, that they are to subdue others to their opinions, reasonings and speculations, are enthusiasts or impostors, madmen or knaves. Almighty God has given no other light to men to distinguish truth from false-hood, or imposture from revelation, but their reason; and in all the addresses which he himself makes to them, appeals to that reason. He has formed us in such a manner, as to be capable of no other kind of conviction; and consequently can expect no other from us: It must therefore be the last degree of impudence, folly, and mad-ness, in impotent, fallible and faithless men, to assume greater power over one another, than the Almighty exercises over us all.

The appointing judges in controversy, is like setting peo-ple at law about what they are both in possession of. A man can have no more than all that he is contending for; and therefore I can compare the quarrelling of two men about their religion, to nothing else in nature, but to the battle between Prince Volscius and Prince Prettyman in *The Rehearsal*, because they were not both in love with the same mistress.[3]

G   *I am, &c.*

NO. 124. SATURDAY, APRIL 13, 1723.

❧   *Further Reasonings upon Enthusiasm.*

SIR,

Besides the flaming enthusiasm mentioned in our last, which is there supposed to be inspired by a super-abundance of spirits, labouring for evacuation; and shaking, disordering, and sometimes bursting its tenement to get ready vent (like gun-pow-

3. The encounter occurs in act IV, scene 2, of Buckingham's play.

der in a granado or mine, or subterraneous fire enclosed in the bowels of the earth); there seems to me to be another sort of religious enthusiasm, not at all mischievous, but rather beneficial to the world; and this has shewn itself in several ages, and under several denominations. There is much to be read of it in the mystick writers in all times. Hermits seem to be inspired with it, and several sects have built their innocent superstitions upon it; as the Alumbrati in Spain, the Quietists in Italy, the French Prophets lately amongst us;[1] and I doubt, a very great part in Europe, called Quakers, owe their rise and increase to it. Having mentioned this last sect, I think myself obliged to declare that I esteem them to be a great, industrious, modest, intelligent, and virtuous people; and to be animated with the most beneficent principles of any sect which ever yet appeared in the world. They have a comprehensive charity to the whole race of mankind, and deny the mercies of God to none. They publickly own, that an universal liberty is due to all; are against impositions of every kind, yet patiently submit to many themselves, and perhaps are the only party amongst men, whose practices, as a body, correspond with their principles.

I am not ashamed to own, that I have with great pleasure read over Mr. Barclay's *Apology for Quakerism*;[2] and do really think it to be the most masterly, charitable, and reasonable system that I have ever seen. It solves the numerous difficulties raised by other sects, and by turns thrown at one another, shews all parts of scripture to be uniform and consistent; and as Sir Isaac Newton, by allowing him gravitation, has accounted for all the phenomena of

1. The Alumbrados, or "Illuminati," of Spain were a loosely knit Spanish religious group of the sixteenth century given to prayer and contemplation and believing in the importance of visions and revelations. Quietism was brought to Italy in the 1660s by the Spanish cleric Miguel de Molinos and soon became immensely popular among the clergy in Rome. Molinos taught the importance of passivity and of destroying the self-conscious will as an obstacle to meditation and divine inspiration. "The French Prophets" refers to a French Protestant sect that arose following the Revocation of the Edict of Nantes; they exhorted their coreligionists on the imminence of the Apocalypse and the fall of Babylon. The group became quite active in England for a time and its millennialist views had a profound effect on the doctrines later adopted by the Shakers.

2. Robert Barclay (1648–1690), *An apology for the true Christian divinity: as the same is held forth, and, preached by the people, called, in scorn, Quakers, being a full explanation and vindication of their principles and doctrines* (London, 1678).

nature, so if we allow Mr. Barclay those operations of the spirit, which the Quakers pretend to feel, and which he says every man in the world has and may feel, if he watch its motions, and do not suppress them; I think that all the jangling vain questions, numerous superstitions, and various oppressions, which have plagued the world from the beginning, would cease and be at an end.

But this postulatum will not be granted, and I fear will never be proved; though such a discovery be much to be wished, and the opinion of it alone must render those very happy, who can persuade themselves that they have attained to it. Mr. Asgil wrote and published a book,[3] to prove that all true believers (that is all who had attained a spirit like this) shall be translated without passing through death; and, as I doubt not but he believed his own dream himself, so if he had published it before any man had actually died, I cannot see how it could have been answered, or how it can be answered now, but by opposing fact to it, and by making the words *eternal death* signify eternal life in torments, which liberty no language will bear in other disputes; and yet his doctrine cannot be assented to, without supposing that no man ever had faith but Elias and Enoch;[4] which is a very wild supposition.

For the same reason, I cannot concur with Mr. Barclay, in believing that all men who cannot find this spirit in themselves, do or have suppressed it; for I believe that there are many thousands in all respects equally virtuous with himself, who have actually tried all experiments of watching, internal prayer, outward and inward resignation, separation from worldly thoughts and actions, acquiescence of mind, and submission to the operations of the deity, yet have found themselves, after all, just where they set out; nor could recollect any thing that happened to them in those intervals, but absence of thought; and therefore, till I can feel something in my self, or discover some traces in others, which I cannot account for from lower motives, I shall take the liberty to call the

3. John Asgill (1639–1738), *An argument proving that according to the covenant of eternal life revealed in the Scriptures, man may be translated from hence to eternal life, without passing through death altho the human nature of Christ himself could not be thus translated till he passed through death* (London, 1700).

4. That is, Elijah and Enoch, both noted for their piety and both spared the pain of seeing death, having been bodily translated into heaven.

pretenders to it, enthusiasts: though I must confess that all or most religious parties have laid claim to this spirit upon certain occasions, and have bestowed it upon their founders, or particular men amongst them; and the Quakers only say, that all men have it, and may exert it, or rather permit it to exert itself if they please.

It is supposed that the power so claimed is Jesus Christ operating within us; and as it is allowed by all that the least drop of his natural blood was enough to atone for the sins of the whole world; so one might imagine that the least portion of his godhead, working within us, might be too hard for and overcome the depravity transmitted to us by our first parents, or at least be able to engage our attention or acquiescence, which is all that is supposed requisite to the farther progress and effusion of his deity. It is very hard to conceive, that we can serve God by sequestering for a time all the faculties which he has given us; by sending our wits out of doors, to make room for grace, and by believing that the spirit of God will never exert it self but in an empty head; and therefore I shall presume to believe, till I am better informed, that as the Almighty shews and exhibits to us the visible world by the medium of the outward senses, which he had before given us, so he dispenses all that we do know or can know of the invisible one, through the vehicles of our reasoning faculties.

We have not yet been able thoroughly to discover any vacuum in nature, but as soon as any body gets out of a place, another leaps in; if therefore a man can once drive his wits out of house and home, some other being of a different kind will certainly get into their room, and wind is always at hand crowding for preferment; which, in various shapes, has a great share in human transactions, and always has contributed much to the great revolutions in empire and superstition, such as have often overturned the world. But to return to my dream.

A clock, or other machine, made by a skilful artist, will have certain and regular motions, whilst it continues in that state; but if it gather filth, meet with obstructions, or its springs and wheels decay and wear out by time, or be hurt by accidents, it moves irregularly, or not at all. Experience proves the same in the mechanism of animals, who have infinitely finer contextures, as consisting of thousands of tubes, veins, arteries, nerves, and muscles, every one of which, in a certain degree, contributes to the operations of the living engine; and as all these are more tender and delicate, and consequently more susceptible of injuries, than the parts which constitute and give motion to other organized bodies, so they are much more easily put out of order: and we find in fact, that a cold which stops perspiration, and hinders the evacuation of the super-abundant particles of matter, disorders the whole fabrick, clogs and interrupts its action; and that those effluviums which cannot find their proper vent through the pores, overshadow and oppress the brain, and render the mind unactive, and incapable to perform its functions, till they are let out by larger passages, as by bleeding, or vomiting, or forced out by sweating, or other violent action, or by fasting, and taking in no new supplies, there is time given to them leisurely to expire; but if they require quicker vent than these conduits can give, then fevers, or other violent distempers ensue, when the brains of men are so oppressed, that they see visions, appearances of angels, demons, and dead men, talk incoherently, and sometimes surprisingly, and have obviously different sensations, affections, and reasonings, from what they have at other times.

The same is true of madmen, who through wrong organizations at first, or through the indisposition of the organs afterwards, persuade themselves that they are princes, prophets, or messengers from heaven; and certainly often utter flights, and sallies of imagination, which are amazing, and that never fall from them in their lucid intervals, and which are often passed upon the whole world for inspiration; insomuch, that in several ages, and in several countries in our age, they have been and are thought to be divinely inspired. Now madness shews itself in a thousand shapes; and as has been said in my former paper,[5] there is scarce a man living but at times has more or less of it, though we denominate it from a train of irregular actions; and many kinds of it certainly do not fall within common observation, or scarce within any observation.

5. See Letter No. 123 (Apr. 6, 1723).

When we see men in the main of their conduct seemingly act with prudence in such things as we understand, we are apt to take their words in such things as we do not understand; especially if we see them do such actions, shew such emotions of spirit, and utter such discourses as we cannot otherwise account for, though we perceive the same done by men in known distempers, and in sleep, and often feel it in our selves: For it is incredible to those who have not seen or observed it, what energy and strength men shew in convulsive distempers, when too they often vent surprising discourses, without knowing what they say; and there are few men, who do not sometimes strike out sudden and extemporary thoughts and expressions, without being able to observe by what traces they came into their minds; and fanciful and conceited men easily persuade themselves, or are persuaded by others, to believe that at those times they are inspired from above.

But if we compare things which we do not know, with those which we do, I think we may account for them both by the same principles in nature. Men, as has been said, in sleep see visions, hold discourses, and sometimes very good ones, with phantoms of their own imaginations, and can walk about, climb over houses and precipices, which no man who is awake durst venture to do. Men in distempers see spirits, talk and reason with them, and often fancy themselves to be what they are not. Melancholy men have believed that they were glass bottles, pitchers, bundles of hay, prophets, and sometimes that they are dead; and yet, in all other actions of life, have behaved themselves with discretion; and as these things happened often, few or none are surprised at them, and therefore treat them only as subjects of jest or merriment; but if they had happened but once, or seldom, we should either have not believed them, or have recurred to miracle and witchcraft for the solution. No man wonders at the sun's rising every day, and yet all are amazed and frightened by seeing a blazing star once in their life-time, though that is certainly the less wonder of the two.

Now what stretch will it be upon our imagination, to believe that once in an age, or more, a catching distemper of the mind should actuate a man or two, and communicate itself afterwards to others of the same complexion, of the same temperament of juices, and consequently of the same dispositions of mind; all which certainly are as infectious as those of the body, though not so observable? We assimulate to the passions, habits, and opinions of those whom we converse with; and their tempers are catching. This indeed is not true in all instances; neither does a plague infect every body, but only those who have proper juices, and suitable dispositions of body to receive it. We see often, that the yawning of one man, will make a whole company yawn; and that the sight of men in convulsive distempers will throw others into the same; as many people were agitated with the same motions and spirit of prating with the French Prophets, though they went to see the Prophets fall into their trances, with a design only to divert themselves; which trances undoubtedly were an unusual kind of epileptick fits, which often actuate the organs of speech without the patient's knowing it, and have often been mistaken for divine trances, and his incoherent rhapsodies been esteemed revelations.

If we may believe Mr. Barclay, and Mr. George Keith, in his *Magick of Quakerism*[6] (who was once of that sect, and afterwards took orders in the Church of England), the same thing has happened to many others who went to insult the Quakers and were caught by their shakings, groanings, and the solemnity of their silent meetings, and became afterwards steady converts. I think it is Thucydides, who tells us, that at Abdera, a city in Greece, upon a hot day, all the spectators who were present in the theatre to see *Andromache* acted, were suddenly seized with a madness, which made them pronounce iambicks; and the whole town was infected with the distemper, which lasted as long as that weather continued.[7] And he tells us too of another sort of madness, which seized the young women of Athens, many of whom killed themselves; and the magistrates could not stop the contagion, till they made a decree, that those who did so should be exposed, and hung up naked.[8] There seems to be no difficulty, in conceiving that the

6. *The Magick of Quakerism, or The Chief Mysteries of Quakerism Laid Open* (London: Printed for B. Aylmer, 1707).

7. The incident is in fact recounted by Lucian, *Quomodo historia conscribenda sit*, 1. Lucian gives the play as Euripides' *Andromeda*.

8. The events were reputed to have occurred in Miletus, not Athens, and are described in Plutarch, *Moralia*, 249c.

effluviums, which steam from the body of an enthusiast, should infect others suitably qualified, with the same distemper; as experience shews us, that the minute particles, which are conveyed by the bite of a mad dog, cause madness, and will make the person infected bark like the dog who bit him. And such particles in other instances may be conveyed through the pores, and in a common instance undoubtedly are so; for many people will swoon if a cat be in the room, though they do not see her. And all infectious distempers must be communicated by those passages.

Some distempers or dispositions of body, make men rave; others make them melancholy: Some give them courage, impetuosity, prodigious energy of mind, and rapturous thoughts and expressions; others sink and depress their spirits, give them panick fears, dismal apprehensions, melancholy images, and secret frights; and they will all account for such sensations from their former imbibed prejudices by early education, and by long use become familiar to them. One of these distempers will make a flaming false prophet, and the other a despairing penitent, in spite of the mercies of God; and afterwards physick or abstinence shall cure the first, and a bottle of wine, now and then moderately and cheerfully taken, in agreeable company, shall make the other a man of this world again.

Opium in different constitutions will work both these extremes, and other drugs will give temporary madness. The oracular priests of old well understood this secret of nature. The high priestess of Delphos sucked inspiration from the fumes of an intoxicating well, which disordered her brain, made her rave and utter incoherent speeches, out of which something was found out to answer the devout querist, and tell the meaning of the god: And in the temple, as I remember, of Amphiaraus,[9] where oracles were conveyed in dreams, the humble and submissive votary was let down into a deep hole, that had several fantastical apartments, where he saw sights and apparitions, which his mind was prepared to receive before by physick, suitable diet, and sometimes by fasting; and then he was wrapped up in the skins of victims, rubbed

9. A prophet and hero of Argos and one of the Seven against Thebes. He was granted immortality by the gods, and his temple was made an oracular shrine.

and impregnated with intoxicating drugs, which made him dream most reverently; and when he related his visions, it was very hard luck if the priests could find nothing in them for their purpose: but if that happened to be the case, the same operation was tried over again; and if they had no better fortune then, the god was angry with the impious seeker for his sins, and so was become sullen, and the poor miscreant was sent away as an excommunicate person (if he had the good luck to escape so), and perhaps hanged himself in his way home.

We see and feel, by constant experience, that our thoughts in dreams are lascivious, frightful or pleasing, according to the temperament of our bodies, the food which we eat, or as our spirits are oppressed or cherished by it. We see too that drunken or distempered men are overcome by liquor or diseases, and made to talk, reason, and act differently from what they do in sobriety and in health; and we all confess such discourses and actions to be the indispositions of their organs, and the operations of external or internal material causes, and will yet not account for other sensations equally extravagant from like mediums, though we cannot shew any difference between them: However, as it is not to be denied but Almighty God has sometimes communicated himself to particular persons by secret impressions upon their senses and understandings, so I dare not affirm, that he may not, and does not do so still; nor will I dogmatically assert, that any one who pretends to feel his divine spirit is a liar or enthusiast; but I think I may safely affirm, that no one is concerned in his visions or revelations but himself, unless the other feels them too, or he can prove the truth of them by miracles.

Almighty God, as has been said, has given us reason to distinguish truth from falsehood, imposture from revelation, delusion from inspiration; and when we quit that light we must wander through endless mazes and dark labyrinths, and ramble wherever fancy, imagination, or fraud leads us. If Mr. Barclay had meant only, by the testimony of the spirit, that natural faculty, or principle which the deity has inspired into all men to regulate their actions, and to acknowledge his divine bounty (which principle I call reason), and could have reconciled the workings of his light to

the only one which I can find in myself, I could readily have subscribed to a very great part of his system; for I must confess that it
is most beneficent to the world, in my opinion, most agreeable to
the scriptures, and makes them, or rather shews them, to be most
consistent with themselves, and comprehends every thing which
has been since said by the best of writers for liberty of conscience,
and against all sorts of religious impositions. And this he has done
with as much wit, happy turn, and mastery of expression, as is consistent with the plainness and simplicity affected by those of his
sect, and for the most part used in the holy writings.

T   *I am, &c.*

NO. 125. SATURDAY, APRIL 20, 1723.

*The Spirit of the Conspirators, Accomplices with Dr.
Atterbury, in 1723, considered and exposed.*[1]

SIR,

I intend to consider in this paper, the behaviour and spirit of the
conspirators; and to shew what enemies they are, even to such
as are favourable to them. But, before I proceed to enquire into
the avowed causes of all this outrageous disaffection, I will freely
own, that many things have been done which cannot be justified;
some, perhaps ignorantly, many ambitiously, and others, it is to be
feared, traitorously, to help the conspirators, by provoking the
people, and by rendering the administration odious. Sure I am,
that there are many pregnant appearances that look sadly this way;
and can be construed no other way; and that these measures gave
much sorrow and indignation to the best friends of the government, as I doubt not but they did pleasure and hopes to the disaffected, who saw how fast, by such steps, their views were advanced.
Treason is most successfully carried on by unsuspected traitors, as

1. In May 1722, a number of conspirators were implicated in a plot to capture
the royal family and to proclaim the Old Pretender as King. Among those suspected of being involved was Dr. Francis Atterbury, then Bishop of Rochester,
who was arrested and confined to the Tower for some months.

friends are easiest betrayed and undone by friends. The cry therefore of the conspirators against unpopular proceedings,[2] was all
hypocrisy, and false fire: They saw their mischievous influence,
and rejoiced in it: They thought that they were saved the danger
and trouble of plotting; and that all that they had to do was to hold
the match ready, while other people were laying the train; and to
put their sickle into a harvest not of their own sowing. How near
they were to reaping this harvest, is now apparent.

Every good man will condemn unjust measures, let them
come from what quarter they will: But the conspirators could not
with a good grace condemn the worst, even supposing the resentment sincere. The wildest and wickedest things done by their own
party, have been constantly and zealously defended and promoted
by them: And they have steadily acted for or against a party, from
passion or faction: Nor has the love of their country, and the good
of the whole, separated from party, ever swayed them in one publick action, that I remember. Neither is it any defence of them, that
others, who professed larger, and more humane and publick principles, have fallen too often into the same partiality and been too
often governed by the same narrow, selfish, and passionate spirit.
Who have ever sworn more blindly to a steady faith in their demagogues, than the conspirators? Who have ever more notoriously
shewn, that they knew no other measures of right and wrong, of
religion and impiety, than the measures espoused or opposed by
their own leaders! What job has been so vile, that they have not
blindly approved? Or what scheme so just, that they have not
fiercely condemned? Just as this scheme, or that job has taken its
rise from this or that quarter.

Nor was the spirit of faction ever more manifest than in
the present conspiracy: What did the conspirators want, but plunder and places? But what advantages was their country to reap
from the violent change, which they were bringing upon it? Before

2. Although there were strong indications that Dr. Atterbury took part in the
plot, there appears to have been insufficient evidence to obtain a legal conviction. As a consequence, the government brought in a bill of pains and penalties, depriving Atterbury of his spiritual offices and sending him into exile.
Such a bill, by which Parliament can condemn an individual while circumventing the protections afforded the accused by the normal legal process, was
justifiably unpopular and was widely criticized.

they could have accomplished it, the nation and every thing in it must have been thrown into convulsions, and a chaos. What order could they bring out of this confusion? What amends could they make for unsettled or plundered property, a trade stagnated or lost, harvests destroyed, contending armies, bloodshed, slaughter and battles, general desolation, universal terror, every man's sword against his neighbour, the foreign sword against all, and dyed with the blood of Britons, his Majesty deposed, and perhaps butchered? For it could not be possible, even for them to suppose, that his Majesty and his family, possessed of so much power in his native dominions, supported by such numbers, such wealth and dependences in Great Britain, and by so many powerful allies abroad, could be effectually expelled by their bigotted idol, and his champions, but after a long and fatal civil war, fought within our bowels: A war in which most of the contending powers of Europe would have been parties, and which must have ended in the utter loss of our liberties, which ever side had prevailed.

In answer to this black catalogue of woes will they urge, that England and English liberty, and the Protestant religion, would have been indeed destroyed; but that they, the conspirators, would have had places? And yet what else can they urge? For this is the sum of their reasoning, whatever disguises they would put upon it. Such was their spirit; and I wish it were as new as it is shocking and horrible. But alas! it is as old as men: and every country upon earth, that has been undone, has been undone to satiate the ambition of one, or a few, who aimed at seizing or extending power.

The complaints of miscarriages, of wrong steps, and abuse of power, came awkwardly and absurdly from their mouths, whatever grounds there may have been for such complaints. What security could the conspirators give us, that, contrary to the nature of man, and of power, and to their own nature and conduct, they themselves would be humble in grandeur, and modest in exaltation, and occupy power with moderation, self-denial, and clean hands? They who would overturn the constitution, and the foundations of the earth, and fill the land with violence, war and blood, to come at that power! Can we conceive it impossible that any regard to the publick good, and to publick property, would have the least influence over those men, who would sacrifice the publick, and annihilate all property, for the gratification of personal ambition and rage? Or how should the love of liberty and peace bind these men, whom neither the laws of humanity, and of their country, nor the religion of an oath, nor the awful gospel of Jesus Christ, can in the least bind?

They exclaim against armies and taxes, and are the cause of both, and rail at grievances of their own creating. Who make armies necessary, but they, who would invade, and enslave, or destroy us by armies, foreign popish armies? Who make taxes necessary, but they, who by daily conspiring against our peace and our property, and against that establishment which secures both, force us to give part to save all? And who, but they, can give a handle and pretence to such as delight in taxes and armies, and prosper by them, to continue and increase them? They are not only the authors of those great grievances, but of all the evils and subsequent grievances which proceed from them. Had the conspirators succeeded, can we think, or will they have the face to say, that they would have ruled without armies? The yoke of usurpation and servitude is never to be kept on without the sword. They who make armies necessary now, would have found them necessary then: Nor would they have ridiculously and madly trusted to their merit and popular conduct, when in this very instance they shew that no means were too black, no pitch of iniquity and cruelty too horrid, for the accomplishment of their treason; and general plunder and devastation, conflagrations and murder, were the concerted specimens of their spirit, and to be the hopeful beginnings of their reign. Did King James, whose misfortunes they caused and lament, did he, or could he, pretend to support his religion, and his arbitrary administration, without the violence of the sword, without a great and popish army? Is the Pretender of a different religion, or more moderate in the same religion? Or does he disavow his father's government, and propose a better and milder of his own? Does he pretend to come or to stay here without armies? And are not governments continued, and must be, by the same means by which they were founded? A government begun by armies, and the violation of property, must be continued by armies, oppression and violence.

What is here said of taxes and armies, may be said of the suspension of the Habeas Corpus Act.[3] They complain of suspension as a heavy evil; and by their incessant plots and rebellions, make long and frequent suspensions inevitable. By their eternal designs and attacks upon us, they force us upon the next means of self-preservation; and then complain of oppression, because we will not suffer them to oppress and destroy us. It is therefore owing to them, that the subject is taken from under the protection of the common law, and left to the discretion of the court. Who says that this is desirable? But who makes it necessary, or gives a pretence for it?

We were all justly filled with the apprehension of losing Gibraltar, and thought that no doom was too bad for the traitor that had agreed to give it up (if there ever were such a traitor in his Majesty's service); and the conspirators exclaimed as loudly as any. But behold their baseness and insincerity in this, as in other complaints, and their extensive enmity to their country in every instance! By the conspiracy it appears, that they laboured with foreign powers to have Gibraltar taken from Great Britain, on purpose to engage the nation to part with their government and their religion, in resentment for the loss of that single though important fortress.

The late management of the South-Sea was another topick of resentment and complaint, and a just one, whatever unjust uses the conspirators made of it. It is reasonable to believe that in their hearts they rejoiced in it, since from the universal displeasure, confusion, and losses, occasioned by it, and from the bitterness caused by those losses, they drew hopes and a good omen to their conspiracy, which else must have been impotent and languishing. The tender and slow prosecution of the execrable managers, the gentle punishment inflicted upon them, and the obvious difficulties thrown in the way of any punishment at all,[4] were fresh provoca-

3. Attempts to forestall the Jacobite plot of 1722, which included the seizure of the Bank of England and the Tower, led to the suspension of the Habeas Corpus Act for one year.

4. It was not until May 1721 that Parliament enacted the South Sea Sufferers Bill, which called for the confiscation of a substantial portion of the estates of

tions to a plundered and abused nation, and fresh stimulations to the conspirators. They saw, that great numbers, who had always hated them and their Pretender, were now, under heavy misfortunes, and in the present agonies of their soul, brought to think not unkindly of him and his cause, or to be entirely indifferent about it. They said they were undone, and could not be worse undone; and that nothing in human shape, or in any shape, could use them so ill as the directors had; the execrable, rich, and unchanged directors!

But of all men it least concerns the conspirators to be noisy about the hellish management of the South-Sea scheme; since one of the first and most certain consequences of the conspiracy would have been the utter ruin of the whole South-Sea stock, and of all the many thousands who have their property in it. The Bank, and all other publick funds, would have had the same fate; nay, one of the first steps would have been the plundering of the Bank, and the seizure of all the books of the great companies.

This was so much the design of the conspirators, that one reason given by themselves for delaying the execution of the plot, was, that a principal conspirator, who had a great deal of stock, might have time to sell out. So that they who did so virtuously and disinterestedly exclaim against the abuse of publick credit, would have sunk and destroyed for ever not only the publick funds, but the foundation of all publick credit and publick happiness, publick and private property.

The conspirators likewise profess a loud zeal and concern for the Church; and papists, nonjurors and perjured traitors, were to deliver a Protestant church from a Protestant government, which protected her, to be better protected by a popish bigot, and his popish monks, who all think her damned. A zeal therefore for the Church was to justify the most hideous impieties, a general perjury, foreign invasions, and the final overthrow of all liberty, virtue, and religion: The reformed Church of England was, for a protecting father, to be surrendered to a nursling of the Pope's, who by his religion is, and must be, a determined enemy to the

---

the directors of the South Sea Company. Many, Trenchard and Gordon among them, were outraged by the delay in acting against those responsible for the bubble, and they thought the punishment ludicrously mild.

whole Reformation in general, and to the Church of England in particular; and is under the menaces and horrors of damnation, if he do not exert his whole policy and power to extirpate the Protestant name, and introduce a religion which is worse than none; as it professedly tolerates no other, and persecutes conscience, which is the source and seat of religion, the only source that any religion can have. While there are men, and societies of men, there will be religion; and where dread and tyranny are taken away, different religions: And yet no religion is preferable to a cruel religion; a religion that curses and oppresses toleration, which is a principle inseparable from Christianity; a religion which buries the Bible, or burns it, and all that read it, and damns all meekness and mercy; a religion that defaces the Creation, cheats, impoverishes, oppresses, and exhausts the human race, and arms its apostles with jails, tortures, gibbets, impostures, and a bloody knife.

Every other complaint of the conspirators might with the same facility and truth be turned upon them. But this paper is already too long. I will therefore conclude with observing, that the conspirators have, by the assistance of malicious calumnies, blind prejudices, gross ignorance, and constant misrepresentations, misled and abused their party, and governed them by abusing them: That they have wickedly taught them to hate a government, which, with all the faults, true or false, that their worst malice can charge it with, does just as far excel that which they would introduce, as the blessings and beauties of liberty transcend the horrid deformities of slavery, and the implacable and destroying spirit of popish tyranny: That they have wickedly taught them to be weary of their present free condition; which, with all its disadvantages, debts, and taxes, is easy and happy, greatly and conspicuously happy, in comparison of any condition of any people under any popish prince now upon earth: That they have, by perpetual delusion and lies, worked them to a readiness, nay, a passion, to venture and sacrifice their whole property, rather than pay a part to secure the whole; and to wish for a revolution, a popish revolution, which will neither leave them their property, their conscience, nor their Bible!

G   *I am, &c.*

NO. 126. SATURDAY, APRIL 27, 1723.

Address to those of the Clergy who are fond of the Pretender and his Cause.

SIR,

I have in my last, considered the spirit of the conspirators in general; I will in this address myself to those of the clergy, who have joined with them, or are well affected to them. That there are some such, no body doubts; and our enemies boast, I hope, unjustly, of a great majority: But let them be many or few, none can be affected by what is hereafter said, but those to whom it is applicable.

I shall not here urge the sacred ties which you are under; ties, sufficient to bind any conscience, which is not past all tenderness and sense of feeling; ties, awful and solemn enough to restrain minds that any religion can restrain; and ties, from which no lawless breach of the Coronation Oath, nor any act of tyranny, has disengaged you; though, according to your own doctrines, your peculiar and favourite doctrine, so often thundered in the ears of Englishmen, *No act nor acts of tyranny can dissolve the bonds of allegiance.* But I would reason with you upon the point of more weight and moment with you, your secular state and interest.

Pray what violence has been offered to your dignities and immunities? What breach made upon your livings, and revenues? What good has been done to religion at your expence? What arbitrary indulgences have been granted to dissenters, or legal ones, besides that of worshipping God? Is it a sin against you, to suffer them to exercise religion in a way different from you; when every man who worships God, must worship him his own way, in the way which he thinks God will accept, else he cannot worship him at all? What other worship will God accept, but that which conscience dictates? Every other worship is hypocrisy; which is worse than a false religion proceeding from a good conscience. He who complies with a religion which he condemns or despises, worships not God, but the pride of priests; and is therefore their friend and favourite:

while the upright man, who adores his God in spite of them, and will not dissemble in so nice and sacred a point, is reckoned a capital foe. The religion of one's country, to any man who dislikes it, is cant, and no more than the religion of Lapland. Besides, would your own pride suffer any of you to comply with the religion of Scotland, or Geneva,[1] if you were there? On the contrary, do you not constantly encourage there, what you constantly exclaim against as schism here, a separation from the established communion?

The state which makes you what you are, and gives you what you have, may by the same right and power confer what favours, privileges, and bounties it pleases, upon any other different bodies of men; nor could you in modesty, or common sense, complain, that a legislature disposed of its gifts and graces according to its own wisdom and discretion; and yet you have not even had this nonprovocation. What dissenter, what Presbyterian, has been preferred to the preferments of the Church, or any other, unless all who are faithful to the government and to their oaths, be dissenters? And will you pay dissenters this compliment? None but churchmen are preferred in the Church, or in the state. No preferments are continued vacant; the church revenues are not lessened, nor impaired, but every day increased. All the usual and legal advantages of the Church are secured to churchmen, and none but churchmen possess them. All their honours, all their emoluments, are in their hands, and they are protected in them; nor are any hardships done them, or suffered to be done them, but that of restraining them from putting hardships, distresses and shackles upon others; and that of confining a bishop, and some of his lower brethren, for treason against their God and their oaths, their religion and their King.[2] And the outrageous and brutal resentments which they have shewn for this necessary, this legal proceeding, shew what friends you are to that establishment, which maintains and supports you in such ease, honours, and plenty; and which he, and such as he, would have destroyed: You indeed make it more

1. That is, a church devoid of episcopal elements.
2. The reference is to Bishop Atterbury and a few members of the lesser clergy who were implicated in the plot and subsequently imprisoned.

and more manifest, that your greatest quarrel to the government is, that it will not put swords into your hands to destroy it. Will you after this complain, that the government will not particularly distinguish you, you only, and your deluded party with honour, trust, and esteem, for this your declared infidelity and enmity to the government?

But the Convocation,[3] you cry, does not sit. This you think a crying evil: But before we agree with you in this thought, you ought to shew us what good their present sitting would do. And if you would shew too what good their sittings ever did, or ever can do, you would inform many who are in utter ignorance as to this great affair. Do convocations always, or at any time promote peace and indulgence, and the tender charity of Christianity? Have their furious contentions for ecclesiastical union ever increased Christian union? Has their fierceness for garments and sounds, and the religion of the body and the breath, had any good effect upon humanity, sincerity, conscience, and the religion of the soul! Have not some of them, and some not very late ones, gone to open war with moderation and common sense; and with such as only offended by reconciling religion with moderation and common sense, and by proving that our Saviour lied not when he declared that his kingdom is not of this world?[4] How did the late Convocation particularly, and their champions, agree with their Head and Saviour, the great Bishop of souls, upon this article?[5] Will such as you say, that for the interest of this government the convocation ought to sit? And ought it to sit for any other interest? Be so good to lay before us the services done, and the instances of zeal shewn by the late Convocations, to this Protestant establishment.

3. The assemblies of the clergy of the Church of England at Canterbury and York. Following the Revolution of 1688, the Lower House of the Convocation of Canterbury was dominated by High Churchmen, often Jacobite in sympathy.

4. John 18:36.

5. In 1717, Benjamin Hoadly preached a series of sermons before George I in which he denied the existence of any visible church authority. This followed by a year Hoadly's publication of a pamphlet attacking the nonjuring clergy—those who had refused to swear allegiance to the crown—and defending the supremacy of the state over the church. The debate that ensued (known as the Bangorian Controversy) reached the Canterbury Convocation, where the attacks on Hoadly were so bitter that the King felt impelled to prorogue it.

Another of your common-place cries is, that the clergy are contemned. What clergy, gentlemen? Are any contemned but the profane, the forsworn, the rebellious, the lewd, the turbulent, the insatiable, the proud, and the persecuting; such as will be unavoidably contemned, and ought to be contemned, by all who have conscience, virtue, loyalty, and common honesty? And will you say that the clergy, or the body of the clergy feel, or ought to feel, this contempt? Why should the just doom of the traitors to their order affect the credit of the clergy, or fill with apprehensions such as are not traitors? If they have their crimes, what credit or respect is due to the criminal? And if any of them respect the crime, what respect is due to them from those who abhor traitors and treason, which all good men abhor?

Your little regard to conscience, and your wanton contempt of oaths, are sad proofs how small power the Christian religion, or any religion, has over you. What can bind the man whom oaths cannot bind? Can society have any stronger hold of him? And are not they enemies to society, and to mankind; they who violate all the bonds by which societies subsist, and by which mankind are distinguished from wild beasts? You boast of your succession from the apostles: Do you do as the apostles did? Or would they have deserved that venerable name, or found credit amongst men, or made one convert from heathenism, if they had been the ambitious disturbers of government; and, by profanely trampling upon oaths, had published to the world by their practice, an atheistical contempt of all conscience and religious restraints? The apostles, rather than disown their faith and opinion, and dissemble a lying regard for the Gentile deities, for a moment, were miserable in their lives, and martyrs in their death; nor could racks, wheels, fire, and all the engines of torture and cruelty, extort from them one hypocritical declaration, one profession that their souls contradicted. Neither they, nor their pious followers, needed to have been martyrs, had they been guided by a spirit that taught religion and conscience to stoop to worldly interest and luxury.

You say, I have heard some of you say, that you are forced to swear. How were you forced? Can conscience be forced? You may as well say, that men may be forced to like a religion which they hate. Can any excuse be an excuse for perjury? Were Shadrach, Meshach and Abednego forced to worship Nebuchadnezzar's golden image?[6] Were the first reformers forced to adore a wafer for a god? Was St. Paul to be forced to offer incense, and worship idols? Or, if he had, would his preaching have been of any effect, or ought to have been? Either the gospel condemns the prostitution of conscience and religion to ease and interest; or such prostitution, if the gospel allowed it, would condemn the gospel. You must therefore either renounce the gospel, which in practice you do; or condemn yourselves, which I do not hear you do: And in honour to the Christian religion, the peaceable, the sincere, the conscientious and disinterested Christian religion, all men who are sincere Christians, or only honest moralists, must condemn you, and abhor your practices.

But how were you forced? Either you must swear fidelity to a government which protects you, and takes nothing from you; or you must quit the advantages, and not eat the bread of the government (for, that the government gives you all that you have, I am ready to prove whenever you please). Now if you have really tender consciences, you would not swear: But if your tithes and rents be dearer to you than your consciences, then it is plain that your consciences are not tender. It is a very hardened conscience that is not dearer to a man than his belly. Your perjury therefore is pure wantonness, and an utter absence of all honesty, conscience, and shame. Are these qualifications proper to direct the lives and consciences of others; and to promote in the minds and practices of others, the scrupulous and upright religion of our blessed Saviour?

Cease, for God's sake, to use that holy name, or use it better. Can you bring people to him, by shewing yourselves daily apostates from him? Cease mentioning the holy martyrs, you who are a disgrace to martyrdom, and act directly contrary to the spirit of the martyrs; nay, would make a martyr of that religion for which they died. For shame rail not at atheism, speak not of atheists, you who give essential proofs of the blackest atheism. What is

6. Despite Nebuchadnezzar's demand that they worship the Babylonian gods, the three refused and were cast into a fiery furnace (Daniel 3:12–30).

atheism but an utter disbelief, or, which is really worse, an utter contempt of the deity? And what is a stronger demonstration of that contempt, than a daring, a practical contempt of conscience, his deputy within us, and a wanton and solemn invocation of his awful name to hypocrisy, deceit, and determined falsehood? This is making the godhead a party to infidelity, and to treason against himself: It is mocking God, and abusing men, and making religion the means of damnation. What can equal this horrible crime, the root and womb of all crimes? Or what words can describe it? This, gentlemen, is your advantage: No language suffices to paint out your wickedness: You are secure that your picture can never be fully drawn, or the world see it in half its blackness and deformity.

Will you after this scold at the morals and impiety of the age? You, who lay the broadest foundation for all immorality and wickedness, by letting loose the minds of men from all the strongest bonds of virtue and of human society, the inviolable engagements of conscience, and the awe of the Supreme Being! After you have thus proclaimed, in the most effectual manner, that you have no religion, or that religion has no power over you, will you continue to fill the world and weak heads with canting conjectures and barren speculations, as if religion consisted in whims, dreams, and non-entities? And when you have, as far as your authority and example go, deprived Almighty God of the essential worship arising from social virtue, peace, charity, and good conscience towards God and man, will you be still adding further indignities to the deity, be representing him chiefly pleased with unmanly grimaces, words without meaning, the nonsense of metaphysicks, the jargon of logick, and the cant of mystery?

But this subject is too long for one paper: I shall therefore continue it in my next. In some following letters[7] I shall shew my poor deluded countrymen, by what wretched guides in church and state they are conducted, and whose jobs they are doing, to their own undoing.

G   *I am, &c.*

7. See Letters 128, 129, and 130 (May 11, May 18, and May 25, 1723).

NO. 127. SATURDAY, MAY 4, 1723.

The same Address continued.

SIR,

I proceed in my address to the disaffected part of the clergy.

Are not you the men who professed such blind, such unconditional submission to princes, the most oppressive and tyrannical princes; and damned all who would not go your mad, your impious, and your impracticable lengths? And are not you the first to bring home your own damnation to your own doors, by shewing that no obligation, human or divine, can with-hold you from rebelling against the most legal government, and mildest prince? To assert that the government is not a lawful government, is to assert your own perjury; and by disowning the government, you disown all honesty and conscience. The government is founded upon reason, upon laws, and consent, the only foundation of any government; and it is administered with equity, and without the blemish of violence, or of dispensing arbitrarily with laws: And yet this government is to be resisted, betrayed, and overturned; while a government founded upon the chance of blood, upon the hereditary sufficiency of men, and successive chastity of women, and which acts by discretion, cruelty, or folly, is of divine appointment, and irresistible. What can be more monstrous! And what capricious and hard-hearted folly would you fix upon the good and all-wise God! By which you only shew, that your hallowed nonsense, if you be in earnest, is as signal as your wickedness.

As to the Pretender's right, I know not what it is; unless it be, that because his supposed father violated his Coronation Oath and the laws, usurped a tyrannical power, and oppressed and enslaved these nations five and thirty years ago, therefore his supposed son has a lawful right to enslave them now. And I defy you, with all your distinctions, and men of distinctions, to produce a better argument upon this head of right. Besides, how can the Pretender think that you have any the least regard to his right, when you have so often and so solemnly sworn that he had none? Dispossess yourselves, if you can, of the spirit of faction, and of groundless displeasure and revenge; and then try if you can find any divine, any unalterable right in the Pretender. He has in truth no right, but what your own unruly and restless passions give him. We all know what would cure you of your opinion of his title, of your fondness for his person. The constitution will not stoop to you; the government will not be governed by you; you have not the power; you have not the revenues of the ancient ecclesiastics before Henry VIII's days; nor would you, if the Pretender were here: And if you had not, in three months you would be fierce for sending him abroad again, as you did his supposed father; or using him worse. Of this I am certain, that if he ruled as his present Majesty does, you would treat him, and obey him, and honour him, just as you do his present Majesty. Plead no longer your consciences, which you have so long, and so often, and so vilely prostituted, and still prostitute! No body will receive the plea.

Before you can pretend to make your notions and authority pass with others, you must shew that you yourselves are guided by any notions of right or wrong. If you would clear yourselves from the guilt, the horrid guilt of constant and repeated perjury; shew how faithfully, how religiously you have kept your oaths. If you would not be thought disaffected, shew by some particular instances your faith and attachment to the government, from the Revolution to this day. What have you done to prevent or repress plots, assassinations, and rebellions; to render them odious in the hearts of your people, or to satisfy the world that they were odious in your own? And is not this the duty of Christians and preachers, and your sworn duty? In a stupid dispute about grimace and forms, or about paltry distinctions and empty words, you are all in flame and uproar, and fill your pulpits, and your people, and the nation, with your important nonsense, and the danger of sense: But when church and state were just going to be swallowed up by popery and tyranny, what alarms have you rung? What resentment, what attachment to the establishment and your oaths, have you shewn? What honest testimony have you borne?

And what have you done, Gentlemen, since the discovery of this horrid conspiracy? You that from your lofty rostrums have scattered poison and epidemical distempers over the land, as if out of Pandora's box; what antidotes have you applied to the venom which you have dispersed? What satisfaction have you made for all the mischiefs which you have done, and which stare you in the face? What sermons have you preached? What discourses have you printed? What detestation have you shewn against this monstrous design; levelled at the life of the prince who protects you; against the religion which you ought to support, and which supports you; and against the liberties and estates of your countrymen, from whose mistaken confidence you derive all your power and wealth?

What has been done by the governors of the universities to promote loyalty either in tutors or pupils, and to support the principles upon which the Revolution stands? What charges have been given by archdeacons (to say nothing of their betters), to enforce obedience to this government upon the foot of liberty? How many seditious priests have met with punishment or discountenance from their superiors? though we all know what resentment they would have found, if any one had dared to have opened his mouth against the power and pride of his order?

What care has been taken in the licensing or approving of school-masters, who are almost all Jacobites! What a bitter and disaffected spirit is there in the charity-schools, and all schools! Is there a contest any where between two candidates, but the most disaffected has the vote and interest of the country clergy? And is not the same partiality practised in most of the colleges of the universities?

Reconcile, if you can, your wild conduct to any semblance of religion, or of common sense and common honesty. If a Protestant dissenter [is] to be let into a place by the good pleasure and indulgence of the law; what books, scolding, and fury! But when the Pretender and popery are to be let into England, to the utter subversion of religion and property, and against law and oaths; what resignation! what silence! Though you are sworn to oppose them, strongly and solemnly sworn, and have no provocation not to oppose them, but that the happiness and estates of the laity, and the tenderness shewn to dissenters (by which our people and our riches are increased, and our Christian spirit is shewn) disturb the pride of the narrow persecuting ecclesiasticks, always insatiable and discontented, always plotting and railing while the wealth and dominion of mankind are not entirely theirs.

It would be endless to enter into all the late and publick instances of your perjury, your disaffection, and furious spirit. I shall mention but one, but one that is a disgrace to our nation; an instance of a mean priest, destitute of name and parts tried and comdemned for sedition, yet almost deified for his insolence and crimes.[1] Ignorant of the laws, and despising his own oaths, he publickly attacked the constitution, and libelled it. He asserted the irresistibleness of all governments good or bad, though our own was founded upon resistance. For this daring offence he was impeached and tried; tried by one part of the legislature before the other, and condemned by all three: So that the business of the nation, and of Europe, stood still for many weeks, till this groveling offender had a hearing, and his sentence; a sentence, which would have come more properly for him from the chairman of a pettysessions, than from the mouth of a Lord High Chancellor of England!

What reverence might not have been expected to such a trial as this, what acquiescence in the issue of it, especially from those who contended, daily and vehemently contended, from the pulpit and the press, for submission, unlimited submission, to governors, though tyrants and oppressors! But instead of this, as if they intended to publish to the world, that the meanest of the order, how vile and insolent soever, is not to be touched for the most enormous crimes, even in the most legal, open, and honourable manner, even by the whole legislature, the most solemn and august judicature upon earth; there was such a hideous

1. Dr. Henry Sacheverell, chaplain of St. Savior's, Southwark, whose sermons violently attacking the Whig government and its policy of toleration and espousing the doctrine of absolute nonresistance were enthusiastically embraced by those with High Church and Tory sympathies. In Dec. 1709, the Whig-dominated Commons condemned two of his sermons as seditious and, despite much opposition, impeached Sacheverell for high crimes and misdemeanors. He was found guilty but, largely because of his immense popularity, was given only a nominal sentence.

stir made; such a horrible outcry and spirit were raised; such inso-
lences, tumults and insurrections ensued; such contempt was
shewn of power and magistracy; such lies and libels published
against those who possessed them; such lying encomiums were
bestowed upon the sentenced criminal; such profane compliments
were made him; such profound and insolent respect was paid him;
as if there had been neither religion nor order in the land, but
both had been banished out of it by many of the avowed and hired
advocates for religion and order; who, all the while they were thus
reviling and resisting authority, had still the front to press and
preach absolute non-resistance to authority, and to reward what
they themselves were doing with damnation: unless it were safe
and laudable to resist the most lawful power, but sinful and dam-
nable to resist that which is lawless. For, after so many oaths to the
government, and so many abjurations of the Pretender, they durst
not say that the government was unlawful. But the rage and
uproar which they were in, even before the sentence, were as great
as if the priesthood it self, nay, all nature was to have been overturned by the apprehended whipping of a profligate priest.

A sufficient lesson is this to all governments, how this sort
of men are to be trusted with power, who dare thus act in spite of
all power! and a strong proof to all men how little regard is due to
the opinions and doctrines of these men, who do not regard their
own doctrines! who teach what no man ought to practise, and
themselves will not! who are perpetually contradicting themselves,
and one another, and yet are never in the wrong! and who would
not suffer the meanest, or worst of their order, to be subject to the
united and original power of one of the greatest states in the
world!

Sure this cannot be forgot whilst there is a king, or liberty,
in Israel!

G   *I am, &c.*

NO. 128. SATURDAY, MAY 11, 1723.

Address to such of the Laity as are Followers of the disaffected Clergy, and of their Accomplices.

SIR,

I have already addressed two of these letters to the disaffected clergy;[1] and will in this apply myself to the disaffected laity, their followers.

I cannot help saying, Gentlemen, that it argues your great lowness of sense, and depravity of manners, to be thus blindly inflamed by such forsworn apostates, such lying and disaffected monks, men of such vile morals: You see their unruly spirit, their unhallowed conduct, their daring and impious perjuries; and yet will you be led by them into wickedness as great, if possible, as their own; the wickedness of unprovoked rebellion; of overthrowing a government, which, in spite of their malice and lies, does really protect you in your religion and property; and of sacrificing a Protestant Church, that you think yourselves fond of, to a popish Pretender, who is bound by his religion to destroy it?

And what is all this noise about? For whose sakes, think you, Gentlemen, that all this combustion is made? Do you believe that they are serving your interests, or their own? Have they in any instance, or any age, shewn any regard, any concern for your persons, your religion, or your interests? If they pretend to have done so, they speak as falsely as they swear. Remember all the reigns since Queen Elizabeth's time to the Revolution; those reigns that oppressed you, and that Revolution that saved you. Did they not make it the whole business of their zeal, of their addresses and their preachments, to give up your persons, your consciences, and your fortunes, to the pleasure and lust of the prince; and damned you if you defended either? Did they not impiously make our Saviour the author of their inhuman nonsense, and Christianity a warrant of indemnity for oppressing, robbing, chaining, and killing you? And did they not fill the kingdom with atheistical volumes

---

1. See Letters 126 and 127 (Apr. 27 and May 4, 1723).

of sermons, books, and addresses, full of profane compliments and curses upon this vile head? And have they ever since publickly and expressly renounced these destroying principles? When their own interest is concerned, no principles can bind them, as we all see and know; but as to the power of princes over laymen, over you, Gentlemen, have they not always asserted it to be boundless and discretionary, and always left you at the mere mercy of royal lust and madness? It is true, they will not now suffer you to bear a prince whom laws can bind; nor would they formerly suffer you to preserve yourselves from tyrants, which neither God, nor man, nor the good of mankind, could bind.

As soon as the great Queen Elizabeth was dead, who was resolved to be truly what she was called, Head of the Church; and in order to be so, kept her priests in a just and becoming subordination, and would not suffer them to meddle with or prate about her government (for which to this day you have never heard them spare to her memory one good word); and when a weak prince succeeded her, many of the leading clergy advanced all the vilest tenets of popery: They declared, that the Church of Rome, contrary to the express words of the *Homilies*, was a true church[2] (which they might as justly have said of the Church of Hell) at the same time that they denounced damnation against all foreign and domestick Protestants for being no churches at all. So much did they prefer their own notional power of ordination before the precepts of our Saviour, and the essentials of religion! They persuaded the King to appoint three bishops to re-ordain the Scotch presbyters; which imposition put that kingdom in a flame,[3] as

2. The Preface to the first edition of the *Homilies*, issued in 1547 during the reign of Edward VII, takes note of the "manifold enormities which heretofore have crept into his Grace's realm through the false usurped power of the Bishop of Rome and the ungodly doctrine of his adherents, not only unto the great decay of Christian religion, but also (if God's mercy were not) unto the utter destruction of innumerable souls which, through hypocrisy and pernicious doctrine were seduced and brought from honoring thee alone, true, living, and eternal God, unto worshipping of creatures, yea, of stocks and stones, from doing the commandments of God, unto voluntary works and fantasies invented of men, from true religion unto popish superstition."

3. In 1610 three ministers of the Scottish Church were called to London by James I and there consecrated as bishops. These three, in turn, consecrated ten others on their return to Scotland. Finally, in 1612, presbytery was abol-

being in effect told, that they were in a state of damnation before, and that their ministers had no lawful call to serve God without episcopal dubbing. And thus he had like to have lost one of his kingdoms, to gratify the pride of a few crack-brained ecclesiasticks.

Then it was that professed papists and popish principles grew in request: Liberty of conscience was once given to them by proclamation, and always connived at and indulged; whilst Protestant dissenters, and the best churchmen too, under the odious name of Puritans, were every where reviled and persecuted. Then it was that your parents first heard, in this Protestant church, of the power of the keys, the indelible character, the uninterrupted succession, the real presence, the giving the Holy Ghost, the divine right of kings and bishops; all tending to aggrandize the clergy, and to enslave the laity. Then was invented that nonsensical apothegm, *no bishop, no king*; which his Majesty echoing several times upon oath at the conference at Hampton-Court, the Archbishop declared, that doubtless his Majesty was inspired, and spoke by the special assistance of God's spirit.[4] Then the bishops thought it was their time, with the Archbishop at their head, to present a memorial to the King, demanding an exemption of their courts from the civil jurisdiction; and the ecclesiastical power was every day swelling, nay carried to such a pitch in the High-Commission Court,[5] as to draw the Parliament upon them. And to induce his Majesty to support them in their nonsense and roguery, they made him a present of all your persons, lands, and liberties. It became the current doctrine amongst the prerogative clergy, and books were published by some of them, approved and applauded by all, to maintain, that the King was exempt from the restraint of laws; that

---

ished and episcopacy became the legal church system, causing bitter resentment throughout Scotland.

4. The Hampton Court Conference was held in Jan. 1604, attended by the English bishops and the Puritan leaders. It was presided over by James I and had as its object consideration of the Puritan demands for Church reform, including modification of episcopacy.

5. The Court of High Commission had as its main purpose the extirpation of heresy and the enforcement of conformity in worship. By the beginning of the seventeenth century it also became the normal court of appeal from lower ecclesiastical courts in doctrinal and disciplinary matters. It was abolished in 1641 but revived in modified form by James II from 1686 to 1688.

he need not call Parliaments, but might make laws without them; and, that it was a favour to admit the consent of his people in giving subsidies.

This weak prince left one as weak behind him; one who having, as is said, been once destined to the priesthood, and being a bigot by nature as well as education, the ecclesiasticks found in his reign a proper season and a proper soil to sow their tares in, with a fair prospect of a plentiful harvest. Popery came into the kingdom like a torrent; arbitrary power appeared undisguised, and in the most glaring colours. The King, by positive order to the chancellor, forbade the laws against papists to be put in execution;[6] and, notwithstanding the constant protestations of Parliaments, protected Romish priests against legal prosecutions. Popish books were licensed by Laud; and Protestant ones, which defended the Articles[7] and the opinions of the Established Church, were forbidden, suppressed, and published in the Star Chamber.[8] Montague, who was impeached by Parliament, for his attempts to introduce popery, was not only protected, but made Bishop of Chichester.[9] Laud issued injunctions, by his own authority, for reforming the Church, and bringing it nearer to popery: He had the sauciness to declare publickly, that he hoped to see the time when no jack gentleman should dare to keep on his hat before the meanest curate. The bishops disclaimed all jurisdiction from the crown in Bastwick's trial;[10] and the independence of the Church upon the

6. In Mar. 1672, Charles II issued a Declaration of Indulgence suspending all penal laws against both Catholics and Protestant dissenters and permitting Catholics to hear mass in private.

7. The Thirty-Nine Articles, comprising the doctrinal formulae of the Church of England adopted by Convocation during the reign of Elizabeth I.

8. The Court of Star Chamber was originally created to prevent miscarriages of justice in the inferior courts resulting from undue influence. Its jurisdiction was illegally expanded under Henry VIII and Elizabeth to encompass any disobedience to the sovereign's proclamations, regardless of how arbitrary. The court was abolished in 1641.

9. Richard Montagu (1572–1641), at one point chaplain to James I. Attempts to impeach him failed for lack of the King's signature.

10. In 1633, John Bastwick, an English physician, published two treatises in Latin attacking the Roman Catholic ceremonial. This was taken by Archbishop Laud to be a veiled attack on the rituals of the Church of England and Bastwick was tried, found guilty, and sentenced to prison by the Court of High Commission. At the same time, Bastwick was tried by the Court of Star Cham-

state was openly asserted. Then came in the altar, and the unbloody sacrifice upon it, with the antick and foppish consecration of churches and church-yards, and many other monkish fooleries, to draw us to a nearer conformity with Rome.

And as priestcraft and tyranny are ever inseparable, and go hand-in-hand, infinite other oppressions were brought upon the poor people, and proved by the priests to be *jure divino*;[11] as, unlawful imprisonments, various monopolies, extorted loans, numerous taxes; all levied without authority of Parliament. Sibthorp and Manwaring, two of Laud's creatures, were set on to preach, that the King was not bound by the laws of the land; that the King's royal will, in imposing loans and taxes, did oblige the subject's conscience, on pain of damnation.[12] His Majesty sent a special mandate to Archbishop Abbot,[13] to license those sermons; and his Grace was suspended for not doing it. It seems that it was lawful then to suspend the greatest clergyman, and first subject of England, for doing his duty, and preserving the laws: And now it is a sacrilegious usurpation of the divine rights of the clergy, to deprive a bishop for the most traitorous conspiracy against his king, his country, and the religion which he himself professes. To make good all these invasions upon publick liberty, a German army was contracted for; and some time after an Irish and popish one was actually raised by Strafford in Ireland.

During these reigns, all the high clergy were the professed trumpets, the setting dogs and spiritual janizaries, of a government which used you like cattle, and starved you, or slew you for profit and sport. They made you conspire against yourselves, by alarm-

---

ber, where he was condemned to pay a substantial fine, to be set in the pillory, to lose his ears, and to undergo imprisonment for life. In 1640, Parliament reversed both proceedings.

11. "By divine law."

12. Both Dr. Robert Sibthorp and Roger Manwaring were clerics. Sibthorp became famous in 1627 for preaching a sermon in which he claimed that the divine command required unconditional and cheerful obedience to the King. In testimony before the House of Lords in 1629, Roger Manwaring declared that the absolute power of the sovereign could be deduced from scripture. Manwaring was impeached later in the same year.

13. George Abbot, Archbishop of Canterbury from 1611 until his death in 1633 and, as such, one of the authorities empowered to license publications.

ing your consciences, and filling them with blind and unnatural resignation to all the excesses of cruelty, plunder, oppression, killing, servitude, and every species of human barbarity: But now that you are protected and secure in standing laws, which the administration has never pretended to dispense with; when you have the full enjoyment of your consciences, which the government in no instance restrains; when you are secure in your estates and property, which the government does not touch, nor pretends any right to touch; when you have as much liberty as mankind can under any government possess, a liberty which goes to the very borders of licentiousness: I say, under all these blessings, blessings unknown almost to all men, but Englishmen; will these implacable and steady impostors let you alone? Are not their spiritual goads continually in your sides, stimulating you to renounce your understanding, your freedom, your safety, your religion, your honesty, your conscience; and to destroy the source of all your own happiness and enjoyments, religious and secular; to exchange a free government, and every thing that is valuable upon earth, for the cruelty, madness, chains, misery, and deformity of popery and of popish tyranny?

Look back, Gentlemen, once more, to later reigns: What testimony did they bear against the barefaced encouragement of popery, and the persecution of Protestants, in Charles II's reign; against his fatal treaties and leagues with France, his unjust wars with the United Provinces, and his treacherous seizure of their Smyrna fleet,[14] to destroy the only state in the world that could be then called the bulwark of liberty and the Protestant religion? What did they say against the terrible excesses, the arbitrary imprisonments, the legal murders, and violation of property, during his reign? Did they not encourage and sanctify all the invasions and encroachments of the court, and cursed all who opposed them, or complained of them? Can they have the forehead[15] to complain of armies, of taxes, or any sort of oppression (however just such complaint may be in others), they who have never shewn

14. In Mar. 1672, four days before the British government declared war on the States General, an English fleet attacked the Dutch Smyrna convoy, escorted by eleven warships, off the Isle of Wight. Contrary to Trenchard's claim, however, most of the convoy managed to escape.

15. Forehead: impudence.

themselves for any government, but what subsisted by armies and oppression? They have been always mortal foes to popular liberty, which thwarts and frustrates all their aspiring and insatiable views; and in every favourite reign preached it as impiously down, as they preached up every growing and heavy oppression.

Nor did they ever quarrel with King James, but consecrated all his usurpations, his armies, and dispensing power, till he gave liberty of conscience to dissenters,[16] and till some of their own ill-contrived oppressions were brought home to their own doors. They then cursed their king, and helped to send him a begging. They resisted him, and upon their principles were rebels to him, and animated others to be so; yet have been damning you and the nation for that resistance ever since: Which is a full confession, that when a popish tyrant plunders and oppresses you, you neither can nor ought to have any remedy; but if he touch but a tithe-pig[17] or surplice of theirs, their heel is ready to be lifted up against him, and their hands to throw the crown from his head, and to put it upon another, with fresh oaths of allegiance and obedience; and to pull it off again in spite of those oaths, or without any forfeiture, or any just provocation. Is not this infamous conduct of theirs manifest to sight? Does it not stare you and every Briton in the face? And yet will you be implicitly led by such traitors to God, to truth, and to you?

How did they behave towards King William, whom they themselves invited over? As soon as he gave liberty of conscience to Protestant dissenters; let them see that he would not be a blind tool to a priestly faction, but would equally protect all his subjects who were faithful to him; had set himself at the head of the Protestant interest, and every year hazarded his person in dangerous battles and sieges for the liberty of England and of Europe, against the most dreadful scourge and oppressor of mankind that ever plagued the earth;[18] they were perpetually preaching and haranguing seditiously, always calumniating him, reviling him, dis-

16. By virtue of James II's two Declarations of Indulgence (of 1687 and 1688), which suspended the penal laws relating to ecclesiastical matters and permitted papists and Dissenters to hold public office.

17. Tithe-pig: literally, a pig given as a tithe; that is, any of the clergy's wealth.

18. Louis XIV.

tressing him, and plotting against him; always endeavouring to render his measures, all his generous attempts for their own security, abortive and ineffectual. Nor did they use the late Queen, their own favourite Queen, or even those of their own party who served her faithfully, one jot better, till she fell into the hands of a few desperate traitors to herself and them; who gave away all the advantage of a long, expensive, and successful war; put France into a condition again to enslave Europe, and to place a popish traitor, an attainted fugitive, upon the throne of these kingdoms[19] (which he had undoubtedly done, if unforeseen accidents had not prevented it): And then what encomiums, what panegyricks, what fulsome and blasphemous flattery, did they bestow upon her person and actions, and have bestowed ever since?

Is not this, Gentlemen, using you like slaves, and worse than spaniels; making you the tame vassals of tyrants, and restless rebels to lawful governors? Is not this using you like insensible instruments, void of reason and of conscience, of prudence, and of property? Is this teaching! this the price of their revenues and ease! this the function of ministers! Or can human invention, animated and aided by human malice, draw the character of more unlimited, merciless, and outrageous enemies?

T   *I am, &c.*

NO. 129. SATURDAY, MAY 18, 1723.

❧   *The same Address continued.*

GENTLEMEN,

You are abused: You are blindly governed by certain chiefs, who can have no view but to dispose of you; to make sale of you for their own proper advantage. By prating pedants, and dis-

19. The reference is to Queen Anne, whose ministry, after 1710, was led by Robert Harley (later the Earl of Oxford) and Henry, Viscount Bolingbroke. It was this ministry that initiated secret negotiations with France, with whom England had been at war since 1702, finally agreeing to a peace treaty whose terms most Whigs regarded as almost traitorously favorable to France. Both Oxford and Bolingbroke were later implicated in attempts to overturn the Act of Succession and restore the Stuart Pretender.

affected monks, and by party cries, and party revelling, and hogs-heads of October,[1] you are brought to adore this duke, that lord, and the other knight or squire; and to think the publick undone, unless it be under the sole management of these your idols, who would effectually undo it. They once had places: Had you then more money, more trade, more land and liberty, by any wise or virtuous conduct of theirs, than you have now? And did they not take that opportunity of your generous confidence in them, to betray you basely to France and the Pretender? And have they not ever since been labouring, by plots and rebellion, to accomplish that which, from the shortness of their reign, and the sudden change, they could not then accomplish by power?

Power and places are still their only aim: And to come at them, you see, they would make war upon heaven and earth, and involve you in blood and popery. But you cannot all have places, Gentlemen: Your only ambition ought to be the security of your property, and to live like freemen. And are you not free? Is not your property secure? or can these men accomplish their designs and conspiracies, but at the expence of your estates and your free-dom? They seek their own grandeur, and all their advantages, from your ruin and servitude. You must pay the whole and long reckoning at last. You must fill the empty coffers of new shoals of *banditti* who must be rewarded out of your pockets for their villain-ous merit and pretended sufferings. You will have a whole and black flight of harpies to glut, who with ravenous and unhallowed claws will devour your substance, and your children's bread. All foreign debts, all the demands of Spain and Rome, will be brought upon you for payment; and all that you have will be too little to satiate needy traitors, whom you madly want to save your all; which is not touched, nor can be hurt, but by them, and is but too little to defend you from them.

Think you to be then without armies? No: Instead of occa-sional troops, which their wicked plots and devices, and your own disaffection, have brought upon you, you will see your country and your houses filled with popish armies, perhaps foreign popish armies. You will be told, that Protestant and English ones, which

1. Hogheads of October: new wine.

already betrayed the father, will betray the son, and cannot be trusted: That your frequent rebellions render you unfit to be relied on; and that if you turned out a Protestant prince, whom you yourselves called in, you will be apt, upon the least disgust or caprice, to turn out your hereditary King, as you did his father.

Think you that your present debts will be cancelled, and your taxes made easy? No; your taxes and your funds will be continued: But, instead of being applied, as they are, to pay off lawful debts contracted for your security, they will be seized by this new government, and called lawful prize. It will be said, That they were given to keep out your lawful king, and ought to be made use of to keep him in: That if you were so prodigal of your wealth for the support of rebellion and faction, can you refuse these revenues, which are now no longer your own, but in possession of the enemies of the establishment, who chiefly gained them at first by stock-jobbing and extortion, and now keep them as the prizes of disloyalty and treason; can you refuse these revenues (so ill got, and as ill applied) to secure your lineal government, founded upon a long succession of your natural princes? These revenues therefore, which are now your property, and the property of your neighbours and relations, will then be united to the crown, fix an absolute power there, and entail lasting and irretrievable slavery upon yourselves and your posterity, and destroy at one blow the whole property and trade of three great kingdoms. At present, if prudent methods be taken (which surely necessity must at last make us take) these great debts may be paid honestly off, and we again see ourselves a happy and disengaged people. But upon such a dreadful turn as the conspirators intended, they will be thrown into a free gift, and your taxes will be made perpetual, to perpetuate your slavery.

Do you expect any redress of any kind from such a Parliament as can then be chosen, if any be chosen? No; hope it not. All that would serve you faithfully in it, will be called enemies and traitors to the new, and friends to the late rebellious establishment. Such therefore will not dare to offer themselves to your choice; and, if they did, would be mobbed, or imprisoned. You must choose only such as are recommended to you, the ragged and famished tribe that are brought over; men of desperate fortunes, the beggarly plotters against your present happiness, fiery and implacable bigots, half papists, engaged malcontents, or rapacious vultures; all gaping for prey, all determined to every measure of oppression, and to sacrifice you and your country to their ambition and want. You will then find time for repentance, when it is too late, when all the grievances which you now so wantonly complain of will fall upon you in earnest, and an hundred fold, without hope of remedy or end.

Nor can this blessed condition be brought upon you, but after the horrid prelude of a long and cruel civil war. You will first see your country in blood, your cities burnt, your houses plundered, your cattle taken from you, your stocks consumed by dragoons, and your sons, your neighbours, and relations, murdered before your faces. Flatter not yourselves, that his Majesty will easily quit the many thousands of his subjects, who will certainly and resolutely stand by him; or that he will want the assistance of all the foreign powers who are interested in his establishment, or even in making this great kingdom wretched, impotent, and poor. No, Gentlemen, you will have armies of Germans and of Dutch poured in upon you on one side, Spaniards and Russians on the other,[2] and perhaps French on both sides. Irish papists will come over in shoals; Hosts of Highlanders will fall like snow from the north; and all the necessitous, the debauched, the ambitious, the rapacious, the extravagant, and the revengeful, amongst yourselves, will think these your calamities their harvest: They will banquet in your plunder; and for a share of you, will greedily join to devour you. Is this a condition like that which you now enjoy?

How would you like to see your churches dressed up like toyshops; to see vermin of various fashions, shapes, and colours, crawling about in them, antickly dressed up in an hundred fantastical garments; to see the same vermin, at other times, filling and polluting your streets, haunting your houses, debauching and cor-

2. German and Dutch armies would, of course, have supported the crown, while, at the time of writing, events in the Baltic and the Mediterranean suggested that both Spain and Russia, for diplomatic reasons, might well support the Pretender's claims against George I.

rupting your wives, perverting your children, devouring your substance, and lording it over you? You will hardly know, thus
transmogrified, the old faces which you have been used to, the
faces of those impious wretches, who would bring all these frightful mischiefs upon you. That they are ready and prepared for this
ungodly change, is evident from their maintaining and asserting
all the vilest and most formidable tenets of popery; and by their
uniting in all the traitorous intrigues, in all the basest and bloodiest
councils of papists. But that the papists would protect or prefer
them afterwards, is more than doubtful: It is not likely, that they
will trust those whom by experience they know no trust can bind.
They know that those who have betrayed you, and a King who has
protected and preferred them, will betray also even papists. They
know, that neither religion, nor conscience, not honesty, nor hardship, has any share in their present disaffection, which has its
whole root in pride and avarice, and the lust of rapine and power;
and that they will in a moment turn upon them as soon as the first
preferments go by them, or they cannot all catch the preferments
and wealth which they so immoderately thirst after.

Your present deceivers, therefore, will not then be
trusted. All ecclesiastical prizes will be the prizes of foreign ecclesiasticks, or of those who have been ever staunch Catholics at
home. The others will be left to certain contempt, beggary, and
if possible to shame. It will not be forgot what servile adoration
they paid, what hollow compliments they made, to the late King
James; adoration that bordered upon blasphemy! Compliments
that interfered with the incommunicable attributes of God! And
how faithlessly, how readily, afterwards they betrayed him, when
all his favours did not fall in their lap, and as soon as they found
that for them alone his tyranny was not exerted. It will be
remembered how cheerfully, or rather how revengefully, they
ran into the Revolution; and when they could not engross the
whole advantages of it, and could not make King William their
instrument and bully, how they were continually libelling King
William and the Revolution, continually prating, preaching, and
plotting against both, notwithstanding their constant oaths, their
constant abjurations and imprecations.

For God's sake, Gentlemen, think what you are doing: Your lives, your estates, your religion, your conscience, your trade, your country, your honour, are all at stake, and you are wantonly throwing them all away; you are pursuing a false and miserable shadow; and it would be happy for you, were it only a shadow: In reality, you are going to catch in your embraces, superstition, beggary, and servitude. I approve your love and pursuit of liberty, which ever was, and ever will be, a grateful and charming sound in my ears; and I will be always ready to lead you, or to follow you, in that virtuous and noble pursuit. This is wisdom! This is honour! But honour is to be acquired by honourable means, and not by rapine, perjury, and murder.

I thank God, we have yet the means left within our constitution to save ourselves. We have, in spite of malice and contumelies, an excellent, meek, and benevolent prince, who has in no one instance of his reign attempted to strain his prerogative above the laws; which we defy his bitterest enemies to say of the best of their favourite kings, his predecessors. He has every disposition to make a people great and happy, and will be always ready to gratify them in every thing that they can reasonably ask for their security. But if we would make ourselves secure, we must make him secure. It cannot be denied, but there have been some excesses of power, and that we have suffered under many publick calamities: None of them are, however, imputable to him; but to the corruption and intrigues of those who betrayed him and us, and to the constant conspiracies of traitors, which deterred honester men from a severe animadversion upon their crimes, when they saw them pursued by those who rejoiced in those crimes, with no design to rectify abuses, but to inflame discontents.

To whom, Gentlemen, do we owe all our present debts and misfortunes? Even to those who opposed all the measures for raising effectual supplies in the first war, and ended the second by a scandalous peace,[3] which left us in insecurity and danger, and

3. The War of the Spanish Succession and the War of the Quadruple Alliance, which was concluded in 1720 when Spain joined the Alliance. The War of the Quadruple Alliance allied Britain with France, its natural enemy. In addition, for a time it appeared that the cessation of hostilities with Spain would come only at the cost of returning Gibraltar to that country.

made more taxes and more debts necessary to our security. To whom, as I have observed in a former paper, do we owe standing armies, such frequent suspensions of the *habeas corpus* bill, and so many consuming pensions?[4] Even to those, who, by their constant plots, conspiracies, and rebellions, have given occasions, or pretences, for these great evils and excesses. And now that they have brought all these mischiefs, and many more, upon us, and forced the government upon measures which perhaps would not have been thought of, certainly would not have been complied with, they would impudently throw upon his Majesty the burdens and imputations, which they alone ought to bear, and impiously dethrone him, and undo their country, for their own crimes.

You are born, Gentlemen, to liberty; and from it you derive all the blessings which you possess. Pray, what affection have these your leaders ever shewn to the cause of liberty? It is plain that they have never taken the sacred sound into their mouths, but to profane it; nor pretended to cherish it, but in order to destroy it, and make it an unnatural ladder to tyranny. As often as dominion has been in their own hands, liberty became a crime, and a sign of sedition; and as often as they wanted to destroy power, that is, as often as they were out of it, they prostituted the spirit of liberty to the service of treason. Hence their late cries for liberty, to animate you against a government that protected it; and under the pretence of affecting liberty, to introduce a tyranny that would destroy the soul, body and property. They could, however, have made no dangerous progress in this mischief and hypocrisy, if those who have always professed, and whose interest it would have been always to have supported and practised, free and benefi-cent principles, had not deserted those principles, and armed by that desertion the enemies to all that is good and virtuous, with an opportunity of turning liberty upon herself. Let the real friends to the government support the maxims upon which it stands, and upon which only it can stand, and they have nothing to fear from the well or ill-grounded popularity of its enemies.

4. See Letter No. 125 (Apr. 20, 1723). The term "consuming pensions" carries the sense of "wasteful pensions."

Such, Gentlemen, are your leaders, and such are the grievances which they cause, and complain of: To cure them, they would introduce the compleatest and most comprehensive of all, a total overthrow of church and state. They have reduced us to unhappy circumstances; but let us not make them infinitely worse, and destroy ourselves for relief; let us not, like silly and peevish children, throw away what we are in possession of, to attain what is out of our power, and which attained would undo us: Let us put on resolutions suitable to our present condition. Let all honest men join with the greatest unanimity in all measures to preserve his Majesty and our establishment; and then we may rest assured, that his Majesty will do every thing to preserve us. We may then ask with confidence, and he will give with pleasure. When the kingdom is in this desirable calm and security, we shall not need so many troops, nor will his Majesty desire them. We may lessen the publick expences, pay off gradually the publick debts, increase the trade, wealth, and power of the nation, and be again a rich, easy, and flourishing people.

I cannot help persuading myself, that the gentlemen at present in the administration, who have observed and condemned so justly the fatal and unsuccessful measures taken by some of their predecessors, the terrible consequences that have flowed from them, and the dreadful advantages that they gave to the common enemies of his Majesty, of themselves, and of us all, are already convinced, that there is no possibility of preserving our happy establishment long, but by gaining and caressing the people, by making them easy and happy, by letting them find their account in his Majesty's reign; and by giving no handles for just reproach, or pretences for contumely, to those who would make no other use of them but to destroy us all.

G   *I am, &c.*

NO. 130. SATURDAY, MAY 25, 1723.

？ *The same Address continued.*

SIR,

I have in my last and former papers[1] given you some faint images of hypocrisy, pride, tyranny, perjury, atheism, and restless ambition, of the Jacobite and disaffected clergy, who constantly mislead you, and constantly abuse you. I shall in this inform you what are their views, what the butt and mark to which they direct all their actions; what the idols to which they sacrifice their honour, their conscience, their religion, and their God. It is even to their ambition and pride. It is to get you into their power; to have the disposal of your persons, your opinions, and your estates; to make you ignorant, poor, miserable, and slavish, whilst they riot upon your fortunes, prey upon your industry. They look abroad with envious, with wishing eyes, at the revenues, grandeur, and power of the Romish clergy; they remember with regret, how they lost all those fine things at the Reformation, and have never lost sight of them since; but been constantly involving you in factions, in misery, often in blood, to recover them again.

Popery is the most dreadful machine, the utmost stretch of human politicks, that ever was invented amongst men, to aggrandize and enrich the clergy, to oppress and enslave the laity. All its doctrines, all its views, all its artifices, are calculated for the sole advantage of the priests, and the destruction of the people, at the expence of virtue, good government, common sense, and the gospel. It is an open conspiracy of the ecclesiasticks against all the rest of mankind, to rob them of their estates, of their consciences, and their senses; and to make them the dupes and tame vassals of saucy and ambitious pedants. Look into their doctrines and their practices, and see whether you can find the least appearance of honour, morality, common honesty, or religion, in them; or any thing but pride, hypocrisy, fraud, tyranny, and domination. What do

1. See Letters 126 through 129 (Apr. 27 through May 18, 1723).

they mean by the power of the keys, binding and loosing, of excommunication, of their being mediators and intercessors between God and you; what do they mean by their pardoning sins, and having the sole power of giving the sacraments, which they tell you are necessary to salvation; what, by their doctrines about purgatory; but to persuade you, if you are foolish enough to believe them, that your future happiness and misery depend upon them? and then they well know that you will give the most that you have in this world, to be secure in the next.

What do they intend by telling you that bishops are of divine institution; by the power of ordination; and that they can alone make one another? What, by the indelible character; by uninterrupted succession from the apostles; by their being able to give the Holy Ghost, and having it themselves; but to create reverence to their persons, submission to their authority, and to render themselves independent of the civil government? And then they know that the civil government will be dependent on them. What purpose does it serve, to make you believe that tithes (which they hold by laws of your making) are of divine institution; that it is sacrilege to resume lands or donations, once given to the clergy, and that they can never afterwards be alienated; but constantly to increase their riches, and consequently their power and dependence, till by the natural course of things they come to be possessed of all? What do they mean by their holy water, their extreme unction, their exorcisms, their consecration of churches and church-yards, and their absurd notion of transubstantiation, but to gain adoration to the priestly character, as if he was able by a few canting words to change the nature of things, bless dead earth and walls, and make a god out of a meal? Why so many monasteries and nunneries, so many religious orders of men and women, so many fraternities, colleges, and societies of different kinds, but to engage great numbers of young people and potent families in their interest? Why so many antick garbs, so many rich vestments, so many gaudy shrines, so many decked images, used in their worship, and so much pompous devotion? Why organs and so much musick, so many singing-men, and singing-boys, but to attract the eyes and ears, and to amuse the understandings of the gaping herd, to make them forget their senses, and the plain natural religion of the gospel, and to engage men and ladies of pleasure in the interests of so agreeable a devotion.

How comes it to be a part of religion, not to confess our sins to God, but to the priest? It lets him into all the secrets of families, the power of imposing what severe penances he pleases upon superstitious penitents, and of commuting for those penances; acquaints him with all designs to the disadvantages of his order; gives him opportunities of debauching women himself, and procuring them for others; and holds them devoted to his will by the knowledge of their most important concerns. And lastly, what do they mean by the terrible engine of the Inquisition, and by their hellish doctrine of persecution for opinions; but to keep all men in awe of them, and to terrify those whom they cannot deceive? These are the favourite doctrines of popery! These the doctrines which they are concerned for! If you be rich or powerful, you may be as wicked as you please, and no body shall molest you; nay, the priests shall be ready to assist you, to pimp for you, and to pardon you. The same is true of the speculative opinions held by that church, that do not affect their power and pride: They suffer their several orders to differ about them, and do not trouble themselves what the people believe concerning them; nor are any of the people at all concerned in them. The absurd notions and ridiculous worship of the papists are only foolish things; but the power of popery is a terrible thing. If a man adore rotten bones, and use antick gestures towards them, he makes a fool of himself, but hurts not me; but if he would rob me, torture me, or burn me, for not playing the fool too, it is time to keep him at a distance, or to hold his hand. It is the power of popery, the cruel, the insatiable, the killing spirit of popery, that is to be dreaded. This, Gentlemen, is the power, this the terrible condition, that many of your Protestant instructors would bring you under, and which you are to guard against.

These wicked doctrines, these absurd opinions, were all abolished, all renounced, by the first reformers, but kept alive by the corrupt part of the clergy, and have been growing upon you ever since: They have been connived at by some, openly asserted by others, and I wish I could say, as openly discountenanced by the rest. It would fill a volume, instead of a paper, to enumerate all the clergymen, in the highest repute amongst their own order, who have abetted most, if not all of these monstrous opinions; and I have heard as yet of none of them who have been censured by any publick act of their body. I confess, that many of the corrupt amongst them have renounced the Pope's authority, as believing that they might find fairer quarter from a King whom they educated and hoped to govern, than from a foreign prelate, and his needy priests, who would plunder them, oppress them, and give away their revenues to his creatures, and to lazy monks and friars. They hoped too, that some favourable opportunities might happen to get away the regale[2] from the crown; and we never had a prince whom they could entirely govern, or who would not be governed at all by them, but they have laid claim to it, and attempted it. But what stood always in their way, and made all their designs impracticable, was the power of Parliament, and the liberties of the people, who preserved the prerogative of the crown to preserve themselves: They therefore levelled all their batteries against publick liberty, and laboured to make the prince absolute; as finding it much easier to flatter, mislead, or bargain with one man (and often a weak one) than to deceive a whole people, and make them conspire against themselves: and if persuasion, bigotry, and fear, would not make him practicable to their designs, they knew that poison and the dagger were at hand.

But now two hundred years' experience has convinced them, that the people will not suffer the crown to part with the regale, nor would they themselves part with their liberty; and till they do so, there is no possibility of settling a pompous hierarchy, and gaining the domination which they aspire to: They therefore are reduced to accept barefaced popery, and throw themselves under the protection of the Holy Father: And that is the game which they are now playing. What else can they propose by a popish revolution, but to share in the power and tyranny that attend it? They have not sufficient stipends for the daily mischiefs which they do: They want greater revenues, and an ecclesiastical inquisition. Now, at whose expence, think you, must this accumulation of wealth which they thirst for be acquired? How must this

2. Regale: the prerogatives of royalty.

Babel of authority which they pant after be raised? Not at the expence of the Pretender, by whose assistance they must gain them: No, Gentlemen; from your coffers these riches must be drained: Over you this tyranny must be exercised: The utter extinction of our liberties must constitute their grandeur: The single seizure of your lands and properties must support their domination: You must be the poor harassed slaves of a monstrous two-headed tyranny: be constantly and inhumanly crushed between the upper and the nether millstone of the regale and pontificate; and, in any dispute betwixt them, be given to Satan on one side, and to the executioner on both.

Many of you are in possession of impropriations and of abbey-lands, and are protected by the constitution in those possessions, which these reverend cheats would rob you of; and only want an arbitrary and a popish government to enable them to commit that robbery, to strip you to the skin, and to reduce the English laity to be once more humble cottagers and vassals to the monks, friars, and other ecclesiastical gluttons, to whom the whole riches of a great nation will be no more than sufficient wages for cheating and oppressing it. I bring you, Gentlemen, no false charge against the Jacobite clergy: Do they not claim your estates publickly from the press and the pulpit; and from the pulpit and the press charge you with sacrilege, and damn you for keeping them? Yes, Gentlemen, these reverend and self-denying teachers damn you for keeping your own legal possessions, and for eating your own bread. Now I would leave you to reason upon this conduct of theirs, to consider how nearly it affects you, whither it tends, and what sort of Protestants these doctors are. If the publick take nothing from them which they occupied since the Reformation, why should they destroy the government, but in hopes of destroying the Reformation, to get possession of popish lands, and popish power; which, while the Reformation and the government subsist, they can never possess?

That this, Gentlemen, is what they aim at, it is impossible to doubt. Lesley,[3] long their favourite and director, who knew their

3. Charles Leslie (1650–1722), Anglican cleric and, although an opponent of Roman Catholicism, a strong supporter of the Stuart dynasty. Indeed, in 1710, he joined the Stuart Pretender in exile. Leslie was the author of numerous pamphlets endorsing the nonjuring cause and attacking Deism. The work here cited is *A Letter from Mr. Leslie to a Member of Parliament* (London, 1714).

inclinations, knew their views, and the best way to apply them and to gain them, in his *Letter to the Clergy* (as I think it was) which was to usher in the rebellion at the beginning of his Majesty's reign, promises them an independence upon the crown, and that they should choose their own bishops. It is dominion, it is power, which they court; it is themselves whom they adore: When have they ever considered you or your interests, when they thought they could make a bargain for themselves? When King James applied to the bishops, upon his fear of an invasion from your great deliverer, and desired them to propose the nation's grievances, what grievances did they represent but their own trifling complaints? They said nothing of standing armies, how much soever they complain of them now. Who are their favourites? Even papists and nonjurors, known rebels, or men of rebellious principles, the most ambitious and wicked amongst the clergy, the most debauched and stupid among the laity. What sermons have they preached, what books have they wrote, against popery, though their flocks be every day decreasing? What exhortations against popish principles, which are constantly growing upon us? Whom do they treat as their avowed enemies, but friends to the Revolution, the most steady friends to the Establishment which they have sworn to, the Protestant dissenters, and such of their own body as regard their oaths, and the principles of the Reformation? What have you gained by all the favours lately shewn to them? Which of them have been obliged by these concessions? You have given them the first-fruits:[4] You have in effect repealed the statute of mortmain;[5] You have given them a shorter method to recover their tithes: You have increased their number and riches by building more churches: You have sat still, whilst they have been destroying the moduses[6] through England,

4. In ecclesiastical law, the first year's profits from a benefice or clerical living, originally transferred by the incumbent to the Pope and, after the Reformation, to the crown. After 1703, the first fruits were paid into a fund, known as Queen Anne's Bounty, whose purpose was the augmentation of poor livings.

5. A statute whose purpose was the prevention of lands coming into ownership by religious corporations, whose landed property remained perpetually in the same hands (in one "dead hand"). The various statutes prevented all sales or gifts of land to religious institutions without the King's license.

6. Modus: a money payment in lieu of a tithe.

buying up your advowsons,[7] extorting upon their tenants, and making those estates more precarious, which were always before esteemed as certain interests as any in Great-Britain: Has all this obliged them? Has it taught them moderation? On the contrary, it increases their demands upon you. Be assured, that they will never be satisfied, never think that they have enough, whilst you have a penny left; and when they have got all your lands, they must ride and enslave your persons.

Will you bear, Gentlemen, such constant and impudent insults? Will you still be governed by such abandoned deceivers? Are you men, free-men, rational men; and will you beat this wild and priestly war against human nature, against freedom, and against reason? Will you indeed believe them, when they pretend any regard to you and your interest? And is it upon your score that they practise perjury and rebellion themselves, and promote it in others?

T   *I am, &c.*

NO. 131. SATURDAY, JUNE 1, 1723.

Of Reverence true and false.

SIR,

The word *reverence* has had the fate of many, indeed of almost all, good words, and done much mischief: It signifies a solemn regard paid the persons of men of gravity, of religion, and of authority. By these qualifications men are entitled to it. But when the pride and craft of men who have no real gravity, no real religion, or a foolish one, and only a pretended or an absurd authority, would annex reverence only to grave or grotesque names, it becomes as ridiculous to men of good sense, as it seems awful to such as have none. Reverence belongs only to reverend qualities and reverend actions. As to names and habits, the more grave they

7. Advowsons: the right to nominate a person to a vacant ecclesiastical benefice.

are, the more ludicrous they become, when worn by persons who live loosely, and act ludicrously.

Garments signify nothing themselves. They grow first solemn, by being worn by men of character and solemnity: But the most solemn garment becomes contemptible and diverting upon the back of a droll, a buffoon, or upon a cheat or mountebank of any kind. The gravest man alive drest up in the cap and coat of a harlequin, would look like a harlequin; and the gravest speech that he could make, would be laughed at: Yet a coat of many colours was a coat of value in the East, in Jacob's time, and his favourite son Joseph wore one. Nor do our own ladies lose any respect by wearing all the colours of the peacock and the rainbow. On the other side, the gravest clothes put upon burlesque animals, will look burlesque. A monkey in a deep coat, and a broad beaver, would be still more a monkey, and his grimace would be still more diverting grimace; and a hog in a pair of jack-boots, and a coat of mail, would make no formidable figure, notwithstanding his warlike equipment.

These two last instances of the monkey and the hog may be farther improved, to shew the spirit of false reverence. A monkey in a red coat, and a hog in armour, would give no offence to a soldier, because his character consists in actions which these creatures cannot perform nor mimick; and consequently these animals, though accoutered like a soldier, cannot ridicule a soldier. But if you put a popish mitre, and the rest of that sort of gear, upon a hog, the useless and stupid solemnity of the animal gives you instantly the idea of a popish bishop, and if you are not a papist, will divert you: Or, if you dress up a baboon in the fantastical habit of a Romish priest, that animal which can chatter much and unintelligibly, and can really do most of the tricks which the priest himself can do, does genuinely represent the original; and therefore creates true mirth, and fully shews, that there cannot be much reverence in that which a baboon can perform as well, for aught I know better, as he is naturally a creature of grimace and humour. And the said bishop and priest could not with any temper bear the sight, their rage and impatience would be still farther proofs, that the monkey did them justice, that the trial was successful, and the mirth occasioned by it just. Such sport would indeed be tragical in popish countries; which is but another confirmation that false reverence cannot bear ridicule, and that the true is not affected by it.

Many of the ancient Greek philosophers took great pride, and found mighty reverence, in the length and gravity of their beards. Now an old goat, who had as much gravity and beard as any of them, had he been placed in any of their chairs, would, doubtless, have provoked the philosopher, and diverted the assembly. Pomp and beard were therefore ridiculous, since they could be ridiculed: But nothing that constitutes a philosopher, neither genius, nor virtue, nor useful learning, nor any thing that is good for something, can be ridiculed, at least justly ridiculed. The odd dance of judges and bishops in *The Rehearsal*,[1] does neither ridicule bishops nor judges, because they never practice such odd dances: But if these grave men met and gambolled together as they do there, the ridicule would be strong upon them.

It is a jest to expect from all men great reverence to that which every man may do, whether it consist in reading, or repeating, or wearing, or acting. Where is the difficulty or merit of saying certain words, or of making bows, or of spreading the arms, or crossing them, or of wearing a long coat, or a short cravat? It is impudence and imposture to demand singular and vast respect to small and common things. Superior virtue and capacity, publick actions and services done to mankind; a generous and benevolent heart, and greatness of mind, are the true objects and sources of reverence. But to claim reverence to prating, to cuts, and colours, and postures, is stupid, ridiculous and saucy. The *a-b-c* of a tinker is as good as a Pope's *a-b-c;* and it is open cheating and conjuring to pretend, that the same words have not the same force out of the mouth of a cobbler as out of a cardinal's mouth. When any one of these mighty claimers (I had almost said clamourers) of reverence from their visionary empire of words and tricks, can by the magick of their art remove a mountain or a mole-hill, or raise a house, or a dead insect, or kill a heretick, or a grasshopper by a charm, I am ready to bow down before them: But while I see any of them living

1. The senseless dance performed at the behest of the King in act V in the Duke of Buckingham's play.

like other men, or worse, and doing nothing but what so many chimney-sweepers (who can read) may do as well; I can consider such who do so only as solemn liars, and seducers; and as much worse than fortune-tellers, as they cheat people out of much more money, and fill their minds with worse terrors.

The Roman augurs made no such base use of their power, and of their ghostly trade, which was instituted, at least practised, for the ends of good policy; and, as far as I can find, they had no revenues: I would therefore have respected them, as they were great officers of the Roman state. But had an augur, as an augur, demanded reverence of me for his long staff, his tricks, and divinations, I should have done what Cato the elder wondered they themselves did not do as often as they met, laughed in his face,[2] as I would in the face of any man who pretended to be my superior and director, because his coat was longer than mine, or of a different colour; or because he uttered words which I could utter as well, or played pranks which a posture-master could play better.

I will reverence a man for the good which he does, or is inclined to do; and for no other reason ought I. But if under the pretence of doing me good, which I neither see nor feel, he pick my pocket, and do me sensible harm, or would do it; how can I help hating and despising him? If he turn religion into selfishness, and a plain trade, or by it destroy morality; if he set himself up in God's stead, and by pretending boldly to his power, abuse his holy name, and oppress his creatures; if he exclaim against covetousness, and be governed by it; and practice every vice which he condemns; if he preach against the world, and yet have never enough of it; and against the flesh, and yet be visibly governed by all its worst passions and appetites; if he take immense wages for promoting the welfare of society, and yet disturb, impoverish, and enslave it; how can I reverence him, if I would? And is he not lost to all modesty if he desire it?

If men would preserve themselves from superstition, and servitude, and folly, they must beware of reverencing names and accidents. A wise man does not reverence rulers for their insignia

2. The remark appears in Cicero, *De Divinatione*, 2.24.52.

and great titles: As there is no use of rulers, but to do service to mankind, he reverences them for that service done: If they do none, he despises them: If they do mischief, he hates them. What are men reverenced for, but for the good talents which they possess, or for the useful offices which they bear. Now if a man have never a good quality, or having such, abuse them; or if he do no good with the office which he bears, but harm (which he must do, if he do no good), every omission by which many are hurt, being a crime against many; how am I to reverence him, for taking away by his conduct the only cause of reverence? If he give me cause to hate him, am I for all that to love him? Either there is no such passion as hatred, which none but a madman will say, or it must be raised by the causes, that raise it; and what are those causes, but mischief done, when good is due, and expected; or the disappointment of a great good; which is a great mischief.

But when people are taught to reverence butchers, robbers, and tyrants, under the reverend name of rulers, to adore the names and persons of men, though their actions be the actions of devils: Then here is a confirmed and accomplished servitude, the servitude of the body, secured by the servitude of the mind, oppression fortified by delusion. This is the height of human slavery. By this, the Turk and the Pope reign. They hold their horrid and sanguinary authority by false reverence, as much as by the sword. The Sultan is of the family of Ottoman, and the Pope St. Peter's successor; they are therefore reverenced, while they destroy human race. The Christians hate the Turk, and call him a tyrant: Protestants dread the Pope, and call him an impostor. Yet I could name Christians who have tyrants of their own, as bad as the Sultan; I could name Protestants who have had impostors of their own as cruel as the Pope, had their power been as great, and their hands as loose. Men see the follies and slavery of others; but their own nonsense is all sacred, their own popes and sultans are all of heavenly descent, and their authority just and inviolable. But truth and falsehood, wisdom and folly, do not vary with the conceptions and prepossessions of men. Affliction and misery, oppression and imposture, are as bad in Christendom as in Turkey, in Holland as in Rome. Protestant rulers have no more right than the Sultan to oppress Protestants; and the Pope has as good a title as a Protestant parson to deceive Protestants. God forbid that all religions should be alike; but all who make the same ill use of every religion, are certainly alike; as are all governors, Turkish, popish, or Protestant, who make the same ill use of power.

If therefore all governors whatsoever, of what conduct soever, [are] to be reverenced, why not the Turk and old Muly of Morocco, who are both great governors, and have as much a divine authority to be tyrants as any governor of any name or religion ever had? And if all clergy whatsoever [are] to be reverenced, why not the Druids, and the priests of Baal, and the priests of Mecca and of Rome? But if only the good of both sorts [are] to be reverenced, why have we been told so much of the mighty respect due in the lump to priests and rulers? Is there any other way in common sense to gain respect, but to deserve it? Could the Romans reverence their governor Nero for robbing them of their lives and estates, for burning the city, and for wantonly making himself sport with human miseries: could the first Christians reverence him for dressing them up in the skins of wild beasts, and setting on other wild beasts to devour them: or for larding them all over with pitch and tallow, and lighting them up like lamps to illuminate the city?

If we reverence men for their power alone, why do we not reverence the Devil, who has so much more power than men? But if reverence be due only to virtuous qualities and useful actions, it is as ridiculous and superstitious to adore great mischievous men, or unholy men with holy names, as it is to worship a false god, or Satan in the stead of God. Are we to be told, that though we [are] to worship no god but the good and true God, yet we are to pay reverence, which is human worship, to wicked men, provided they be great men, and to honour the false servants of the true God, whom they dishonour? Or, that any sort of men can be his servants or deputies in any sense, but a good and sanctified sense? And if they be not, are we for the sake of God, to reverence those who belie him, and are our enemies? Or, am I to reverence the men, though I detest their actions and qualities which constitute the characters of men? Can I love or hate men, but for what they are, and for what they do? We ought to reverence that which is good, and the men that are good: Are we therefore to reverence wickedness and folly, and those who commit them? Or, because they have good names and offices, which are to be honoured, are they to be honoured for abusing those good things, and for turning good into evil?

We must deserve reverence before we claim it. If a man occupy an honourable office, civil or sacred, and act ridiculously or knavishly in it, do I dishonour that office by contemning or exposing the man who dishonours it? Or ought I not to scorn him, as much as I reverence his office, which he does all he can to bring into scorn? I have all possible esteem for quality; but if a man of quality act like an ape, or a clown, or a pick-pocket, or a profligate, I shall heartily hate or despise his lordship, notwithstanding my great reverence for lords. I honour episcopacy; but if a bishop be an hypocrite, a time-server, a traitor, a stock-jobber, or an hunter after power, I shall take leave to scorn the prelate, for all my regard for prelacy.

It is not a name, however awful, nor an office, however important, that ought to bring, or can bring, reverence to the man who possesses them, if he act below them, or unworthily of them. Folly and villainy ought to have no asylum; nor can titles sanctify crimes, however they may sometimes protect criminals. A right honourable or a right reverend rogue, is the most dangerous rogue, and consequently the most detestable.

> *Omne animi vitium tanto conspectius in se*
> *Crimen habet, quanto major qui peccat habetur.*[3]

Juvenal

G   *I am, &c.*

---

3. "However much greater the sinner's position, by so much more will the blemishes of his spirit stain his soul." Juvenal, *Saturae*, 8.140–41.

NO. 132. SATURDAY, JUNE 8, 1723.

Inquiry into the Doctrine of Hereditary Right.

SIR,

We have had a world of talk both in our pulpits and our addresses, about hereditary right, and I think that no one has yet fully explained what it means; I will therefore try whether I can unfold or cut asunder the Gordian knot. It is a divine, unalterable, indefeasible right to sovereignty, dictated or modified by the positive laws, and human constitutions or national governments. In France, Turkey, and the large eastern monarchies, it descends wholly upon the males. In the kingdom, or rather queendom of Achem,[1] it falls only upon females. In Russia formerly it descended upon all the males jointly, and it would not operate upon the females at all. In Poland the nobility have an human right to confer part of this divine right, but not all of it, upon whom they please;[2] and in old Rome the soldiery often made bold to confer it: But in England and other countries, all of it falls upon the male who chances to be born first; and so on to the next, according to priority of birth; and for want of males to the eldest female, contrary to other inheritances, which descend upon females equally. However, though this same right be absolute and unalterable, yet it is often limited and circumscribed by human laws, which ought not to be transgressed, yet may be transgressed with impunity, unless it interfere with another divine right, which is the divine right of the high clergy. In all other cases, it is boundless and unconditioned, though given and accepted upon conditions.

1. Achin, located at the northern end of the island of Sumatra. The kingdom reached its height during the first half of the seventeenth century. Following the death of the sultan in 1641, his widow was placed on the throne and three more queens succeeded her before the more religious Muslim elements restored male rule in 1699.

2. Since the latter half of the sixteenth century, the crown of Poland, whose powers were considerably circumscribed, was determined by election by the nation's gentry.

There is one circumstance particularly remarkable in the exercise of this divine right; namely, that it may make as bold as it thinks fit with other divine right (except as before excepted), of which we have a late and very pregnant instance, approved by very good churchmen, and all our able divines, who thanked God, publickly for thus exercising it; that is, when the Queen made that honourable peace which executed itself.[3] Then the unalterable divine right of the dauphin to the kingdom of Spain was given to his younger son, and the indefeasible divine right of the present King of Spain, to the monarchy of France, was assigned over to a younger branch of the house of Bourbon; and sometime before, the divine right of the last Emperor to the Spanish dominions, was given to the present Emperor. Nay, it seems that this alienable, unalienable, indivisible right, is divisible too. The divine right to Sardinia, is given to the Duke of Savoy; that of Naples, Sicily, and Flanders, to the Emperor; and that of Gibraltar and Port Mahon to us, as long as we can keep it; which I hope we are now in a fair way to do. All the rest of this divine right, besides what is thus disposed of, remains where it was before, and where it should be.

But there are certain human ingredients, experiments, and operations, which are necessary to attain to this divine right. In most countries, and particularly in our own, the priests must have a finger in modelling the same; nor will it come down from above, and settle here below upon any prince whatsoever, unless they say certain words over the married couple, which they alone have the right to say: But in Turkey, India; and other Mahometan and pagan countries (*heu Pudor!*[4]), this same divine right is to be got without the benefit of their clergy, and will make its conveyance through the channel of a strumpet; yet in most nations all is not well, unless the clergy say grace over it; but then it is of no consequence who it is that gets the divine babe, so he be but born

3. That is, the Peace of Utrecht ending the War of the Spanish Succession, which recognized Philip, the son of the Dauphin, as King of Spain rather than his older brother, in return for which Philip renounced any possible future claim to the French throne. The treaties of Utrecht further provided that Spain cede to Savoy the island of Sicily; to Austria, the Spanish Netherlands and Sardinia; and to Britain, Gibraltar and the island of Minorca. In 1720, Savoy and Austria exchanged Sicily for Sardinia.

4. A Greek exclamation meaning "Alas, the shame!"

in wedlock; and in a late instance it appeared no ways necessary whether he were born in wedlock or not, or of whom he was born, so he were but born at all.[5] Now, sir, you must know, that this is a mystery, and like some other mysteries, wholly inexplicable, yet may be explained by the Jacobite clergy; but then you are not to understand the explication, but are to take their words for it; and we all know that they are men of probity, and will not deceive you. From this divine right all other rights are derived, except their own, which comes down from above too; and if the possessors of these two divine rights can agree together, all is as it should be; otherwise, you are to take notice, that God is to be obeyed before man, and the regale is to bow down, like the sheaves in Joseph's dream, before the pontificate.

But this is not all: There are some circumstances very particular and whimsical in this divine right. Though, as has been said, it may be conveyed away, yet nothing passes by the conveyance in many cases: Part of it may be granted and conceded to its subjects, and yet they have no right to keep what is so given, always excepting the high clergy, who may take it without being given. I had almost forgot another conveyance of this right, which is conquest, or, in other words, the divine right of plunder, rapine, massacre: But the right is never the worse for the wickedness of men; for howsoever they get possession of sovereign power, the right is that moment annexed to the possession, unless in special cases, still preserving a right to the Jacobite clergy, to give a right to whomsoever they else please. This same right is of so odd and bizarre a nature, that it receives no addition or diminution from the consent of men, or the want of that consent. It is lawful to swear to it, when there is an interest in doing so; yet it is no ways necessary to believe what you swear, or to keep your oath. It is not to be resisted; yet in particular cases it may be opposed. It is limited, and yet unlimitable. You may make laws to bind it, yet it is treason and damnation to defend those laws, unless you have the *verbum sacerdotis*[6] on your side.

5. In June 1688, James Edward, later known as the Old Pretender, was born to James II and his wife, Maria of Modena. It was commonly held, especially among Whigs, that Maria was not in fact pregnant and that a new-born infant was smuggled into her bed chamber in a warming pan.
6. "The word of a priest."

What contradictions, absurdities, and wickedness, are men capable of! We have a set of abandoned wretches amongst ourselves, who seem to have a design to destroy [the] human race, as they would human reason! Every doctrine, every opinion, which they advance, is levelled against the happiness of all mankind. Nothing conduces to virtue, to true religion, to the present or future interests of men, but is represented as destructive to piety. We are to be the vassals of tyrants, the dupes of impostors, the zanies of mountebanks, or else are in a state of damnation. Men, for whose sakes government was instituted, have no right to be protected by government. Religion which was given by Almighty God to make men virtuous here, and happy hereafter; has been made use of to destroy their happiness both here, and hereafter. Scarce any thing is discovered to be true in nature and philosophy, but is proved to be false in orthodoxy: What is found to be beneficial to mankind in their present state is represented hurtful to their future; nay, some are risen up amongst us, who are such implacable enemies to their species, that they make it sin to take proper precautions against the danger of the small-pox, even when they are advised by the most able physicians, and when these physicians are most disinterested.

What can be more cruel, wicked and detrimental to human society, or greater blasphemy against the good God; than to make government, which was designed by him to render men numerous, industrious, and useful to one another, designed to improve arts, sciences, learning, virtue, magnanimity and true religion, an unnatural engine to destroy the greatest part of the world? to make the rest poor, ignorant, superstitious and wicked; to subject them like cattle, to be the property of their oppressors; to be the tame slaves of haughty and domineering masters, and the low homagers[7] of gloomy pedants; to work for, to fight for, and to adore those who are neither better nor wiser than themselves; and to be wretched by millions, to make one or a few proud and insolent? And yet we are told, that this is the condition which God has placed us in, and that it is damnation to strive to make it better.

All these mischiefs, and many more, are the inseparable consequences of an indefeasible hereditary right in any man, or

7. Homagers: vassals.

family whatsoever; if it can never be alienated or forfeited: For if this be true, then the property of all mankind may be taken away, their religion overturned, and their persons butchered by thousands, and no remedy attempted: They must not mutter and complain; for complaints are sedition, and tend to rebellion: They must not stand upon their defence, for that is resisting the Lord's anointed: They must not revile the ministers and instruments of his power; for woe be to the man who speaketh ill of him whom the king honoureth. And all this has been told us by those who have never shewn any regard to authority, either human or divine, when it interfered with their own interests. What shall I say; what words use to express this monstrous wickedness, this utter absence of all virtue, religion, or tenderness to the human species: What colours can paint it, what pen can describe it!

Certainly, if government was designed by God for the good, happiness, and protection of men, men have a right to be protected by government; and every man must have a right to defend what no man has a right to take away. There is not now a government subsisting in the world, but took its rise from the institution of men; and we know from history when, and how it was instituted: It was either owing to the express or tacit consent of the people, or of the soldiers, who first erected it; it could have no more power than what they gave it; and what persons soever were invested with that power, must have accepted it upon the conditions upon which it was given; and when they renounced those conditions, they renounced their government. In some countries it was hereditary; in others elective; in some discretionary; in others limited: But in all, the government must have derived their authority from the consent of men, and could exercise it no farther than that consent gave them leave. Where positive conditions were annexed to their power, they were certainly bound by those conditions; and one condition must be annexed to all governments, even the most absolute, that they act for the good of the people; for whose sake alone there is any government in the world. In this regard there can be no difference between hereditary and elective monarchies; for the heir cannot inherit more than his ancestor enjoyed, or had a right to enjoy, any more than a successor can succeed to it.

Then the wise question will arise, what if any man, who has no natural right, nor any right over his fellow creatures, accept great powers, immense honours and revenues, and other personal advantages to himself and his posterity, upon conditions either express, as in all limited constitutions, or implied, as in all constitutions whatsoever; and yet either by deliberate declarations, or deliberate actions, publickly proclaim, that he will no longer be bound by these conditions, that he will no longer abide by his legal title, but will assume another that was never given him, and to which he can have no right at all; that he will govern his people by despotick authority; that instead of protecting them, he will destroy them; and he will overturn their religion to introduce one of his own; and instead of being a terror to evil works, will be a terror to good: I ask, in such a case, whether his subjects will be bound by the conditions, which he has renounced? Do the obligations subsist on their part, when he has destroyed them on his? And are they not at liberty to save themselves, and to look out for protection elsewhere, when it is denied where they have a right to expect and demand it, and to get it as they can, though at the expence of him and his family, when no other method or recourse is left?

And now, O ye gloomy impostors! O ye merciless advocates for superstition and tyranny! Produce all your texts, all your knotty distinctions! Here exert all your quaint eloquence, your quiddities, your *aliquo modo sit, aliquo modo non;*[8] appear in solemn dump, with your reverential robes, and your horizontal hats, with whole legions of phantoms and chimeras, and cart-loads of theology, broken oaths, and seditious harangues, and try whether you can maintain the battle, and defend the field against one single adversary, who undertakes to put all your numerous and fairy battalions to flight.

Let us hear what you can say for your abdicated idol. Distinguish, if you can, his case from that which I have represented: Shew that Almighty God gave him a divine right to play the Devil; or, if he had no such right, that his subjects had none to hinder him: Prove that kings are not instituted for the good of the people,

8. "In some measure, yes, in some measure, no."

but for their own and the clergy's pride and luxury: But if they be instituted for the good of the people, then shew that they are left at liberty to act for their destruction, and that their subjects must submit to inevitable ruin, yet kiss the iron rod whenever his Majesty pleases: Shew that it was possible for the kingdom to trust themselves again to the faith and oaths of a popish prince, who, during his whole reign, did nothing else but break his faith and his oaths, and whose religion obliged him to do so; or that it was possible for them to place his son upon the throne which he had abdicated (if they had believed him to be his son), when he was in possession of the most implacable enemy of their country, or of Europe, or of the Protestant religion; and that it would not have been direct madness to have sent for him afterwards from France or Rome, enraged by his expulsion, educated, animated, and armed with French and popish principles; and shew too, that the poor oppressed people had any recourse, but to throw themselves under the protection of their great deliverer, who was next heir to their crown.

If you cannot do this, there is nothing left for you to do, but to shew, that the late King James did not violate and break the fundamental laws and statutes of this realm, which were the original contract between him and his people; and that he did not make their allegiance to him incompatible with their own safety, for the preservation of which he was entitled to their allegiance: Shew that he did not claim and exercise a power to dispense with their laws; that he did not levy the customs without the authority of Parliament; or that he called Parliaments according to the constitution which he had sworn to; and that when he intended to call one, he did not resolve to pack it, and closeted many of the gentlemen of England, and with promises and menaces endeavoured to make them practicable to his designs: Shew that he did not disarm Protestants, and arm papists; set up exorbitant and unlawful courts; cause excessive bail to be required, excessive fines to be imposed, and excessive punishments to be inflicted; that he did not prosecute members in the King's-Bench for what they did in Parliament; and discharge others committed by Parliament;[9] that he did not

9. Several eminent Whigs, members of James II's Parliament, were tried for conspiring against the crown, including involvement in the Rye House Plot. These included Charles Gerard, the eldest son of the Earl of Macclesfield, John Hampden, and Henry Booth, Lord Delemere.

grant fines and forfeitures of persons to be tried, before their conviction; that he did not erect an ecclesiastical commission directly
against an act of Parliament, and suspended, by virtue of it, clergymen, for not reading in their churches a proclamation, which he
issued by his own authority, to give liberty of conscience to papists
and Protestant dissenters:[10] Shew that he did not imprison and try
seven bishops for their humble petition against it, which petition
they were empowered by law to make;[11] that he did not combine
with France and Rome to overthrow the Established Church,
which he was bound to defend, and to introduce another in the
room of it, which was worse than none; that, in order to it, he
brought not professed papists into offices, both civil and military;
sent not, nor received ambassadors to and from Rome, who were
guilty of high treason by the laws of the land, and brought not
from thence swarms of locusts, to devour and pollute every thing
that it produced; turned not out the masters and fellows of Magda-
len-College against law, for not doing what they were sworn not to
do, nor substituted in their room, those who were not qualified by
law to be there:[12] And to make good all these breaches upon our
liberties, that he did not raise a popish army in Ireland, and

10. In 1686, King James restored the Ecclesiastical High Commission, which
had been abolished by the Long Parliament in 1641. The commission was
given final jurisdiction over all religious matters and was empowered to suspend or deprive any ecclesiastic of his living. Some two years later, in Apr.
1688, the King issued his second Declaration of Indulgence, by which he suspended the penal laws relating to ecclesiastical matters and declared that
neither the Test Acts nor the oaths of allegiance and supremacy were to be
applied to office holders. The Declaration was ordered to be read in every
cathedral and parish church, and when a substantial number of clergymen
refused to obey the order, they were suspended from their livings by the High
Commission.

11. Among the clergy who refused to obey the King's order requiring that the
Declaration of Indulgence be read in every church were William Sancroft,
Archbishop of Canterbury, and six other bishops. The seven bishops drew up
a petition against the order and presented it to the King; as a result, they were
charged with seditious libel and tried before the King's Bench in June 1688.

12. In 1687, despite the King's instructions to the fellows of Magdalen College, Oxford, that they elect his own unqualified nominee to the presidency of
the college, the fellows proceeded to elect an applicant from among their number. As a consequence, the High Commission voided the election, decreed the
removal from the college of all its fellows, and placed the college under the
visitatorial jurisdiction of a committee. Some months later the King intruded
yet another of his favorites as president. At the same time, the fellowships were
filled with Roman Catholics and Magdalen College took on the aspect of a
Catholic seminary.

another in England, which had many papists in it, without authority of Parliament.

Shew, if you can, that he ever discovered the least inclination to reform these abuses; but on the contrary, when he could continue them no longer, that he did not desert his people: That he dared to trust himself to a free Parliament, after he had called it, and dissolved it not again, and did not foolishly throw his great seal into the Thames, that no other might be called; and when he resolved to leave his people, that he would suffer his pretended son to remain amongst us. Shew that you yourselves did not help to expel him; that you have not taken oaths, repeated oaths to this government, and abjurations of every other; and that you have adhered to either one or the other. When you have done this, I will allow you to be honest men, good Englishmen, and true Protestants.

T   *I am, &c.*

NO. 133. SATURDAY, JUNE 15, 1723.

Of Charity, and Charity-Schools.

SIR,

I know well, that any one must run a great deal of hazard, who shall advance any opinions against what is vulgarly called charity, though it be ever so much mistaken or miscalled, as for the most part it is, and ever has been. The giving loose money in the streets to canting and lazy beggars, has obtained the name of charity, though it is generally a mischievous liberality to encourage present idleness, or to reward past extravagancy, and is forbid by severe laws. The founding of monasteries, nunneries, and other miscalled religious houses, has passed too upon the world in late ages for charity, though they have ever proved seminaries of superstition and of papal tyranny, discouragements of matrimony, the sources of depopulation, and have made multitudes of people useless to the world and themselves. The giving lands and revenues to saucy, aspiring, and lazy ecclesiasticks, has been reputed a meritorious action; yet such actions have ever destroyed religion, increased the pride and dominion of the clergy, and depressed, impoverished, and enslaved the laity, for whose sakes alone there ought to be any ecclesiasticks at all. The founding and endowing of universities, colleges, and free-schools, carries an appearance of promoting sciences, learning, and true religion; yet they have been made use of to promote the kingdom of Antichrist, to debauch the principles of the nobility and gentry; to deprave their understandings; advance learned ignorance; load their heads with airy chimeras and fairy distinctions; fill states with desperate beggars and divines of fortune, who must force trade for a subsistence, and become the cudgels and tools of power or factions. A learned author justly compares these establishments to the Trojan horse, which carried hosts of armed men within its bowels, to send them out afterwards to destroy kingdoms.

But there is another new-fangled charity risen up amongst us, called *charity-schools*, which, I think, threatens the publick more than all which I have mentioned. I would not be understood to condemn every thing of that nature; for, under a proper regulation, something like it may be commendable: But, as they are now employed and managed, I see no good that can accrue to the publick from them, but apprehend a great deal of mischief. These establishments were first begun and encouraged by pious men, many of them dissenters; and then our high clergy every where exclaimed against them as dangerous innovations, and attempts to subvert the Church, and the national religion. But now they have got them under their own management, and they really prove what they foretold they would prove, they continually make harangues and panegyrical elogiums upon them, and upon the persons who promote them. It is become part of their duty (and much better executed than all the rest), to prate people out of their money; to decoy superstitious and factious men out of their shops and their business, and old doting women out of their infirmaries, to hear too often seditious harangues upon the power of the clergy, and of the reverence due to them, and upon the merit of nursing up beggars to be the blind tools of ambitious pedants; and lectures and instructions are there given them, inconsistent with our present establishment of church and state; and we have scarce a news-paper but gives notice of sermons to be preached upon this occasion.

It is certain that there was almost every where a general detestation of popery, and popish principles, and a noble spirit for liberty, at or just before the Revolution; and the clergy seemed then as zealous as the foremost. But when the corrupt part of them found themselves freed from the dangers which they complained of, and could not find their separate and sole advantage in the Revolution, they have been continually attacking and undermining it; and since they saw that it was impossible to persuade those who were witnesses and sufferers under the oppressions of the former governments, wantonly, and with their eyes open, to throw away their deliverance, they went a surer and more artful way to work, though more tedious and dilatory; and therefore have, by insensible degrees, corrupted all the youth whose education has been trusted to them, and who could be corrupted; so that at the end of near forty years, the Revolution is worse established than when it began. New generations are risen up, which knew nothing of the sufferings of their fathers, and are taught to believe there were never any such. The dread of popery is almost lost amongst us; the vilest tenets of it are openly asserted and maintained; men are taught to play with oaths; and it is become fashionable to revile authority more for its commendable actions, than for its excesses. The principles of our nobility and gentry are debauched in our universities, and those of our common people in our charity-schools, who are taught, as soon as they can speak, to blabber out *High Church* and *Ormond*;[1] and so are bred up to be traitors, before they know what treason signifies.

This has been long seen, and as long complained of; yet no remedy has been applied, though often promised. Those whose duty and business it ought to have been, have had their time and thoughts so wholly engaged in modelling factions, and enriching

1. James Butler, second Duke of Ormonde (1665–1745). Though a supporter of the Revolution of 1688, Ormonde had strong Tory leanings and was a follower of Bolingbroke, whom he joined in exile in 1715 after being impeached by Parliament. Ormonde took part in the Jacobite invasion of 1715 and, in the following year, saw his immense estates confiscated by the crown.

themselves, that this great evil has been suffered to go on, and still goes on; it has been continually increasing, and yet increases; but I hope, at last, that those in authority will take the alarm, will think their own safety, and the safety of his Majesty and his people, are highly concerned to remove a mischief which is levelled at all their and our happiness; and that they will not, like their predecessors, disoblige all their friends to gratify their enemies, whom yet they cannot gratify. If this be not done, any one, without much skill in politicks, may safely affirm, that our present establishment cannot long subsist. A free government must subsist upon the affections of the people; and if those affections be perpetually debauched; if the education of youth be altogether inconsistent with the nature of it; and if it must depend only upon converts, pensions, or armies, its duration cannot be long, without a constant succession of miracles: Armies will soon find their own strength, and will play their own game: Foreign armies will neither be thought on nor borne; and it is to be feared, that our domestick ones, upon every disgust, or prospect of advantage, may fall into the intrigues and resentments of their countrymen, when they grow to be general, and consequently will be of least use, when most wanted. We cannot sure, so soon forget what the Parliament army did formerly, and King James's lately, and what was expected from our own in the late conspiracy;[2] and without such expectations, it had been direct madness to have formed or engaged in such an attempt, and the criminals had been more properly sent to Bedlam than to Tyburn, though they deserved both.

But to apply myself more directly to the charity-schools, I shall endeavour to show, that under the false pretence and affectation of charity, they destroy real charity, take away the usual support and provision from the children of lesser tradesmen, and often from those of decayed and unfortunate merchants and gentlemen, and pervert the benevolence, which would be otherwise bestowed upon helpless widows, and poor housekeepers, who cannot by reason of their poverty, maintain their families.

Every country can maintain but a certain number of shopkeepers, or retailers of commodities, which are raised or manufac-

2. The Atterbury plot of 1722.

tured by others; and the fewer they are, the better; because they add nothing to the publick wealth; but only disperse and accommodate it to the convenience of artificers, manufacturers and husbandmen, or such who live upon their estates and professions; and serve the publick only by directing and governing the rest; but as there must be many retailers of other men's industry, and the greatest part of them will be but just able to support themselves, and with great pains, frugality, and difficulty, breed up their families, and be able to spare small sums out of their little substance to teach their children to write and cast account, and to put them out apprentices to those of their own degree; so those employments ought to fall to the share of such only; but now are mostly anticipated, and engrossed by the managers of the charity-schools; who, out of other people's pockets, give greater sums than the other can afford, only to take the lowest dregs of the people from the plough and labour, to make them tradesmen, and by consequence drive the children of tradesmen to the plough to beg, to rob, or to starve.

The same may be said of servants, who are generally the children of the lesser shop-keepers, though sometimes of decayed merchants and gentlemen, who have given them an education above the lower rank of people, which has qualified them to earn a comfortable subsistence this way, without much labour, to which they have never been used. Now, I have often heard, that one advantage proposed by these charity-schools, is to breed up children to reading and writing, and a sober behaviour; that they may be qualified to be servants: A sort of idle and rioting vermin, by which the kingdom is already almost devoured, who are become every where a publick nuisance, and multitudes of them daily, for want of employment, betake themselves to the highway and house-breaking, others to robbing and sharping, or to the stews; and must do so, if we study new methods to increase their numbers.

I have mentioned another mischief which has flowed from this pretended charity; for it has, in effect, destroyed all other charities, which were before given to the aged, sick and impotent. I am told that there is more collected at the church-doors in a day, to make these poor boys and girls appear in caps and livery-coats, than for all other poor in a year; and there is reason to presume, that less still is given to private charities, where the givers are almost the only witnesses of their own actions: So that this benevolence is a commutation or composition for what was formerly given to widows, orphans, and to broken and unfortunate housekeepers. And how should it be otherwise, when the clergymen in highest repute, stroll about from church to church, nay print publick advertisements of charity sermons to be preached, recommending the merit of this sort of liberality, the service which it does to God and the Church; and but faintly, or perhaps not at all, exhorting to any other: insomuch, that the collections made every winter, by virtue of the King's Letter,[3] for the many miserable in this great town, visibly decrease, though these collections be made from house to house, though the names of the givers, and sums given, be entered down, and though all ministers be directed by his Majesty and the Bishop of London, in their sermons, to press this charity upon their congregations; which is notwithstanding seldom done, unless in a faint manner, perhaps at the end of a sermon; whereas, on the other occasion, the ears of the auditors are deafened with the cry of the preacher, and their passions are all inflamed to a profuse liberality; and those who do not give, and give largely too, must incur reproach and contumely.

Oh! but say some pious, and many more impious and hypocritical people, what would you hinder poor boys and girls from being well clothed, from serving God, and being bred scholars? I answer, that there are few instances in which the publick has suffered more, than in breeding up beggars to be what are called scholars, from the grave pedant and the solemn doctor, down to the humble writer and caster of accounts; to attain which characters, does not require the pains and acuteness that are necessary to make a good cobbler: yet they immediately fancy themselves to be another rank of mankind, think that they are to be maintained in idleness, and out of the substance of others, for their fancied accomplishments; are above day-labour, and by an idle education, require a listlessness to it; and when they cannot find the sort of subsistence which they aspire to, are always perplexing the world,

3. "The King's Letter" refers to the annual winter collections for the poor begun in Dec. 1688, with a letter and donation from William III.

and disturbing other people. So that no education ought to be more discountenanced by a state, than putting chimeras and airy notions into the heads of those who ought to have pickaxes in their hands; than teaching people to read, write, and cast account, who, if they were employed as they ought to be, can have no occasion to make use of these acquirements, unless it be now and then to read the Bible, which they seldom or never do: Besides, they are told by their spiritual guides, that they must not understand it.

What benefit can accrue to the publick by taking the dregs of the people out of the kennels, and throwing their betters into them? By lessening the numbers of day-labourers, by whose industry alone, nations are supported, and the publick wealth increased? By multiplying the number of such who add nothing to it, but must live out of the property of the rest? By taking boys and girls from the low and necessary employments of life, making them impatient of the condition which they were born to, and in which they would have thought themselves happy, to be seamstresses, footmen, and servant maids, and to teach them to read ballads? How much more useful a charity would it be, to give the same sums to their parents to help them to raise their families, and breed up their children to spinning or hard-labour; to help them to maintain themselves, and to depend for the future upon their own hands for subsistence? Whereas, this sort of charity is of no use, benefit, or ease to their parents, who must find them meat, drink, washing, and some clothes, during the whole time which they spend at school, and lose, at the same time, the little that they can otherwise earn, or what they would earn themselves, whilst they employed their children in going on errands, and doing little offices, which they can do as well: And all this for the pleasure of seeing them a little better clothed, hearing them sing psalms, and repeating by rote a catechism made for that purpose.

The pretence that this sort of education will render them more useful members of society, and will make them more virtuous and religious, is a mere chimera. How many are hanged at Tyburn that can write and read; or rather how few that cannot? And generally they all die for high church, and for the right line! Who are greater rogues than scholars, as they are called; And what set of people have supplied the town with more whores than our spiritual fathers, who all have the practice of piety by them? Nothing keeps the herd of mankind so honest, as breeding them up to industry, and keeping them always employed in hard-labour, and letting them have no time or inducements from necessity to rob or cheat, or superfluities to debauch with. Who are the persons who have the conduct, and are at the head of these charity-schools? Are they men of the most exemplary piety and morals? No, I am told quite the contrary: They are, for the most part, staunch Jacobites, or, in other words, furious high-church-men; often men of debauched lives and principles; and the masters of these schools are generally enemies to the establishment. And what use do they make of their power? Why! they supply the children with what they want out of their own shops; get credit and interest amongst their neighbours, for their charitable disposition; make use of that credit to promote disaffection to the government; engage the parents and friends of the children in the interest of a popish Pretender, and breed up the children themselves to fight his battles in due time.

I have been very much diverted to see, now and then, one of these poor creatures skip over a kennel as nimble as a greyhound, to get to the other side of the way, that it might be ready to make a low bow to a parson as he passed by; which order of men they are taught almost to adore; and I have been often told (though I do not affirm, and can scarce believe it to be true), that their duty to the clergy is inserted in a catechism that is or has been taught them; but whether such a catechism be committed to print or writing, or not, it is certain that their duty to God is not half so much, I will not say, inculcated into them, but observed by them, as the reverence and respect which they are made to believe is due to these holy men. And what use will be made of this blind adoration to such persons and their power, we may easily judge by what use ever has been made of it; which I think is well worth the time and thoughts of publick authority, as of all men who wish well to their King, their country, and themselves, seriously to reflect upon, and to provide against, before it be too late, and the mischief be accomplished.

T   *I am, &c.*

NO. 134. SATURDAY, JUNE 29, 1723.

❦   *What small and foolish Causes often misguide and animate the Multitude.*

SIR,

I t is surprizing what minute and contemptible causes create discontents, disorders, violence, and revolutions amongst men; what a small spring can actuate a mighty and many-headed multitude; and what mighty numbers one man is capable of drawing into his disgusts and designs. It is the weakness of the many; when they have taken a fancy to a man, or to the name of a man, they take a fancy even to his failings, adopt his interest right or wrong, and resent every mark of disfavour shewn him, however just and necessary it be. Nor are the resentments and fondness the less violent for being ill-grounded. If a man make them drunk once or twice a year, this injury is a kindness which they never forget; and he is sure of their hearts and their hands for having so generously robbed them of their time, their innocence, and their senses. They are grateful for the mischief done them; and in return, are ready to do any for him. He who restrains them from drunkenness, or even punishes them for it, is a greater and a real benefactor; but such a benefactor as they will never forgive, and he is sure to lose their good will, probably to purchase their hatred.

This shews how much their senses are stronger, than their understandings. They are governed not by judgment, but by sensations; and, one guinea in drink obliges them more than two in clothes; or in any other dry way. Liquor warms their hearts, and fills them with the man who is the author of so much joy. So that to instruct them, feed them, and employ them, are not such sure ways to win them, as to mislead and inflame them, and to waste their time. For this reason, the sober and the sensible clergyman is never so popular, as the loud, the factious, and the hot-headed. Rational and sober instruction is a cold thing, and goes no farther than the understanding: But noise and raving awaken and intoxicate the animal spirits, and set the blood on fire, and have all the effects of wine.

So that in raising parties and factions, inflaming goes a thousand times farther than reasoning and teaching. A foolish speech, supported with vehemence and brandy, will conquer the best sense, and the best cause in the world, without anger or liquor. Sobriety and capacity are not talents that recommend to the crowd, who are always taken with shallow pomp and sound, and with men of little restraints. The debauched and the superstitious have great hold of them: Men who will sin with them, or men who can give them amulets against the vengeance due to sinning. But men who will neither corrupt them, nor deceive them, are to them distasteful Stoicks, or frightful infidels, and sometimes used as such. One may at any time gain an interest in a mob with a barrel of beer, or without it, by means of a few odd sounds, that mean nothing, or something very wild or wicked. Let any superstition, though ever so wild or foolish, be advanced by one who has credit enough to deceive them; let any favourite party watch-word be invented, and pronounced in such a tone and such a posture, it soon becomes sacred, and in the highest esteem; and woe be to him that speaks against a mystery: Every argument shall be an affront and a sign of unbelief; which is a crime always highest, and most hated, when it is best grounded. The managers of the charm, on the contrary, are men of vast reverence, moment, and popularity: and a zeal for the charm, creates guards and revenues to the charmers. If you go about to expose the imposture, and unfold the cheat, you are a foe to all religion, and will believe nothing without evidence. The superstition grows in established repute, and 'tis dangerous to oppose it, till some other, often more absurd, and consequently more prevailing, undermines and exterminates it: For there is that propensity in most men to delusion and grimace, that they seldom recur to the plain and amiable precepts taught in the scripture, and to a religion without shew, pageantry, and ceremonies; but superstition almost always subsists in some shape or other, and grows strong and reverenced in proportion to its weakness, nonsense, and absurdity: As it is admired in proportion as it is foolish or wonderful, it is believed in proportion as it is incredible. So that the credulity of the people for the most part follows the wise improvement of nonsense:

Cupidine ingenii humani libentius obscura credi.[1]

TACIT.

Considering the weakness of man's nature, prone to imaginary fears, to lean upon imaginary props, and to seek imaginary cures, limited deluders are often to be borne; but the worst is, that they will not be limited, but extend their guile to instances where it is not wanted; and from managing his whims, assume a right to direct his property, his eating and drinking, and every part of his behaviour; and turn canting and telling dreams, into authority and ruling.

The Egyptians have been always a most superstitious nation, always under the dominion of their priests, and consequently prone to tumults and insurrections. Their priests were at one time arrived to that monstrous pitch of power and tyranny, that they used to dispatch their kings by a message. If they did but signify their pious pleasure, that his Majesty was to cut his throat he durst not refuse, but must humbly take the knife, and be his own executioner. But the power of the priests was weakened, and the danger of frequent rebellions prevented, by the following stratagem of one of the princes. He considered the madness of the multitude after their gods, and their priests; and that their unity in religious frenzy and nonsense, disposed them to unanimity in their civil rage. He therefore divided Egypt into several districts, and endowed every district with its peculiar and separate deities. He knew, that if they differed about their gods, or divine cattle, and vegetables of worship, and about the rites paid them, they would agree about nothing else, and consequently never to conspire against him. One division had for its deity a monkey, another had a cat, another a crocodile, another a kite; and some adored leeks and garlick, savoury gods of their own planting.

1. "Obscure things are believed more freely because of the greed of human nature." Tacitus, *Historiae*, 1.22.

O sanctas gentes, quibus haec nascuntur in hortis
Numina!———[2]

This dividend of deities had the desired effect. The several districts abhorred all the neighbouring celestial gentry as intensely and madly as they doted on their own; and were ready to spill their blood, either offensively, or defensively, for the honour and interest of these their different divinities. Hence the religious and bloody war between two neighbouring towns, finely described by Juvenal with his usual force and indignation.

> *Inter finitimos vetus atque antiqua simultas,*
> *Immortale odium & nunquam sanabile vulnus*
> *Ardet adhuc, Ombas & Tentyra. Summus utrinque*
> *Inde furor vulgo, quod numina vicinorum*
> *Odit uterque locus; cum solos credit habendos*
> *Esse deos quos ipse colit.*[3]
>
> JUV. SAT. 15

When people are once divided in their affections, every thing, however innocent and indifferent, if it be peculiar to the one, becomes a mark of iniquity, and an object of hatred to the other. A different hat or coat becomes the source of resentment, when perhaps a cloak or a ruff[4] creates friendship and esteem. A judgment is made of the hearts of men by their habit, and particular good or bad qualities are annexed to cloth and colours. There are instances of monarchs deposed and murdered by their people for wearing a foreign dress, or for speaking a foreign language: And there are instances of nations persecuted, wasted, and laid in blood by their princes, for using, or not using, particular gestures and sounds, which their Highnesses had taken a liking to; and of princes used the same way by their people for the same reason.

2. "What a holy nation to have such gods springing up in its gardens!" Juvenal, *Saturae*, 15.10.
3. "Between the neighboring towns of Ombi and Tentyra an ancient feud, marked by everlasting hatred and wounds that never heal, burns even now. Each town is filled with anger against the other because each hates its neighbors' gods, believing their own deities the only true ones." Juvenal, *Saturae*, 15.33.38.
4. Ruff: collar.

If they take an affection to the word *abracadabra,* though they join to it no certain idea, they think themselves justified in oppressing, and sometimes in butchering, all who do not profess the same vehement affection to the same senseless sound. But the man who is loud and mutinous for *abracadabra* is their darling: They grow fond of him for being fond of their word: His fondness is a compliment to them; and they will venture life and limb for a cheat, or a blockhead, who opens his mouth just as they do theirs. Their zeal is the fiercer, because it is blind. If they fall religiously in love with an ape, or an ox, or with those that tend him, as the Egyptians did, he is presently a blasphemer, who does not debase his understanding or forfeit his sincerity, by sacrificing shamefully and devoutly to these brute creatures, and by reverencing and pampering the solemn Merry Andrews[5] that look after them.

The great island of Madagascar is divided into two great parts and parties, who are at fierce strife and everlasting war about a sanctified elephant's tooth, which both own to have come down from heaven, and both pretend to have it; and I am not sure whether it has not worked miracles on both sides: but as neither side will allow the other to have it, they hate one another as much as they love and hate the said tooth. *Great is the elephant of Madagascar, and the tusk which fell down from Jupiter!*

The Turks and the Persians are equally the devout, the blind, and bigotted followers of Mahomet, and differ in no point of doctrine. This doctrinal unanimity, one would think, must be a powerful bond of union, at least of religious union between the two empires. But no such matter. They treat one another as execrable hereticks and infidels, and do not hate the Christians more, though their only or principal difference in opinion is, that the Turks hold Omar for the true successor of Mahomet, and the Persians maintain that Ali was.[6] They tie their religion, at least the efficacy of it, to the succession; and deny that there can be any salvation in any church where the uninterrupted succession is not

5. Merry Andrews: mountebanks.

6. The distinction between Sunni Islam, on the one hand, and Shi'ite Islam, on the other. There are, of course, significant doctrinal differences as well, not the least of which concerns the status of women.

kept up: So that each side is damned in the opinion of each. This hatred and division is increased by another momentous difference, the difference of the colours and caps which they wear. The Turks wear white turbans, and the Persians wear red bonnets. These are such abominable marks of heresy and schism, as deserve to be expiated with blood: And therefore that heresy has always been assigned as a principal cause of their many mutual invasions, merciless wars, and devastations.

I wish I could not say, that the wise and grave English nation have had also their holy and outrageous quarrels about words and motions, crape and cloth, bonnets and colours, and about the eastern and western situation of joint-stools.[7] Thank God it is not quite so bad at present, no thanks to our education.

I would, for a conclusion to this letter, only desire it to be considered, what infamy and contempt it reflects upon the human understanding, and indeed upon the human species, to be thus apt to run into discord and animosities upon such wretched and unmannerly motives; and what monsters and impostors they must be, who begin, or manage, or heighten these absurd and impious contentions amongst any part of the race of men, already too unhappy by the lot of nature.

G   *I am, &c.*

NO. 135. SATURDAY, JULY 6, 1723.

❧ *Inquiry into the indelible Character claimed by some of the Clergy.*

SIR,

I have lately given you[1] the genuine meaning of two very nonsensical words, as they are vulgarly understood, those of *hereditary right*. In this I shall a little animadvert upon two other words in

---

7. The eastern and western situation of joint stools: The term has no precise meaning and is apparently here used solely to express ridicule.

---

1. See Letter No. 132 (June 8, 1723).

as much use, even the *indelible character*. This I choose to do, because no small number of ecclesiasticks, and some, as I have heard, of the highest character, dare to assert, that though the late Bishop of Rochester[2] be deprived of his bishoprick, and expelled the kingdom, yet *He remains a bishop of the Universal Church,* which are some more nonsensical words. Indeed, there is scarce a theological system in the world (legal establishments excepted), but contains almost as many falsehoods as words, and as much nonsense as matter. Give the corrupt priests but some odd, unintelligible, and ill-favoured words, suppose *hic haec hoc*,[3] *trim tram, bow wow, fee fa fum,* or any other sound that is utterly void of any rational meanings, they shall instantly find profound mystery in it, and fetch substantial advantages out of it: Nay, when they are got in full possession of the said word, you are damned if you deny it to be sense, and damned if you endeavour to make sense of it.

The *indelible character*, is one of their beloved phrases, from which they derive great importance and authority; yet it is a palpable contradiction to all common sense. By it they mean a certain invisible faculty, which is peculiar to themselves, of doing certain duties, which they could have done as well before they had it. It is a divine commission, or power, to do that every where, which human powers can hinder them from doing any where. It neither conveys virtue, holiness, nor understanding, and has no visible operation; but authorizes those who are possessed of it to use certain words, and perform certain actions and ceremonies, and act certain motions, all which most other men could pronounce, perform, and act as well as they can, but, they tell us, not with equal effect: But then this effect is no ways visible, nor comprehensible, but through faith, and is far above all human conception.

How then, and by what marks, shall we know that any one has attained to this indelible character? Not from scripture, which is wholly silent about the matter. Not by succession from the apostles, who claimed no such power; as is unanswerably proved in the *Independent Whig*, nos. 6 and 7. Not from reason, the impossibility of it being there fully shewn in nos. 15. And the wickedness

2. Dr. Francis Atterbury, who was exiled by act of Parliament in 1723.
3. The Latin equivalent to "blah, blah, blah."

of pretending to it being as fully shewn in nos. 47 and 48. Not
from the laws of England, which oblige all clergymen to own, that
they receive all jurisdiction and authority whatsoever from the
crown, as is demonstratively proved in nos. 13 and 14 and in nos.
49 and 50.[4] It is as undeniably proved there by numerous texts, as
well as by the whole bent of scripture, that no one Christian has
more power than another, to perform all the offices of Christianity; that the Holy Ghost fell upon all believers alike, and that they
had all the power of doing miracles, after they had received it: And
I think it is as evident, that none of them have now the power of
doing miracles, as this would be with a witness, if a few words pronounced, and few motions performed, should give to any one new
qualities and faculties which he had not before. I am sure, if this be
a miracle, it is an invisible one, much like that of the popish transubstantiation, where, though we are told, that the bread and wine
are changed into flesh and blood, yet to human eyes they appear
to be bread and wine still. We are so far from being told in holy
writ, that elders, pastors, and teachers (for all priesthood is plainly
abolished by our Saviour in any other sense than as all Christians
are priests), are always to choose one another; that even an apostle
in the first of the *Acts* is chosen by the congregation, and by the
casting of lots.[5]

   But these gentlemen are sometimes so modest, as to confess, that holy orders do really convey neither piety, morals, learning, nor increase the natural faculties in any respect: I desire
therefore to know of them, what they are good for, unless to
declare, that such a man has undertaken to execute an office, and

4. *The Independent Whig* (London: Printed for J. Peele, 1721). Letter 6 (Feb.
24, 1720): "Of Creeds and Confessions of Faith"; Letter 7 (Mar. 2, 1720): "Of
Uninterrupted Succession"; Letter 15 (Apr. 27, 1720): "The Absurdity and
Impossibility of Church Power as Independent of the State"; Letter 47 (Dec. 7,
1720) and Letter 48 (Dec. 14, 1720): "All Priestly Power Inconsistent with the
Gospel and Renounced by It"; Letter 13 (Apr. 13, 1720): "The Church Proved
a Creature of Civil Power by Acts of Parliament and the Oaths of the Clergy";
Letter 14 (Apr. 20, 1720): "The Clergy Proved to be Creatures of the Civil
Power by the Canons and Their Own Public Acts"; Letter 49 (Dec. 21, 1720):
"An Inquiry Into Religious Establishments, With a Further Confutation of the
Impious and Absurd Claims of High Priests"; Letter 50 (Dec. 24, 1720): "Of
the Three High Churches in England."
5. Acts 1.15-26.

that he has natural or acquired qualifications sufficient to perform it? And this trust is for the most part committed to clergymen, who are presumed best to understand their own trade; and the ceremony which they use to signify that declaration, is laying on of hands, and a form of words prescribed by act of Parliament; which ceremony has obtained the name of consecration and ordination. Now suppose that the law had appointed another form to be executed only by laymen, as by flourishing a sword over his head, and by putting a cap and long gown upon him; would not the same man with the same qualifications, be just as good a pastor? Or suppose that the bishop, who ordained him, through some mistake, had not himself gone through all the operation, would the person ordained have been ever the worse? There is no appearance that our modern operators have any discernment of spirits; if they had, I presume that we should not have had so many Jacobites in holy orders; and 'tis evident in fact, that whenever the parishes choose their own parsons, they prove at least as good ones as those who are recommended to us by our spiritual fathers. 'Tis certain that our laws know nothing of this gibberish, but declare laymen capable of all sorts of ecclesiastical jurisdiction; and when the bishops consecrate one another, or ordain priests, they do it ministerially from the crown, and formerly took out a commission from the crown to ordain presbyters. Nay, the King now constitutes bishops in Ireland by commission; and they will be valid bishops, and able to perform all episcopal offices, though they were never consecrated. In Scotland, before the Revolution, they were created by patent, and held their sees only during the good pleasure of the crown.

Now let us consider what is the meaning of the word *bishop*, and wherein his office consists. It is a power or jurisdiction given to do certain actions within a certain district, which district is limited by human laws; and he must not execute his power in any other bishop's district, under the penalty of schism, and human punishment. Now what is this jurisdiction? It is a power to name a lay-chancellor if he pleases, who is to enquire after and punish certain carnal crimes, without consulting or taking any notice of the bishop himself, who constituted him; and excommunication is the legal process which he is to use, and the punishment which he is to inflict. The bishop has, moreover, a power to examine into the qualifications of those who desire to be admitted into orders, and to admit them, or reject them, as he finds them capable, or incapable; and after they are admitted, to inspect into their behaviour, in some respects, and to punish them according to stated laws. Now what is this priestly office? It is to read prayers, appointed by act of Parliament, publickly to the congregation; to read aloud certain chapters out of the Bible, appointed by publick authority to be read on particular days; to pick out a text or two every Sunday, and harangue upon it to the people; to administer the sacraments by a form of words prescribed by law, to visit the sick, exhort and rebuke, and to take the tithes. The bishop besides is to be a lord of Parliament, to have one or more thousands *per annum,* and to bless people when they are upon their knees.

Now what part of all this may not be as well executed, by what ceremony soever the person officiating be appointed, or if he be appointed without any ceremony at all? May not a bishop constitute a lay-chancellor to hear smutty causes, and to excommunicate the guilty, till they buy themselves out of purgatory again for a sum of money? Cannot this layman equally enquire into the capacities of those who were candidates for the priesthood, as they call it, and deprive or otherwise punish them as the law directs? Might not he equally sit in the House of Lords, and vote for the just prerogatives of the crown, and the good of the Church; make the most of his revenues (only for the sake of his successor), and say "God bless you" to any one who will ask it upon his knees? Might not a private man, though a bishop's hand had never touched his periwig, read aloud the publick prayers and the chapters for the day, when he can read at all, without any new inspiration; talk half an hour or more about the meaning of a plain text; exhort his parishioners to be good churchmen; rail at and revile dissenters; read the legal form of baptism, and sprinkle an infant; carry about the bread and wine to the communicants; repeat the words appointed in the Common Prayer Book to be said on that occasion; gather in tithes very carefully, and put any one into the spiritual court that does not pay them?

Now, what is deprivation, but by publick authority to hinder them from doing these things; that is to take away the power that it has given them? I think it is agreed by them all, that some of these powers might to taken away, namely, that of the bishops being members of the upper house, with their baronies and revenues, their lordships, their dignities, their spiritual courts, their legal jurisdiction within their former districts; but still, it seems they remain good bishops of the Universal Church; which character is indelible, and can never be taken away. But what they mean by the Universal Church, I cannot guess, unless they mean all Christian countries, or all countries where there are Christians: And then it seems that bishops may ordain presbyters, and bishops and presbyters both may preach and pray, give the sacraments, and excommunicate, wherever there are any Christians; and if the words *Universal Church* will extend to those who are no Christians, then they may do these things through the whole world. But how will this agree with another orthodox opinion, holden I think by them all, that no bishop can execute his office in another's diocese, and no priest in another's parish, against consent, without being guilty of schism? And here almost all Christendom is cut off from their ecclesiastical jurisdiction at once, and a good part of Turkey too, the Christians there having all bishops (such as they are): So that they are reduced to execute this universal power only *in partibus infidelium;*[6] and methinks, since sovereign authority is every where the same, Mahometan or pagan princes should have as much power to hinder any one from conferring offices in his dominions, as Christian princes have to confine him to a small limit, and to hinder him every where else; for no more power is necessary to one than to the other.

But to shew that I am in charity with these gentlemen, and willing to agree with them as far as I can admit, that no government, either Christian, Mahometan, or pagan, has any authority to hinder a good man from doing his duty to God; from saying his prayers, and reading the scriptures publickly; from exhorting his brethren, from giving or receiving the sacraments, or from avoiding ill company; which last is all that is meant in scripture, by what

6. "In the regions of the infidel."

we call excommunication: All which offices, or rather duties, every Christian is empowered by the gospel to execute. And as the clergy have been called upon oftener than once already to shew from scripture, or reason, that these duties, or any of them, are appointed by God, to be performed by any set or order of men whatsoever, independent of other Christians; so I call upon them again to shew it, and I expect that they will introduce plain and direct texts, or, at least, as much evidence as they would pay five shillings upon any other occasion. And if they cannot do this, as I shall presume they cannot, till the contrary appears; then all this artificial cant must pass for juggling, hypocrisy, and priestcraft.

If we will take some of their words for it, there are many things very strange and extraordinary in this divine trust. It may be given here below, but cannot be taken away again; for then it would not be indelible. It is a power to execute ecclesiastical jurisdiction or duty through the whole earth, yet may be confined to dioceses, or parishes. No human authority can hinder those who are possessed of it from executing it; yet their persons may be imprisoned, or put to death, and so be wholly disabled from executing it. They may be rendered incapable of performing it by diseases, by drunkenness, gluttony, and laziness; but not by murder, robbery, treason, blasphemy, or atheism. Non-execution, or wrong execution, is no forfeiture. It is the most tender and important of all trusts; yet no crimes, how heinous or black soever, will disqualify a man from holding and executing it. Whoever has once got it, can never part with it, but carries it with him to the block and the gallows; but whether it there leaves him, authors are silent, or uncertain.

It can be given by one of them to another only by the motion of the hand, but not by act of Parliament, and the consent of the States of a great kingdom, though the head of the church be one of them; yet it must be given according to the command of that one, and by a form of words enacted by all three. Whoever has it, must have a call from the Holy Ghost, yet must be examined whether he have common natural qualifications. When he has heard this call, and his qualifications are found sufficient, he need not execute what he is called to, but may hire another to do it for him; which other must not execute it neither, unless he has an human diocese, or an human parish, or is employed by those who have.

Is not this pretty jargon, worthy to be made an article of faith? Though it has had the ill luck not to get in amongst the rest; and, what is worse, some of the rest directly contradict it.

The same invisible faculty makes him, who is possessed of it, neither wiser nor better; yet he is to be much more respected, and his authority to be much more regarded, provided he be zealous for the notions which are orthodox for the time being; otherwise you may abuse him as much as you please, whether he be Most Reverend, Right Reverend, or only plain Reverend; and you need not then have any reverence at all for him, though the indelible character stick just where it did before. You must know that this indelible character came down by an uninterrupted succession from the apostles; but then it being wholly invisible, and making no alteration in the outward or inward man, there is some difficulty, and we are often at a loss to know who has it. The most common, outward and visible signs are a broad-brimmed hat, a long black gown, and a band; though others hold a cloak, with a cape to it, to be a better criterion. But what will become of us, if some heretick should have formerly usurped these holy garments, without having passed through all the precedent ceremony and operation? What if he should have happened to have consecrated and ordained a great many others, such as have continued the succession? Then, alas! the whole chain of succession may have been broken, never to be pieced again by human skill; and we can never know who amongst us are regular Christians, or in a regular way of salvation. Some are so wicked as to say, that this was the case of many of our Protestant bishops at the Reformation. Which God forbid!

Nay, what is worse, the orthodox differ amongst themselves about what requisites are necessary to continue this line of succession. Many have affirmed, that the Holy Ghost would not inhabit a heretick, a schismatick, a simoniack,[7] or an atheist: And some have went so far, as to assert, that a Christian bishop ought to be a Christian. Now it is certain, that there have been many bish-

7. Simoniac: a buyer of benefices.

ops and popes too, who did not believe one word about Jesus Christ; and if this be a disqualification, then the Lord have mercy upon those who have pretended to receive orders from them, or under them, and upon those who received the sacraments only by succession from such.

Others have ventured to affirm, that no greater power was necessary to take away orders than to give them. If so, the Pope and Church of Rome have taken away all our orders from us, and excommunicated us all to a man. Then too a question will arise, whether any one, who is wholly turned out of the Church, can be a bishop of the Church! If not, all our bench of bishops are gone at once: for we all know that the Church of Rome is a true church; and if the clergy have any authority from scripture, all the ecclesiastical authority in the world was against the first reformers, and they were all excommunicated together. They had certainly no power to separate themselves from the Church of Rome, but what every man in the world ever had, has now, and ever will have, to separate from any church which he thinks to be erroneous, and to disown all ecclesiastical authority, which does not take its force from the laws of the country which he lives under; and then it is only civil authority. I desire of the gentlemen, who have always shewn themselves very happy at distinctions, to clear up those matters to us, that we may know whether we be Christians or not, and in the ordinary way of salvation.

G   *I am, &c.*

❧ *The Popish Hierarchy deduced in a great Measure from that of the Pagans.*

Sɪʀ,

In my last I endeavoured to give you a true anatomy of the *indelible character*, and of the *uninterrupted succession*, from whence are derived most of the absurdities of the Romish Church,

with all the spiritual equipages of their popes, patriarchs, archbishops, bishops, parish-priests, &c. as well as all the powers
claimed by them in the Church. In this I shall give you their genealogy; as also the genealogy of their cathedrals, their altars, their
lighted candles upon them at noonday, their worshipping God
towards the east; and a great deal more of their religious trumpery. I cannot, after the most diligent enquiry, find out the least
countenance for most, if any, of these fine things, in the Christian
religion, and the Jewish is long since abolished. Our Saviour
plainly intended to reduce men to natural religion, which was corrupted and defaced by the numerous superstitions of the Jews, and
by the absurd idolatries of the Gentiles. The doctrine which he
taught, consisted only in worshipping one god, and in doing good
to men; and therefore he instituted a religion without priests, sacrifices, and ceremonies; a religion which was to reside in the heart,
to consist in spirit, and in truth; and to shew itself outwardly in
virtuous actions: But such a religion would not gratify the ambition and pride of those who desired to domineer over their brethren, and to acquire from their ignorance and fears, riches and
authority.

As therefore the Jewish priests had, by their traditions, and
their fabulous legends, corrupted the law of Moses; so the Christian clergy did by degrees blend the gospel, and the plain and easy
precepts of Christianity, with the most absurd parts of the Jewish
traditions, and with the ridiculous foppery of the religion of the
Gentiles; insomuch, that at the Reformation there was not left in
the world any thing that looked like Christianity. The Pope and his
priests had picked out from all other superstitions their most
absurd, cruel, and wicked parts and principles; and having incor-
porated the same with peculiar absurdities of their own, made out
of all such a wild jumble of nonsense and impieties, as has driven
virtue, good government, and humanity, almost out of the world;
given rise to Mahometanism; and both together have almost extinguished the human race; since there is not in those countries,
where these religions entirely prevail, the tenth part of the people
that they could boast in the times of the old Romans, nor in pro-

portion to the numbers which China and Holland can now boast; where the priests have no power, and but little influence.

It would be endless to trace all the numerous absurdities of the Romish Church, and to search the sources from whence they are all taken and stolen. I shall content myself here, to shew that their whole machinery is copied from the religion of Zoroaster and the Persian Magi; and shall quote no other authority than the excellent and learned Dr. Prideaux, but give an account of that impostor and his Magi, altogether in the doctor's own words.[1]

He tells us, that Zoroaster flourished in the reign of Darius Hystaspes[2] (though others say, very long before, as he says, the Magi did, who, without doubt, held many of the same opinions, he having only revived their sect with some alterations), and he taught, that there was one Supreme Being, independent and self-existent from all eternity: That under him there were two angels; one the Angel of Light, and the author and director of all good; the other the Angel of Darkness, the author and director of all evil; that this struggle shall continue to the end of the world, and then there should be a general resurrection, and a Day of Judgment, wherein just retribution should be rendered to all, according to their works; and the Angel of Darkness and his disciples should go into a world of their own, where they should suffer in everlasting darkness the punishment of their ill deeds; and the Angel of Light and his disciples should go into a world of their own, and receive in everlasting light, the rewards due to their good deeds.

This impostor[3] pretended to have been taken up to heaven, and there to have heard God speak to him out of the midst of the fire; and therefore he ordered fire-temples to be built, and erected altars in them, upon which sacred fires were kept and preserved, without being suffered to go out; and all the parts of their publick worship were performed before these publick sacred fires, as all their private devotions were before private fires in their own

1. The following account is taken from Prideaux's *The Old and New Testaments Connected*, pt. I, bk. IV (I:300–18).
2. That is, of Darius I of Persia, who reigned from 521 to 486 B.C.
3. That is, Zoroaster.

houses: Not that they worshipped the fire, but God in the fire; for God having spoken out of the fire, he said, that it was the surest *Shechinah*[4] of the Divine Presence; that the sun being the perfectest fire that God had made, there was the throne of his glory, and the evidence of his Divine Presence, in a more especial manner than any where else; for which reason he ordered them to direct all their worship towards the sun, and next towards their sacred fires; and therefore, they always approached them from the west-side; that having their faces towards them, and also towards the rising sun at the same time, they might direct their worship towards both; for the *kebla* of the Magians[5] being the rising sun, they always worshipped with their faces towards the east.

To gain the greater reputation to his pretensions, he retired to a cave, and there lived a recluse, pretending to be abstracted from all worldly considerations, and to be wholly given up to prayer and divine meditations. Whilst he was in his retirement, he composed the book wherein his pretended revelations are contained; which consisted of twelve volumes. The first contains the liturgy of the Magi, and the rest treat of the other parts of their religion. In this book he commands the same observances about beasts; clean and unclean, which Moses commands; gives the same law of paying tithes to the sacerdotal order; enjoins the same care of avoiding all external and internal pollutions; the same way of cleansing and purifying themselves by frequent washings; the same keeping the priesthood always within one tribe; and several other institutions are also therein contained, of the same Jewish extraction. The rest of its contents are an historical account of the life, actions, and prophecies of its author; the several branches and particulars of his new-reformed superstition; and rules and exhortations to holy living; in which he is very pressing, and sufficiently exact, saving only in one particular, which is about incest, which (the Doctor supposes) is allowed by him out of flattery to the Persian kings, who were exceedingly given to incestuous marriages. This book he pretends to have received from heaven; and accord-

4. *Shekhinah* is the most general rabbinic term for God's immanence.
5. The *qiblah* is the point toward which the Magians turn when worshipping.

ing as the actions of his sect agree or disagree with it, they are esteemed either good or evil.

His priests, as is said, are to be all of one tribe, and none but the son of a priest was capable of being a priest; and his priesthood he divided into three tribes. The lowest were the inferior clergy, who served in all the common offices of their divine worship. Next above these were the superintendents, who in their several districts governed the inferior clergy, as the bishops do amongst us; and above all was the Archimagus, or arch-priest, who was the same as the high-priest amongst the Jews, or the Pope now amongst the Romanists, and is the head of the whole religion: And, according to the number of their orders, the temples and churches in which they officiated, were of three sorts. The lowest sort, were their parochial churches, or oratories, which were served by their inferior clergy, as the parochial churches are now with us; and the duties which they there performed, were to read the daily offices out of their liturgy, and at stated and solemn times to read some part of their sacred writings to the people. In these churches there were no fire-altars; but the sacred fire before which they worshipped, was maintained only with a lamp. Next above these were the fire-temples, in which fire was continually kept burning on a sacred altar; and these were in the same manner as cathedrals with us, the churches or temples, where the superintendent resided. In every one of these were also several of the inferior clergy entertained, who, in the same manner as the choral vicars with us, performed all the divine offices under the superintendent, and also took care of the sacred fire, &c.

The highest church above all, was the fire-temple where the Archimagus resided, which was had in the same veneration with them, as the temple of Mecca among the Mahometans, to which every one of that sect thought themselves obliged to make a pilgrimage once in their lives. Zoroaster settled at Balch,[6] and he and the Archimagus his successors had their residence there; but afterwards it was removed to Herman.[7] This temple of the Archimagus, as also their other fire-temples, were endowed with large

6. Balkh, in modern-day Afghanistan.
7. Kerman, in modern-day Iran.

revenues in lands; but the parochial clergy depended only upon the tithes and offerings of the people. The Doctor observes afterwards, that this impostor having wonderful success in causing this imposture to be received by the King, the great men, and the generality of the whole kingdom, he returned to Balch; where, according to his institution, he was obliged to have his residence, as Archimagus, or head of the sect; and there he reigned with the same authority in spirituals over the whole empire, as the King did in temporals.

The Doctor observes, and perhaps with truth, that Zoroaster borrowed a great part of his new religion from the Jews, especially if he lived so late as he supposes him to have done, with some appearance of reason. But if the impostor took his doctrine of the immortality of the soul, and of rewards and punishments from them too (which he also supposes), it must have been from the Essenes, a sect among the Jews, not exceeding four thousand: For I cannot find any mention made of that doctrine in the books of Moses, which contain their laws, and promise only temporal blessings and punishments: And the Doctor himself, in another place, tells us, that the Sadducees,[8] who were the gentlemen, and men of learning amongst them, did wholly disbelieve the resurrection,[9] future rewards and punishments, angels and spirits, and rejected all the scriptures but the law; and that the Pharisees,[10] though they believed the resurrection, yet only thought it a Pythagorean resurrection, or transmigration of the same soul into another body: And I think it is plain from the New Testament, that the full revealing of this truth was reserved to our blessed Saviour, who brought life and immortality to light: Though it is undoubtedly true, that some of the Jews held it as a philosophical opinion, probably taken from the nations whom they conversed with: But it does not appear to

8. A theologically conservative group consisting mainly of Jewish aristocrats who rejected the beliefs, then common in Jerusalem, in bodily resurrection and in angels and demons.

9. That is, the resurrection of the body, not *the* Resurrection.

10. A Jewish religious party with a large following among the common people, regarded by some as embracing a purely formalistic observance of Jewish ritual. The Pharisees did, in fact, believe in bodily resurrection and in retribution in the world to come.

me, that Moses established it as a sanction to the religion which he revealed, or that it was any part of the Jewish religion to believe it.

But admitting that Zoroaster took the best parts of his religion from the Jews, I think it is much plainer that the Romanists have taken the worst parts of theirs from him; or else they have very luckily or unluckily jumped in the same thoughts. Their Archimagus, high-priest or pope, they can have no where else, unless they borrowed him from the Jews, which would be extremely impudent, since the Christian religion is built upon the ruins of theirs. Their superintendents, whom they call archbishops and bishops, and their parochial priests, whom they do not borrow from the Jews, and who, they say, are not derived from human institution, cannot be derived, in my opinion, from any other source than that of Zoroaster. Where else do they find the division of their priests into several orders, which exactly resemble his, namely, the lower order in parochial temples, to read offices out of their liturgies, or mass-books, and portions of their sacred writings at appointed times? for the Jews had not that oeconomy, nor indeed any synagogue-worship, till long after Zoroaster's time. Where else do they find cathedrals with altars in them, and lighted candles upon these altars, in imitation of the sacred fire of the Magi; and these altars standing to the east, and the worship in them performed with the face towards it? Where else the many inferior priests officiating in such temples, subordinate to the superintendent, and in ease to him? And where else the endowing these temples with lands, and revenues?

Where do they find their *uninterrupted succession &c.* and in consequence their *indelible character*, but in the succession of Zoroaster's priests in one tribe only, who without doubt were all holy, had all a divine right, were particularly favourites of the Divine Being, and clothed with peculiar powers and dispensations? Where had they the absurd and blasphemous opinion of God's being more immediately at the altar, or in the east, than in any other place; unless from the notion and dreams of the Magi, that the Divine Presence was in an especial manner in the sun, or in the fire? Where do they find that the deity is pleased with men's retiring into caves, corners, and monasteries; with their neglecting the affairs of the world, and of their families; with their being useless to society; and with their indulging meditation and the spleen; but in the example and authority of Zoroaster? Where do they find any command for wild jaunts in pilgrimage to the Holy Land, and for idle and enthusiastick devotions to shrines, altars, and chappels, unless in the injunctions of this impostor to all his votaries to visit the temple of Balch? And where else did they adopt the absurd, monstrous, and wicked hypothesis, of the Church's having a different head from the state, and of the independence of the priests upon the civil power?

Most of these opinions and practices are parts of the religion of the ancient Magi; and from thence it is reasonable to presume that the Romish priests have copied them, unless they can shew where else they had them. They cannot, with the appearance of common sense, be deduced from the New Testament; and the Jewish religion has been long since abolished. They have therefore the honour of having restored the old superstition of the Magi, with this material difference, that the latter had more learning, and much more integrity; that they did not do, by the hundredth part, so much mischief; and treated with more humanity those who differed from them.

T   *I am, &c.*

NO. 137. SATURDAY, JULY 20, 1723.

Of the different and absurd Notions which Men entertain of God.

SIR,

In my paper, which treats about the use of words,[1] I have promised to shew how absurd and impious it is for men to fall together by the ears, on account of their difference in trifles, when they scarce agree in any one thing in the world, not even in the attributes annexed to the object of all worship, though they know

1. See Letter No. 120 (Mar. 16, 1722).

nothing of him but from his attributes. I will now perform that promise.

There is no proposition about which mankind have agreed and disagreed so much, as about the meaning of the word *god*. I think, very few instances excepted, they have all agreed that there is such a being; and yet I apprehend, that no two nations, two sects, or scarce two men of the same sect, have essentially agreed in all the ideas which they have annexed to the sound. All have asserted, that he has existed from all eternity, and must for ever exist; and that he has made or produced every thing else: And thus far heathens and Jews, Mahometans and Christians, Protestants and papists, deists and free-thinkers, materialists and immaterialists, Stoicks, peripateticks and Epicureans, are all orthodox; for the last could not have doubted but some being must have existed before the fortuitous concourse of atoms; and in this sense there are very few, if there be one atheist, in the world. But when they go farther, and explain what they mean by the sound, I doubt most, or many of them, are atheists to one another, as not believing in the being which the one and the other call God.

All the differences amongst mankind, as to their belief of the deity, are owing to their different conceptions of him; as they disagree in his attributes, in the modes of his operations, and worship him under various images and representations. As to his substance, essence, the manner or *sensorium* of his existence, we neither know nor can know any thing, nor can have any conception about it, and consequently can believe nothing concerning it; and therefore all that we can believe (besides what I above said every man agrees in) is concerning his attributes, and the *modus* wherein he has communicated or represented himself to us: That is, we can only believe in the ideas which we have annexed in our minds to the word *god*; and if we annex different images to the word, we are of a different religion, or rather are atheists to one another, though we call the object of all our worship by the same name. For since, as I have said, we can only worship our own conceptions or images of the deity, or (by new placing the words) the deity under our conceptions and images, if those images be false, we worship only an idol of our own imaginations, and pay divine homage to nothing. For, what is the difference to us in saying, that another man believes in nothing, or believes in what we know to be nothing, which equally is atheism. From hence I think it appears, that no man has a right to call another atheist, in any other sense, than as I shall make appear, that most men have a right to call those who differ from themselves, in their conception of the deity, atheists.

Now, to begin with the heathens, who worshipped Jupiter, Mars, Venus, Mercury, &c. which were only bare sounds and non-entities: Their paying divine honours to nothing, was worshipping nothing: and believing in nothing, is the same thing in substance as having no belief. And therefore they were certainly atheists, though they did not know themselves to be so. For what is atheism, but not believing in a god? And can any man be said to believe in a god, whose whole belief is in an imaginary being that is not God; though I confess such a fancied belief may influence his actions, and answer many of the purposes of society? It was the same thing when they believed in real beings, as images, stocks, stones, monkeys, garlick, &c. For they worshipped them for powers which they supposed were in them, but which were not in them; and so worshipped those supposed powers, and consequently worshipped nothing, and believed in nothing which was God; and consequently were atheists in fact, though devout religionists in shew, and in their own opinion too.

But without annihilating the heathen deities, the Stoicks and Epicureans (who differed much in the same manner as some of the deists and orthodox do amongst us), were atheists to one another, as not believing in the attributes that each annexed to their different divinities. The Stoicks annexed the attributes of wisdom, mercy, and justice, to the being of the deity; who was supposed by them to dispense those attributes occasionally to the actions and necessities of men. The Epicureans thought the deity to be sufficient in his own felicity; and that he did not concern himself with our affairs here below; but that all things depended upon fate, and an eternal cause, which controlled and was superior to even Jupiter himself; which fate must have been their eternal god, which produced all things at first.

They had no notion of what was meant by *wise, merciful,* and *just,* when applied to the deity; and thought that these could not be analogous to what was meant by the same qualities in men: For they said, that wisdom in men, was only balancing the motives of doing or not doing an action, and choosing which was best; which wisdom was a knowledge acquired by habit and experience, and by observing the relations of things to one another, and conveyed to them through the organs of sense: But they said, that the deity had no organs, but saw all things intuitively from all eternity, and could not err. So they said, that mercy in men was a passion caused by the feeling or apprehension of the sufferings of others: But they believed that the divinity could have no passions, because no agent could operate upon him, he himself being eternal, and before all things, and producing all things; nor could suffer temporary anguish and uneasiness, always produced by compassion. In like manner, they said, that justice was an adherence to certain rules, dictated by superior powers, or agreed upon by men for their mutual convenience; but no rules could be set to the divinity, who the Stoicks confessed had made every thing, and had a right to do what he pleased with his own creatures. He that made the relation of all things, might alter that relation, and dispense with his own laws, when and how he thought fit.

They therefore said, that when those attributes were applied to the deity, nothing could be meant by them, but to express our reverence for him, our admiration of his power, and to sacrifice to him our best conceptions; not that we pretend to define his essence, nor the *modus* of his actions, which are wholly incomprehensible to us. They concluded that he that had done all things could do all things; but did not pretend to know how he did them; but thought themselves very sure that he did not do them as we do, by weighing the difficulties on each side the question, because nothing could be difficult to him; nor could he deliberate, because deliberation would imply doubt; and the deity could not doubt, being necessitated by the excellency of his nature always to do the best.

They thought, that a being that could never have any cause before it, nor without it, or after it, but what it produced, nor any objects to work upon it, must have been always uniform and entire; that is, its attributes, its will, and its actions must have been one with its essence. It must have been constantly moving, or acting or, as late divines very elegantly express themselves, eternally proceeding. For there could be no beginning of action, without being at rest before; and then they said that it must have been from all eternity at rest, as finding it difficult to conceive, that a being that had self-motion should never have exerted that principle till a particular period of time, and in a particular portion of space, when eternity and infinity (its inseparable attributes) can have no periods and limits; nor can any intervals of time and space measure such a being.

Hence philosophers have called eternity a *nunc sans*, or an instant, or punctum, which cannot be divided even in imagination; and though they could not convey any distinct images by that way of speaking, yet they found themselves reduced to it, from the difficulties which would arise in dividing the operations of a being in all respects indivisible. Now, can any one say that these sects believe in God? Certainly the object of the belief of one of them was not God, but only an idol of their own brains, and consequently that sect believed in nothing, and were atheists.

The same observations run through the different sects of religionists in the world, and great numbers of particular men in every sect of religion. Some represent the deity as a capricious, angry, revengeful being, fond of commendation and flattery, prescribing and dictating partial rules to his creatures, laying useless burdens upon them, and making their future happiness to depend upon the actions of others, and upon such performances, or believing such speculations, as are out of their power. Others think that the deity has satiety of happiness within itself, and must be incapable of any passions to interrupt that happiness; and therefore, as we cannot do good or harm to him, the only way to recommend ourselves to him, is to do good to one another. These cannot apprehend, that any man's future felicity lies in another's power; or, that useless speculations or actions, as bows, cringes, forms, grimaces, rotes of words, or any thing but a good conscience, and a virtuous life, can make us acceptable to the deity. Now 'tis certain that there are great numbers of men in the world of both these opinions, and they undoubtedly do not believe in the same being; but some of them believe in a non-entity, and consequently are atheists.

If this argument were to be traced through all its subdivisions, it would fill a volume instead of a single paper; and therefore I shall tire you no farther upon the subject; my design in entering upon it being to warn my countrymen how cautious they ought to be in calling odious names, which may with equal justice be retorted upon themselves. Let us therefore leave such appellations to those who scold for hire; and rest fully assured, that as most certainly there is a God, so he is the best being in the universe, that he expects no more from us than he has given us means to perform; that when we have done all in our power to please him, we shall please him, however, or how much soever, we mistake his being or attributes; and then it will be of very little consequence whom else we displease.

T   *I am, &c.*

NO. 138. SATURDAY, JULY 27, 1723.

🙰   *Cato's Farewell.*

SIR,

As I have with a success which no man has yet met with (if I regard the number of my readers, and the sale of these papers) carried on a weekly performance, under this and another title,* for near four years; in doing which, it was impossible that I could have any other view but the good of my country and of mankind; by shewing them the advantage and the beauty of civil and ecclesiastical liberty, and the odious deformity of priestcraft and tyranny: As I have vindicated Almighty God, and the religion which he has taught us, from the superstition, follies, and wickedness of men, who would prostitute it to ambition and avarice, and

* *The Independent Whig.*

build a visionary empire upon the plain and simple precepts of Christianity; and have endeavoured to remove all the rubbish, grimace, and pageantry, with which it has been long stifled and oppressed, by shewing to the world, and I think proving, that true piety consists only in honouring the deity, and in doing good to men, and not in postures, cringes, and canting terms, and in barren and useless speculations: As I think I have unanswerably shewn that civil governments were instituted by men, and for the sake of men, and not for the pride and lust of governors; and consequently that men have a right to expect from them protection and liberty, and to oppose rapine and tyranny wherever they are exercised; and have thereby vindicated our present establishment, which can pretend to no other title.

As I have done all this openly, and in the face of the world, and have defied and called upon all the merciless and detestable advocates for superstition and slavery, to shew that I have transgressed the rules of morality or religion, or the peace and happiness of society in any respect; and no one has yet dared to enter the lists against me; from whence I may reasonably hope that I have removed many of the prejudices imbibed by education and custom, and set many of my countrymen free from the wild, wicked, and servile notions, strongly infused and planted in their minds by craft and delusion: I shall now with cheerfulness lay down this paper, which I am well informed will be continued by an able hand, under another name, and upon various subjects; and it is probable that I may so far join in the undertaking, as to give my assistance now and then, when proper occasions require it;[1] at least, I am not determined not to do so.

There are some papers, especially those signed Diogenes,[2] which have given an undesigned offence to some, whose persons I honour, and whose opinions I reverence. For I have no regard to the persons, and narrow notions of bigots, who will renounce any opinion as soon as it appears to be rational, and would rather make

1. The six letters that follow, which were first appended to the third edition (1733) of the *Letters* by Gordon, originally appeared in the *British Journal* over the name of Criton.

2. This apology is clearly ironic since none of Cato's letters bears Diogenes' name.

nonsense of it, than not make it a mystery. It is a principle become constitutional to me, that God gave us our understandings to use them, and that we cannot offend him in carrying them as far as they will carry us. However, as the principal question handled in those papers is a matter of mere speculation, understood but by few, and to be understood but by few, the belief or disbelief of it can no way affect human society; and whether it be true or not, the actions of men will be the same, and men will be alike actuated by the motives that operate upon them, and equally pursue what they take to be their advantage upon the whole, at the time, and in the circumstances which they are then in, whether they be obliged to do so, or choose to do so without being necessitated to that choice.

What led me into this thought, is the observation which runs almost through the world, that the bulk of mankind in all ages, and in all countries, are violently attached to the opinions, customs, and even habits, which they have been used to; that sounds, shews, prejudices, vain and idle terrors, phantoms, delusions, and sometimes diet and physick, are more prevalent with them, and operate more upon them than true and strong reasons; and that all animals of the same species act in the same manner, and have the same passions, sensations and affections, with very little alterations: All which I could not account for, but by supposing those operations to be mechanical, and the results of their several constitutions, as they were altered and modified by habit, and by different occasions or motives of making use of them, such as acted upon them.

For the rest, I saw, with a sensible concern, the many mischiefs, which the leaders and deceivers of parties and factions in religion did to the world, by throwing God's judgments at one another, and impiously confining his providence and mercies to themselves; and by applying the common phenomena and events of nature to their own advantage, and interpreting the same as denunciations of his wrath against their enemies; by which unhallowed presumption they have raised up and inflamed implacable hatred, animosities and uncharitableness amongst men of the same nation, who are all brethren. I have therefore shewn, that the Almighty dispenses his favours to all his creatures; that his sun shines upon the just and the unjust; and that it is the highest and most daring boldness in any sort of men to search into, and to pretend to unriddle the secret dispensations of his providence; to know his mind before he unfolds it; to throw about such balls of contention and wrath; and to make the condition of men, already too miserable by the lot of nature, still more miserable.

I saw the many evils and barbarous consequences arising from the idle and foolish stories of witches, spirits, and apparitions, first infused into our tender minds by nurses, chamber-maids, and old women, and afterwards continued and improved by tutors and priests; which impressions and stories the wisest and bravest men often carry about them to their graves, and which make them always uneasy till they go thither; insomuch, that numbers of people dare not be alone, nor go about their necessary affairs, in the night-time; but are kept in constant dread of phantoms and non-entities; and multitudes of innocents have been murdered under the appearance of justice upon Satan's confederates. I have therefore shewn, that there is no foundation in nature, in reason or in religion, for these fairy tales; that they are inconsistent with the mercies, and even with the being, of the great and good God; and that the telling or believing these tales, is endeavouring to give an empire to the Devil at the expence of the Almighty.

It is certain, that the capacities of men would carry them much farther than they are suffered to go, if they were not cramped by custom and narrow education, and by narrow principles taken from those who design and derive advantages from this their ignorance. I have therefore lamented to see men of large and extensive genius, such as seemed designed by nature to carry human knowledge many degrees further than it has yet gone, seemed designed to manumit their country and mankind from the servile and wicked notions infused into them by prating pedants, and babbling impostors; I say, I have lamented to see such extensive capacities employed and conversant only about whims, idle speculations, empty notions, fairy-dreams, and party-distinctions, all tending to contract and imbitter the mind, to stifle and oppress the faculties, and to render men dupes and machines to the ambition, pride, and avarice of selfish and haughty ecclesiasticks, or of corrupt statesmen. Nor can I see how this great evil can ever be

cured, till we change the education of our youth; and let gentlemen be bred by gentlemen, and not by monks and pedants; whom
yet I would suffer to dream on with their bellies full of college-ale,
and their heads full of college-distinctions; but think that they
ought not to be trusted with the education of our nobility and gentry, till they have some themselves.

And now I beg leave again to repeat, that it was impossible
I could engage in this undertaking so troublesome to myself, and I
hope of some benefit to my countrymen, with any view to my own
personal advantage. I hope that no one will think so meanly of my
understanding, to believe that I intended to make my court to any
of the powers of this world, by attacking vice, corruption and folly
wheresoever and in whomsoever they were found. I knew that I
was to walk over burning plough-shares; that I must provoke
numerous and powerful societies and parties; that I must disturb
nests of hornets, and sometimes venture too near the lion's den,
and perhaps within the reach of Jove's thunder; that men in possession of reverence would not bear being told, that they did not
deserve it; that those who rioted in power, and upon the publick
misfortune, would very unwillingly hear that they were trusted
with that power for the publick advantage, and not for their own;
that they were obliged by all the motives of honour, virtue, and
religion, to serve and protect the people out of whose industry and
wealth they were so highly rewarded; and that they deserved the
severest punishment if they did otherwise. I had all this before my
eyes: But armed with innocence, and animated by love to God and
mankind, I resolved to brave the danger, in defiance of the worst
that could happen to myself, in the service of my country; and I
have braved it. I have now the pleasure to see great numbers of my
fellow-subjects approve my endeavours, and embrace my opinions.
I therefore here lay down this paper, and with it the most virtuous
and noble subject that can employ the human soul; the subject of
religion and government.

T and G   *I am, &c.*
                                        CATO

The End of the Fourth Volume.

❧ ADVERTISEMENT TO THE READER.

After Mr. Trenchard and I had agreed to conclude Cato's Letters, *we likewise agreed to publish occasional papers upon such subjects of moment as occurred to us. But as he was not long after seized with the distemper that soon bereft the publick of his valuable life, the pursuit of that design was left altogether to me; and I continued to publish from time to time several papers upon religious subjects, and a few upon political subjects. The latter, six in number, are therefore subjoined to this edition of* Cato's Letters, *as naturally belonging to that collection. The former, which are a much greater number, upon the subject of religion and controversy, I intend to throw together as a third volume of* The Independent Whig, *since they treat of the like matters.*

T. GORDON

957

AN APPENDIX

*Containing additional
letters by Cato*

That ambitious Princes rule and conquer only for their own Sakes; illustrated in a Dialogue between Alexander the Great and a Persian.

SIR,

Man is more selfish than all other creatures; as habit, or imagination, has made more things necessary to his pleasure and convenience, than other animals want for theirs. Lust and hunger are their only appetites; further than these prompt them, they commit no ravages, and they have the plea of necessity for the evils which they do. None of them invade countries for the vanity of a title; nor enslave, plunder, and burn, out of pride. They have no avarice; they do not starve millions to surfeit one, or a few. They have no ambition; they do not destroy for glory. To the disgrace of humanity, and the misfortune of the world, all these mischiefs and abominations come from the impulse of human passions, from a ravenousness and ferocity, worthy only of wild beasts, but practised by men with much more extensive and successful cruelty. The false refinements of reason have taught them to make the earth a wilderness, or a shambles; and to commit oppressions and butcheries, which true reason abhors.

Men are so conceited, that they think they deserve every thing they want, and may do every thing to procure it; and nothing but fear restrains man from dealing with man as nations deal with

961

nations, that is, from devouring one another. There is not a city or country in the world, but, were it let alone, would swallow up all the rest; and cities and countries are compounded of men, and governed by them. And, as every nation is in its own conceit better than another, almost every man in every nation is in his own opinion better than all the rest. Some may ask, whether a poor labourer in a ditch fancies himself as good a man as the lord of the soil? I answer, try him: Offer him the manor, and then see whether, from a mean opinion of his merit, he rejects the offer. Who is it that refuses or resigns greatness, from the inaptness of his talents to sustain it? Titles and honours are only due to merit; but who denies them from a sense of the want of it? On the contrary, are not the weakest and most worthless men the easiest puffed up with the vanity of a gay name; which is so far from giving them any intrinsick advantages, that it really exposes their defects? And do they not make one acquisition, which they merited not, a ground and reason for expecting and demanding, perhaps for extorting, others, which they merit as little? Great men are sometimes supplanted and undone by their creatures; and princes have had the crown taken from their head, and with it their life, by such as they had raised from the dust.

Leave men to take the full reward of their fancied merit, and the world will be thought too little for almost every individual, as Alexander thought it for him. He had the fortune to ravage the world, and from thence believed he had a right to it. *Omnia vult, qui omnia potest.*[1] Men thus let loose, do no more mischief than they can, nor less. The world is therefore a foot-ball; a great scene of contention, revolutions, and misery: It is full of Alexanders.

For the better illustration of this subject, I will here subjoin a dialogue between Alexander the Great and a Persian.

Alex. I find you a man of understanding; and you shall say with security what you please: But sure you must acknowledge that I have acquired everlasting glory in conquering this great empire.

1. "He wants all things who is able to do all things."

Pers. You have done many horrible things for this glory; made havock of mankind, all Asia a scene of blood, and the world a theatre of sorrow and violence, to gain it.

Alex. Is not glory thus gained?

Pers. More is the shame and the pity, that so wicked a thing should have so fine a name. If you had saved us from all the evil, that you have done us, I should have called it glory.

Alex. Great actions are glorious, let the consequences be good or bad.

Pers. Then I perceive there is no difference between good and bad actions; at least great mischief is as good and as glorious for your purpose as great good.

Alex. For the mischiefs that you have suffered, your king must answer: He drew the war upon you.

Pers. How so?

Alex. Xerxes, one of his predecessors, invaded Greece.

Pers. If he did it wantonly, he did wrong, and sacrificed many lives to his pride: But I thought all this had been glory, because you seek glory the same way.

Alex. No, I revenge Greece upon Persia.

Pers. So he did Persia upon Greece, though with less advantage to him, and less detriment to the Grecians. Besides, he is dead, and it is unjust to punish those who hurt you not, for those who hurt your ancestors a great while ago.

Alex. Greece and Persia still subsist.

Pers. They are still called Persia and Greece; but the men of whom you complain no longer subsist.

Alex. Darius, your present Emperor, whom I have so often beaten, still lives, and he oppressed the Greek cities in Asia.

Pers. So he did the Persian cities, and his whole empire; or his governors did it for him. Now if you had come and relieved us, and gone back again, I should not differ with you about the notions of glory: But to invade us, and make us the plunder of armies for another man's crimes, which we condemn, and could not help, is no glory to us.

Alex. I meant his subjects no harm.

Pers. But you have done it as effectually as if you had.

Alex. I could not come at him, without killing his soldiers, and subduing his people.

Pers. Then you should have let him alone, at least till he had molested you.

Alex. He did; he enthralled my brethren the Asiatick Greeks; which I could not brook.

Pers. Give me leave to say, you have enthralled Greece itself, and Asia, and the world. How comes thraldom from Alexander to be better than thraldom from Darius? or why should it be better brooked?

Alex. I see you are no politician: You do not consider, that when I was about to invade Asia, it would have been madness to have left Greece unsubdued behind me.

Pers. The great Mithra[2] shining yonder over our heads, and witnessing our actions, preserve all sober men from madness; and, for the peace of mankind, restore all madmen to their senses! And so, to revenge Greece upon Asia, which a hundred years before would have subdued Greece, you subdued Greece yourself, in order to subdue us harmless Asiaticks, who never saw any of your faces, till you came sword in hand to kill and oppress us for glory. You have arrived at that glory: And now I hope you will leave us, and return home.

Alex. No: Your King Darius still lives.

Pers. What! would you kill him?

Alex. No.

Pers. Then why do you pursue him?

Alex. To have him in my power.

Pers. And make him a captive and a slave; which is worse than killing him. But when you have him in your power, do you propose to set him up again, or in his room another royal Persian, who has not offended you?

Alex. No: Whom can I set up so worthy as Alexander, over the conquests of Alexander?

2. Mithras was the Persian god of light, worshipped in both Hinduism and Zoroastrianism.

Pers. Doubtless none so brave to maintain them. But what right do you claim to the crown of Persia?

Alex. My sword; that sword which has conquered it.

Pers. While that right is in such hands, few will care to dispute it. But were I, who am no conqueror, to drive away my neighbour's flocks and herds, and make them my own, I doubt you would call it robbery, and impale me alive.

Alex. Doubtless: I conquered the Persian empire; but I will protect the Persians in their lives and property: It is suitable to my generosity and justice.

Pers. In conquering us you have destroyed many lives, and much property, against all justice; and reserve the rest for your own use, whenever and as often as you think fit to take them.

Alex. It is the right of war.

Pers. War is then an unrighteous and inhuman thing, and entitles the next invader (if his sword be longer than yours, and his fortune superior) to drive you out, as you have done Darius.

Alex. Who shall dare to brave Alexander? Who contend with the son of a god?

Pers. Methinks you come not very honourably by that divine pedigree, and carnal divinity; which reflects some disgrace too upon your mother, and her husband Philip, and is not much to the reputation of this god of the desert. But who told you that he was your father?

Alex. His priests.

Pers. They would have told me as much, had I been there at the head of an army in quest of a celestial descent. It is no great credit to be akin to the figure of a ram: It is at least as much honour to be akin to the next palm-tree, or to the next marble-quarry, the elements of such inanimate deities.

Alex. Blaspheme not the gods, if thou wouldest avoid their vengeance: They will punish thee, though I forbear.

Pers. If the son forgive me, I will venture the displeasure of the father. I honour that only god, whose bright image I behold in the skies; nor fear the indignation of a piece of a trunk, or of a rock, however fashioned; unworthy kindred of the great Alexander, the most exalted of men, but subject to pain, misfortunes, and grief, and all the symptoms of mortality: The conqueror of Asia, the avenger of Greece, must die. But first, how is Greece avenged?

Alex. By conquering Persia.

Pers. You have ruined both: But of the two you have rather revenged Persia upon Greece. The lesser follows the greater. You are already monarch of Asia; and Greece, which you have enslaved, will be but a province of Persia: You do the very thing which you were so incensed against our former princes for intending. If your sovereignty continue, Persians will in time be sent governors of Greece; nay, you yourself, who are a Greek, wear already a Persian habit.

Alex. I have made the world my own, and will do with it as I list.

Pers. You do so; but it is more than you would suffer others to do, who thought they had a better right. If you be innocent, how were the Persian monarchs faulty?

Alex. I am Alexander, the son of Jupiter, and conqueror of the world.

Pers. Nay, they had sublime titles too, and heavenly alliances. They were lords of the world, and brothers of the sun; a more illustrious and visible deity than Jupiter the ram.

Alex. Their gods could not protect them; and mine have given me their empire. Once more, I am Alexander; the world is mine, and I will keep it.

Pers. Now this is open and fair dealing, worthy the great spirit of Alexander. You had a mind to the world, and you took it; nor think it enough for you. If you had made this frank declaration at first, I should not have troubled you with so much contradiction. If the great and bold mind of Alexander can stoop to dissemble, we are never to expect that men will own the true motives of their conduct. Their reason is just what their passion pleases. All their plausible and framed pretences are resolvable into some selfish appetite, which, like their conceit, is generally unmeasurable.

G   *I am, &c.*

NO. 2. SATURDAY, SEPTEMBER 14, 1723.

Considerations upon the Condition of an absolute Prince.

SIR,

There is no human condition but what carries uneasinesses with it; and I believe it will be difficult to know what condition makes men most happy, or happy at all. There is no judging of it by outward appearances. We often envy others for what they find misfortunes; and pity them for things, which are blessings, and either make them happy, or hinder them from being miserable. Nothing can be happiness in this world but gratifying our desires and inclinations; and yet we can seldom gratify them to any degree, but by turning them into misfortunes; yet we must gratify them in some degree, or else we can have no happiness at all.

To have no desires (if that be possible) is a perfect state of stupidity; and our desires must be always to attain what we do not then enjoy, and often what we cannot compass. This produces uneasiness, or in other words, renders us unhappy in some degree. The man therefore who has fewest desires, or desires the least difficult to be accomplished, has the least unhappiness; but wants many agreeable sensations, which men of more lively and active spirits enjoy. So that, upon the whole, if we balance the account, men have little reason to envy or pity one another: But if there be any difference between them, the condition of absolute princes and great men is by far the most miserable. They have little relish of the enjoyments, which they possess; they are always pursuing things difficult to be obtained, and are in as constant fear and danger of losing what they have, as of gaining what they have not; and if they do gain it they are seldom the better, but often plunged into new difficulties by their success.

Great fortune comes attended with great cares, and much greatness has many incumbrances. This is the condition of a despotick prince, who, having much more business than himself can do, be his diligence ever so great, must share the great weight and multiplicity of his affairs amongst many; who will be but too apt, in the administration of their several parts, to attend more to their own greatness and advantages, than to their master's reputation and security, to justify their ill actions by his authority, and to acquire grandeur and riches to themselves, while they heap obloquy upon him.

This is often the true reason why a good prince is not always popular. People will judge of him by what is done, and not by what he causes to be done; and therefore the publick dislike rarely stops at his servants, who perhaps alone deserve it; but have often the art of involving him in the ill consequences of their own conduct, and of making their crimes complete, by engaging him to support them in their crimes, by persuading him that all their views and actions were for his service, and by frightening him with this false and mischievous maxim, That *a prince must never give up his servants:* A maxim fatal to many princes, and big with nonsense and with ruin to the people, as it makes all ministers, even the weakest and the worst, perfectly unaccountable!

This is an unnatural maxim: Nor have the most absolute monarchs, though their power be erected upon the violent abasement of human nature, and upon the ruins of all goodness, happiness, and virtue, been ever able to practise it, however they may want it, and in speculation pretend to it. The Great Turk is often forced to give up his servants, who must die for his crimes, as well as for their own; so far is he from sacrificing himself for theirs, as this maxim would direct. Nor is there an arbitrary prince in the world but must give up the best minister that he has, if his army demand it; and where the people have any share of power, no well-advised prince will employ a servant whom they justly hate and suspect.

Princes are set in a high place; which, though the most coveted of all, has the least happiness of any other. Those, who have no equals, can hardly have any friends; and a particular friendship and confidence between an arbitrary prince and any of his own subjects, is seldom sincere on either side, especially on theirs; and often fatal to him, sometimes to them. Such princes are most successfully betrayed by their greatest favourites, who are likewise frequently undone for being favourites. Nor can princes, with all their power, raise to the highest place those who are highest in their favour. Interest, or ambition, and sometimes fear, determines their choice; and their first minister is often the man whom they hate most, or dread most, which is the beginning of hatred. Nero hated Seneca and Burrhus; and Lewis XIII hated Cardinal Richelieu; as did King James I towards his latter end, the Duke of Buckingham.[1] Even the crafty, implacable, and diffident Tiberius was forced to continue the traitor Sejanus in his power, places and trust, a good while after he had full proof that he sought his life and empire.

The greatest princes therefore are generally destitute of friends. To purchase friends, they must give them power; and power cancels all friendships. It is the most selfish thing in the world. Those who have it are too frequently faithless to the giver; and when it is taken away, always ungrateful. And this is the reason why they may dislike their ministers, and yet be loth to change them: They know, that to dismiss their servants, is to multiply their enemies. So they are forced to accept faint or false services, to prevent open opposition; which they who have been in their service, and know their affairs and designs, are the best qualified to make.

The opening of one's heart to a friend, is one of the greatest pleasures and reliefs arising from friendship; and private men can practise it, because where the reputation of keeping a secret is greater than the temptation to reveal it, it will be kept: But to whom can a prince lay open his heart in any great and tender point, when by doing it he puts his safety and reputation in the power of another, who must be paid dear for being faithful; and perhaps at last is not so, because he never thinks himself sufficiently paid!

Hence princes and great men are naturally close and reserved, and keep themselves as far as possible within their own power: They know that the fidelity of men is then only greater than their treachery, when the price is greater. Secrecy is indeed so absolutely necessary in great affairs, that he who wants it is utterly unfit for them; and I have known very little men, who, with this

1. In 1624, Buckingham, against James's wishes, maneuvered the King into a war with Spain while allying England with France. This action certainly weakened James's affection for Buckingham, although it is an exaggeration to say that he hated him.

qualification alone, have been thought great men. Sometimes men are dark and cautious from the littleness of their talents; and employments and trust generally make men so.

As to the publick friendships of princes, that is, of princes with princes, it is generally grimace; and there can scarce be any such thing. They are all rivals for power and credit; and all envy, or are envied by, one another. Nor do treaties and alliances allay their jealousies and heart-burnings, but often increase them: They are generally made out of fear, and always imply distrust. Men of power, at least men of equal power, princes or subjects, never agree but from the necessity of their affairs; and they too often seem to be friends, on purpose to execute their malice with the greater certainty. Every particular wants to be master, and to give laws to all the rest; and they often push their mutual diffidence even to ridicule, and fall into violence and quarrels about the ceremonial; which, like some other ceremonies, signifies not a straw to the rest of the world, and yet must be owned to be of considerable consequence to those that deal in it.

Nor are princes more happy in their families. They are unhappy if they have no children, because by it conspiracies are encouraged, as one life is easier destroyed than several. Julius Caesar had no child; and the tyrannicides hoped in him to have destroyed his family. The same consideration was doubtless one motive to the many plots against Queen Elizabeth and King William: If they have children, they are often as unhappy; and there is seldom a good understanding between the incumbent and the next heir; who sometimes takes the throne before it is vacant, and sometimes makes a vacancy: *Imperium habere quam expectare mallet.*[2] And sometimes the father destroys the son, for fear of being destroyed by him; as did Constantine, the first Christian emperor, and Philip II of Spain.[3] And thus the excellent Germanicus owed his murder to the cruel politicks of Tiberius, his uncle, and his father by adoption. Nor do the children of princes hate one another less, than the eldest or the most ambitious generally does his father. The Great

2. "He would prefer to rule rather than to wait for it." Said of Tiberius in Tacitus, *Annales*, 1.7.

3. There is no evidence that the eldest son of Philip II, Don Carlos, who was apparently deranged, was killed by his father.

Mogul almost always sees his sons, and his daughters with them, engaged in wars and blood for their father's empire; and he is their prisoner by turns, as their several parties prevail, and perhaps ends his life in a dungeon. One of David's sons lay with his sister, and was killed by another son, who defiled his father's bed, and endeavoured to dethrone him; and Solomon, as soon as his father was dead, put his eldest brother to death.[4]

Princes are likewise subject to higher dangers, and have more and greater enemies, than other men; and their lives and reputations are more exposed. They have no small enemies, but either neighbouring princes and states as powerful or politick as themselves; or great domestick conspirators, often more terrible; or little assassins, the most formidable enemies of all, as they are the most sure and sudden. Besides, the dangers they are sometimes in are not seen or credited till they are past remedy. Domitian therefore said well, *Conditionem principum miserrimam, quibus de conjuratione comperta non crederetur, nisi occisis:*[5] "It is a miserable lot that of princes, never to be believed as to any conspiracy formed against them till it has had its effect, and they are fallen by it." Sueton. in *Domitian.* C. 21.

I shall refer to another paper my further considerations upon the condition of a prince.[6]

G   *I am, &c.*

鴷   *The same Subject continued.*

SIR,

I have already sent you a letter about the condition of an arbitrary prince: I here send you another; and what is said in both does in some respects concern all princes, especially all princes

4. 2 Samuel 13–16; 1 Kings 2:13–25.
5. "The condition in which princes found themselves was a most miserable one, since when a conspiracy was discovered, it was not believed unless they had been killed." Suetonius, *Domitian*, 21.
6. See Letter No. 3 (Appendix) (Nov. 2, 1723).

who do not make the fixed and standing laws of their country the rules of their government. For though I do not think it possible for any prince, the wisest and most vigilant, and virtuous to avoid all the inconveniences which I have observed usually to attend a crown; yet it is my opinion, that a prince of a legal and limited state, who defends the laws and rights of his people to his people's advantage, will be defended by his people and the laws; that a righteous administration will be too powerful for unrighteous factions, and make him safe in the love of his subjects, against the leaders and deceivers of parties, and against the intrigues of his own servants, who will be obliged to serve him faithfully in their own defence, and cannot distress him where his people love him. But as this has been the condition of few, very few princes, they have generally reduced themselves to the evils and hardships which I have already mentioned in part, and shall now further set forth.

Such princes are generally poor, notwithstanding their great revenues. Their income is scarce ever well husbanded. The great number of officers necessary to gather it in, must all be paid suitable to the grandeur and bounty of a prince; and it is well if they do not finger more of it, much more than their pay; so that it comes into his coffers with large abatements; and the bulk of his rents is far short of the name, yet by that name his wealth is computed; and hence expectations from him are higher than his ability to answer them.

If his money be wasted in his receipts, it is still more so in his issues. His revenues are distributed, as well as collected, by a great number of officers, with great salaries, who, in the payment of his bills, frequently value their own gain more than their master's credit, and keep in their hands for their own use the money which they should pay away for his. For this reason he buys almost every thing extremely dear, sometimes at double, nay, treble its value; because they who will sell have large interest for slow and uncertain payment: Neither is it uncommon, that those who buy for him, combine with those who sell to him, and divide the profits of an extravagant bill: Even officers who do not conspire against his purse out of sordidness, frequently do it to oblige their friends; so that he is at least cheated on one side. I have known a piece of ground sold to a king at fifty times its value, and an old house for not much less; and the like enormous prices received for a piece of painting, for a horse, and for a paltry rarity, which, for the benefit of a friend, they who had his ear persuaded him to purchase.

But besides all this, let his revenues be as great as they will, the demands upon them are commonly greater. Every service done him costs him dear; and it is well if he pays not equally dear for disservice and treachery; a price which yet he is obliged sometimes knowingly to pay, to deceive and flatter an enemy, or a false friend, whom he dares not crush. The pretensions too of those who never served him, but fancy that they did, or that they can, are infinite; and they will be too apt to distress him without provocation, if he do not reward them without cause, or beyond their merit. Whatever they do for him, or think they can do, claims a high price, not according to its worth, but according to their own conceit, and to his grandeur; and all his gratuities are expected to be great, how small soever they and their pretensions are who expect them: Others, who think they can hurt him, will make a virtue of not being mischievous; but not a virtue which is to be its own reward, but such a virtue as will seek revenge where it is not rewarded; so that he must pay as well for false services, and for no services, as for real services; his foes for sparing him, and his friends for defending him, and both rather according to the measure of their own selfish value and importance, than suitably to reason, or even to his ability.

And as such princes are, I think without exception, oppressors of their people, they must fear those whom they oppress, and depend for their security either upon a nobility or an army, or upon an army only; two sorts of men equally ambitious and insatiable, who will expect to riot upon the spoils of the prince, as he does upon the spoils of the people, and will turn upon him if he disappoint their avarice and pride, nor spare him if he spare his subjects.

The Roman emperors were no longer safe than they were feeding the soldiery with largesses, and sometimes all that they had to bestow was not a sufficient bribe to save their lives. The immense revenue of the whole Roman world was too little for the soldiery alone, though the provinces were ransacked, tortured, and exhausted, to increase it. The emperor was but a name: The soldiers were the state, the governors of the state, and the gentle landlords of Europe, Asia, and Africa; as the Great Turk is at this day but the creature and property of the janizaries, who are the real disposers of the Turkish diadem, and the real governors, or rather emperors, of Turkey. He who has the name, is but the gatherer of their rents; and they hold him in such alarms, that he is scarce secure of his life for a day, and in such necessities, that to satiate them, he is forced to be daily killing and plundering his bashaws, glutted with the plunder of the provinces; which to supply this constant and progressive plunder, are reduced to regions of gloomy solitude and desolation: And all this wealth of so great and so fine a portion of the earth does but end in a fee to a tribe of rogues, renegades, and vagabonds, to save their master's life.

No prince's coffers are full enough to answer all demands; and as to the places and bounties which he has to bestow, he may engage by them a number of people in his interest; but he makes a greater number of enemies, because to every such favour there are many pretenders, and all are disgusted but he who gains it; and the boundary between disgust and enmity is so very small in such cases, that it is scarce to be measured, or indeed discerned. Where twenty people aim at the same thing, he can make a friend of but one.

Hence such a prince must be subject to perpetual and painful hypocrisy, by being obliged to soften disappointments with good words, which, perhaps he does not mean; and with fair promises, which he cannot keep. It behoves him to please all that he can please, and to provoke none wilfully; for, in spite of his greatest complaisance, many will be provoked by disappointments which he cannot prevent.

No sort of men are under such great restraints as to liberty of speech princes as are; nor can the greatest power give them this freedom with any safety. For, besides that a loose in mirth and jests affects their dignity, and weakens its awe, their words are all thought to have design in them, and are readily caught up and misapplied, especially where they seem any way to relate to their own power, or to the persons of men. Caesar did at least hasten the conspiracy again him by a miserable pun of his: He said, that Sulla, who had resigned the dictatorship, was a novice in letters; he could not dictate.[1]

From these words of his, perhaps spoken in pure jest, the measure of his ambition was taken, though I think there were much better proofs against him. Galba was murdered by his guards, for an honest unwary speech of his: He declared, he would choose soldiers, and not purchase them:[2] And Cassius Chaerea,[3] captain of the guards to Caligula, put that prince to death, for rallying[4] him upon his effeminacy.

All satirical railleries are the more felt, and the least forgiven, the higher they come. A sarcasm from a superior is an insult, because it cannot be returned. No man cares to bear a severe jest, which only serves to shew him how much lower he is than the person who makes it; and therefore no wise or good-natured man will make such jests. Greatness is so naturally apt to be proud, that we generally expect no better from it, and are ready to see pride in great men where they really have none, or shew none; and because we hate pride, we are apt to hate greatness, which we consider as the cause of pride: an imputation which all great men can never be too careful to avoid; and let them be ever so careful and complaisant, they will never wholly avoid it: And therefore stateliness of behaviour, and imperious airs, are signs of great want of sense, and the certain causes of hate.

Great men can never be too well-bred. We are naturally quick-sighted enough to see the difference between us and them, and can only be reconciled to it by their treating us as if there was none; but supercilious pains taken on their side, will surely create distaste and enmity on ours. We think that they owe us a sort of amends for being greater than we; and if they can pay us with affa-

1. See Suetonius, *Julius Caesar*, 77, which reports that Caesar publicly declared that Sulla was an ignorant person for having abdicated the dictatorship.

2. Suetonius, *Galba, Otho, Vitellius*, 16.1.

3. Tribune of a praetorian cohort, Gaius *Cassius* Chaerea is credited with fashioning the conspiracy by which Caligula was assassinated in A.D. 41.

4. Rallying: making fun of.

bility and condescension, they pay easily, and have no occasion to complain.

Caesar was never forgiven for receiving the Roman magistracy sitting: And some passionate expressions of King Charles I against the Parliament, did him more mischief than all his former encroachments upon the constitution; as these expressions created personal enemies, and a fear and distrust of his spirit and sincerity. His father, still less capable of supporting the dignity of a crown, and of preserving the affections of his people, had such a wild mixture of timidity and pride, and familiarity, that many of them hated him, more despised him, and yet none feared him. He would sacrifice his reputation with his people to the titillation of a poor pun, and manifest his passion for absolute power, rather than smother a wretched witticism, or a quaint conceit, hardly worthy of a country school-master. When a fit of bouncing was upon him, then he was the oldest king in Europe, and, he trowed,[5] the wisest, and would be master of the purses of his subjects; but when the Parliament had put him into a fright, then they had an humble sermon from him, larded with scraps of Latin, upon the duty and restraints of a sovereign; and logick was chopped, and distinctions were made, upon that head.

His private conversation was low and cheap; and when the crown was off, the King was never seen; his tongue never lay still, and his usual themes were far unworthy of royalty: He delighted in sifting metaphysical questions, and in discussing dark points in divinity, and in smutty and familiar jokes; and it was usual with him to fall upon men with rude language and ill breeding: His condescension to others was as full of meannesses, and the obscenities and fulsome style of his letters are below the lowest mechanick. It was impossible to know him and reverence him. Those who were raised by him, and most obliged to him, treated him with contempt, and hectored him when they could not wheedle him: And it was usual with him to give and take such language, as no gentleman would give or take. He was particularly free of his oaths and his kisses, practices beneath a great or a grave man. He was so ignorant of his

5. Trowed: believed.

character, and so fond of logick, that from a great king he descended to be a disputant on one side in a squabble of divines. His reputation abroad was as low as at home. He talked much of king-craft; but his maxims, which he was always uttering, were poor ones, and foreign princes derided him. In their treaties with one another, they either took no notice of this keeper of the balance of Europe, or always outwitted him. In his own negotiations with them, they over-reached and baffled him, even to wantonness; and treated his long letters and his learned labours with small regard: His premonition to princes, and his books of divinity, had no influence on the powers of Christendom.

King Charles II had more sense, and more accomplishments: He had the parts and address of a gentleman; but he was too ludicrous for a King. He had many pleasant stories, and told them well: He made very good jests, and diverted his friends over a bottle. But the monarch suffered in the merry companion, and his good-nature was the occasion of many ill-natured railleries. His great familiarities with his subjects made them very familiar with the dignity of the diadem; and he never made so many jests as were made upon him. The freedoms which his own dear friends the wits used with their sovereign, and their sarcasms upon so great a prince, are astonishing.

Scarce any of the words of a prince fall to the ground; they therefore ought to be cautious what words they utter. Whatever he says, and his manner of saying it, will be apt to make impressions either to his advantage or disadvantage. His sayings quickly fly abroad, and are at the mercy of every interpreter; and when once his words are publick, it depends no longer upon himself what meaning his words shall bear. The publick rarely distinguish the man from the King; but with them in every thing he acts and speaks as a King, and consequently by all his words and actions that come abroad, his royal dignity is affected, though they regard neither.

My next letter shall be upon the same subject.

G   *I am, &c.*

NO. 4. SATURDAY, NOVEMBER 9, 1723.

ϾϾ   *The same Subject continued.*

SIR,

The actions of a prince are more liable to censure than his words. His words, which can be heard but by a few, may be misrepresented; and this his friends may plead in his defence: But his actions publish themselves; and all men will pretend to judge what all men see, and what concerns all men. Nor must he expect to be judged by the motives, and intention of his conduct, but by the effects. Those motives, however just and necessary, are not always such as he can avow; and if he mean one thing, and pretend another, he cannot with a good grace take it ill that his sincerity is suspected.

Henry III of France dispatched Monsieur Bellievre[1] away to England as his ambassador extraordinary, to interpose his royal credit with Queen Elizabeth, for the life of Mary, Queen of Scots; and great consequences were expected from so much zeal and ostentation. Nor was ever any thing more strong, laboured, and pathetick, than Monsieur Bellievre's speech upon that occasion. In it all the topicks of mercy, of consanguinity, of charity and forgiveness, of good policy, of the sacredness of the blood of princes, and the ill example of shedding it, were urged and exhausted with great earnestness and art. The French King's pious concern for his sister-in-law was dressed up in moving colours, and warm arguments were fetched from the safety and reputation of Queen Elizabeth herself. Never was such a dolorous farce! The ambassador had private orders to solicit in his Majesty's name the execution of Queen Mary, and alleged the same arguments for that execution.

Now the whole of this conduct, so full of contradiction and insincerity, was necessary to his condition. It concerned that prince's reputation with his people, and with all the Catholicks in Europe, to interest himself in the life of a Catholick queen, his brother's wife: If he had not, he had furnished the Guises and the

1. Pomponne de Belliévre, who had earlier been dispatched by Charles IX to Switzerland to justify the massacre of St. Bartholomew.

League, already too popular and powerful, with a new advantage against him.[2] They had already charged him with heresy, though he had murdered a world of hereticks to demonstrate his Catholick zeal. But it concerned him full as nearly, that that Queen should neither be restored to Scotland, nor succeed Queen Elizabeth in England, and thereby strengthen the hands of the League, and her uncles, the Guises, against him.

Queen Elizabeth, who was a wise princess, acted the same double part in the same affair. The security of her life and her crown was precarious while the Queen of Scots lived; and yet the life of her royal cousin and sister was so dear to her, that the importunity and repeated addresses and petitions of Parliament, with all the doughty casuistry and logick of her spiritual counsellors, the bishops, could hardly prevail upon her tender conscience to rid herself and her realm of so dangerous an enemy; and after she had submitted her many scruples to the love and fears of the people, and to the holy reasonings of the bishops, she was forced to be surprised into the signing of the death warrant; which, after all, she never meant to have executed, but only kept over the sentenced queen *in terrorem*. But this her merciful purpose was frustrated by the officious zeal of Secretary Davison;[3] for which the poor man was disgraced.

This was all illusion. No person upon earth wished more passionately for the death of Mary, Queen of Scots; but she did wisely to save appearances. She had good reasons for what she had done; and reasons equally good for not bearing her testimony to the rightfulness of putting a queen to death.

Queen Elizabeth escaped the bloody hand of her sister Mary, by the policy of King Philip her husband, which got the bet-

2. Mary Stuart was not only the widow of Francis II of France but the daughter of Marie de Guise, the sister of Louis, Cardinal of Guise, and Francis, Duke of Guise. The League, of course, is the Holy League, which sought to elevate the Guises to the throne of France.

3. William Davison (c. 1541–1608), secretary to Queen Elizabeth, to whom the warrant for the execution of Mary, Queen of Scots, was entrusted. Following Mary's execution, Elizabeth claimed that she had instructed Davison not to part with the warrant. Accordingly, Davison was thrown into prison. He was tried before the Court of Star Chamber and, although acquitted of evil intention, he was fined and sentenced to imprisonment during the Queen's pleasure.

ter of his bigotry and natural cruelty.[4] His wife had no children, and the crown must descend either to her sister Elizabeth, who was a Protestant, or to the Queen of Scots, who was a papist, and also Queen of France. He hated Protestants, but loved his interest better; and saved the princess, to prevent so much power from falling into the French scale. This was just policy; but he durst not own it: It would have made him odious to the court of Rome, and to the popish world.

Thus princes themselves become subjects; subjects to the censure of their people: And to please them, or to avoid their displeasure, are often obliged to disguise their actions, often to disown the motives of their best actions, and sometimes the actions themselves. This acting in masquerade is a restraint which most princes, the most haughty and unlimited, must undergo. Not Louis le Grand, nor the Great Turk, durst declare to his people, that he oppressed them to satiate his pride or avarice; that he went to war through ambition, and spilled their blood for fame.

Caesar, the mighty and successful Caesar, had no other deity but false glory! But, with all his power and fortune, he was not powerful enough to declare, that he shed human blood, and enslaved the world, only to make more noise than any man in it; for this great glory of his was no more but noise and mischief. His purpose of war with the Parthians was only to gratify his restless spirit, and to employ the spirits of the Romans, which, by enslaving them, he had incensed; and he was no longer easy and safe, than he was fighting and killing. But this was a secret not fit to be told, and the honour and benefit of the Romans were boldly pretended; that is, the Romans were to have certain losses, and no purchase, for the honour and benefit of the Romans: For, if he had conquered all Parthia, which was no ways probable, Rome would have been never the better, but, on the contrary, must have sacrificed many Romans to the pride and pleasure of Caesar.

4. The measures taken by Philip of Spain to protect Elizabeth from Mary Tudor's hostility were largely due to his desire to curry favor with the English people. Philip was aware that if Elizabeth were put to death it would place Mary, Queen of Scots, as the next heir to the English throne, which would be tantamount to making England a satellite of France.

Oliver Cromwell sought the Lord upon all occasions, and all that he did was the Lord's doings; and because many of the saints preached it, numbers believed it. Now, though this was downright impudence, which, to a wise man, is worse than silence, yet it passed with a party. Parties generally act implicitly: Watchword and cant pass with them for reason, and they find great conviction in a few solemn unmeaning sounds. The partisans of Caesar vindicated their purpose of making him a king, by a foolish old prophecy never heard of before, that none but a king could conquer the Parthians. They could not have devised a better argument; it convinced the whole party, and filled their mouths with an answer to the stiff-necked republicans. Had Cromwell been declared King, I doubt not but his preachers would have found a revelation for it, and probably the coronation sermon would have abounded with texts that gave him the diadem. It would not have been the first nor the last time that the Bible has been made a great courtier, and heaven the voucher of wickedness and falsehood. The last argument of the Spanish clergy for the expulsion of the Moors, was a bell in the church of Vililah, which rung of its own accord; and though it uttered nothing but sound, yet expressly commanded that expulsion, and fully satisfied King Philip's conscience.[5] It was a miracle; and what should miracles be worked for, but for the confusion of infidels and hereticks? And who should see the design of miracles executed, but those who interpret miracles?

Princes must say something for their best and worst actions; which is a confession, that they are not so unaccountable as some would make them. Their reputation is at the mercy of their people; and when their reputation is lost or lessened, they cannot possess their crowns in much peace, nor indeed in much safety. Hence nothing is so tender as the reputation of a prince, and nothing ought to exercise his thoughts and fears more. He must not measure his publick fame by the fine tales told him by

5. In a memorial to King Philip III, Don Juan de Ribera, the Archbishop of Valencia, offered this proof that the heavens supported the Church's petition that the Moors be expelled from Spain: the church bell in the town of Vilila had rung of itself for several days. Bowing to pressures from the Church, Philip expelled the Moors in 1609.

those who are well paid for the tales, and dare not always tell him truth, for fear of losing that pay. It would be more to his advantage to hear the worst things that are said of him; for while he is falsely told that all things go well, he will never think of altering his conduct, how wrong soever he is; and going on in an error for want of honest information, has been the ruin of many princes. They cannot go abroad for truth, and rarely hear it at home; and the evil day has come upon them when they thought themselves most secure; or if they have heard part of the truth, it has come disguised to their ears; and the complaints of the people, forced from them by oppression, have been represented as the clamours of malcontents, and as the voice of faction. And it is very true, that faction often rails without ground; but it is as true, that faction often derives its chief power from complaints that are well-grounded. Nor is it at all good reasoning to justify every thing which faction condemns.

—*Fas est & ab hoste doceri.*[6]

Some men, especially great men, would never hear of their faults, were it not for their foes; and princes might often have learned better lessons of government from the satires made upon them, than from their many panegyricks. Their panegyricks consecrate their worst actions, and never find any thing to be mended; but in satire there is always some truth, and often a great deal; and where there is no truth, there is no satire.

It is the interest of a prince, to know what his subjects think of him and his government: It is a duty which he owes to himself as well as to them; and though he may hear of many evils and grievances which are fathered upon him, and yet not owing to him, he will probably at the same time hear of many that he has power to remove, or to mitigate. Let him do his best, he will have many enemies; but this is no reason why he should not lessen their number, by lessening the cause all he can.

It is a hard matter for a prince to learn his true character at second-hand: His surest way is to learn it from himself, from the

6. "It is right to be taught, even by the enemy." Ovid, *Metamorphoses*, 4.428.

measures which he pursues, and from the effects which they ought to have upon the minds and fortunes of men. His friends will sanctify or palliate his greatest faults; and his foes will make crimes of his greatest virtues. If he be a bigot to a reigning superstition, wise men will despise him; and if he despise superstition, the bigots, who are always the majority, will curse him. Nor will the most able and upright administration be of any merit with them, if he do not season his administration with the blood of infidels and hereticks, and exclude the best and soberest part of his subjects, from any share in his protection and paternal mercy; and if he fall in with this religious fury, he destroys or provokes his soberest and best subjects. So that to be a saint one way, he must be a devil on the other; a character very common in the world: And if he do not exercise his rage for enthusiasts, he must expect to feel theirs, and to have his humanity and wisdom exposed and treated as atheism. To butcher, or be butchered, is the lot of a prince who rules over bigots; a sort of madmen, who would father their own frenzy upon the deity, and make him thirst after the coolest human blood to assuage it. The Spanish Inquisition is a priestly slaughter-house, a dreadful tribunal erected against the lives, consciences, and faculties of men; and yet no King of Spain could attempt to suppress it, without expecting to lose his life in the attempt. Nor is it in the power of the Pope to suppress popery. And the Great Turk, absolute and irresistible as he is, were he to turn Christian, could not live half an hour.

Princes are under the same difficulty, when they would cure another mighty evil in their government. Standing armies are standing curses in every country under the sun, where they are more powerful than the people; and yet it is hardly possible for a prince that rules by an army, to part with his army, or to set up any new authority over them. He will find them armed against himself, as well as against his people or his neighbours; and he cannot relieve his subjects, if he would. The Asiatick governments, and all that are like them, are modelled for the destruction of [the] human race; and yet the best and wisest man that ever lived, were he at the head of one of those governments, must act according to its bloody maxims, or quickly perish. Brutus, in the place of the Great Turk, must have been a Great Turk, and observed all the essential principles of that savage monarchy. Human wisdom cannot give freedom to Turkey; and if the laws of liberty, practised amongst us, were to be followed there, especially in cases of treason, there would be an end of the empire in a month, and every bashaw would be an independent king. Great empires cannot subsist without great armies, and liberty cannot subsist with them. As armies long kept up, and grown part of the government, will soon engross the whole government, and can never be disbanded; so liberty long lost, can never be recovered. Is not this an awful lesson to free states, to be vigilant against a dreadful condition, which has no remedy.

This therefore is the situation of the best arbitrary prince, as to his conduct and popularity. The good that he would do, he cannot do; and the good that he does, he sometimes dares not own. He is often hated for his best deeds, and slandered for his noblest qualities: If he rule by soldiers, he must oppress his people; and if he favour his people, he is in danger from his soldiers. Where there are factions, he is sure of one of them for his foes; and is exposed to the cruelty of the bigots for his mercy to all men. As to limited princes, who have the laws for the rules of their actions, and rule their actions by those laws, and study in all things the happiness of their people, they may be secure from the convulsions which are scarce separable from absolute monarchies; nor are they necessitated to exercise the violence and fraud by which the others subsist, unless they have the misfortune to govern a people mad with enthusiasm and bigotry: And there is no remedy but to overcome the enthusiasm, or to be carried away with it; to comply in some instances with reigning and popular prejudices; to elude their force by seeming to yield to them; and in time, by patience and prudent management, wholly to destroy them.

T   *I am, &c.*

NO. 5. SATURDAY, NOVEMBER 30, 1723.

❧ *Considerations upon the Condition of Prime Ministers of State.*

SIR,

I have considered, in three former letters,[1] some of the many evils that encompass royalty: I shall here consider the condition of great ministers; who are far from being so happy as they appear. Those who view them at a distance, are apt to measure their happiness by their greatness; and, as they do in other things, to take appearances for proofs. They see the elevation of great men, the shew that they make, the numbers that follow them, and the obedience and adoration which are paid them; and from all this infer a suitable degree of felicity. This is wrong reasoning. The world affords not more unhappy men, than those who seem to abound in happiness, by abounding in certain things, which others, who have them not, consider as the means of happiness. The increase of fortune is followed by an increase of cares; and riches and power, so much the aim of all men, as the chief causes of worldly happiness, are no more capable of giving it, than of giving health, strength, or beauty; but often become real misfortunes, and the bitter sources of misery in various shapes. All which will be more manifest from an enquiry into the condition of a great man.

In his pursuit of greatness he will meet with many rough rebukes, and many shocking disappointments. Things, upon which he had set his heart, will often fail him; and the next hopes of his ambition be often frustrated. Little men and small accidents will frequently do him great and essential harm; and the chance of a day destroy the schemes of years. Those who are his equals, will not care to see over their heads one who they think ought to be at their elbow; and when he offers to break out of his rank, will be apt to give him an invidious pull backwards. They will not care to see their companion become their master; and such as are yet greater

1. The three preceding letters (Sept. 14, Nov. 2, and Nov. 9, 1723).

than he, will not love one who would be as great as they, and when he is as great, would be greater; one, who, having been accustomed to mount above his equals, aims visibly at equalling his superiors or at having none.

Here are the beginnings of numerous conspiracies against him and his ambition; conspiracies that will watch his steps, retard his advancement, blast his views, and perhaps his reputation; and, when he has gained ground, be ready to set him back again: They will often reduce him to difficulties, often to despair, or to painful patience, and make his ascent tedious and tiresome: They will be heavy weights upon him while he rises, and thorns in his side when he is risen; and possibly push him over a precipice at last.

In his state of exaltation he will find new difficulties to encounter, besides most of the old ones increased; and the grandeur which he had so long and so painfully pursued, he will now find to be chiefly pomp and name, the reputation of happiness without happiness: He will meet with a thousand mortifications which a private character is a stranger to, and which but for his elevation he would have never known. He will never be able to oblige all who are able to hurt him, if they be not obliged; nor to terrify all who can distress him, if they be not terrified. By this power he will think himself entitled to honour and submission; and where he misses the same, as certainly he often will, his vexation will be as great as are the notions which he entertains of his worth and power; and those notions being generally sufficiently selfish, that is, extreme, that vexation must likewise be extreme.

Hence a disappointment in small things often gives men great disturbance; not from the value of the thing, but from the value which they put upon themselves; and great men are not apt to value themselves less than other men are, but much more, and, at least, in proportion to their greatness. A private man's vineyard could not be of much importance to a king; but a king thought it of great importance to be refused, when he had set his heart upon having it. Ahab could not brook this refusal of Naboth; and therefore "Ahab came into his house heavy and displeased; and he laid him down upon his bed, and turned away his face, and would eat no bread." I Kings xxi. 4. Archbishop Laud was equally discontented, and more enraged, by a jest of Archy, the King's fool, upon the mad and unsuccessful pranks which his Grace was playing with religion in Scotland; so enraged, that though Archy was a professed and allowed buffoon, and had made many jests equally severe upon the King himself without offence, yet of so fierce and unforgiving a temper was the Archbishop, and so much a greater man than his Majesty, that poor Archy was by a solemn act of council banished the court, for offending his meek Grace of Canterbury.[2]

Such instances shew, that trifles are capable of mortifying the most exalted men, because the most exalted men think that they ought to be balked and ruffled in nothing, and expect to be protected by their exaltation from all contradiction and opposition: Whereas greatness, which must be supported by much action, and by the co-operation of many persons, does, by increasing their necessities and views, increase also their anxieties and disappointments. They will need many helps, and be obliged to embark in many designs; and both the helps and the designs that they relied on will often fail them. And as they will find the cause of that failure in the shortness of their power, it will be natural for them to be trying expedients to enlarge their power: If those expedients miscarry, as they frequently will, their uneasinesses are multiplied by an attempt to cure them: If they succeed, the success will only imbitter their enemies, and probably help to strengthen them, by furnishing them with a popular handle for reproach, and for alarming the publick. And as to their friends, who are only to be made so by giving each his lot in the power which they assist to raise, it is not to be expected that they will raise it so high, as no longer to want their assistance, unless in cases perfectly desperate, when in the last struggle of parties one or other must inevitably swallow all; and then the respect of persons must carry it.

2. The fool was Archibald Armstrong, court jester to James I and to his son, Charles I. He was noted for his outspokenness and, after the death of the Duke of Buckingham in 1628, he reserved his rudest comments for Laud, whom he vilified at every opportunity. Following the Scottish Rebellion in 1637, Archy is reputed to have twitted Laud, who was on his way to the council chamber at Whitehall, with the words, "Who's fool now?" As a consequence, the council that same day banished him from the court.

But I speak here of the usual contention for the usual advantages of power, which is not to be acquired without difficulty and struggles, unless where by the maggot of a prince a favourite is raised in a day; as King James I from a stripling, without name or experience, or any fitness for business, made young Villiers[3] his first minister for his handsome face. But, however it may be thus hastily got, or rather given, that minister found that it was not easily kept: for, though he was possessed of his master's whole authority, and invested, in effect, with royalty; and though that weak timorous king did not at first, and afterwards durst not, refuse him any thing, how absurd, extravagant, and arbitrary soever; and though the civil and military lists were filled with his creatures and family; yet he was not too big to be shaken: His foundation, as strong and broad as it was, felt many terrible convulsions; and if King Charles I who had likewise taken him for his minister, or rather for his master, had not loved him better than he loved the constitution, and parted with the Parliament rather than part with Buckingham, his fall must have been as swift as his rise, as it was afterwards sudden by the hand of an assassin.[4]

Cardinal Richelieu, infinitely more able, and far more powerful, as that monarchy, which he governed with a high hand, was more absolute than ours, was never free from difficulties, dangers, and embarrassments: And though by his great talents and good fortune he overcame them almost as fast as they arose; yet still they arose as fast as he overcame them. The intrigues of the cabinet against him were so many, so powerful, and so constant, that, though he had almost all Europe to contend with, he declared, that one chamber (meaning the cabinet) embarrassed him more than all Europe. The plots against his power were perpetual, and there were frequent plots against his life: Cardinal de

3. George Villiers, whose advancement was meteoric. He was brought to the King's notice in Aug. 1614 when he was twenty-two years old, and by Jan. 1618, had been created Viscount Villiers and Baron Waddon, Earl, and, finally, Marquess of Buckingham. Twelve months later he was made Lord High Admiral of England. In 1623, he was raised to a dukedom.

4. In 1628, Buckingham was assassinated by an officer whom he had failed to promote, as he had promised. The assassin's action, although motivated by a sense of private wrong, was applauded by the Commons, which had earlier pronounced Buckingham a public enemy.

Retz (then the Abbot de Retz) owns himself to have been engaged in one, and Monsieur Cinqmars died for another.[5] Cinqmars was the King's favourite, and the King knew his design, though it does not appear that he approved it; but it is certain that he hated the Cardinal, as did all France.

As his power grew, his crosses and danger grew; so much are they mistaken, who from the growth of power expect equal ease and security. Cardinal Richelieu had the entire power of France in his hands, her armies, her garrisons, and her finances: The King was no more than his pupil; and every thing that obeyed the monarchy, obeyed him. Mazarin, who had the same authority, but seems to me to have been rather a little tricking Italian than a great politician, underwent so many insults, disgraces, dangers, and disappointments, that none but a man mad with ambition and avarice would have held his place upon such miserable terms.

G   *I am, &c.*

NO. 6. SATURDAY, DECEMBER 7, 1723.

⚑   *The same Subject continued.*

SIR,

I t is true, that the ministers whom I mentioned in my last were arbitrary ministers, and committed acts of power, which made them justly terrible; but it is equally true of Cardinal Richelieu, that his justest and his wisest actions created him the most powerful enemies, and the greatest danger: And it is true of every minister, that the good which he does is as odious to faction as his errors are, often more; and that his services to the publick are, in some instances, through misrepresentations, from envy, made distasteful to the people, who must feel those services before their distaste be removed. And if he has made, or they believe that he has made, any ill steps (a case by no means rare), they will be apt to believe

5. Henri Coiffier Ruzé, Marquis de Cinq-Mars. In 1642, he formed a conspiracy with the Duke of Bouillon and others to overthrow Richelieu, for which he was tried and condemned to death.

that all his steps are ill, to confound the good and the bad, and to hope no good from him. Nor has he any ready way of removing those ill impressions, but by some such sudden and signal act of praise and popularity as perhaps he has no opportunity to perform; and to remove them by degrees, and by a continued series of worthy actions, perhaps the term of his life, or of his power, is not sufficient. And as sometimes the most glorious actions are done with ill views, he who does them will not be more adored by some, than he will be dreaded and reproached by others. And hence the beginning or increase of factions, which almost always extol or condemn implicitly, and by no other rule but that of blind affection and blind antipathy.

And as faction, on one side, will be watching, thwarting, and exposing all that he does; his own party, on the other, will be making advantages of his distresses, and consequently be distressing him more; and he will find it harder to defend himself from his friends, and to preserve their dependence, than to disappoint his foes: Every party hangs together by interest, and every particular means his own. It is impossible to gratify all; and all that are not gratified are disobliged: Whoever therefore is at the head of a party, has but an uneasy station. Whatever blaze he may make, and however absolute he may seem, his disappointments often equal his triumphs; and when we say that he carries all before him, it is because we see his successes, but not his difficulties.

Besides, he has equal trouble and solicitude from small as from great matters. For every little favour which he has to bestow, he has numerous little suitors, as well as several great ones, who become suitors for the small, and think their reputation concerned not to be denied. So that perhaps there are a dozen considerable men soliciting earnestly for one inconsiderable place, and each ready to resent a refusal, and to disappoint him in something of greater moment, if he disappoint them in that, as he must do most of them. Sometimes he has twenty embarrassments of the like nature upon his hand, besides many greater; as particularly, when several considerable men are all candidates for some considerable thing, which can only be given to one; and all the rest are made enemies, or cool friends.

And as there is no greatness without emulation, his attacks from rivals must be incessant, and frequently powerful and dangerous. They who follow power, will themselves never want followers; and such as aim at his place, will never want creatures, nor consequently strength. It sometimes happens that one of his own creatures, whom he trusts (as he must trust somebody), shall make use of that trust to supplant him; a method which, I think, is as frequent as any other; and hence he is sometimes persuaded by his false friends into measures which they intend shall destroy him. Sometimes schemes are offered him, which they know he will reject; and then his non-compliance, however honest, is made a crime, and the cause of his disgrace; and he often bears the reproach of the evil counsels which he opposed. Sometimes a step taken to subdue his rivals, shall end in exalting them; and sometimes an advance made to win his enemies, throws him into their power. Add to all this the difficulty of managing the humours of a prince, and of pleasing the people at the same time. A hard task! Princes are afraid of a minister who has too much credit; and he cannot serve them, if he has none. Neither is the favour of the most powerful prince able always to preserve a minister. The demands of the people, or of a great party, often make his dismission unavoidable; of which there are endless instances. Cardinal Richelieu, indeed, found a way to govern the French king and the French nation, in spite of themselves; but I have already shewn what uneasinesses he underwent.[1] No prince will love a minister whom he dares not part with; and no minister will care to be of so little importance as to be parted with at pleasure.

It is another plague of greatness, that he who has it has scarce any leisure, any agreeable moments to throw away upon amusements and indolence; even when he is doing no business, the cares of business follow him, with a concern for preserving and enlarging his power, always attacked from one quarter or another, and always liable to be attacked in some weak place or other. The necessity of receiving and of making many applications, of raising some creatures, and gaining others; of disappointing the machinations and assaults of enemies; of making many dispatches, or

1. See Letter No. 5 (Appendix) (Nov. 30, 1723).

directing them to be made; of giving access and part of his time to such as have or claim a right to see him, who will always be many, and always resent it if they cannot see him; and of concerting and pursuing favourite projects: I say, all this must either engage him entirely, or he cannot expect to stand. Perpetual industry and anxiety are generally the terms upon which he stands; and if he be idle or recluse, his affairs will be in confusion, and he himself pursued with clamour, as neglectful of the publick, and unequal to his trust. Nor will the partiality and authority of the prince be able to protect him long, at least without exposing his own reputation for the idleness of his minister.

When therefore a minister is strongly addicted to his pleasures, it is a great misfortune to a prince, to the people, and himself. A man whose head is often warm with wine, or perpetually possessed with women or gaming, must often neglect business, or do it hastily. This is not only postponing, but sacrificing the publick to pleasure. Thus the Duke of Buckingham involved us in two wars at once, with France and Spain for disappointed lust;[2] and thus the invasion of Italy by Francis I, the unfortunate Battle of Pavia, the loss of a noble army, the long captivity and imprisonment of that great king, were the effects of the passion of one of his ministers for an Italian beauty, whom he was resolved to enjoy once more, at the peril of his master and of his dominions.[3]

It is true that the pleasures of a minister, which do not affect the publick, ought not to offend it; but it is as true, that how-

2. English participation in the Thirty Years' War (1625–1630) was brought on by the dispatch of English troops to Holland, which was looked on as an act of war by Spain. The second conflict, the Anglo-French War (1626–1630), was set in train by the Duke of Buckingham's expedition to La Rochelle in support of Huguenot forces.

3. In 1521, the claims of Francis I to Navarre and Naples embroiled France in a war with the emperor Charles V, in which Italy was the principal battleground. In 1525, the forces of Charles V inflicted a humiliating defeat upon the French army at Pavia. Francis I, who stood at the head of his troops, was badly wounded and captured by the imperial army. He remained in captivity in Madrid until the following year, when he agreed to surrender all his claims in Italy. The minister whom Gordon mentions as intoxicated by "an Italian beauty" is Guillaume Goufflier, Seigneur de Bonnivet, Admiral of France. Gordon is here apparently relying on Pierre de Bourdeille, Seigneur de Brantôme, who, in his *Recueil d'aucun discours*, relates that Goufflier's passion was alone responsible for Francis's invasion of Italy and the disasters that followed.

ever private and personal they are, they will give publick offence; and it is his misfortune that they can scarce ever be hid. His haunts and diversions will soon be observed and known. Several people must be trusted, some of them will certainly whisper; and private whispers about publick men will grow to be publick rumours; and amongst the rigid and precise, or those who pretend to be so, the man of pleasure always passes for a debauched man.

A minister is liable to the same or greater censure of misrepresentation in the making or enlarging his fortune. Men may, by accidents, by conspicuous parts, by the caprice of a prince, or by the partiality and weight of a party, arrive at greatness without the assistance of wealth: But wealth is, doubtless, a great help to a man who would rise; and he who is careless of acquiring it, judges ill. It is one of his greatest stays, and sometimes his only one. Now, however fairly he comes by it, it is odds but part of it, if not the whole, will be ascribed to corruption. Ill-natured comparisons will be made between what he had, which will be generally lessened; and what he has, which will be more generally aggravated; and the fruits of private management and industry will be called publick plunder. So that as the neglect of riches is imprudent, the accumulation of riches is unpopular. I have known great ministers go poor out of employment, when it was thought that their estates were immense; and what others had got was sometimes reckoned ten times greater than it proved.

The last thing which I mention upon this subject is, that men who have once tasted of greatness, can scarce ever after relish a private life. The toils, tumult, and anxieties, inseparable from power, make them often sick of it, but never willing to leave it. Self-love tells them, that as nothing is too much for them, so they are constantly worthy to keep what they have; and as the displacing them is a contradiction to this opinion, and the putting others in their room a declaration that others are more worthy, their pride is and continues inflamed, and they are never to be cured of hatred or emulation towards their successors. So that, besides the loss of power, and consequently of homage, pomp, and submission (a tribute always dear to all mankind), they live ever after angry and affronted; and if they have any pleasure, it is when things go wrong under their successors. Nor can old age and infirmities, unless they be such as render them utterly unfit for business, cure them of this uneasiness and painful ambition. England affords instances of men who have lived forty years after their dismission from power, in a constant struggle to regain it: At fourscore they were in the midst of intrigues: When they had lost all other appetites, their lust of power was in its vigour; upon the brink of the grave, their eyes were unnaturally turned backwards to secular grandeur, and their souls bent upon dominion.

This is one of the greatest curses which attend power, that they who have enjoyed it, can rarely ever after enjoy retirement; which yet they are always extolling, and seeming to long for, while it is out of their reach. In the hurry and solicitude of employment, beset with cares, fears, and enemies, they see the security, ease, and calm of recess; but are never to be reconciled to the terms upon which it is to be had. What! Descend from on high, and from giving laws to a nation, be lost in the multitude, and upon a level with those who adored them, and see others adored in their room; others, whom probably they hated, probably despised! This is a sorrowful and a dreadful thought to ambition; and they consider their discharge as a sentence of ignominy and exile.

G   *I am, &c.*

FINIS

Index

This book is set in New Baskerville, based on the original fonts of John Baskerville, an eighteenth-century printer and typefounder. Many of his contemporaries found his types too delicate and over-refined, especially because his printing methods produced an unusually crisp image. In 1760 Benjamin Franklin wrote to him of having heard a friend say that Baskerville's types "would be a means of blinding all the readers in the Nation owing to the thin and narrow strokes of the letters." New Baskerville retains the delicacy and elegance of the original face while slightly increasing the x-height to increase legibility.

This book is printed on paper that is acid-free and meets the requirements of the American National Standard for Permanence of Paper for Printed Library Materials, Z39.48-1992. ∞

DESIGN BY BETTY BINNS, BROOKLYN, NEW YORK

COMPOSED BY ALEXANDER GRAPHICS, INC., INDIANAPOLIS, INDIANA

PRINTED AND BOUND BY WORZALLA PUBLISHING COMPANY, STEVENS POINT, WISCONSIN